A COMPLETE RECORD OF
Walsall Races
1755 - 1876

Published by
Mount Chase Press
109 Mount Street, Hednesford, Cannock, Staffs. WS12 4DB

Copyright John Griffiths 2015

The right of John Griffiths to be identified as the author of this work has been asserted
by him in accordance with the Copyright, Designs and Patents Act 1988.

ISBN 978-0-9551382-6-3

No part of this publication may be reproduced, stored in a retrieval system, or transmitted
in any form or by any means, electronic, mechanical, photocopying, recording, or otherwise,
without the prior written permission of the author.

Every effort has been made to obtain copyright ownership for some of the illustrations and
photographs reproduced in this publication, but in certain cases this has proved impossible,
apologies to anyone whose copyright has been unintentionally infringed.

*The maps plus the illustration of The Woolpack Inn and the jockey portraits of
George Calloway, Robert Denman and George Whitehouse are all the copyright of the author.*

Printed in the UK by 4edge Limited

CONTENTS

	Acknowledgements	4
	Introduction	5
	Racecourse map	6
Chapter One	1754 – 1799	7
Chapter Two	1800 – 1819	12
Chapter Three	1820 – 1839	28
Chapter Four	1840 – 1859	52
Chapter Five	1860 – 1879	78
Chapter Six	The 1940s Revival	114
Chapter Seven	The Jockeys	126
Chapter Eight	The Trainers	146
Chapter Nine	The Colours	156
	Bibliography	159

ACKNOWLEDGEMENTS

No publication of this nature can be entirely credited to one person and I would like to thank the following people for their contribution in helping me to achieve my aim of compiling this record of Walsall Races.

Chris Pitt for sharing his vast knowledge of racing history with me, for his encouragement to help me see the project through, and last, but definately not least, for introducing me to Chas Hammond whose knowledge of jockeys, both past and present, is second to none.

The staff at Weatherbys Group Limited who have answered all of my many requests for information, with great patience.

To the staff at Walsall Local History Centre, and fellow researcher June Ellis who has passed information to me regarding the racecourse while conducting the monumental task of transcribing the diaries of Peter Potter, land agent to Lord Bradford.

Tony Hunt of Hednesford for supplying many vital pieces of information regarding the Hednesford training grounds.

Edwin Metcalfe, also of Hednesford for supplying information about his great grandfather, Thomas 'Badger' Metcalfe.

Gary Burgess, a great racing fan for as long as I have known him, who allowed me to use a copy of his very rare 1870 racecard and also a copy of his print of the racecourse which is shown on the title page.

Mike Glasson and Ian Bott of Walsall Leather Museum for their contributions and assistance.

Maureen and the late Colin McPherson of Hednesford who gave me valuable information regarding Colin's fathers association with the legendary trainer Tom Coulthwaite of Hazel Slade and Flaxley Green.

Paula Bryars who discovered several important documents held at the Staffordshire Record Office relating to the Hednesford training grounds.

The staff at the William Salt Library, Stafford, the Staffordshire Record Office and Birmingham Library, all of whom pointed me in the right direction for research material.

Finally, to my wife Margaret, who has put up with our home being covered in fragments of leather falling from the bindings of my ancient and ever disintegrating *Racing Calendars* and *Baily's Racing Registers*, seemingly everytime I remove one from the bookshelf.

Introduction

This book was first published in 2005 but without ISBN registration, something I always regretted in the years that followed its publication. This update has given me the opportunity to put this right.

So what's new? The title has changed to *A Complete Record of Walsall Races 1754-1876*, this is due to the Hednesford training grounds chapter being removed. In 2010 Anthony Hunt and myself produced and published a new book dealing in depth with this subject, see page 160 for details. Although one chapter has been removed the page count has increased by ten due to additional pages in Chapter Six, the 1940s race revival organised for the Mayor's War Aid Fund. In the original book only the 1942 meeting was included but a further eight meetings during wartime were discovered in late 2014 and these have now been added. Chapter Seven, The Jockeys, is another that has grown as more information has been discovered and included.

The inspiration for this book came from a question I asked myself in the autumn of 2002, *'how good were Walsall Races.'*

First thought was of an informal gathering of local farmers and gentry, one of them saying *'I've got an 'oss that can run fasta' than any of y'own.'* Throwing down the gauntlet, another replied *'I'll bet it cor, we'll find out tomorra',* and so, as the saying goes, the rest is history!

The origins of the third oldest race meeting in Staffordshire (at the time of the course closure) very probably began in this way. The men of vision in the town quickly realised the importance of supporting an annual race meeting to coincide with the Wake and Fair week in late September would make more people aware of the then, little market town.

My initial thoughts regarding the meeting was that it remained, throughout its history, an informal gathering at best, but research has proved otherwise.

It took several years before the races were run under Newmarket Rules or, the Rules of Racing, eventually however it happened, and continued up to the closure of the course. Organised and fashionable, a course measured out and licensed by the rulers of racing, the statistics of each meeting recorded in the annual bible of the racing fraternity, the *Racing Calendar*. Unbelievably, this was Walsall Races.

The little course, set in later years, in the heart of the town, was never going to be an Epsom or an Ascot, but to the people of Walsall it was their chance to be at the heart of the 'Sport of Kings' for two days a year. Whatever the moral issues of racing are, the sport gave the majority of our ancestors, as it has me, a great deal of pleasure and spectacle over the years.

Finally, I would like to dedicate this book to the memory of two well respected, nationally known jockeys of yesteryear. The first being Walsall's own son, George Whitehouse (1815-1869), a good jockey who rode in excess of 350 winners but is forgotten by racing historians, he retired in 1856 and died at his home, Rose Cottage, Upper St. John Street, Lichfield thirteen years later. Secondly is Charles Marlow (1814-1882) who, after a racecourse accident sank into obscurity and died penniless and forgotten in the workhouse. His final resting-place is a paupers grave in Devizes, Wiltshire.

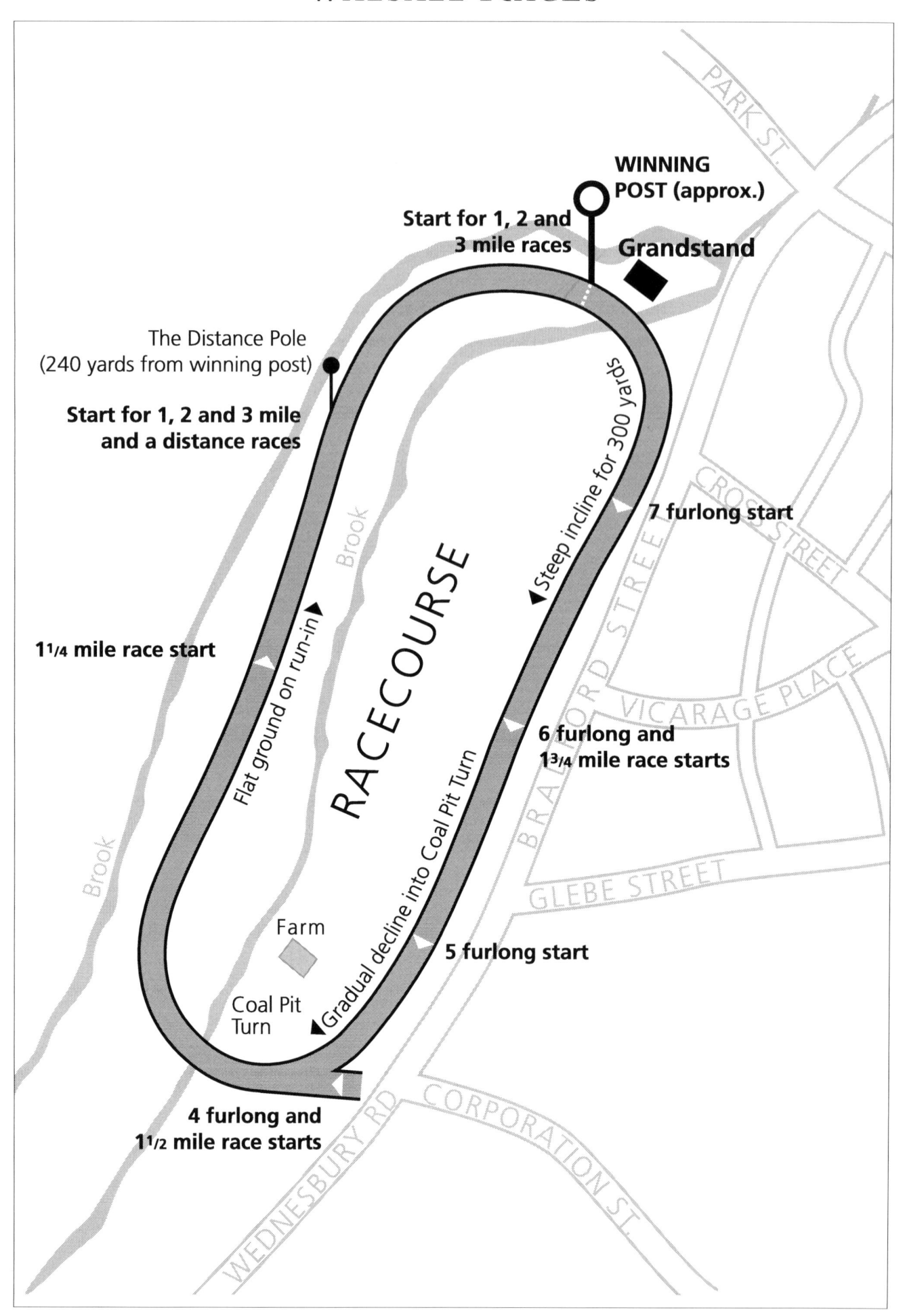

WALSALL RACES

WINNING POST (approx.)

Start for 1, 2 and 3 mile races

Grandstand

The Distance Pole (240 yards from winning post)

Start for 1, 2 and 3 mile and a distance races

Brook

Steep incline for 300 yards

7 furlong start

1¼ mile race start

Flat ground on run-in

RACECOURSE

Brook

6 furlong and 1¾ mile race starts

Gradual decline into Coal Pit Turn

Farm

5 furlong start

Coal Pit Turn

4 furlong and 1½ mile race starts

PARK ST.
CROSS STREET
BRADFORD STREET
VICARAGE PLACE
GLEBE STREET
WEDNESBURY RD
CORPORATION ST.

WALSALL RACES

CHAPTER ONE
1754 - 1799

Walking from Bradford Place, around The Cenotaph and up Bradford Street today, it is difficult, if not impossible, to realise the path taken skirts the perimeter of the old Walsall Racecourse. The race meeting coincided with the Walsall Fair, and for two days every year from around the mid-eighteenth century until 1876, horse races were run on land known as the Long Meadow. The land was owned by Lord Bradford who was obliged to allow the freeholders of the Parish to feed and graze cattle from Lammas Day to Candlemas each year; this must have made the going at times a little testing.

Whatever the activities in that part of town on Friday and Saturday nights today, they become somewhat insignificant compared to the sheer mayhem created by our ancestors on race days - and nights! With spirits already high from the Walsall Fair the previous day, the races succeeded in prolonging the suffering for the many citizens of the town, and in later years, particularly those residing in Bradford Street. Both Fair and races brought with them their own selection of traditional shows, merry-go-rounds, swings and vendors of every description to entertain the public, and extract their cash. There was music and dancing, eating and drinking, buying and selling, swearing, shouting, weariness and disappointment, cocking contests, dogfights and pugilism, organised bouts or those spontaneous events that come about by the consumption of too much alcohol. The wheels of work stood still in Walsall of old in the last week of September.

The origin of horse racing goes back many centuries, coming to Britain with the Romans. The oldest English racecourse is Chester where records exist of organised meetings on the Roodee since 1511 and continue today. James I, whose preference was for hunting rather than racing, established Newmarket in Suffolk as a sporting centre in 1605, quickly seeing the opportunities afforded by the town's heath land, he purchased The Griffin Inn and made it into a royal hunting lodge. His continued patronage of Newmarket led to many horse races and matches being held by his courtiers to pass the time while James I continued his pursuits in the hunting field. Because of these activities Newmarket Heath racecourse was opened in 1636. Charles I, James' son was far more enthusiastic about racing than his father and built the first grandstand there but just as the future was looking good for racing, thunderclouds were gathering in the form of Oliver Cromwell, whose policies and Puritanical government were to change Britain forever. After Charles I execution in 1649, the Puritan government banned horse racing throughout the kingdom. With the restoration of the monarchy in 1660 the sport began again under the enthusiastic racing king, Charles II. It was on his orders that the Spring and Autumn meetings at Newmarket were established and remain today as one of the highlights of the flat racing season. The Rowley Mile Course at Newmarket is named after Charles II who was known as 'Old Rowley', a name taken from his favourite hack. Such was his enthusiasm for racing he became an arbiter on all turf matters and disputes, reputedly showing more zest for these than official state matters. To ease the burden of ever increasing state and turf duties, Charles appointed the exotically named William Tregonwell Frampton as Keeper of the Royal Running Horse. Frampton came from a sporting family in Dorset and was a keen follower of cock fighting, as well being a heavy gambler with a reputation for sharp practice. He continued his reign of turf supremo far longer than Charles' reign as monarch, retaining his appointment under William III, Queen Anne, George I and II. Guarded for many years by his close associations with the monarchy, Frampton had a great deal of influence, particularly at Newmarket, it is reputed that much of the legislation introduced by him was as much for his benefit as anyone else's. He died at Newmarket in 1727 at the grand old age of eighty-six.

The Jockey Club was founded in 1752 as a club for owners and breeders to advance the breeding of thoroughbred horses. It was said in those early days that to be a member you had to be a relative of God - and a close one at that.

The first important administrator of the Jockey Club was Sir Charles Bunbury who ruled from 1768 to 1820, he was the first of the three men known as Dictators of the Turf, he was followed by Lord George Bentinck and finally by the formidable Admiral Rous. The Jockey Club's first conquest was, not surprisingly, Newmarket, where they took control over the happenings on the Heath, eventually buying the course. Other racecourses began to refer disputes to them and many courses adopted to run their races under the Newmarket Rules or Rules of Racing as they are now known. From the

1754 - 1799

outset of the Jockey Club it was realised that a competent administrator from outside the Club would be required to record the details and organise the many Matches being run. In 1770 they appointed the thirty seven year old James Weatherby to the combined office of Secretary to the Jockey Club and Keeper of the Match Book. In 1773 Weatherby published the first official *Racing Calendar*, this bible of the turf was followed by the *General Stud Book*. Both publications are still in existence today following a very similar format to the originals. The *Racing Calendar* is an annual record of all the races run on British racecourses, listing the runners, owners, the betting, and, from the mid 1820s, the jockeys. Surprisingly, trainers names didn't appear on a regular basis until much later.

It must be remembered that in the mid eighteenth century racing, as everyday life, was run by the 'ruling few' and jockeys and horse trainers were merely servants there to do a job. Woe betide any of them that didn't perform their duties to the letter. This may seem a far cry from races on the Long Meadow but eventually, the Race Committee responsible for organising this annual event in Walsall, adopted the Jockey Club's Rules of Racing.

The exact origins of Walsall Races are unknown, but it would appear they came about as additional entertainment to enhance the reputation of the century's old Walsall Fair, also known as the Michaelmas or Cheese and Onion Fair - the latter because of the large amounts of both products being sold.

In some previous articles written about Walsall Races, it has been said that the first meeting was held in 1777, but in fact it was at least twenty-three years earlier than this. Research has shown that the first positive indication of horse racing taking place on the Long Meadow appeared in *Aris's Birmingham Gazette* on the 15th September 1755 and states:

> 'This is to give notice, that on Wednesday and Thursday the 24th and 25th inst. will be a Main of Cocks fought at John Newton's in Walsall for Two Guineas a Battle and Ten the Main, to weigh twenty one in the Main and Ten for the Bye Battles, between the Gentlemen of Birmingham and Walsall. Feeders Thomas Probin and John Newton. At the same time the Races as usual; and on the 26th will be a Match run for fifty pounds, betwixt two Gentlemen of the same Town; they both ride their own horses, being eighteen stone each.'

At eighteen stone each, I would think Walsall already held the dubious distinction of holding the slowest horse race ever!

Very little is known of the course itself at Walsall, other than the fact that it was oval, about a mile in circumference and the horses ran in a clockwise direction. The location of the winning post and judge's chair has never been accurately determined, neither before nor after the grandstand was built in 1809. It is fair to assume that after that date it was in close proximity to the grandstand, but where exactly is lost in time. It is known that the runners would set off up the hill, which we now know as Bradford Street, they would continue towards Corporation Street and turn right at what was known as 'Coal-pit Turn.' After negotiating the turn, the runners would head back towards town along a flat piece of ground, which is now occupied by the railway.

In Staffordshire at this time there were only two other courses organising meetings on a regular basis, and consequently have a longer history than Walsall Races - they are the courses at Lichfield and Stafford.

Years later, many other towns and villages in the county joined the growing list of organised race meetings but many of these tended to run for a few years and then disappear, only to reappear phoenix like after several years absence, some of course, were never heard of again. Newcastle-Under-Lyme was the fourth town to join the list in 1786, others included, Bloxwich, Brewood, Burntwood, Burton-Upon-Trent, Cannock, Hednesford, Leek, Meynell, North Staffs (Stoke), Penkridge, Rugeley, Shenstone, Stone, Tamworth, The Potteries (N.E. Staffs), Uttoxeter and Wolverhampton.

Many of the horses that ran in these early races would not be thoroughbred animals with bloodlines traced back to the so-called Pillars of the Stud Book, the Darley Arabian, Byerley Turk or the Godolphin Arabian, far from it, at best, they would have been hunters or half-breeds with a turn of foot, or so their owners thought - and hoped!

Between 1755 and 1765 the annual announcements in *Aris's Gazette* for the races were rather succinct, giving details of the venue and dates only, mentioning nothing of the conditions the races were to be run under or the runners, and in later editions of the paper, the results. In 1766, the races were run on Thursday 25th and Friday 26th September, two days after the Walsall Fair, the announcement included *'sport as usual in the Meadows, which are greatly improved'*. It fails to state if the improvements were to do with the racing itself or the amenities afterwards, because on both evenings, after racing, a Ball would be held at the Town Hall. Tickets could be obtained from Mr Hemming at one of Walsall's most famous inns, The Green Dragon; prices for tickets were 2s 6d for one night, or 5s 0d for both nights.

The races in 1767 were held on Thursday 24th and Friday 25th September, and to follow on from the success of the previous year, with the addition of the Ball, it was onward and upward for the Race Committee. On the Thursday evening there was an Assembly at the Town Hall followed by the Ball on Friday evening. This was preceded by a Concert of Music, with ticket prices the same as the previous year and obtainable from Misters Balam and Smart, booksellers, the Town Hall, and of course Mr Hemming. If this entertainment was a little genteel for your tastes and you had a liking for more adventurous pursuits to while away the night, a word in the right ear could point you to many of the drinking establishments, in particular the New Inn or The Woolpack, where cockfights, cards and gambling continued well into the early hours.

In the same year, another interesting sideshow took place in Pelsall, ten days after the races on Monday 5th October in the form of a race for footmen. It was to be run at Thomas Rowley's at the Maypole and each entrant had to pay one guinea entrance fee which had to be in by twelve noon and was to be run for in one four mile heat. There had to be at least three reputed footmen entered or the race was cancelled. The prize for the winner was a silver cup valued at three pounds fifteen shillings followed by a good Ordinary afterwards.

1754 - 1799

From 1767 to 1775, there are no official announcements in *Aris' Gazette* for the races taking place but it is difficult to believe that some form of the sport did not take place on the Long Meadow during this period.

At the time of the next official announcement for the Races in 1776, more details were published than previously. The appointment of Stewards is mentioned for the first time, although names of those early enforcers of the Rules is omitted. The Rules and Orders of the Jockey Club, to give them their full title, were being implemented by many courses throughout Britain. Walsall however, did not appear on the hallowed pages of the *Racing Calendar* until 1785, although the Race Committee was already applying some of the rules, or their interpretation of them, to its race entry conditions. The Jockey Club were aware that 'the gentlemen of the turf', were being less than honest about the age of the horses that they ran, hopefully to eliminate this blatant dishonesty, they ruled, as early as 1773, that a certificate would have to be produced proving the age of all intended runners.

In late September 1776, there was entertainment in abundance in Walsall, on the Monday evening there was to be a 'Display of Grand and New Fireworks' by Monsieur Caillot from Burgundy, followed by the Fair on Tuesday and the races on Wednesday and Thursday with the now usual Ball at the Town Hall after racing. With all this excitement, food and drink a plenty, it is little wonder that things occasionally got out of hand in what was at this time, a quiet market town.

The announcement for the 1776 meeting appeared in *Aris' Gazette* on 16th September and read: -

'On Wednesday September 25th, 1776, will be run for, on Walsall Meadows, a purse of fifty pounds; free for any horse, mare or gelding, that never won that value at anyone time, (matches excepted). Four year olds to carry 7 stones, five year olds, 7 stones 7 pounds, six year olds, 8 stones 2 pounds, and aged horses, 8 stone 9 pounds, bridle and saddle included; the best of three, three mile heats. On Thursday September 26th, 1776, will be run for on the same course a purse of fifty pounds, give and take, for any horse, mare or gelding that never won that value at any one time (matches excepted). 14 hands aged, to carry 9 stones, all higher or lower to carry weight in proportion, allowances 7 pounds for every year under seven, and enter to J. Sherratt's, The New Inn, Walsall, on Wednesday, September 25th, between 9 and 12 o'clock in the morning, or double at the post. The winners of the first day's plate will not be suffered to start for the second day's plate, except agreed upon by the Stewards, who are authorised to settle all matters in dispute. No less than three reputed running horses to start for each day's plate, if only one enters, to be allowed two guineas, if two enter, to be allowed a guinea each. The winner of each day's plate to return to the Stewards forty pounds towards the next year's plate - There will be a Ball at the Town Hall each night as usual.'

It is interesting to note in the quote, of a type of race included in the programme, a 'give and take plate.' It shows that the Race Committee was influenced by the contents of the Racing Calendar, as in the first edition, the Jockey Club published a table of weights to be allocated in Give-and-Take Plates. Instead of weight being allocated by the age of the horse, in these plates, the height of the horse determined the weight. Give-and-Take plates made it difficult to obtain a dishonest advantage over your opponents, as the height of a horse was there for all to see.

From 1776 through to the early nineteenth century, race entry conditions and the programme remained almost the same, with a few minor alterations. The entry fee for the races in 1777 was 10s 6d per race, but a year later, possibly due to lack of entries the previous year, the fee had been cut to 5s 0d in an attempt to entice prospective owners. Entries for Wednesday's race had to be made at The New Inn, whilst the entries for Thursday's race were made at the Angel Inn, also in Park Street; it appears that dual places of entry were to become the normal practice from now on. What the logic was in this change is difficult to say. Maybe it had more to do with the quality of the ale, or, why visit one hostelry when you can visit two?

The Ball for 1777 was held at the Town Hall, for two nights as usual, with tickets available from the Green Dragon, tea and coffee included. At the same hostelry, a public breakfast on the bowling green on Thursday morning was available with a good band too; all this for 1s 0d.

It was during the meeting of 1778 that the first reported incident concerning the races was published. During the running of one of the heats on Wednesday, September 25th, a man rode across the course as the runners were passing by. He was knocked from his horse and badly injured. He also succeeded in bringing down one of the runners, the jockey escaping with fractures and a dislocation. This was common in those days, and many racecourses had similar problems due to large amounts of mounted spectators present and insufficient identification of the actual course. The courses were distinguishable by posts and ropes only, and at many courses, posts only. These could easily be trodden down by an enthusiastic crowd and with no policing available, mayhem soon followed. It was not uncommon for mounted spectators to ride alongside a horse they had backed, urging the jockey to give his all in an attempt to save the luckless spectator's guinea or two.

It was not only spectators that were in danger, jockeys were the ones most exposed to the perils of the racecourse as this quote from the 1774 *Racing Calendar* shows: -

'As many fatal accidents happen by Riders being thrown or jammed against the posts, which are commonly square, and much larger than necessary, it is earnestly recommended to all Clerks of Courses, where new posts are erected, to have them made round, of light brittle wood, not above three inches in diameter, and two feet higher than usual; and where the old ones are suffered to remain, to have the edges taken off, and the bottom sawed nearly through, so that they may fall with any strong pressure.'

By the mid 1780s, races at Walsall were still being run under the same conditions as they had for at least the last thirty years, but further a field, by courtesy of the Jockey Club, progress was being made. From around 1670 to 1775, all-important races were run in heats but the future lay in what was called 'dash' racing, one race that settled the matter there and then. The first major change came at Doncaster in

1754 - 1799

1776 where a 'dash race' for three year old colts and fillies took place over one and three quarter miles and was called the St. Leger Sweepstake, the first of the Classic races. Three years later the 12th Earl of Derby and his entourage devised a race for three year old fillies over one and half miles to be run at Epsom and known as The Oaks, the name coming from the Earl's house. In 1780 Lord Derby and Sir Charles Bunbury, seeing that the St. Leger and Oaks were proving to be a success, devised another race to be run at Epsom over the same distance as The Oaks but for three year old colts and fillies. The name of the race, so reputation has it, was decided on the toss of a coin between Lord Derby and Sir Charles. Had it gone the other way, we would have had over two hundred years of the Bunbury Stakes instead of what we know as The Derby Stakes. The inaugural race was won by Sir Charles's Diomed. These early Classic races brought a relatively new word into the vocabulary, sweepstake, each race entrant subscribed a part of the prize. This was becoming increasingly popular as it increased the prize-money and attracted larger fields.

The Classic races are a long away from the little oval circuit on the Long Meadow, but by 1785 Walsall Races did have something in common with racing's elite, they were all governed and sanctioned by the same body, the Jockey Club. This was the year that the town's races appeared in the pages of the eleventh edition of the *Racing Calendar*, hopefully to the delight of the local gentry who organised the event. The racing programme was virtually no different to previous years, two races consisting of three, three mile heats with entries to be made at the same hostelries, one on Wednesday and other on Thursday. Because of this inclusion, the first official details of the races are known. The first known winning owner at the course was Mr Robert Benton whose grey mare Sally won the Gentlemen's Subscription Purse of £50 on Wednesday, September 26th, beating Mr Sifton's light bay mare, Maltbury Maid. The race on the following day saw Mr Sifton's Maltbury Maid gain revenge over Mr Benton's horse by relegating him to third place, as in the final heat the horse was withdrawn leaving the second place to Mr Woolford's bay mare, Lady Legs.

An article from *Aris' Gazette* read: -

'There was excellent sport on Wednesday, every inch of ground being sharply contested by Mr Sifton's bay and Mr Benton's grey mare and was won with difficulty by the latter, and on Thursday, afforded three excellent heats. The company was as great, respectable and genteel as ever appeared at Walsall.'

It was around this time that the organisers of the Races realised that the tradesmen of the town were taking liberties regarding the setting up of stalls and booths etc. on the race ground itself. The tradesmen were profiting handsomely from this initiative and not paying a penny in any form of rent to the organisers for the privilege. This practice had to stop, a new paragraph was inserted into the announcement in an attempt to alleviate the problem. Another problem causing concern was that of stray dogs on the course, the paragraph read: -

'No person to erect any Booth, Shed, or any other Place for the Purpose of selling Liquors, but what are Subscribers: and no Wagon, or Fruit Stall or Standing will be permitted unless Subscribers. Proper Persons will be employed to destroy all Dogs that are bought upon the Course.'

The official results of the meeting were:

Wednesday 26th September 1785
GENTLEMEN'S SUBSCRIPTION PURSE of £50, weight for age.

Mr Robert Benton's gr. m.	**Sally**	2	1	1
Mr Sifton's light b. m.	**Maltbury Maid**	1	2	2
Mr Dunkin's br. h.	**Little Jacob**		drawn	
Mr Moore's bright b. m.	**Whimsy**		drawn	

Thursday 27th September
GENTLEMEN'S SUBSCRIPTION PURSE of £50, weight for age.

Mr Sifton's light b. m.	**Maltbury Maid**	2	1	1
Mr Woolford's br. m.	**Lady Legs**	3	3	2
Mr Benton's gr. m.	**Sally**	1	2	dr

The races for 1786 were very much a copy of the previous year regarding the actual events, which took place on Wednesday and Thursday, 27th and 28th of September. The winner of Wednesday's contest was Mr Atkinson's Young Warrior beating Varges, owned by Mr Saunders' of Hednesford with Mr Young's Tally-Ho third. This race took five heats to decide the outcome instead of the advertised three. At the end of the third heat, due to a dead heat in the second and no clear winner at the end of the third, two further heats were required before the day's sport concluded.

The horses that contested Wednesday's race ran fifteen miles before a winner was declared. With the inevitable false starts that occurred frequently in those days, either by accident or design, the meeting would be approaching dusk before a conclusion was reached. In between each heat there was a half-hour interval while the jockeys weighed in and out and the horses would be scraped and rubbed down in preparation for the next stage of the contest.

The official results of the meeting were:

Wednesday 27th September 1786
GENTLEMEN'S SUBSCRIPTION PURSE of £50, weight for age

Mr Atkinson's b. g.	**Young Warrior**, 5 y-o, 8st.	2	0	2	1	1
Mr Saunders' b. m.	**Varges**, 5 y-o, 8st.	4	0	1	2	2
Mr Young's b. h.	**Tally-Ho**, 6 y-o, 8st. 9lbs.	3	4	-	-	-
Mr Ratcliff's br. h.	**John Sharp**, aged, 9st.	1	3	2	dr.	-

Thursday 28th September
GENTLEMEN'S SUBSCRIPTION PURSE of £50, weight for age

Mr Atkinson's b. m.	**Peggy**	1	2	1
Mr Young's b. m.	**Tally-Ho**	2	1	2

1754 – 1799

There is no mention at these early meetings at Walsall of how the betting was arranged. It was usual for the nobility and gentry to gather around what was known as the 'betting post' to place their wagers. Here, wagers were placed between individuals, each wager being logged in the gentleman's betting book. Settling of bets struck did not always take place immediately after the race as happens today, but had to wait until 'settling day', when the gentlemen concerned would gather to reap their rewards or pay off their debts. It is likely that betting in Walsall took place on a similar format, with the venue for 'settling day' probably being the Green Dragon.

It is known that the races took place in 1787 and 1788, but whatever criteria allowed inclusion in the *Racing Calendar* previously, it was missing in these years, and in consequence, the official results.

The next entry in the *Racing Calendar* was 1792; the conditions and rules for race entry remained the same as in previous years with the inclusion of additional charges of 7s 6d that the winner of each days' Plate must pay to the Clerk of the Course for scales and weights. The meeting consisted of three races, a Subscription Purse of £50, to be run on Wednesday and Thursday 26th and 27th September, with an additional race in the form of a Silver Cup for ponies, the announcement in Aris' Gazette read :-

'On the same day [Thursday], a Silver Cup will be run for by Ponies that never started for above the sum of £10, and not more than 13 hands high each, the best of three, two mile heats – Aged to carry 6 stones 1 pound, all under, 6 stones. Three to start or no race. Entrance is 5 shillings or double at the Post.'

Even the little ponies had to work very hard for their moment of fame, only to find that their efforts were not officially recorded.

Although the meeting was due to take place on the last Wednesday and Thursday of September, it didn't actually take place until one week later, this delay may well be the reason behind Thursdays race being cancelled.

The venues for making entries had changed, included in this year's list were the George Inn on The Bridge, the Angel Inn, Park Street and the Bulls' Head Inn, Upper Rushall Street. It makes one think that the Race Committee may well have consisted of men who ran the drinking establishments of the town.

The official results of the meeting were:

Wednesday 3rd October 1792

GENTLEMEN'S SUBSCRIPTION PURSE of £50, for horses of all ages.

Mr Shelton's b. h.	**Merry Andrew,** aged	2	1	1
Mr Pearce's ch. m.	**Lucy,** 5 y-o,	1	2	dr
Mr Lockley's ch. h.	**King Hiram,** aged	dis.	-	-

The Green Dragon, photographed in 2004, is the last of Walsall's famous old inns that is still standing. The original building is the tall white building, much of the organisation of Walsall Races happened within these walls, as did much council business, at one time it was also known as the Town Hall. One of the early licencees of the Green Dragon, Thomas Fletcher, later built the George Hotel in 1781, which became the town's premier hostelry.

WALSALL RACES

CHAPTER TWO
1800 - 1819

At the time of the first Races in the mid eighteenth century, Walsall was a thriving market and light industrial town. The town itself was surrounded by open farmland and the manufacturing industry consisted not of saddlery, as is usually associated with Walsall, but lorinery – buckle-making, ironmongery, stirrup makers and bit makers.

Walsall is one of the few towns to have census records that go back to 1801 and 1811 thanks to the foresight of a prominent citizen of the period, Thomas Pearce, a future Clerk of the Races or Course, as the position is known today. Pearce held many posts in the town including that of churchwarden, borough constable, vestry clerk, overseer of the poor and insurance agent. This early man of action was described by one of his contemporaries, James Gee, as 'Bonaparte in miniature,' this comment, bearing in mind the period, must have been as bigger insult as one could get! Almost two hundred years later, historians and researchers are grateful for the foresight of Thomas Pearce for publishing the town's first local history book in 1813, titled, *The History and Directory of Walsall*.

The total population of Walsall at the turn of the century was approximately 10,400 people living within the Borough and Foreign, and according to the reports of the day, 10,399 of them attended the Races on the Long Meadows.

1802

After a ten-year absence, the Races were again included in the pages of the *Racing Calendar* in 1802 for only the fourth time in their fifty-year history. It is clear that the Race Committee were determined to build on their past achievements and ensure that Walsall Races became an annual and fashionable event that the town could be proud of, and would equal any in the county. Between 1802 and up to the closure of the course in 1876, there were only six years that the town's name was missing from the *Racing Calendar*, twice due to outbreaks of cholera and the remaining four years due to lack of funds.

The meetings in the early part of the nineteenth century had few runners but this was as much down to the logistics of getting horses to the racecourses. In truth, the majority of horses that ran at the meetings were no better than average, with the occasional very good horse appearing from time to time; good, bad or indifferent, they still had to get to the course and the only way was by walking them. With Walsall being approximately ten miles from Hednesford and its training grounds, it comes as no surprise to find that a high percentage of the runners on the Long Meadow had this relatively short walk to 'work'. Not only did Hednesford have excellent conditions to train horses on, the ground didn't break down into a quagmire at the first drop of rain, it was also very well placed to serve Lichfield, Stafford, and in later years, Rugeley, racecourses.

On the 25th September 1802 an advertisement for the meeting was run in the *Staffordshire Advertiser* and opened with the following statement:-

'On Wednesday the 29th of September, will be run for on **Walsall New Course**, *the Corporation's and Gentleman's Subscription Purse of Fifty Pounds etc ………'*

Quite what constituted as a 'new course' is now sadly unknown as no maps from this era exist. Six years later in 1808 even more change were made to the course, these are also unknown. Safety issues even in those days were something all responsible Clerks of the Races had to be aware of, and the Clerk for Walsall Races, John Hawkes, was no exception; the same advertisement continued: -

'The Course for running will be properly marked out, and it is requested gentlemen will not ride upon it – Parents are desired to keep their children off the Course during the time of running – Dogs found upon the Course will be destroyed.'

The meeting consisted of just two races, the Corporation and Gentlemen's Subscription Purse and the Subscription Purse, the formers title being extended due to the Corporation providing added money of ten guineas to boost the prize fund.

Although only two official races were run for, there was additional entertainment available for the sporting fraternity in the form of matches, organised by individuals for their own pleasure, but no doubt enjoyed by all of the spectators; details of these informal events were unfortunately not recorded.

The Earl of Stamford became the first member of the nobility to enter a runner at Walsall. His three year-old chestnut filly, Elfrida contested the Subscription Purse on the second day – and finished last.

1800 – 1819

The official results of the meeting were:

Wednesday 29th September 1802
GENTLEMEN'S SUBSCRIPTION PURSE
of £50, weight for age

Mr Lord's ch. c.	**Turntoe**, 3 y-o	1	1
Mr Bloss' iron gr. c.	**Marquis**, 4 y-o	3	2
Mr Davis' gr. m.	**Vanity**, 6 y-o	2	3

Thursday 30th September 1802
GENTLEMEN'S SUBSCRIPTION PURSE
of £50. Three-mile heats

Mr Jones' b. h.	**Orange Flower**, 4 y-o	1	1
Mr Lockley's br. h.	**Attainment**, 4 y-o	-	-
Mr Saunders' b. m.	**Eliza**	-	-
Mr C. Smith's br. h.	**Citizen**, 5 y-o	-	-
Earl of Stamford's ch. f.	**Elfrida**, 3 y-o	-	-

Stewards: Charles Adams and Charles Berrington
Clerk of the Races: John Hawkes

1803

The meeting for this year proved to be a disappointment for the organisers with only one principle race, the Town Subscription Purse, the remaining races consisting of matches. Some of these 'matches' were a contradiction of the term; one was advertised as a match between a pony and a horse, the latter won of course but not before the gallant pony had won one of the three heats.

The Gentlemen's Subscription Purse was not run as there were only two entries, and the conditions stipulated there must be a minimum of three horses going to the post.

It would appear that the safety warnings issued the previous year were not heard by everyone, as this was the year of the first known fatality on the course. During the second heat of the Town Subscription Purse on Friday September 30th, Mrs Jane Spittle of Wednesbury attempted to cross the course as the six runners were passing. Inevitably, she was struck by one of the horses and killed instantly. Two hundred years ago this tragic event was looked upon as an inconvenience to the real proceedings of racing horses, the *Staffordshire Advertiser* simply commented, *'that it was a very good race.'*

Winner of the race was Mr Brookes' colt, Bay Mostyn, the favourite, who beat his five rivals after two of the three heats had been run. Joseph Kellerman, owner of the runner-up, Mary, was more used to seeing his rose and black colours carried at courses like Newmarket, York and Chester, quite what the attraction was to run a horse at Walsall is unknown.

The official results for the meeting were:

Thursday 29th September 1803
TOWN Purse of £50, for all ages.

Mr Brookes' b. c.	**Bay Mostyn**	1	1
Mr Kellerman's ch. m	**Mary**	2	2
Captain Graham's colt	**by Beningbrough**	5	3
Mr Dyott's b. m.	**Eliza**	3	4
Mr Ladbroke's ch. m.	**Marlanne**	4	5
Mr Hawkes b. h.	**Hop Planter**	6	dif.

A MATCH FOR 50 GUINEAS

Mr Sirdefield's br. m. pony,	**Miss Hotupon**	1	1
Mr G. Fleming's ch. m. pony,	**Frolic**	2	2

Friday 30th September 1803
A MATCH FOR 50 GUINEAS

Mr Booker's br. m.	**Little Stretton** 7st. 7lb.	1	2	1
Mr Sirdefield's br. m pony,	**Miss Hotupon** a featherweight	2	1	2

A MATCH

Mr Dace's pony, **North East** beat Mr Day's pony, **South West**.

1804

Fortunately John Hawkes, the Clerk, did not ignore the tragic incident in 1803, included in the announcement for the meeting for the following year an additional paragraph was added regarding safety on the course and read: –

'Whereas several accidents have happened on the race ground, by the foot people standing within the cords during the time the horses are running; to prevent the same in future, an additional number of course keepers are engaged for that purpose, as no person whatever will be suffered to be within the cords, during that time, it is hoped everyone will peaceably comply with this regulation. Any person insulting the men upon their duty, will be prosecuted.'

It appears the spectators of Walsall Races obeyed Mr Hawkes warning, as there were no reported incidents for many years to come.

With the town swelled by the influx of people for the Fair and the Races, the last week in September must have been the most profitable period of the year for the innkeepers, theatre owners and traders in Walsall. The innkeepers were still maintaining the tradition of the 'ordinaries' during daylight hours and a ball after racing each evening at the George Inn one night, and the Dragon the following night.

The theatre in The Square (known as The Old Square today), opened in 1803 and continued entertaining the public well into the night with Mr Watson's Company from the Theatre Royal, Cheltenham, and Mrs. Nunn's Company of Comedians. The money to erect the theatre was raised by subscription, in shares of fifty pounds. Every subscriber received interest on the investment, along with a silver ticket transferable at pleasure.

The official records show three races recorded, two on Wednesday, the Corporation and Subscription Purse plus a Sweepstakes race, and on Thursday, the Town Subscription Purse. James Lord, a trainer from Hednesford, made his presence felt when his horses won two of the races and finished second in the other.

The official results of the meeting were:

Wednesday 26th September 1804
GENTLEMEN'S SUBSCRIPTION PURSE of £50,
weight for age. Three mile heats.

Mr Pigot's colt	**by Woodpecker**, 4 y-o	3	1	1
Mr J. Lord's ch. f.	**Danceaway**, 4 y-o	3	3	2
Mr Reece's b. m.	**Duchess**, 4 y-o	1	2	dr.

High odds on Mr Pigot's colt.

1800 - 1819

A SWEEPSTAKES of 50 guineas.
Three mile heat.

Mr J. Lord's ch. f.	**Danceaway**, 4 y-o	1	
Mr Tinkler's bl. f.	**Raval**, 4 y-o	2	
Mr Booker's b. c.	**by Screventon**, 4 y-o	dr.	

Danceaway the favourite.

Thursday 27th September 1804
SUBSCRIPTION PURSE of £50.
All ages. Three-mile heats

Mr J. Lord's b. g.	**Cockspinner**, 4 y-o	1	1
Mr T. L. Brookes's b. h.	**Bay Mostyn**, 4 y-o	2	2
Mr J. C. Whateley's b. h.	**Prior**, 5 y-o	fell	dis
Mr Pigot's colt	**by Woodpecker**, 4 y-o	dr.	
Mr Reece's b. m.	**Duchess**, 4 y-o	dr.	

5 to 4 Bay Mostyn against the field.

1805

Cockfighting was continuing its popularity at the Woolpack in High Street and the New Inn in Park Street. To cope with the demand for this rather extreme of 'sports,' Charles Perks opened a larger cockpit in 1805 at the bottom of the yard behind the New Inn in Park Street.

John Clifton from Lancashire began to enter horses at the meeting, and his colours of yellow jacket with a brown hoop became a familiar sight on the racecourse over the next few years. Clifton was a successful owner with many winners at various courses around the country. His luck, however, appeared to nearly always desert him at Walsall, recording just two winners in a ten-year period - but it never stopped him trying. His first winner at the course was a four year-old bay mare named Josephina, who won the Corporation and Gentlemen's Subscription Purse in 1805. Josephina was by the 1787 Derby winner, Sir Peter Teazle, and contested several more races on the Long Meadow but never again caught the judge's eye. On the opening day of the Walsall meeting in 1806, John Clifton was at Doncaster to watch his horse, Fyldener, run, and win, the final Classic race of the season, the St. Leger Stakes. The year after, with no horse of the quality of Fyldener to worry about, he was back watching his runners at Walsall.

In 1805 another owner, a Mr Skinner, entered his horse Duckling in the Town Subscription Plate, and this was possibly the best horse yet to appear at Walsall. Duckling was a five year-old bay mare that had previously won four times before coming to Walsall, including three successive wins at Reading, Warwick and the prestigious King's Plate at Lichfield. Her superior ability was proven when she won the first two heats of the three-heat event easily, and if this wasn't enough, she beat her nearest rival carrying thirty one pounds more in weight.

It was around this period that it was announced that all jockeys riding at Walsall must wear colours to distinguish themselves from the other

A watercolour illustration of the original Woolpack Inn which had close associations with Walsall Races. Many cockfights were held on the premises to keep the sportsmen of the old town happy after the days racing. These premises were demolished in 1892 to make way for a new mock Tudor building that bore the same name, see inset above, photographed c.1905. © John Griffiths.

1800 – 1819

runners. This rule was made compulsory by the Jockey Club as long ago as 1762 for races and matches held at Newmarket. The idea soon spread to many other courses but it didn't reach Walsall until forty-three years later. Any rider who didn't go out in colours had to pay a fine of one guinea to the Clerk of the Races. Up until this announcement was made many of the jockeys were indistinguishable from the spectators. Jockeys at this time were allowed to wear spurs and they carried a most evil whalebone whip capable of cutting into horseflesh and inflicting considerable injury on the unfortunate animal. The riders and training grooms of this era were rough men, on and off horses, and many of them were as bent as a paper clip, but probably no more so than the nobility and gentry they rode for.

Not for the first time, the meeting proved to be a disappointment with just two races being contested, a Sweepstakes race was included in the card on Wednesday, but this failed to attract the minimum required entries and was cancelled. New initiatives were tried in the form of hunter races to be ridden by gentlemen riders only, usually the horses owner, at first they were rather spasmodic events but in later years became a regular event, proving popular with both owners and racegoers alike.

The official results of the meeting were:

Wednesday 25th September 1805

CORPORATION AND Gentlemen's Subscription Purse of £50, for 3 and 4 y-o horses.
Three mile heats. 3 y-o to carry 6 st. - 4 y-o 7st. 4lbs.

Mr John Clifton's b. f.	**Josephina,** 4 y-o	1	1
Lord Grey's br. f.	**Georgina,** 3 y-o	2	2
Mr Saunders' br. f.	**Brown Bess,** 4 y-o	3	3

Thursday 26th September 1805

TOWN SUBSCRIPTION PURSE of £50.
Three-mile heats. Horses of all ages.

Mr Skinner's b. m.	**Duckling,** 4 y-o, 8st. 6lb.	1	1
Mr John Clifton's ch. c.	**Welsh Harp,** 3 y-o, 6st. 3lb.	4	2
Mr Glossop's b. c.	**Skylark,** 4 y-o, 7st. 7lb.	3	3
Mr Anson's gr. c. by	**Moorcock,** 3 y-o, 6st. 3lb.	2	4

Stewards: Walter Spurrier and William Nicholls.
Clerk of the Races: John Hawkes.

1806

In an effort to raise the profile of the meeting in this year, the Race Committee managed to organise a record number of five races to be run over the two days.

Scheduled for Wednesday 24th September were two races, the customary Subscription Purse of £50 and a Sweepstakes of 10 guineas each, followed on Thursday by the age old Town Subscription Purse of £50 and two Sweepstake races of 10 guineas each, one for three year olds and one for hunters.

Rather disappointingly, the outcome of only two of the five races was officially recorded in the Racing Calendar. Of the remaining races, it is not known if they took place, but it seems unlikely that all three races would have fallen by the wayside due to a lack of runners. The most likely explanation for their omission is that they were simply not recorded.

The two races of which the results are known were both predictable affairs, with one horse in each event dominating. On Wednesday the Corporation and Gentlemen's Subscription Purse unfortunately became a match between Mr Smith's brown mare, Hebe, and Mr Storey's chestnut filly, Lady Fair. The weights were in favour of the latter, who was giving almost three stones to her solitary opponent, Hebe. The difference in weight proved to be insufficient as far as Lady Fair was concerned, both she and her jockey could only watch as Hebe disappeared into the distance to win two of the three heats comfortably.

Thursday's race, the Town Subscription Purse, did provide something in the way of sporting entertainment with four runners, although this event was also dominated by one horse. The horse concerned was Mr Butler's five year old bay mare, Miss Coiner, who defeated her opponents easily, even though carrying top weight. Welsh Harp, who had run second in a race the previous year for the well known northern owner John Clifton, had changed hands, and was now owned by a Mr Birchall. Running in the new colours of Mr Birchall had not changed anything, the colt could only finish second and third in the heats to Miss Coiner. Lord Grey was still waiting for his first winner on the Long Meadows when his colt, St. Domingo, was placed second. The remaining member of the quartet, Mr Goodall's colt, Ptarmagan, proved no threat to any of his opponents, finishing last in both heats.

The official results of the meeting were:

Wednesday 24th September 1806

CORPORATION AND GENTLEMEN'S SUBSCRIPTION PURSE of £50.
For horses of all ages. Three mile heats.

| Mr Smith's br. m. | **Hebe,** 5 y-o, 8st. 6lb. | 1 | 1 |
| Mr Storey's ch. f. | **Lady Fair,** 3 y-o, 5st. 11lb. | 2 | 2 |

Thursday 25th September

TOWN SUBSCRIPTION PURSE of £50.
Three-mile heats. Horses of all ages.

Mr Butler's b. m.	**Miss Coiner,** 5 y-o, 8st. 6lb.	1	1
Lord Grey's ch. c.	**St. Domingo,** 3 y-o, 6st. 5lb.	3	2
Mr Birchall's c.	**Welsh Harp,** 4 y-o, 7st. 9lb.	2	3
Mr Goodall's b. c.	**Ptarmagan,** 3 y-o, 6st. 3lb.	4	4

Stewards: James Adams and Richard Adams
Clerk of the Races: John Hawkes

1807

Predictability was once again the name of the game with regard to the meeting, three races dominated by two horses. In the opening race on Wednesday 23rd September, the Sweepstakes race of three, three mile heats, was won by Hebe, still in the same ownership as when she won so convincingly in 1806. She may have been a year older, but her ability to dominate races hadn't deserted her, with only two opponents,

1800 - 1819

she won two of the required three heats with considerable ease, just as she had done the previous year.

Lord Grey, of Enville Hall near Stourbridge had been a supporter and subscriber to Walsall Races for many years, without success. In 1807 his luck finally changed and he recorded his first two winners, with the same horse. In recording these victories, he also became the first member of the nobility to record a winner at the course. The horse, Belinda, that carried his colours of light blue silks and black cap to victory in the Corporation and Gentlemen's Subscription Purse was sired by the 1794 winner of the St. Leger, Beningborough. Following on from this, the three year old filly won the only race on Thursday, the Town Subscription Purse, five runners contested the event including the easy winner from the previous day, Hebe. In this race Mr Smith's mare, Hebe, found Belinda, and two other contestants, full of running, and she could only finish fourth of the five runners. Weight undoubtably played a big part in Hebe's defeat, she was conceding weight to all of her opponents, including two and half stone to the winner, that combined with the exertions of her victory the previous day, proving a little too much.

The official results of the meeting were:

Wednesday 23rd September 1807

A SWEEPSTAKES of 10 guineas each, with 20 guineas added.

Three mile heats.

Mr Smith's br. m.	Hebe. 6 y-o, 9st.	1	1
Mr Goulburn's gr. h.	Grimaldi, 5 y-o, 8st. 9lb.	2	2
Major Morris' br. f.	Fay, 4 y-o, 7st. 1lb.	3	3

CORPORATION AND Gentlemen's Subscription Purse of £50.
For horses of all ages. Three mile heats.

Lord Grey's b. f.	Belinda, 3 y-o, 6st. 2lb.	1	1
Mr Goulburn's gr. h.	Grimaldi, 5 y-o, 8st. 7lb.	2	2
Mr Bowker's br. c.	Plunder, 4 y-o, 7st. 4lb.	3	dr

Thursday 24th September 1807

TOWN SUBSCRIPTION PURSE of £50.
Three-mile heats. For horses of all ages.

Lord Grey's b. f.	Belinda, 3 y-o, 6st. 2lb.	1	1
Mr Bowker's br. c.	Plunder, 4 y-o, 7st. 4lb.	5	2
Major Morris' br. f.	Fay, 4 y-o, 7st. 1lb.	4	3
Mr Smith's br. m.	Hebe, 6 y-o, 8st. 11lb.	2	4
Mr Brown's ch. c.	by George, 3 y-o, 6st.	3	5

1808

In the announcement in Aris' Gazette of September 19th 1808 there appeared another significant statement regarding the course:

> 'On the morning of Wednesday, September 28, will be run for, on Walsall New Course.'

A later quote from the announcement states: -

> 'A capital New Course has been made at considerable Expense, and every Exertion will be used to keep it clear and in good Order.'

A capital new course, how did it differ from the old course, were there further course alterations from those made in 1802? From a researchers point of view, many questions are asked by that statement, with no answers forthcoming. In all probability the course did undergo alterations of some kind as the following year the grandstand opened. At this time there were few maps of the town showing the area the racecourse covered. The only maps of this period show the boundaries of the Borough of Walsall, and the racecourse was in the Foreign. It will probably never be known how the new course differed from the old one; the most probable explanation is rather contradictory. It was not a new course as one would think, but the existing one, with a more permanent definition of its lines and possibly an accurate measurement of the course. In later years it was known that the course was 1,740 yards in length – 20 yards short of one mile, well maybe not that accurately measured!

Whatever the changes in the course were, it shows the Race Committee were not content to see the town's annual sporting event continue in the same vein that it had done for the last fifty years. As was said earlier, this was the era of Thomas Pearce, and it does raise the question of how much influence Walsall's 'Bonaparte in miniature' had in these new initiatives. Given his past record within the town, it would seem highly unlikely that his name didn't appear somewhere on the proposals for developing the new course.

To test the new facilities five races were arranged over the two days of Wednesday 28th and Thursday 29th of September. Mr J. Lockley had the distinction of owning the first winner on the new course with his bay filly, Peggy Bucknall who beat four other horses of considerably better pedigree. The prize money for this race was one hundred guineas, which was quite a sum in those days at a provincial racecourse. The owner of the second horse was Nathaniel Gooding Clarke of Handsworth, a man whose name was to feature, along with others, in future developments of the racecourse.

Lord Grey who had problems winning at Walsall in previous years now couldn't stop. After recording his first two winners the year before, he continued his success with another double on Thursday, with a chestnut horse named St. Domingo.

The official results of the meeting were:

Wednesday 28th September 1808

In the morning,
A SWEEPSTAKES of 100 Guineas. One two mile heat.

Mr J. Lockley's b. f.	**Peggy Bucknall**	1
Mr N. Clarke names b. f.	**by Hambletonian**	2
Major Morris' b. f. by	**Warter**	3
Lieut. Col. Crum's ch. c.	**Juniper**	dr
Earl of Stamford's br. f.	**Petronella**	dr

In the afternoon,
THE CORPORATION PLATE
of £50. Three, three mile heats.

Mr C. Smith's br. m.	**Miss Blanchard**, 4 y-o	5	1	1
Mr John Clifton's br. m.	**Josephina**, aged	3	2	dr
Mr Butler's b. m.	**Miss Coiner**, aged	4	3	dr
Mr Richardson's b. m.	**Miss Whitley**, 4 y-o	2	dr	-
Mr J. Lockley's b. f.	**Peggy Bucknall**	1	dr	-

1800 - 1819

Thursday 29th September 1808

In the morning,

A SWEEPSTAKES of 60 Guineas. Three, three mile heats.
Horses of all ages.

Lord Grey's ch. h.	**St. Domingo**, 5 y-o	1	1
Major Morris' b. c.	**Wildair**, 4 y-o	2	2
Mr Richard Dyott's gr. c.	**Lichfield**	dr	-
Major Wilson's b. c.	by **Hambletonian**, 3 y-o	dr	-

The same morning a match between two hunters, carrying 8st. each, the best of 3 two mile heats for 50 guineas. A good race, the horse beating the mare by only half a neck.

In the afternoon,

THE TOWN PLATE of £50. Three, three mile heats

Lord Grey's ch. h.	**St. Domingo**, 5 y-o	1	1
Lord Oxford's b. h.	**Tudor**, 5 y-o	2	2
Major Morris' b. c.	**Wildair**, 4 y-o	3	3
Mr C. Smith's br. m.	**Miss Blanchard**, 4 y-o	dr	-
Mr John Clifton's b. m.	**Josephina**, aged	dr	-
Mr Butler's b. m.	**Miss Coiner**, aged	dr	-

Stewards: Lord Bradford and Nathaniel Gooding Clarke.
Clerk of the Races: John Hawkes.

1809

With little detailed information available regarding the Races for earlier years, 1809 is one year that has been referred to in every publication or article that has been written about the meetings on the Long Meadow, as this was the year the grandstand was opened.

To give an impression of what Walsall was like in those days, we must move on seventy years to the demolition of the grandstand in 1879. In the Walsall Red Book for that year, W. C. Owen, reminisces over the demise of the grandstand and part of his article describes the town in 1809, before the town expanded and the soot and grime of industry had completely enveloped the area: -

'At our feet flows the open 'mill fleam,' with a foot bridge for passengers, while vehicles drive through it. The George Inn is there, and that and the building where now is the office of the 'Red Book,' are the only two of any size in the open space. On the side opposite to the 'George' runs the main brook, crossed by a bridge at the bottom of Park Street. Near the right hand corner are some magnificent forest trees, and there is a lonely walk through the fields towards the Wisemore. Park Street has some good houses, but most of those in the street are mean, low buildings. Of course there is no Station Street. At the top is the Town's-end Bank, literally the town's end, and all beyond is open country, with at most a few old cottages. Bridge Street is only partially filled, but the houses are of a very respectable class, and it is certainly a 'residential' street. There is no Lichfield Street, and the main road from Lichfield comes to the bottom of Lower Rushall Street, which street, as a glance at its buildings will amply testify, is occupied by many of our local aristocrats. On the other side of the town there is no Bradford Street, but a nice walk through fields alongside the 'mill fleam,' till we reach the Grand Stand, where the walk divides, one branch continuing along the banks of the stream, and the other going to the right of the Stand and then over the main brook to the Pleck. From the racecourse to the canal there are green fields, and no ironworks to bound the view, and across the fields can be seen the small group of houses which is all that goes to make the Pleck. Caldmore and Palfrey are unbuilt upon. The Windmill is a hamlet near Walsall, and the Vicarage a neat, rural mansion. On the hill, near the Church, is the ancient building where formerly the Grammar School was located; while the space around is densely crowded with small buildings, and a 'Crooked alley' gives access to New Street. The hill from the Church to High Street is filled with dwellings, and the narrow flight of steps between them is the only thoroughfare. Up the Church steps, along the south side of the Churchyard, under the chancel, and out at the 'light gates,' is a public footway. The Old Church is still standing, but soon to be condemned. There are no policemen, no gaslights, no railways; in fact, Walsall is more of an agricultural than a manufacturing town, and on Tuesdays, at the top of High Street and Upper Rushall Street are busy throngs of farmers' wives and daughters selling the produce of their dairies and poultry yards, while pigs are there in thousands, for Walsall has one of the most flourishing pig markets in the kingdom. The old Market Cross in the upper room of which was held the Blue Coat School, has just disappeared, and its pillory, stocks, and whipping posts are no more.'

What a wonderful picture those words paint of a Walsall long since disappeared, but little changes in some respects – there are still no policemen and the town is full of pigs, after dark, most nights of the week anyway!

The area of the Grandstand covered 165 square yards, and the completed structure cost £1,300, the money for the project was raised by subscription in shares of £25, each subscriber receiving interest on his money and a free admission ticket. The word ticket is rather misleading, it was in fact a bronze coin (see below). The land upon which the grandstand stood was leased from the owner, Lord Bradford for ninety-nine years, commencing on March 25th 1809 and expiring on March 25th 1908 at an annual rent of one shilling. As events turned out, the races ceased thirty-two years before the lease was due to expire.

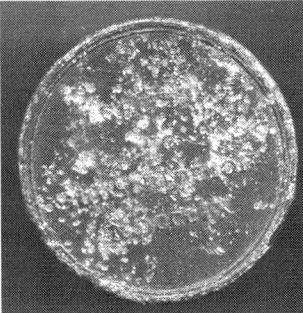

Artifacts from Walsall's past do not come much rarer than this original 1809 Grandstand Subscription Ticket for the races. Three of these 'tickets' came up for sale at a major London auction house some years ago. It measures 40mm in diameter and is 3mm thick. The first word on the back is possibly "Second" followed by "Subscription MDCCCIX". (Reproduced by courtesy of Gordon Garrity).

1800 - 1819

WALSALL RACES 1809

On Wednesday, September 27, will be run for, in the MORNING, a SWEEPSTAKES of TWENTY GUINEAS each, for three year-olds, Colts to carry 8st. 5lb. and Fillies 8st. 2lb. one two mile heat.
Lord Bradford's b.c. by Cheshire Cheese
Mr Crockett's ch. c. Sandy by Sorcerer
Mr Whitmore's b.c. Glassblower, by Expectation

In the Afternoon, the Corporation and Gentlemen's Subscription Purse of £50, by Horses &c. of all Ages, three year-olds to carry 7st. four year-olds 8st. 2lb., five year-olds 8st. 12lb. six year-olds 9st. and aged 9st. 2lb. Mares and Geldings allowed 3lb. the best of three-mile Heats.
Lord Bradford's b.h. Sir Guy, by Sir Peter, 5y-o
Mr R. Hawkes' br.f. The Inconstant, by Sir Peter, 4y-o
Mr J. V. Barber's br.c. Sir Anthony Rowley, by Sir Peter, 3y-o
Mr Spurrier's ch.f. by Delpini, Dam by Dungannon, 3y-o
Mr Goulburn's ch.h. Romeo, 5y-o
Mr Crocket's ch.c. Sandy by Sorcerer, 3y-o
Mr Smith's br.m. Miss Blanchard, 5y-o

In the AFTERNOON, the TOWN SUBSCRIPTION PURSE of FIFTY POUNDS, by Horses of all Ages, Weights, Distance, and other Particulars, the same as for the Wednesday's Plate.

All Horses, running for either of the above Plates, that have won one 50l. this Year, to carry 3lb. of two or more 5lb. extra, and must stand at the House of a Subscriber of one Guinea, and be plated by a Smith subscribing 10s. 6d. or pay double Entrance, by which Payment any Horse, duly qualified, may enter on the Day of running, the Stewards having directed that all Post Entrance shall be made to the Clerk of the Course at or before Ten o'clock in the Morning of that Day.

The Owner of each Horse, &c. must pay two Guineas Entrance and 10s. 6d. to the Clerk. The Entrance Money to go to the second best Horse, &c.

No less than three reputed running Horses, &c. to start for either of the above Plates; if only one enters, to have ten Guineas; if two, five Guineas each, and their Entrance Money returned; but if agreed upon by the Stewards that two shall start, the Refuser to forfeit his Entrance, and the other who does not refuse to have ten Guineas.

To start each Day in the Morning at Eleven, and in the Afternoon at Three o'clock.

Certificates of the Age of each Horse, &c. to be produced at the Time of Entrance, which is Monday the 25th September, between the Hours of Four and Six o'clock, at the George Inn, Digbeth.

All Disputes to be finally determined by the Stewards, or whom they appoint.

The Winners of the above Plates to receive the same without any Deduction.

HENRY CROCKET, Esq., JOHN WALHOUSE, Esq., Stewards
Mr J. HAWKES, Clerk of the Races.

No Person will be allowed to erect a Booth, Shed or Stall, on the Race Ground, until they have agreed with the Clerk and paid one Guinea for each Booth, Shed, Carts, Stalls, &c. in Proportion.

Ordinaries, Balls, and Cocking, as usual. Plays each Evening during the Race Week at the Theatre, by Mr Watson's Company, from the Theatre Royal, Cheltenham.

To prevent Disputes, and the better to distinguish the Race Horses, the Owners at the Time of Entrance to declare what Colour they intend to ride in, and any Jockey not riding the Colour specified to forfeit one Guinea to the Clerk.

N.B. An elegant new Grand Stand has been erected, at great Expense, for the Accommodation of the Nobility and Gentry attending the Races.

The announcement for Walsall Races published in Aris' Birmingham Gazette, 4th September 1809.

The principles involved in the lease from Walsall were, James Adams (gentleman), John Stubbs (banker), John Vaughan Barber (gentleman of Rushall Street) and John Clements Whateley of Birchills. Other men involved from out of the immediate area were, Henry Crocket of Little Onn Hall, Nathaniel Gooding Clarke and Joseph Stubbs, both of Handsworth and John Walhouse of Hatherton.

The architect for the new structure was Mr B. Wyatt of Sutton Coldfield; the builders were local men, William Nevill a builder, and Thomas Carter a carpenter, both of Dudley Street. The main walls of the building were of brick with a timber frontage, the engraving made in 1813 shows what an elegant building it must have been, small by comparison to some of the grandstands being built at other courses. The organisers of the races may well have felt that a structure of this nature would increase their standing within the racing fraternity and show that Walsall was serious about its sport, but the real reason, as with every other grandstand built, was to separate the nobility and gentry from the 'riff-raff'. This is highlighted in the final paragraph from the announcement for the meeting which was published in Aris' Gazette on September 4th 1809 and reproduced in the panel above. Thomas Pearce in *The History and Directory of Walsall* states: -
  'It [the grandstand] filled at the races which took place on the 27th and 28th of September, in the same year, with a numerous and respectable company.'
There are no plans or descriptions of the interior of the new building it is difficult to say how it functioned, apart from allowing race-goers of the right class to watch the races in relative comfort.

There is no mention of a weighing area, but this is not unusual as the majority of courses at this time, and for many years to come, weighed the jockeys outdoors. In the one and only known photograph of the grandstand, on page 111, there appears to be a large beam protruding from the wall, on the far right of the building, it is possible that this could be the beam from which the scales were suspended. The facilities had improved but the racing itself was little different to previous years. Henry Crocket, one of the Stewards for this year, won the first race on Wednesday morning when his chestnut colt, Sandy won the Sweepstakes over two miles. This race had been reduced to a match when Lord Bradford withdrew his horse from the running, leaving only Mr Whitmore's colt Glassblower, the 1/2 odds-on favourite, to challenge Sandy.

The Sweepstakes run on Thursday had a change to its conditions, this year the horses contesting the event were to carry Leicester Cup weights.

At the end of the season, in early November, the Race Committee at Walsall must have looked back on what was a memorable year for them. Their efforts to develop the course in 1808 and the building of the elegant little grandstand would give them confidence in promoting the meeting in the future as a fashionable event, worthy of inclusion on anyone's calendar.

1800 – 1819

The official results of the meeting were:

Wednesday 27th September 1809
In the morning,
A SWEEPSTAKES of 20 Guineas each.
One, two mile heat.

Mr Crockett's ch. c.	**Sandy** by Sorcerer, 8st 5lb.	1
Mr Whitmore's b. c.	**Glassblower**, 8st. 5lb.	2
Lord Bradford's b. c. by	**Cheshire Cheese**	dr

In the afternoon,
A SUBSCRIPTION PURSE of £50 for all ages.
Three mile heats.

Mr Hewitt's br. f.	**Lady Earn**	2	1	1
Mr Tarratt's ch. g.	**Sunflower**	1	2	2
Mr Turner's	**Maid of Durham**	3	3	3

Thursday 28th September 1809
In the morning,
A SWEEPSTAKES of 10 guineas each,
with 20 guineas added by the Stewards, for all ages,
carrying Leicester Cup weights. Three mile heats.

Mr Goulburn's ch. h.	**Romeo**, 3 y-o	2	1	1
Mr C. Smith's br. m.	**Miss Blanchard**, 5 y-o	1	2	dr

In the afternoon,
A SUBSCRIPTION PURSE
of £50, for all ages.

Mr Hewitt's br. f.	**Lady Earn**	1	1
Mr Tarratt's ch. g.	**Sunflower**	2	dr

Stewards: Henry Crockett and John Walhouse.
Clerk of the Races: John Hawkes.

1810

In 1810 the *Staffordshire Advertiser* concluded their report on the meeting with the following quote: -

'These Races were well and respectably attended; and from the spirit manifested by the gentlemen of the town for their engagement, will, we have no doubt, shortly vie with the best in the county.'

Thomas Pearce took over as Clerk of the Races from John Hawkes who had held the position since the late 1790s. If Pearce applied himself to his new position as enthusiastically as he had to the other posts he held, Walsall Races may well 'vie with the best in the county', even if there were only three other contenders, Lichfield, Stafford, the oldest in the county, and Newcastle-Under-Lyme, which first appeared in the *Racing Calendar* in 1786.

The annual announcement in Aris' Gazette published on September 10th states that the Races will take place on the last Wednesday and Thursday of the month as usual but the official results read somewhat differently. They state that the meeting took place over three days and not two. Why this happened is not clear. The most probable reason was that bad weather, prevented Thursday's meeting from concluding and it was decided to 'add-on' to Friday. Whatever the reason behind the first three day meeting, accident or design, it still had the same races listed in the programme as in previous years. In earlier meetings it appears all of the runners had to pay a fee for the use of scales and weights, from this year only the winners of the races had to pay the ten shillings and sixpence for the privilege. The cost of one entry was two guineas plus 10s 6d to the Clerk. This entrance money was given to the horse placed second.

The earliest known illustration of the new grandstand erected in 1809. This was published in Thomas Pearce's History and Directory of Walsall in 1813. (Walsall Local History Centre.)

1800 - 1819

The official Steward's for this year were Sir Robert Lawley from Canwell Hall near Sutton Coldfield, and a name well known in Walsall during this period, Phineas Hussey of Little Wyrley Hall. It was not unknown for the Stewards to appoint other people to officiate in their place and not turn up, however, it would be difficult to think of this happening whilst 'Bonaparte in miniature', Mr Pearce was in office.

On the third day of the meeting the first ever handicap race at the course was run, the Handicap Sweepstakes over three three-mile heats. The winner was Mr Keen's horse Parvula who had already won on the previous day, taking the other Sweepstakes race.

What makes this year memorable is that one jockey, Richard Spencer from Hednesford, rode all of the winners. If the walkover on the first day is added to the tally, Spencer rode eight winners over the three days. He was a very well respected, and well-known, horseman, whose fame did not stop at the boundaries of Staffordshire. *The Sporting Magazine*, in 1839 wrote after his death, *'...the late Mr Richard Spencer, who was in his time one of the best country jockeys we had.'* After Spencer had died, the house was taken over by Thomas Saunders who was to become, along with his son, a famous trainer in the Hazel Slade and Hednesford areas. Thomas' son, William, trained horses for Rugeley's most infamous son, Dr. Palmer in the 1840s and 50s.

The official results of the meeting were:

Wednesday 26th September 1810
In the morning,
A SWEEPSTAKES of 10 guineas each with 20 guineas added by the Stewards. Three mile heats.

Mr Richard Dyott's gr. h.	**Lichfield**, 6 y-o	walked over

In the afternoon,
THE CORPORATION & GENTLEMEN'S PURSE
of £50 for all ages. Three, three mile heats.

Earl of Stamford's b.m.	**Belinda**, 6 y-o, 9st. 2lb.	3	1	1
Mr Carter's b.f.	**by Sir Ulic**, 3 y-o, 7st. 4lb.	2	3	2
Mr Ashmole's b.h.	**Smallhopes**, 4 y-o, 8st.	1	2	dr

Thursday 27th September 1810
In the morning,
A SWEEPSTAKES of 20 guineas each, for 3 year olds.
One, two mile heat.

Mr Astley's br.f.	**Elve**, by Sorcerer	1
Mr Crockett's ch.c.	**by George**	2
Mr Denham's b.c.	**by Beningborough**	3
Sir Robert Lawley's br.c.	**brother to Baron**	dr

In the afternoon,
THE TOWN SUBSCRIPTION PURSE of £50.
Horses of all ages.

Mr Keen's b.m.	**Parvula**, 4 y-o, 8st. 4lb.	1	1
Mr Fisher's br.m.	**Amulet**, 4 y-o, 8st 4lb.	2	2
Mr Hodson's ch.c.	**Sandy**, 4 y-o, 8st. 5lb.	3	3
Mr Carter's b.f. by	**Sir Ulic**, 3 y-o, 7st. 4lb.	dr	-
Mr Ashmole's b.h.	**Smallhopes**, 4 y-o, 8st. 7lb.	dr	-
Earl of Stamford's b.m.	**Belinda**, 3 y-o, 9st. 2lb.	dr	-

Friday 28th September 1810
A HANDICAP SWEEPSTAKES of 5 guineas each,
with 40 guineas added by the town. Horses of all ages.

Mr Keen's b.m.	**Parvula**, 4 y-o, 8st. 11lb.	1	1
Mr Hodson's ch.c.	**Sandy**, 4 y-o, 7st. 4lb.	3	2
Mr Fisher's b.m.	**Amulet**, 4 y-o, 7st. 12lb.	2	dr
Mr Crockett's ch.c.	**by George**, 3 y-o, 6st. 7lb.	dr	-
Mr Denham's br.c.	**by Beningborough**, 3 y-o, 7st	dr	-

Stewards: Sir Robert Lawley and Phineas Hussey.
Clerk of the Races: Thomas Pearce.

1811

The first meeting in the second decade of the nineteenth century saw additions to the race programme in the form of a Silver Cup and another new race called the Welter Stakes. The latter event proving to be a disappointing affair as only two horses entered instead of the three required to make a race.

The subscribers for the Silver Cup totalled eight for its inaugural running, but subscribers do not necessarily make runners at the post, and the event was reduced to a match, won by Mr J. P. Dyott's horse, Bronte. One of the conditions of entry for this race was: -

'Horses must be the property of an Officer, Non-Commissioned Officer or Private of the South Staffordshire Southern and Western Local Regiments of Militia.'

With conditions as restrictive as that it is surprising there were as many as eight subscribers.

The two Stewards for the meeting, Sir John Wrottesley of Wrottesley Hall near Albrighton and Thomas Giffard of Chillington Hall near Brewood, entered horses but were unsuccessful in taking any of the prize money. The race went to Walton, owned by Mr Keen, who had now had three wins from three runners in the last two years.

The official results of the meeting were:

Wednesday 25th September 1811
In the morning,
A SWEEPSTAKES of 10 guineas each,
with 15 guineas added by the Stewards. For horses of all ages, carrying Leicester Cup weights. Three, three mile heats.

Capt. Chambers'	**Morgiana**, 4 y-o	3	1	0	1
Mr Shaw's b. c.	**Occator**, 4 y-o	1	3	0	2
Mr Brown's ch. h.	**by George**, 4 y-o	2	2	dr	-
Mr J. V. Barber's	**Stilton**, 5 y-o	dr	-	-	-
Mr Boultbee's ch. c.	**Rifler**, 5 y-o	dr	-	-	-

A SILVER CUP of £50, with £10 added by the town,
for all ages. One, three mile heat.

Mr J. P. Dyott's b. h.	**Bronte**, aged	1
Mr T. Gibbons' jnr. gr. g.	**by Regulus**	2

THE CORPORATION & GENTLEMEN'S SUBSCRIPTION PURSE of £50 for
horses of all ages. Three, three mile heats.

Mr Tomes' r. h.	**Mahogany**, 4 y-o	1	2	1
Mr Brade's b. m.	**Georgiana**, 4 y-o	2	1	2
Mr J. Elliott's ch. f.	**Cora**, 3 y-o	3	3	dr
Mr Shaw's b. c.	**General Graham's**	dr	-	-
Mr Brown's ch. c.	**by George**	dr	-	-

1800 – 1819

Thursday 26th September 1811
In the morning,
A SWEEPSTAKES of 10 guineas each,
with 15 guineas added by the town. for 3 year olds.
Colts to carry 8st. 5lb., fillies 8st. 3lb. One, two mile heat.

Mr Keen's gr. c.	by Walton	1
Mr Shaw's b. c.	General Graham	2
Sir Thomas Stanley's b. c.	by Rememberancer	3
Mr Thomas Giffard's b. f.	by Vermin	4
Mr J. V. Barber's b. f.	Claudia	5

Two others withdrawn.

THE TOWN SUBSCRIPTION PURSE
of £50, for all ages. Three, three mile heats.

Sir Thomas Stanley's b. c.	by Rememberancer	1	1
Mr J. V. Barber's b. f.	Claudia	2	3
Mr John Clifton's	Jessamy	3	2
Mr Shaw's b. c.	Occator	dr	-

THE WELTER SWEEPSTAKES did not fill.

Stewards: Sir John Wrottesley and Thomas Giffard.
Clerk of the Races: Thomas Pearce.

1812

The grandstand was obviously having the desired effect in attracting the nobility and gentry. There were entries from Sir John Wrottesley, Sir Robert Lawley, Earl Wilton, Edward Anson (Steward), the Honourable G. A. Bridgeman, Richard Moores Fletcher, Edward J. Littleton, Lord Oxford, Colonel Walhouse, John Vaughan Barber, Ralph Benson and Sir Thomas Mostyn. Benson was a new name to add to the dignitaries that ran horses at Walsall, a resident of Staffordshire, his colours of blue and white hooped jacket and blue cap were more well known at the more prestigious courses like Newmarket, York, Chester and Epsom.

Colonel Walhouse must have been well pleased with his choice of jockey in the opening race on Wednesday morning. With the race again reduced to a match, the Colonel must have fancied his chances, only to see them disappear when his horse took hold of the bit and bolted leaving the eventual winner, Lord Oxford's runner, Tinker Barnes to win as he pleased. Let us hope none of the fruit stalls were in easy reach or the lad riding the Colonel's horse may as well have been in the stocks as on horseback.

If the Race Committee were having problems attracting runners, the cockpit in Park Street was having no such problems with their entries, for the second time in six years the facilities were enlarged yet again.

The official results of the meeting were:

Wednesday 23rd September 1812
In the morning,
A SWEEPSTAKES of 10 guineas each,
with 15 guineas added by the Stewards. For three year olds.
One two mile heat.

Lord Oxford's	Tinker Barnes	1
Colonel Walhouse's b. f.	by Staveley	bolted

Four horses withdrawn.

In the afternoon
THE CORPORATION & GENTLEMEN'S SUBSCRIPTION PURSE
of £50 for horses of all ages. Three, three mile heats.

Lord Oxford's	Glauvina, 4 y-o	4	1	1
Earl Wilton's	Berenice, aged	1	2	2
Mr West's b. m.	Locket, 5 y-o	2	dr	-
Sir Thomas Mostyn's	Nobody, 4 y-o	3	dr	-
Mr Fletcher's gr. f.	Juno, 4 y-o	dr	-	-

Thursday 24th September 1812
In the morning,
A SWEEPSTAKES of 10 guineas each,
with 15 guineas added by the Stewards.
Horse of all ages carrying Leicester Cup weights.
Three mile heats.

Mr Fletcher's gr. f.	Juno, 4 y-o	1	1
Mr T. L. Brookes's	Oliver Cromwell, 4 y-o	2	2

Six others withdrawn.

In the afternoon,
THE TOWN SUBSCRIPTION PURSE of £50,
for horses of all ages. Three, three mile heats.

Mr Palfrey's	Worcester, 4 y-o	1	1
Lord Oxford's	Glauvina, 4 y-o	2	dr
Mr Atherton's b. m.	by Milo, 4 y-o	3	dr
Earl Wilton's	Berenice, aged	dr	-
Mr West's b. m.	Locket, 5 y-o	dr	-

Stewards: Honourable G. A. Bridgeman and Edward Hanson
Clerk of the Races: Thomas Pearce.

1813

One thing that was becoming apparent in 1813 was the confusion caused by the ambiguity of some of the race distances. In previous years the announcements and results had always described some distances as 'three, three-mile heats,' this year, and for subsequent years, it became 'three, mile-heats.' Certainly races were run over the longer distance, and longer, during this period. It may be that both are correct and the race distance was changed in 1813. The *Racing Calendar* certainly has the distance down as the latter description, and as we all know, the word of the Jockey Club, or their agents, Weatherbys, is sacrosanct.

The number of runners in 1813 was similar to previous years with some good races taking place, inevitably, there always seemed to be at least one race that suffered and this year was no exception. The second race on Wednesday was reduced to a match and then a walkover when the other runner failed to show at the post.

Another member of racing's elite joined the throng on the Long Meadow, the Right Honourable, Mr J. C. Villiers, whose first runner on the course, Merryfield, won the Corporation and Gentlemen's Subscription Purse from three other runners easily.

As well as new owners coming to the course, a new race was devised for this year, the Staffordshire Stakes for none thoroughbred horses. Three of the seven entrants were sired by the same horse, an un-named full brother to Stamford, a

1800 - 1819

prolific sire of many winners. Presumably the dam of these three entrants was only half-bred, as Stamford's brother was most certainly a full-blood horse. The pedigree showed too, the three of them finished, first, third and fourth.

The meeting was brought to a close on Thursday afternoon with a good race for the Town Subscription Plate. The race was won by Mr Shaw's Don Julian ridden by Richard Spencer, with Sir Thomas Stanley's Da Capo second and Mr Bowker's Tom Bowling taking third spot.

The official results of the meeting were:

Wednesday 29th September 1813
In the morning,
A SWEEPSTAKES of 10 guineas each with 15 guineas added by the Stewards. For three year olds. Three mile heats.

Mr Walhouse's b. h.	**Don Julian**	1	1
Mr Carr's b. m.	**Glauvina**, 5 y-o	2	2

Two horses withdrawn.

The same morning
A MATCH for £50. One two mile heat.

Mr Dalby's b. m.	**Express** by Mast	walked over
Mr Mellish's br. m.	**Miss Fanny**	drawn

In the afternoon
CORPORATION AND GENTLEMEN'S SUBSCRIPTION PURSE of £50. Three, three mile heats.

Rt. Hon. J. C. Villiers b. h.	**Merryfield**, 5 y-o	1	1
Mr Pengree's b. g.	**Mount Pleasant**, 4 y-o	2	2
Mr Brade's b. c.	**Sangcado**, 4 y-o	bolted	
Mr Shaw's b. h.	**Don Julian**	dr	-

Thursday 30th September 1813
In the morning,
A SWEEPSTAKES of 10 guineas each, with 15 guineas added by the Stewards. For three year olds. Two mile heat.

Lord Grey's b. c.	**Cossack**, *(R.Spencer)*	1
Mr Crockett's b. c.	**by Sancho**	2
Sir Thomas Stanley's b. c.	**by Williamson's Ditto**	3

Four others withdrawn.

The same morning
THE STAFFORDSHIRE STAKES of 5 guineas each, for horses foaled in the County of Staffordshire, not thoroughbred. Three two mile heats.

Mr Ward's b m,	**by brother to Stamford**, *(H. Arthur)*	1	1
Mr Edden's	**Fisherwick**	5	2
Mr Heeley's b. m.	**by brother to Stamford**	3	3
Mr Richmond Aston's b. g.	**un-named**, 5 y-o	4	4
Mr Barber's ch m,	**by brother to Stamford**	2	dr
Mr W. Mold's Snowdrop,	**by Alligator**	6	dr

In the afternoon,
THE TOWN SUBSCRIPTION PURSE of £50, for horses of all ages. Three, three mile heats.

Mr Shaw's b. h.	**Don Julian**	1	1
Sir Joseph Stanley's b. c.	**Da Capo**	2	2
Mr Bowker's ch. h.	**Tom Bowling**	3	3

Glauvina and Merryfield withdrawn.

Stewards: Sir Joseph Scott and M. Walhouse.
Clerk of the Races: Thomas Pearce.

1814

On the first day of the meeting in 1814 three runners contested the opening race on Wednesday morning, the Earl of Stamford's, Stella, Ralph Bensons', Uncle Toby and the equally quaintly named, Uncle Dick owned by a Mr Thompson. All of these horses had worked hard throughout the season, running in twenty-seven races between them and winning just eight of them. The winner, Stella, had won twice before coming to Walsall, once at Newton near Manchester and again at Worcester, followed by a walkover at Shrewsbury. Again it is worth remembering, the horse had to be walked to all of these venues. The Earl of Stamford had another horse running at the meeting on Thursday named Platowna whose previous race at Worcester in August had caused both owner and jockey some embarrassment. The Stewards at Worcester were not happy with the riding of the horse and both of the connections were reported to the Jockey Club who issued the following statement in the annual *Racing Calendar*: –

'With respect to the unfair riding in this race, we are authorised to say that the owner of Platowna, on being satisfied of the truth of the charge, immediately wrote a severe reprimand to his rider, threatening to discharge him from his service if ever guilty of a like offence.'

His Lordship and his servant, the jockey, both receiving a slap on the wrist from the powers that be, who weren't finished yet. The Jockey Club also felt the Worcester Stewards had acted improperly and continued the statement to reprimand them: –

'At the same time it was suggested to us [Jockey Club stewards], the Steward would have done well to wait his Lordship's determination, rather than publish the transaction in the way it was done, which besides being of itself a severe punishment to the rider, might by some to be thought to reflect on his employer.'

Upset the Jockey Club if you dare, but if you do, you must take the consequences of public humiliation, nobility or not.

Another member of the nobility, Lord Grosvenor, joined the growing band of the elite men of the turf running horses at the course, and his baptism couldn't have been simpler. His horse Zadora arrived at the post with no opposition and completed the formalities of a walkover to claim the prize.

The official results of the meeting were:

Wednesday 28th September 1814

In the morning,
A SWEEPSTAKES of 10 guineas each with 10 guineas added by the town. Horses of all ages. Three mile heats.

Lord Grey's b. m.	**Stella**, 6 y-o	3	1	1
Mr Thompson's b. h.	**Uncle Dick**, 6 y-o	2	2	2
Mr Benson's	**Uncle Toby**, 5 y-o	1	3	dr

In the afternoon
CORPORATION AND GENTLEMEN'S SUBSCRIPTION PURSE of £50. Horses of all ages. Three, three mile heats.

Mr Dunn's ch. c.	**Alexander Little**, 4 y-o, 8st. 3lb.	2	1
Lord Grey's b. m.	**Stella**, 6 y-o, 9st.	1	dr

1800 - 1819

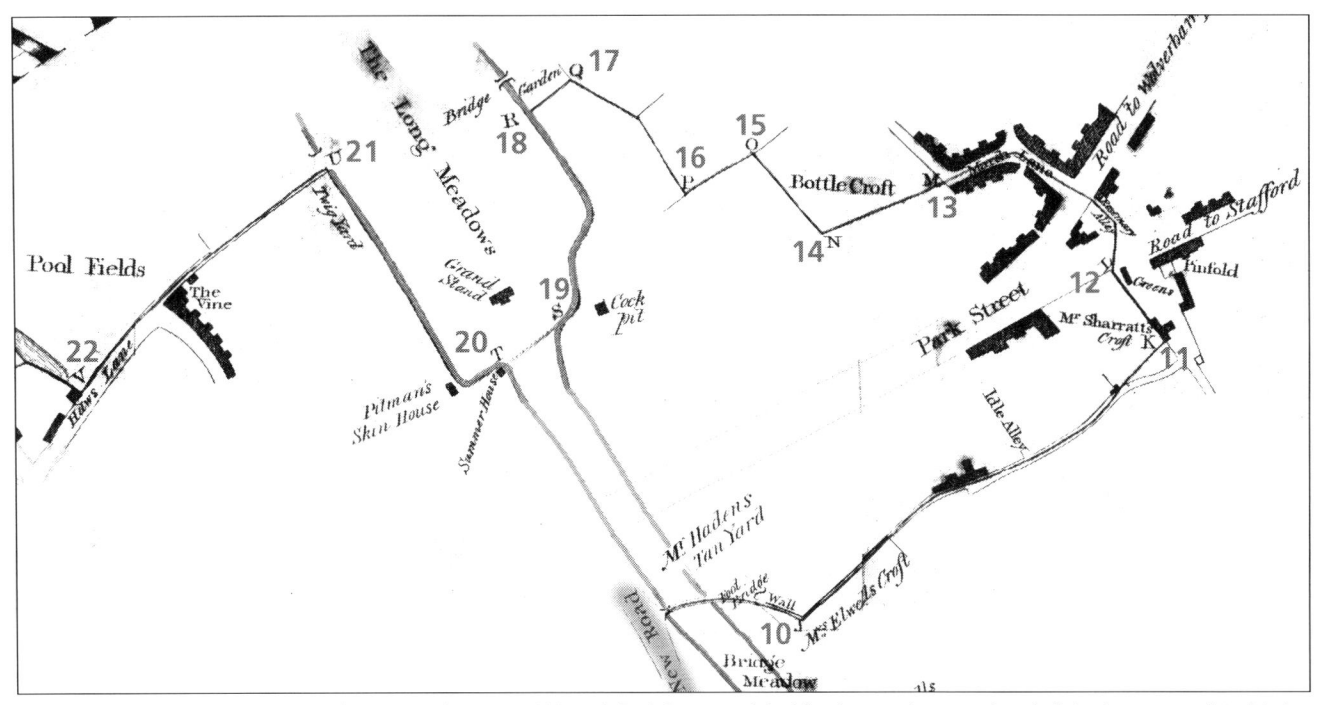

The area around the Long Meadow (racecourse) in 1814. Although Park Street and the Vine Inn can be seen there is little else to associate it being the town centre that we know today. The two light grey lines show the watercourses surrounding the Long Meadow. The road marked New Road is what we know as Bridge Street. (Walsall Local History Centre.)

Thursday 29th September 1814

In the morning,
A SWEEPSTAKES of 10 guineas each,
with 10 guineas added by the Stewards.
For three year olds. Two miles.

Lord Grosvenor's b. f.	**Zadora,** 8st. 5lb.		walked over

In the afternoon
A PLATE of 50 guineas,
for beaten horse of all ages. Three mile heats.

Mr Benson's b. h.	**Uncle Toby,** 5 y-o, 9st. 3lb.	1	1
Lord Grey's b. f.	**Platowna,** 4 y-o, 8st.	3	2
Mr Thompson's b. h.	**Uncle Dick,** 6 y-o, 9st. 3lb.	4	3
Mr Galloway's b. c.	**by Sorcerer,** 3 y-o, 6st. 10lb.	2	4

Stewards: Edward D. Scott, Esq. and Edward J. Littleton, Esq.
Clerk of the Races: Thomas Pearce.

1815

As will be seen by the results, this year proved confusing with regard to who owned what. For the first race on Thursday morning, Diabolis, a winner on Wednesday under the ownership of John Walhouse, turned out for the race in the colours of John Clifton. If this is correct, Clifton was just as lucky as Walhouse, the horse trotted up, winning both heats comfortably. It would appear, as if there were any doubt, both Clifton and Walhouse knew a good horse when they saw one. Diabolis was previously owned by Major Bowers, a Yorkshireman, who ran the horse no less than fourteen times in 1814 at numerous courses in the north of England. The horse won seven of the fourteen races, including a five-heat affair over one and three-quarter miles on the Knavesmire at York. Viceroy, the runner-up to Diabolis the previous day when owned by Edward Littleton, turned out twenty four hours later under the ownership of Richard Fletcher, son of the owner of the George Inn. Likewise, Rosabella who had run under Mr Jones' name was entered the day later as being owned by Mr Scott. The most likely answer to the discrepancies in ownership came about from a mistake by the publisher's of *Aris' Gazette*. The more suspicious of us would say some rather sharp horse dealing was going on between racing hours at the George, or the Dragon, possibly a hand of cards or a cocking contest was the cause for a change of ownership.

Walsall was also honoured this year, or so it thought, by an entry from Lord Derby no less. His Lordship is reputed to have had horses in training with Thomas Saunders at Hednesford. It is fair to assume that the horse entered for the Sweepstakes, Rinaldo, was one of these. Disappointingly, the horse was withdrawn and the famous black jacket and white cap were never seen on the course.

The official results of the meeting were:

Wednesday 27th September 1815

A SWEEPSTAKES of 10 guineas each with 10 guineas added by
the town. Horses of all ages. Three mile heats.

Mr J. Walhouses's	**Diabolis**	1	1
Mr E. J. Littleton's	**Viceroy**	2	2
Lord Derby's	**Rinaldo**	dr	-

CORPORATION AND GENTLEMEN'S SUBSCRIPTION PURSE
was cancelled due to lack of runners

continued

1800 - 1819

Thursday 28th September 1815

In the morning,

A SWEEPSTAKES of 10 guineas each, with 10 guineas added by the Stewards. For three year olds. Two miles.

Mr H. Crockett's	**Arthur O'Bradley**	1
Mr E. J. Littleton's	**Pallas by Evander**	2
Mr Jones'	**Rosabella**	3
Mr T. Hawkes	**b. f. by Waxy**	dr

In the afternoon

A PLATE of 50 guineas, for beaten horse of all ages. Three mile heats.

Mr Clifton's	**Diabolis**	1	1
Mr Hill's	**Miss Platoff**	2	2
Mr Bayley's	**ch. c. by Newcastle**	3	3

A HANDICAP SWEEPSTAKES of 50 guineas

Sir. T. M. Stanley's	**Tamerlane**	1	1
Mr Fletcher's	**Viceroy**	2	dr
Mr Jones'	**Rosabella**	3	2
Mr Hill's	**Nogo**	dr	-

1816

Aris' Gazette admirably describes the meeting that took place on Wednesday 25th and Thursday 26th September, with the following quote: -

> 'These races maintain their accustomed celebrity. The heats for the Plates were well contested, and gave general satisfaction. The weather proving favourable, the concourse of spectators assembled on the ground from all quarters, was immense. The Ordinaries were very respectably attended; and the Race Assemblies, on similar occasions, for beauty and fashion, never exceeded. The Grand Stand, from the fashionable display of well-dressed ladies, made a most brilliant appearance.'

The races may have maintained their accustomed celebrity but they also maintained their accustomed small fields, only fifteen horses to contest the races over two days. Wednesday's racing consisted of two matches and a three horse race. Thursday's events were a walkover in the morning Sweepstakes after everyone withdrew leaving John Walhouse's un-named black filly with the minimum of exertions to take the money, followed by a five horse race in the afternoon. This race was won by Lord Grey with his horse Prince of Orange and although he had runners in later years, this was to be the final time his light blue colours would catch the judge's eye. The horse that finished runner-up in this race, Little Thomas, was owned and bred by Joseph Painter from Dean's Hill, Stafford, a man who had an excellent reputation in Staffordshire for the breeding of thoroughbred horses and hunters.

Sir Thomas Stanley, well known at the larger courses, had been entering the occasional runner at Walsall since 1811. Finally, in 1816 he broke his 'duck' when his bay gelding, Charioteer carried his colours of blue jacket with yellow sleeves to victory in the Corporation and Gentlemen's Subscription Purse.

The official results of the meeting were:

Wednesday 25th September 1816

In the morning,

A SWEEPSTAKES of 10 guineas each with 10 guineas added by the town. For three year olds.

Mr. E. J. Littleton's b. f.	**by Sir David**	1
Mr. H. Crockett's	**b. c. by Sir Oliver**	2
Lord Grey's b. f.	**Melisa, sister to Stella**	dr
Mr. T. Hawkes's b. c.	**by Newcastle**	dr

A MATCH for £50. To be ridden by gentlemen over two miles.

Mr. J. Baldwin ch. m.	**Clara by George**	1
Mr. W. Taylor's br. m.	**Annette**	2

In the afternoon

CORPORATION AND GENTLEMEN'S SUBSCRIPTION PURSE of £50. Horses of all ages. Three, three mile heats.

Sir Thomas Stanley's b. g.	**Charioteer**	1	1
Lord Grey's	**Prince of Orange**	2	3
Mr. Vincent Corbett's br. f.	**Mervinia**	3	2

Thursday 26th September 1816

In the morning,

A SWEEPSTAKES of 10 guineas each, with 10 guineas added by the Stewards. Three mile heats.

Mr. J. Walhouse's bl. f.	**sister to Toolly**	walked over

In the afternoon

A PLATE of 50 guineas, for beaten horse of all ages. Three mile heats.

Lord Grey's	Prince of Orange	1	1
Mr. J. Painter's	Little Thomas	3	2
Mr. V. Vever's	Lady Byron	4	3
Earl Grosvenor's b. f.	Larissa	2	dr
Mr. I. Millington br. m.	Jersey	dist.	-

1817

Research for this years meeting, held on Wednesday 24th and Thursday 25th September, was made all the easier by the discovery of *'Milward's List of Walsall Races.'* Frederick Milward, an enterprising printer and stationer of High Street, produced a printed sheet containing the results from the Races. It is not known when Milward began to produce this invaluable, and now rare little guide to events on the Long Meadow, or indeed when it ceased production. The list contains the most comprehensive information available for Walsall Races for this period. The Racing Calendar and the Sporting Magazine did not include the names of the early jockeys until about nine years later; Milward's List contained this information, as well as the owner's colours, and pedigree of the runners and the weights they carried. After putting so much work into the leaflet it is surprising that Milward didn't print the runners in consecutive order, as they crossed the line. Instead he printed them as they had originally been entered, in three of the race results the winners appear last in the list. For the

1800 – 1819

information contained in this single side leaflet, Mr Milward can be excused this small oversight.

Lord Rossmore was another member of the nobility to run horses at this years meeting for the first time when he entered three horses, Sunflower, Fandango and Carolan. His Lordship must have been delighted with his first visit to Walsall, Sunflower won, Fandango was second and Carolan was third in their respective races.

Vincent Corbet, another owner to have a runner at the course for the first time, saw his chestnut filly, Parthenope win the first contest of the meeting on Wednesday morning, Henry Arthur senior was the jockey that carried Corbet's colours of orange jacket and blue cap to victory.

Another owners name that appeared in the list of entries this year was that of Beardsworth, not once but twice, in the same race. One was a Mr C. Beardsworth and the other was John Beardsworth, the latter, a name that would become familiar at Walsall, and many other courses, over the next twenty years.

John Beardsworth, a very successful Birmingham horse and carriage dealer, began his turf career in 1817 at the Walsall meeting. The horse that began his colourful and controversial career on the turf was a six year-old gelding named William. Beardsworth's turf baptism did not have a fairy tale ending however, the horse was withdrawn after the first heat had been run.

After this less than auspicious start, Beardsworth's turf career progressed and he had many successes on racecourses throughout England, including a Classic winner that carried his crimson colours to victory in the 1830 St. Leger at Doncaster. Beardsworth ran horses on an almost annual basis at Walsall until his death in 1835, and quite possibly owned the best horse ever to grace the Long Meadow in its one hundred and twenty year history, a horse called Independence. It was another thirteen years before this fine horse came onto the racing scene and a brief history of him is covered in future pages.

John Beardsworth was certainly one of the characters that early nineteenth century racing was seemingly full of. Beardsworth liked to win, and if it meant bending the rules to breaking point, so be it. On more than one occasion he upset the Senior Stewards of the Jockey Club and only his great charm and wit got him out of some very deep water. He was ridiculed by the nobility who were so green with envy at his success they must have looked like the cabbages many of them undoubtedly were.

Thomas Pearce and the other members of the Race Committee must have delighted with the quality of horses now running at Walsall in comparison to those that ran ten years previously, even though the numbers of runners was still low. Napoleon Bonaparte may have been defeated five years earlier, but Walsall's version of the dictator, Thomas Pearce, was still going strong.

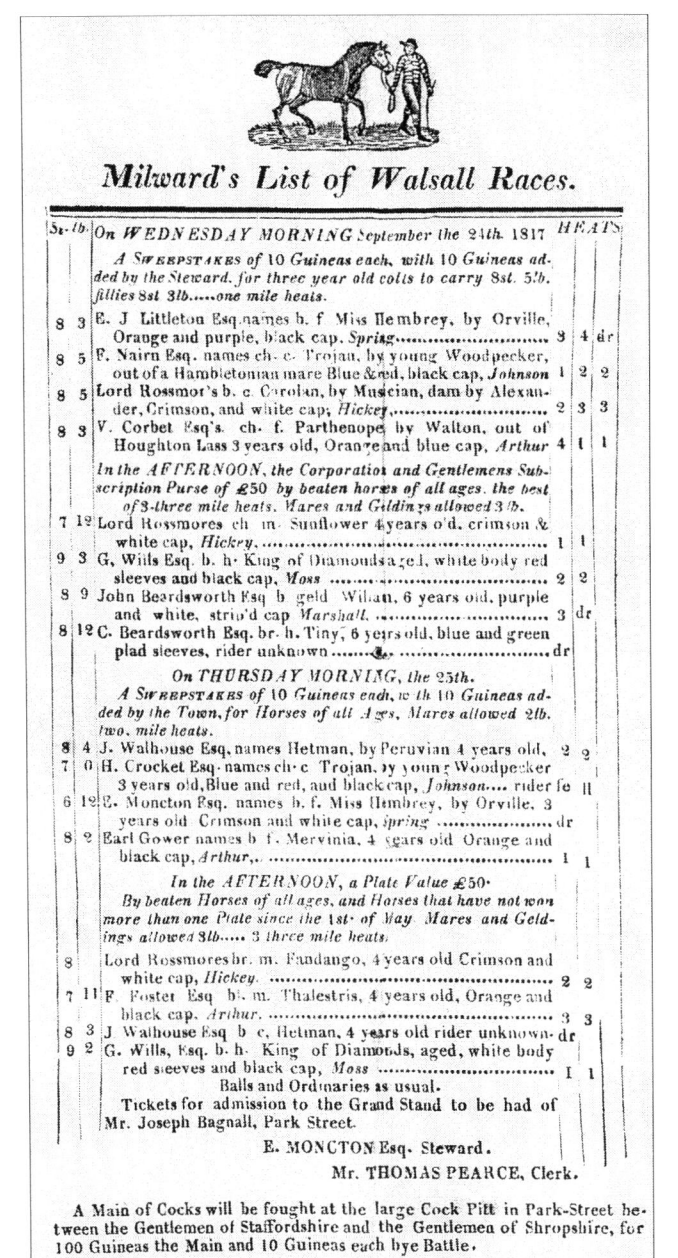

A copy of the extremely rare, Milward's List of Walsall Races for 1817. (Reproduced by courtesy of Walsall Local History Centre)

The official results of the meeting are repeated showing the correct finishing order:

Wednesday 24th September 1817

In the morning,
A SWEEPSTAKES of 10 guineas each with 10 guineas added by the Stewards. For three year olds.
Colts to carry 8st. 5lb, fillies 8st. 3lb.

Mr V. Corbett's ch. f.	**Parthenope**, *(H. Arthur)*	4	1	1
Mr F. Nairn names ch. c	**Trojan**, *(Johnson)*	1	2	2
Lord Rossmore's b. c.	**Carolan**, *(Hickey)*	2	3	3
Mr E. J. Littleton b. f.	**Miss Hembrey**, *(Spring)*	3	4	dr

In the afternoon
CORPORATION AND GENTLEMEN'S SUBSCRIPTION PURSE of £50.
Horses of all ages. Three, three mile heats.

Lord Rossmore's ch. m.	**Sunflower**, *(Hickey)*	1	1
Mr G. Wills' b. h.	**King of Diamonds**, *(Moss)*	2	2
Mr J. Beardsworth's b. g.	**William**, *(Marshall)*	3	dr
Mr C. Beardsworth's br. h.	**Tiny**	dr	-

1800 - 1819

Thursday 25th September 1817

In the morning,

A SWEEPSTAKES of 10 guineas each,
with 10 guineas added by the Town.
Horses of all ages, two mile heats.

Earl Gower names b. f.	**Mervinia,** *(H. Arthur)*	1	1
Mr J. Walhouse names	**Hetman**	2	2
Mr H. Crocket names	**Trojan,** *(Johnson)*	fell	-
Mr E. Monckton names	**Miss Hembrey,** *(J. Spring)*	dr	-

In the afternoon

A PLATE of £50,
for beaten horse of all ages and horses that have
not won a Plate since 1st May.
Three, three mile heats.

Mr G. Wills' b. h.	**King of Diamonds,** *(Moss)*	1	1
Lord Rossmore's br. m.	**Fandango,** *(Hickey)*	2	2
Mr F. Foster's bl. m.	**Thalestris,** *(H. Arthur)*	3	3
Mr J. Walhouse's b. c.	**Hetman**	dr	-

1818

On Monday 28th September Aris' Gazette published a report of the meeting part of which read:-

'The course was, as usual well attended, although the weather on the first day was exceedingly unpropitious.'

The meeting was held on Wednesday 23rd and Thursday 24th September with two races on each day, opening the proceedings was a Sweepstakes of 10 guineas, run in one-mile heats. Only two runners were declared so presumably the added money given by the Stewards was withdrawn. Only two heats were required to obtain a winner, Mr H. Lowe's filly Sybil winning both comfortably from a previously well thought of colt of Lord Anson's named Tattoo.

At least the Corporation and Gentlemen's Subscription Purse gave something like a horse race for the spectators in the afternoon. Four runners started, but this too became a procession for Vincent Corbet's filly, Parthenope who won two of the three, two-mile heats with ease, the minor placings were filled by Lord Rossmore's Sentorious second and the Rt. Hon. J. C. Villier's horse Gresador third. The fourth horse, owned by J. Stevens was Single Peeper who started but didn't complete the first heat.

The sport on Thursday was as unspectacular as the first day; a match began the days racing in the Sweepstakes race, victory going to Sybil again. On this occasion the reports have the owner listed as E. J. Littleton. Sybil won the first two heats with ease from another of Mr Corbet's runners, Mervinia.

The most contested race was the final one in the afternoon, a Plate valued at £50; seven started the race with only the names of the first and second horses being recorded in the *Racing Calendar*. The outcome was in Mr Drages's favour, his colt Aylesbury winning two of the three heats, beating Single Peeper.

The official results of the meeting were:

Wednesday 23rd September 1818

In the morning,
A SWEEPSTAKES of 10 guineas each with 10 guineas added by the Stewards. One mile heats.

Mr. H. Lowe's ch. f.	**Sybil**	1	1
Lord Anson's b. c.	**Tattoo**	2	2
Three horses drawn.			

In the afternoon
CORPORATION AND GENTLEMEN'S SUBSCRIPTION PURSE of £50.
Horses of all ages. Two mile heats.

Mr. V. Corbett's ch. f.	**Parthenope**	1	1
Lord Rossmore's b. c.	**Sentorious**	2	2
Rt. Hon. J. C. Villier's	**Gresador**	3	3
Mr. J. Steven's b. g.	**Single Peeper**	dr	-

Thursday 24th September 1818

In the morning,
A SWEEPSTAKES of 10 guineas each,
with 10 guineas added by the Town.
Two mile heats.

Mr. E. J. Littleton names	**Sybil**	1	1
Mr. V. Corbett's br. m.	**Mervinia**	2	2
Two horses drawn.			

In the afternoon
A PLATE of 50 guineas,
for beaten horse of all ages. Three mile heats.

Mr. Drage's b. c.	**Aylesbury**	2	1	1
Mr. J. Stevens's b. g.	**Single Peeper**	1	2	2

Five others horses unplaced but not listed.

1819

The meeting for this year was held on Wednesday 29th and Thursday 30th September, comprising of four races as usual. For the first time in several years there was not a walkover or a match in sight. All of the races were well contested and gave the large crowd that assembled on the Long Meadow two days of good sporting entertainment.

The dignitaries who attended the meeting and the ball afterwards included, Viscount and Lady Anson, and Miss Phillips, Earl Gower, Sir John Wrottesley and family, Sir George Pigot and family, Misters George and Edward Monckton, Mr and Mrs. Walhouse, Colonel Walhouse, Lady Scott, Mr Scott and Mr and Mrs. Edward Anson. Several of the above had runners at the meeting and the course was also host to John Tomes and John Twamley from Warwickshire, both well-known owners who frequented many courses. The two of them would have cause to remember Walsall for both the right, and wrong reasons. John Twamley's horse Warwick, won both heats well, and so the race, or so his connections thought. Unfortunately, when the jockey weighed in for the second heat he was found to be under weight, by two pounds! Rules are rules, and the Walsall Race Committee obviously adhered to them, declaring the horse 'distanced,' in

1800 - 1819

other words, disqualified. The race was given to John Tomes' horse, Northwood.

John Beardsworth returned, running a colt, sired by the unusually named Williamson's Ditto, in two races; both attempts at recording his first winner at Walsall failed. The best the un-named colt could do was to finish second in the Corporation and Gentlemen's Subscription Purse.

The Earl of Stamford brought a high spirited animal out for the first race on Wednesday morning named Duke Michael, the horse won the first heat comfortably but then bolted and was ruled out of the race. Entered in the Sweepstakes race twenty-four hours later, Duke Michael still had his own ideas about racing, and bolted again, before he had even started this time.

In conclusion, this meeting appears to have been one of the best in recent years, both in terms of the number of runners and the quality of racing.

The official results of the meeting were:

Wednesday 29th September 1819

In the morning,
A SWEEPSTAKES of 10 guineas each with 10 guineas added by the Stewards. One mile heats.

Mr. E. J. Littleton names b. c.	**Northwood**	3	1	1
Earl Gower names br. c.	**by York**	4	2	dr
Earl of Stamford's b. c.	**Duke Michael**	1	bolted	
Mr. V. Corbett's b. f.	**by Haphazard**	2	dr	-
Mr. F. Nairn names br. c.	**by Clinker**		bolted	

One horse drawn.

In the afternoon
CORPORATION AND GENTLEMEN'S SUBSCRIPTION PURSE of £50. Horses of all ages. Two mile heats.

Sir Thomas Mostyn's b. f.	**Finance**, 4 y-o	1	1
Mr. J. Beardsworth's ch. c.	**by Ditto**	4	2
Mr. G. Monckton's br. c.	**by Dick Andrews**	2	3
Mr. J. Twamley's ch. c.	**Warwick** by Sorcerer	5	f
Mr. J. Turner's b. g.	**by Eagle**	3	br.d.

Thursday 30th September 1819

In the morning,
A SWEEPSTAKES of 10 guineas each, with 10 guineas added by the Town.

Mr. John Tomes's b. c.	**Northwood**	2	1
Mr. J. Twamley's ch. c.	**Warwick** by Sorcerer	1	dis.
Earl of Stamford's b. c.	**Duke Michael**	bolted	-

Three horses drawn.

Warwick's rider was two ounces short of weight and the heat was given to Northwood, Warwick deemed distanced.

In the afternoon
A PLATE of £50.

Mr. V. Corbett's b. f.	**by Haphazard**	1	1
Mr. J. Twamley's ch. c.	**Warwick** by Sorcerer	4	2
Mr. John Tomes's b. c.	**Northwood**	2	3
Mr. J. Beardsworth's ch. c.	**by Ditto**	3	4
Viscount Anson's b. c.	**Aylesbury**	5	5

Two horses drawn.

WALSALL RACES

CHAPTER THREE
1820 - 1839

1820

This year proved almost as good as the previous one, with each race, except one, filling well and giving some excellent racing.

Mr Painter, the horse breeder from Stafford, got the proceedings off to a good start when his three year-old colt by Haphazard, ridden by Richard Spencer, won the first two heats of the Sweepstakes race comfortably.

Vincent Corbet, obviously a man with a good eye for a horse, continued his success from previous years by winning the principle race of the day on Wednesday afternoon when his bay filly, Victorina, ridden by Henry Arthur, beat the other four runners with ease.

The only race of the meeting that was reduced to a match was the first event on Thursday morning, the Sweepstakes race. With only two runners, it nevertheless proved to be quite a battle with the Earl of Dartmouth's un-named horse providing Henry Arthur with another winner, beating Viscount Anson's Hobgoblin, by two heats to one. The distance for this race was now entered as being 'twice round and a distance,' in other words, two miles two hundred and forty yards. A distance in racing terms being two hundred and forty yards or two hundred and twenty metres.

The final race on Thursday afternoon had the most runners of any of the races so far, seven in all. The horse that finished in third place, Montemar, was owned by a Mr Fidler, let us hope it was just by name and not by nature. The persistent Mr Beardsworth was once again in attendance, searching for his first winner on the course, but 1820 was not to be his year, one runner came third and the other fell.

The *Staffordshire Advertiser* in summing up the proceedings assures us that the race meeting and the ball were very well attended, giving a list of the nobility and gentry who were present. Lord Hatherton who also attended the Races on Wednesday was not so complimentary, in the book, *The Diaries of Lord Hatherton*, he states: - ' *September 27th 1820. Went to Walsall races, a bad meeting.*' His Lordship doesn't appear to be that interested horse racing, as the sport of kings is rarely mentioned throughout the book, and when he does, it is always the negative aspects of the events he relates to.

The official results of the meeting were:

Wednesday 27th September 1820

In the morning,
A SWEEPSTAKES of 10 guineas each with 10 guineas added by the Stewards. For three year-old colts, one mile heats.

Mr. J. Painter's br. c.	**by Haphazard,**		
	(Richard Spencer)	1	1
Mr. Whitehurst's b. c.	**by Cavendish**	2	2
Mr. John Walhouse's	**Loyalty by Rubens**	3	3
Sir J. G. Egerton's ch. c.	**un-named colt**	4	4

Two horses drawn.

THE CAVALRY SWEEPSTAKES of 10 guineas each.
To be ridden by gentlemen of the Walsall Troop of Volunteer Yeomanry Cavalry. Two mile heats.

This race was either not run or the result was not published.

In the afternoon
CORPORATION AND GENTLEMEN'S SUBSCRIPTION PURSE of £50.
Horses of all ages. Two mile heats.

Mr. V. Corbett's b. f.	**Victorina**, 4 y-o		
	(Henry Arthur)	1	1
Mr. Stevenson's b. c.	**Ashbud**, 3 y-o	3	2
Mr. J. Beardsworth's b. c.	**by Petronious**, 3 y-o	4	3
Earl of Dartmouth's b. g.	**un-named**, 5 y-o	5	4
Mr. Denham's br. c.	**by Blucher**	2	dr

Thursday 28th September 1820

In the morning,
A SWEEPSTAKES of 10 guineas each,
with 10 guineas added by the Town.
All ages, twice round the course and a distance.

Earl of Dartmouth's b. f.	**un-named**, 4 y-o			
	(Henry Arthur)	2	1	1
Viscount Anson's ch. c.	**Hobgoblin**, 5 y-o	1	2	2

Three horses drawn.

1820 - 1839

In the afternoon
A PLATE of £50.
For beaten horses of all ages. Two mile heats.

Mr. Whitehurst's b. c.	by Cavendish, 3 y-o	2	1	1
Sir George Pigot's b. f.	Fair Salopian, 4 y-o	1	6	2
Mr. Fidler's b. c.	Montemar, 3 y-o	3	2	3
Mr. Stevenson's b. c.	Ashbud, 3 y-o	4	5	dr
Mr. Pickernell b. m.	Patience, 4 y-o	5	3	dr
Mr. J. Beardsworth's b. h.	Cameleon, 6 y-o	6	4	fell
Mr. Lewis's b. c.	Noyeau, 3 y-o	7	dr	-

Two horses drawn.

Stewards: Viscount Anson and George Monckton.
Clerk of the Races: Thomas Pearce.

1821

This year the poor weather played a part in the proceedings, all of the races were well contested but the state of the going made life difficult for the runners on both days. Aris' Gazette states: – 'The company at these races was very numerous, and the grandstand was crowded with fashion.'

Not surprising if it was pouring down with rain. Admission to the grandstand for subscribers was included with your annual subscription of five guineas, but tickets could also be purchased from Valentine and Throsby, stationers of High Street, and John Farrington at the Excise Office.

For the second contest on Wednesday morning, a new race was inserted into the programme, the Cavalry Sweepstakes. The race was to be ridden by the Gentlemen of the Walsall Troop of Volunteer Yeomanry Cavalry. Either Walsall didn't have sufficient volunteers to support a race of this kind or the result of the contest wasn't published. Hopefully, for the honour of Walsall, it was the latter.

In the race on Wednesday afternoon there were five runners entered, the winner was named Loyalty and owned by Sir George Pigot. It was during the running of the third heat a horse named Tagus fell, probably due to the effects of the going, and its rider, Gallaway, was severely injured in the fall. No further details are reported regarding the incident, which is a pity because it would be interesting to know if the jockey was in fact a young George Calloway, a rider that rode many winners at Walsall in later years, and on his retirement from riding, became the judge at Walsall. It is feasible that it may be Calloway (or Gallaway) as he was born in 1803, making him seventeen at the time of the accident and many of the newspapers of this period were not to particular about spelling, especially peoples names.

John Beardsworth finally had his first winner on the course when the filly Laena, who won in fine style, beat John Tomes' horse Duplicate, with Quicksilver, the 6/4 favourite, owned by Earl of Stamford, third.

Throughout the years of racing at Walsall it seems the Stewards had little to do, apart from watching the proceedings from the grandstand, but this year they were called in for a ruling regarding two of the runners in the final race of the meeting. The other owners objected to the winner, Sir Thomas Mostyn's Alderman Wood, on the grounds that it wasn't qualified to enter, along with Mr Jackson's Minerva who finished second. The argument arose from a misunderstanding of the conditions of entry for the race, and the words that created the problem were 'for beaten horses only.' Sir Thomas and Mr Jackson read those words as 'for beaten horses that had run anywhere', when the actual meaning was 'for beaten horses that had run at the current Walsall meeting.' The Stewards couldn't make a decision, after all it was quite late in the day, and you can drink a lot of wine between eleven in the morning and early evening! The matter was referred to the Stewards of the Jockey Club whose decision ruled against Sir Thomas and Mr Jackson. As neither of their horses had run previously at the meeting, they were disqualified and the Plate was awarded to third horse Duplicate, owned by John Tomes'.

Much bending of rules was common place during this time. Today we know it as gamesmanship, but now, as then, it is cheating, and many of the most notable of men in racing were not adverse to using a little 'gamesmanship' if it helped their cause.

Many tricks were employed to attempt to gain the upper hand against a rival, false starts being one. When a much fancied horse who was known to be nervous went to post, the other jockeys would deliberately cause false starts. After several of these, the fancied horse would get upset and sweat up. A couple more aborted attempts and the unfortunate animal would be reduced to a shivering heap in equine form, then they would start. With the nervous wreck unable to get anywhere near its usual form, the jockeys, who could bet at this time, and for a great many years to come, would make a nice killing in the betting ring by getting the favourite out of the way.

The 'pulling or stopping' of horses was the favoured method of preventing them from winning, the jockey would simply, if that is the correct term when talking of such a high spirited animal, hold onto the reins for dear life and so preventing the horse from having its head. During this period, stopping a horse was really a case of how good is one's imagination. Bribery was the favoured method but poisoning and the drugging of horses were the more extreme and not uncommon methods of getting the job done. Undoubtably, at least one of the methods mentioned above occurred sometime during the long history of Walsall Races, but exactly when and how is impossible to say. There was an occasion in the 1860s when the crowd suspected some malpractice had been going and an ugly scene developed on the course.

When so called 'easy' money comes into the equation, all common sense and logical thoughts disappear down the nearest drain, along with some poor unfortunates money.

The official results of the meeting were:

Wednesday 26th September 1821

In the morning,
A SWEEPSTAKES of 10 guineas each with 10 guineas added by the Stewards. One mile heats.

Mr. J. Beardsworth's b. f.	Laena	1	1
Lord Anson's b. c.	Patriarch	2	2
Sir. George Pigot's	Chancellor	dr	-
Mr. F. Giffard jnr.	Gleaner	dr	-

1820 - 1839

In the afternoon
CORPORATION AND GENTLEMEN'S SUBSCRIPTION PURSE of £50. Horses of all ages. Two mile heats.

Sir George Pigot's b. f.	**Loyalty**	5	1	1
Mr. Hutchinson's b. h.	**Tagus**	1	3	fell
Earl of Stamford's b. c.	**Peter Leley**	2	2	2
Mr. J. Twamley's ch. h.	**Warwick**	3	4	dr
Mr. J. Beardsworth's b. h.	**Vampyre**	4	5	dr

Thursday 27th September 1821

In the morning,
A SWEEPSTAKES of 10 guineas each,
with 10 guineas added by the Town.
Two mile heats.

Mr. J. Beardsworth's b. f.	**Laena**	1	1
Col. Walhouse's	**Duplicate**	2	2
Earl of Stamford's b. c.	**Quicksilver**	3	4
Mr. J. Thompson's b. h.	**Fitz Langton**	4	3

Earls of Stamford's Quicksilver was the favourite at 6-4 against.

In the afternoon
A PLATE of 50 guineas,
for beaten horse of all ages. Three mile heats.

Sir Thomas Mostyn's b. h.	**Alderman Wood**	1	1
Mr. Jackson's b. f.	**Minerva**	2	3
Mr. J. Tomes's b. h.	**Duplicate**	3	2
Mr. J. Thompson's b. h.	**Fitz Langton**	4	dr
Mr. J. Beardsworth's b. h.	**Vampyre**	5	4

Objection was made to the qualification of Alderman Wood and Minerva, and the question is left to the Jockey Club.

1822

Once again, *Aris' Gazette* sums up the proceedings in late September on the Long Meadow succinctly with the following statement: -

'These races were more numerously attended than usual, and the concourse of spectators was immense. Nearly one hundred noblemen and gentlemen dined at the ordinary, and there was a large and brilliant company at the ball. Mr Pearce, by whose active exertions the course has been kept in a better state than most others, and equal to any in the kingdom, received the unanimous thanks of the parties present. Lord Dartmouth and Mr John Mytton are appointed Stewards for next year, when to the plates and stakes run for on the present occasion, will be added a Gold Cup, value 100 Guineas, and another Sweepstake of 25 Guineas.'

Every year the newspapers report on the Races, the spectators are always more numerous than ever before, it would appear it was as difficult to park your barouche then, as it is to park a car today!

Thomas Pearce, who had been Clerk of the Races since 1809, stepped down from the post this year; he had done yet another excellent job in getting the racecourse up to its present standard, and for acquiring the Gold Cup race to be run for in 1824. It is fair to assume that this man was the driving force behind any new initiative that occurred at the course in the last twelve years. His predecessor was John Newton, landlord of The Dragon.

This year saw the first two year-old race ever run at Walsall when a Sweepstakes of twenty-five guineas each, to be run over half-a-mile was added to the programme. Two year-old races had been part of the racing scene for almost thirty-five years, the oldest established race being the July Stakes at Newmarket, founded in 1786. The line up for Walsall's first venture into racing youngsters consisted of four horses, Mr Yate's chestnut filly, Squib, Mr Alderson's bay colt, The Tartar, Viscount Anson's un-named bay filly by York and John Beardsworth's chestnut filly, Lady Caroline. The winner of the inaugural two year-old race was Mr Yates' filly, Squib.

John Beardsworth had his second winner at Walsall in this year when his bay colt, Sir William won the opening race of the meeting on Wednesday 25th September. It was in actual fact a match and not a race as the only other contender was a horse called Gallivant, who obviously didn't live up to his name and was beaten easily over two heats by the colt.

The most popular race of the meeting proved to be the new event on Thursday afternoon, the Sweepstakes of five guineas each, for none thoroughbred horses. This race attracted ten subscribers with eight declaring to run, and all had to be ridden by gentlemen riders, all of whom had to be Members of the Walsall Troop of Yeomanry Cavalry. The winner, on the running of the race, was Mr Beaumont's, Old Sportsman who won two of the three heats; unfortunately, his owner/rider, rather foolishly, dismounted before coming to the weighing chair. The judge declared him 'distanced' and the race was awarded to the runner-up, Mr Perk's grey horse, Comet. This race had the distinction of having the oldest runner ever on the Long Meadow when a Mr Wilson optimistically entered his twenty-five year-old mare, Fly; she was unplaced in the first heat but gave the other runners the fright of their lives when finishing third in the second heat, this must have taken the running out of the old girl and Mr Wilson sensibly withdrew her from the final heat.

The official results of the meeting were:

Wednesday 25th September 1822

In the morning,
A SWEEPSTAKES of 10 guineas each with 10 guineas added by the Stewards. For three year olds, one mile heats.

Mr. J. Beardsworth's b. c.	**Sir William**	1	1
Mr. Roberts's b. c.	**Gallivant by Fyldener**	2	dr

Three horses drawn.

A SWEEPSTAKES of 10 guineas each. with 10guineas added.
Two mile heats.

Mr. Moody's b. h.	**Alderman Wood,** 6 y-o	1	4	1
Mr. Dockeray's b. h.	**Paintbrush,** 5 y-o	2	0	2
Mr. T. Flintoff's b. g.	**Hassan,** 3 y-o	3	3	dr
Mr. J. Tomes's b. h.	**Duplicate,** aged	4	0	fell

Two horses drawn.

THE CORPORATION (MAIDEN) PLATE of £50.

Mr. Massey's ch. f.	**Ynysymaengwyn,**	4	1	1
Mr. H. Arthur's b. m.	**Elwina**	1	4	2
Mr. J. Beardsworth's ch. f.	**Lady Jane**	2	2	3
Mr. Robert's b. c.	**Gallivant by Fyldener**	3	3	4

1820 - 1839

Thursday 26th September 1822

In the morning,
A SWEEPSTAKES of 25 guineas each.
For two year olds - four furlongs.

Mr. Yates's ch. f.	**Squib** by Soothsayer	1	
Mr. Alderson's b. c.	**The Tartar**	2	
Viscount Anson's b. f.	**by York**	3	
Mr. J. Beardsworth's ch. f.	**Lady Caroline**	dr	

THE TOWN PLATE of 50 guineas. Three mile heats.

Mr. J. Painter's br. h.	**The Main**	1	1
Sir George Pigot's b. m.	**Loyalty**	2	dr

A MATCH for £50. Two mile heats.

Mr. Eld's br. f.	**by York**	1
Mr. Spilsbury's gr. m.	**by Crabstock**	2

A SWEEPSTAKES of 5 guineas each, for horses not thoroughbred.
To be ridden by Members of the Walsall Troop of Yeomanry Cavalry.

Mr. Perks's gr. h.	**Comet**	6	2	2
Mr. James's br. h.	**Confidence**	3	5	3
Mr. Barber's bl. h.	**Jack**	4	7	4
Mr. Green's br. h.	**Spectacles**	7	6	5
Mr. Green's b. h.	**Georgius**	0	8	6
Mr. Wainright's b. h.	**Waterloo**	8	4	7
Mr. Wilson's b. m.	**Fly** (25 years old)	0	3	dr
Mr. Beaumont's br. h.	**Old Sportsman**	5	1	1

Old Sportsman came in first but was disqualified due to his rider dismounting before coming to the weighing chair. The race was awarded to Comet by the Stewards.

A PLATE of 50 guineas.
Given by the Coal and Iron Masters. Two mile heats.

Mr. J. Painter's	**Coxcomb** by Fitzjames	1	1
Mr. Canning's	**black colt by Gleaner**	2	2

1823

In the race report for 1822 taken from *Aris' Gazette,* it may be remembered the announcement of the two Stewards for this year, Lord Dartmouth and John Mytton. Whether or not Lord Dartmouth had heard of Mytton prior to them being thrust upon each other in their administrative capacity is not known, but at the end of the meeting, probably neither he, nor Walsall, would forget Mytton in a long time.

John Mytton, known also as Jack and Squire Mytton, hailed from Halston in Shropshire and was descended from a very respectable family that could trace its ancestry back to the twelfth century. He was born on September 30th 1796, and died at the age of thirty-eight, but during those years he was M.P. for Shrewsbury, High Sheriff of Shropshire and Merioneth and Major of the North Shropshire Yeomanry Cavalry. To say he was eccentric is somewhat of an understatement. It is a very thin line between sanity and insanity, and which side of it John Mytton was, is open to question. He owned a pet monkey named Jacko and a brown bear that he once rode into the dining room at Halston Hall to entertain his guests at a dinner party he was giving. One night during a bout of hiccups at his ancestral home he set fire to his nightshirt in an attempt to shock himself out of the 'accursed infliction.' His high living antics, drinking sessions and sense of humour were legendary wherever he went, his bravery in all walks of his life were without question, a fearless rider across open country and a man, who few, if any, got the better of. One of his friends reckoned Mytton hadn't been sober for twelve years. The Squire, when told of this replied, *'yes, that's about right.'* For at least one night in late September 1823, Walsall was to be his host; there is a song from the late 1950s by the Chris Barber Band with Ottilie Patterson that sums it up perfectly, *'There'll be a hot time in the old town tonight,'* and I'll bet there was too!

A very good friend of Mytton was the celebrated sporting writer Charles Apperly, otherwise known to the sporting world as Nimrod. It was around this time he became a regular at Walsall Races along with many other sporting men of the day including Peter Burgess from London, Dick Fryer, Bob Thacker, Tom Evans, Joe Curtis, Jack Jesson etc. With champagne in abundance at ten shillings and sixpence (52.5 pence) per litre at the George Hotel it was said the gathering would upset tables, smash glasses and generally cause mayhem after drinking their fill. Then it was time to dress for the ball in the evening and start all over again!

An engraving of the celebrated sporting writer, Nimrod (Charles Apperly). It was he that wrote the book, The Memoirs of the Life of the Late John Mytton, first published in the Sporting Magazine in 1837.

1820 - 1839

The George Hotel circa 1890. The hotel was built around 1781 by Thomas Fletcher. In 1823, his son, Richard Moores Fletcher (pictured above) altered the building considerably. He added the four columns to the front of the building which were taken from Fisherwick Hall near Lichfield, the home of the Marquis of Donegal. (Reproduced by courtesy of Walsall Local History Centre)

John Beardsworth, already well known at Walsall, teamed up with John Mytton and became what is known today as his racing manager. Thomas Flintoff at Hednesford trained the majority, if not all of Beardsworth's horses and it was with this same trainer that Mytton placed many of his horses. Mytton's association with Beardsworth cost him dear however. By 1830 his fortune had severely diminished, from having upwards of fifteen to twenty horses in training each year, he was down to his last two. This was to be the final year his colours of green and white jacket, black cap would be seen on a racecourse.

Mytton's first runner at Walsall was a horse named Fair Barbara who was pulled up in the second race on the Long Meadow for two year-olds. With only three runners, the race proved to be a disappointing affair, what in effect was a match, it was won by Colonel Yate's grey, Fille de Joie beating John Beardsworth's colt by Blucher.

The first race on Wednesday morning was reduced to a match, and was won by Sir George Pigot's filly, Active who beat John Beardsworth's horse Birmingham. The naming of the latter was a trademark of Beardsworth; many of his horses were named after towns and villages. This horse, however, was not the horse of the same name that gave Beardsworth his only Classic winner in 1830.

The Maiden Plate on Wednesday afternoon had a good turn out of runners, eight in all going to post. One of these runners was Thomas Wadlow's of Shifnal, another Shropshire man of a somewhat different nature to his fellow Salopian, John Mytton. This was Wadlow's first runner at Walsall, after running well in the first heat to finish third, the horse threw its jockey and so ended the owners chance of having his first winner with his first runner. Thomas Wadlow along with his sons, Thomas and Henry, continued to support the Races right through to the demise of the meeting in 1876.

In the second race on Thursday, John Mytton turned the tables from the previous day when his famous horse, Whittington, beat Beardsworth's Birmingham over two heats in a four horse race. That would be enough for the Squire, a fifty percent success rate from two runners, time to get over to the George Inn to celebrate, and maybe tar and feather the Mayor of Walsall whilst riding naked on his brown bear with his pet monkey, Jacko, on his back for good measure, after all, it was the week of his birthday!

The final race of the meeting was a Plate of fifty guineas, won convincingly by Mr Massey's filly, Ynysymaengwyn. This horse won the Maiden Plate equally convincingly at the meeting last year.

The official results of the meeting were:

Wednesday 24th September 1823

A SWEEPSTAKES of 10 guineas each with 10 guineas added by the Stewards. One mile heats.

Sir George Pigot's b. f.	Active	1	1
Mr J. Beardsworth's b. c.	Birmingham	2	dr

A MATCH for 50 sovereigns. One mile heats.

Mr Barber's b. m.	Blue Ruin	2	1	1
Mr Perks' g. h.	Comet	1	2	2

A MAIDEN PLATE of £50. Two mile heats.

Viscount Anson's br. c.	by Sir Oliver, 3 y-o	1	1
Mr Smith's b. c.	Little Driver, 3 y-o	5	2
Mr J. Tomes' b. m.	Fair Phillis, 4 y-o	2	3
Mr Williams' br. g.	Tripoli, 5 y-o	4	4
Mr Charlton's b. h.	Gallivanter, 4 y-o	7	5
Mr Hassall's b. f.	Fair Helen, 3 y-o	6	6
Mr Wadlow's bl. f.	by Ambo, 3 y-o	3	•
Mr Simmons' b. m.	Gratitude, 5 y-o	dr	-

• *Rider thrown.*

Thursday 25th September 1823

A SWEEPSTAKES of 25 guineas each. For two year olds. Four Furlongs.

Col. Yates' gr. f.	Fille de Joie	1
Mr J. Beardsworth's b. c.	by Blucher	2
Mr John Mytton's	Fair Barbara	dr

1820 - 1839

A SWEEPSTAKES of 10 guineas, with 10 guineas added.
Two mile heats.

Mr John Mytton's br. c.	**Whittington**, 3 y-o	1	1
Mr J. Beardsworth's b. c.	**Birmingham**	4	2
Mr Walhouse names ch. c.	**Hero**, 3 y-o	2	3
Mr J. Painter's br. h.	**The Main**, 6 y-o	3	dr

A PLATE of £50. Two mile heats.

Mr Massey's ch. f.	**Ynysymaengwyn**, 4 y-o	1	1
Mr West's br. h.	**Sharper**, 4 y-o	4	2
Mr J. Beardsworth's ch. f.	**Paradigm**, 4 y-o	2	3
Mr Whitehead's b. g.	**Young Sir Peter**, aged	3	dr

Stewards: Earl of Dartmouth and John Mytton.
Clerk of the Races: Thomas Pearce.

1824

The report in Aris' Gazette covering the meeting for 1824 gave the following statement: -

'At Walsall Races the sport was excellent and the company never on a similar occasion more numerous; the ball was also most fashionably attended. The performances at the theatre, under the patronage of the steward, Captain Yates (whose attention to the interest of the races has left a lasting impression), produced a bumper to the Manager, Mr Chamberlain. The ordinaries were well provided by the respective landlords of the George Hotel and Dragon Inn; great festivity prevailed at the tables and many toasts were drank with three times three. Ten gentlemen subscribed their names at ten guineas each for a gold cup to be run for at the Races next year, to which Major Giffard and John Monckton, Esq. are appointed stewards.'

The facts of the report in the *Staffordshire Advertiser* read somewhat differently to the above statement, recording the details of only two races, which would hardly warrant the comment of 'the sport was excellent'. It is known that at this time a great many horses in the area were suffering from a form of equine distemper and this may have played a part in the shortened programme. Sir Thomas Stanley, who had runners at Walsall in the past, lost his well-bred colt by Cestrian through this complaint only a few weeks after it had won at Lichfield and Shrewsbury.

When the race for none thoroughbred horses was introduced in 1822 the Race Committee possibly had no idea they were to prove so popular amongst owners, and the viewing public; if truth be told, they were the most competitively contested races on the card in many years. Although only five runners went to post for the first race on Wednesday it turned out to be a first class race with all three heats being required to decide the winner. Mr R. Sudbury's horse, Woodman, won the first heat by half a length from Mr S. Perks junior's grey, Escape. In the second heat, Woodman again passed the post first but was disqualified after passing the wrong side of one of the posts and the heat was awarded to Richard Barber's, Clara. The rider of Woodman made no mistakes in the third heat, winning that with ease, and consequently, the race.

In the only other reported race, the Maiden Plate, John Beardsworth recorded his second winner at Walsall when his un-named colt by Cestrian won the race after two heats.

The *Staffordshire Advertiser* ended their concise race report with the following paragraph: -

'We understand the races of next year are expected to be very superior to any in this neighbourhood. There is a Gold Cup already subscribed for by ten Gentlemen at 10 gs. each, and many other Gentlemen are expected to become subscribers. Besides this, there is a two year-old Stake of 15 gs. each. A three year-old Stake of 10gs. each. An All-age Stake of 10gs. each. A Hunter's Stake of 5gs. each and a Cavalry Stakes of 5gs. each; also two Plates of 50gs. each.'

It is obvious the Race Committee decided a revamp of the race programme was necessary, hence the above comments. After another year of failing to get the Gold Cup into the programme, it finally looked as though it was going to happen in 1825.

The official results of the meeting were:

Wednesday 25th September 1824

A SUBSCRIPTION PURSE of 50 sovereigns, for horses not thoroughbred, to be ridden by Members of the Walsall Troop of Yeomanry Cavalry.

Mr R. Sudbury's b. h.	**by Woodman**	1	0	1
Mr S. Perks' jun. gr. h.	**Escape**	2	3	2
Mr Richard Barber's b. m.	**Clara**	3	1	3
Mr E. Adams' b. m.	**Pauline**	4	4	4
Mr John V. Barber's b. h.	**Abraham Newland**	5	dist	-

In the second heat Woodland came in first, but passed the wrong side of a post, the heat being awarded to Clara.

A MAIDEN PLATE of 50 sovereigns.

Mr J. Beardsworth's gr. f.	**by Cestrian**	1	1
Mr Smith's b. c.	**Little Driver,**	2	2
Mr J. Lambs's br. g.	**Tripoli,**	3	dr

1825

Wednesday, September 28th saw the opening of the meeting in 1825 with four races due for the first day. The first two races were somewhat of an anti-climax, the first was a walkover and the second was reduced to a match, although the press report states that it was a good race. Again, the race for none thoroughbreds proved to have the most runners in any of the races over the two days, with six horses going to post. The race was still restricted to all of the horses being ridden by gentlemen, or amateur riders as they are known today, who, this year made no errors of judgement as in previous years, that resulted in disqualification. The race went to Joseph Painter's horse, Fitzwilliam, who was so far unbeaten in all of his races. Not surprisingly, he won the event easily from the second horse, Sir Edward owned by Edward Phillips, another well-known horse breeder from Bushbury near Wolverhampton.

The horse that took the first prize of the day with a walkover, Mr E. Yate's, Madame Poki, turned out for the final race on Wednesday afternoon, the Corporation Plate over

1820 – 1839

three, two-mile heats. After the first heat Mr Yate's must have thought his luck was in when the boy riding his horse found he couldn't hold the filly when she bolted. This usually meant disaster, but in this instance it turned out to be the opposite. Madame Poki obviously kept to the course, even though the boy riding had no control over her, to everyone's amazement, she won. In the second heat she was beaten after only a mile had been run and could only finish third to Lord Anson's horse, Sligo, who also won the final heat and the race.

Thursday finally saw the running of the inaugural Gold Cup, ten horses originally subscribed to the event in 1824 but there were only three when it came to the actual running. The race was run over three miles and a distance with only the one heat to decide the winner, which was John Beardsworth's, Arachne, a superbly bred bay filly by the outstanding 1815 St. Leger winner, Filho Da Puta, a stallion that was a favourite of Beardsworth's and gave him many future winners with his offspring. This season alone, Arachne had won ten races valued at £840, a considerable sum for the period.

The race report for 1825 was taken from the *Birmingham Journal* who's article read:

'There are ten subscribers to the cup to be run for next year. The Saddlers' Ironmongers of Walsall, have come forward with a new plate, which, no doubt, will be a very handsome one, and give general satisfaction; as there is probably, no class of tradesmen to whom the sports of the turf tend so greatly to benefit as the Saddlers' Ironmonger. The company at these Races was very large, and the sport good. The ordinary at the George, on the first day, was well attended; but on the last day, at the Dragon, it was quite neglected.'

The official results of the meeting were:

Wednesday 28th September 1825

A SWEEPSTAKES of 10 guineas each, with 10 guineas added by the Stewards. For three year olds. One mile heats.

Mr Yates' b. f.	Madame Poki	walked over

A SWEEPSTAKES of 15 sovereigns each, with 20 added. For two year olds. To start at the bottom of the hill.

Mr Yates' b. f.	Claudia, 8st. *(John Spring)*	1
Mr J. Beardsworth's b. c.	by Milo, 8st. 3lb.	2

THE CORPORATION PURSE of £50. Horses of all ages. Two mile heats.

Lord Anson's b. c.	Sligo, 4 y-o, 8st. 7lb. *(John Spring)*	0	1	1
Mr J. Twamley's ch. f.	by Blucher, 3 y-o, 6st. 10lb.	0	2	2
Mr Yates' b. f.	Madame Poki, 3 y-o, 7st. 1lb.	1	3	dr
Mr Tongue's b. h.	The Agent, 5 y-o, 8st. 10lb.	0	4	dr

A SWEEPSTAKES of 5 sovereigns each, for horses not thoroughbred, to be ridden by gentlemen riders. Two mile heats.

Mr J. Painter's b. g.	Fitzwilliam, 5 y-o, *(Mr Meek)*	1	1
Mr E. Phillips' br. g.	Sir Edward, 6 y-o	2	2
Mr Kempson's b. g.	High Lurcher, 4 y-o	4	3
Mr John Jesson's	Wolverhampton Mary, aged	5	4
Mr S. Perks' b. g.	by Hambleton Jack, 4 y-o	3	fell
Mr R. Barber's b. g.	by Hercules, 4 y-o	5	dr

Thursday 29th September 1825

A SWEEPSTAKES of 10 guineas each, with 10 guineas added by the Town. Two mile heats.

Mr J. Painter's br. f.	Sarsparilla, 4 y-o, 8st. 2lb. *(John Cheswas)*	1	3	1
Mr J. Beardsworth's b. h.	Libertine, 5 y-o, 8st 5lb.	3	1	2
Mr Gisbourne's br. h.	Charnwood, 5 y-o, 8st. 12lb.	4	2	dr
Mr Tongue's ch. h.	Mazame, 5 y-o, 8st. 12lb	2	dr	-

A GOLD CUP in specie, by 10 subscribers of 10 sovereigns each. Horses of all ages. Three miles and a distance.

Mr J. Beardsworth's b. f.	Arachne, 3 y-o, 6st. 10lb. *(Picken)*	1
Mr Adams' br. f.	Susan, 3 y-o, 6st. 10lb.	2
Mr Gisbourne's br. h.	Charnwood, 5 y-o, 8st. 10lb.	3

A HANDICAP SWEEPSTAKES of 5 sovereigns each, with 30 added. Two mile heats.

Mr Tongue's ch. h.	Mazame, 5 y-o. 8st. 4lb. *(Farlow)*	1	1
Mr Hill's gr. f.	Niobe, 4 y-o, 7st. 5lb.	2	2

A MATCH for 50 sovereigns. 10st. 7lb. each. Two mile heats.

Mr Sudbury's b. g.	Worthy, 4 y-o	1	1
Mr Kempson's b. g.	High Lurcher, 4 y-o	2	2

1826

The grand aspirations of the Race Committee of two years ago were rapidly diminishing. The race programme for 1826 reverted more or less to what it was ten years ago, except for the Gold Cup, which retained its place on the card.

The Sweepstake race for two year-olds attracted three subscribers, and the event itself became a match on race day between Squire Mytton's filly, Lark and John Beardsworth's Loraine. This was the last runner Mytton had at Walsall before his death eight years later; unfortunately he went out on a loser, being beaten by John Beardsworth of all people.

The two races that had been the backbone of Walsall Races for over sixty years, the Corporation Purse and the Town Subscription Purse were suffering with regard to entries for both events. The reason was quite simple, racing was now very fashionable and to hold a meeting put the town or village on the map. In 1814 the only competition Walsall had was from the three other Staffordshire courses mentioned previously, now there were eight courses in the county. Meetings were also being held 'down the road' at Stourbridge, and also at Dudley and Tipton, although the latter venue had been holding meetings spasmodically since 1807. The upsurge in the new meetings gave owners an additional choice of venues, and as the horses were still walked to the meetings this meant they couldn't always get them to another course in time to compete.

One race that was consistently attracting runners since its introduction was the Sweepstakes for none thoroughbreds

1820 - 1839

and to be ridden by gentlemen. Initially nine subscribed for the event and four lined-up to contest it. The winner was the top weight, Mr Payne's gelding, Gossoon, carrying twelve stone seven pounds and ridden by Mr Pickernell

The Gold Cup was now the premier race of the meeting, but after only two years of running, this was also struggling for runners. The initial signs for the race were good, with twelve owners subscribing, on race day this was reduced to just three contenders, Mr Gleaves' Miller of Mansfield, Sir George Pigot's Granby and Mr Massey's Claudia. The latter horse had won the Town Subscription Purse on the previous afternoon, beating only one other horse. This time she was found wanting and could only finish third to Granby who beat Miller of Mansfield by a head after an excellent race. The jockey who rode the winner was William Lear from Brewood.

The Corporation Purse was the final race of the meeting, with the Miller of Mansfield making amends for his defeat in the Gold Cup a couple of hours earlier to take the prize easily in two heats.

The official results of the meeting were:

Wednesday 27th September 1826

A SWEEPSTAKES of 25 sovereigns each.
For two year olds, four furlongs.

Mr J. Beardsworth's b. c.	**Loraine**, 8st. 13lb. *(John Spring)*	1	
Mr John Mytton's br. f.	**Lark**, by Rubens, 8st.	2	

One horse drawn.

A SWEEPSTAKES for 5 sovereigns each, with 10 added.
For horses not thoroughbred. Gentlemen or yeoman riders.
Two mile heats.

Mr Payne's b. g.	**Gossoon**, aged, 12st. 7lb.	5	1	1
Mr Cary's b. g.	by Young Beninborough, 5 y-o, 11st. 12lb.	1	3	2
Mr Calvert's gr. g.	**Equinox**, 4 y-o, 11st.	4	4	2
Mr J. Painter's b. g.	**Fitzwilliam**, 6 y-o, 12st. 5lb.	2	2	dr

THE TOWN SUBSCRIPTION PURSE of 50 sovereigns.
For three and four year olds. Two mile heats.

Mr Massey's b. f.	**Claudia**, 3 y-o, 7st.	1	1
Mr Twamley's ch. f.	**Tintoretto**, 3 y-o, 7st. 3lb.	2	2

Thursday 28th September 1826

A GOLD CUP, value 100 sovereigns, the surplus in specie.
For horses of all ages. Three miles and a distance.

Sir G. Pigot's b. c.	**Granby**, 3 y-o, 6st. 12lb. *(William Lear)*	1
Mr Gleaves' br. h.	**Miller of Mansfield**, 5 y-o, 8st. 9lb.	2
Mr Massey's b. f.	**Claudia**, 3 y-o, 6st. 10lb.	3

Miller of Mansfield the favourite.

A SWEEPSTAKES of 10 sovereigns, with 10 added.
For horses of all ages. Two mile heats.

Mr Gisbourne's b. f.	**Susan**, 4 y-o, 8st. 2lb. *(Henry Arthur)*	1	1	1
Mr J. Beardsworth's b. c.	**Chesterfield**, 3 y-o, 7st.	2	dr	

THE CORPORATION PURSE of 50 sovereigns.
For horses of all ages. Two mile heats.

Mr Gleaves' br. h.	**Miller of Mansfield**, 5 y-o, 9st. 1lb., *(Norman)*	1	1
Mr Gisbourne's br. h.	**Cinder**, 6 y-o, 9st. 4lb.	2	2
Mr Longmore's gr. g.	**Alpha**, 4 y-o, 8st.	3	3

1827

There were six races to be contested for over the two days and one of these was a match between two ponies on Wednesday September 26th, a case of déjà vu for the Race Committee.

The Sweepstakes race for none thoroughbreds saw an entry from John Jesson, whose family name is remembered today by Jesson Road. This was his first known runner at Walsall, and unfortunately the venture did not end in glory, the horse, quaintly named Julia, came last of the three runners, being distanced in the final heat.

John Beardsworth was making his annual assault at Walsall with just two runners, Loraine, a winner last year, and a newcomer, Chesterfield. Both of his runners finished out of the money, the duo being beaten in their respective races by the same horse, Thomas Giffard's colt by Ambo.

Mr Gleave again entered his horse, Miller of Mansfield, in the Gold Cup, and for the second successive year was beaten, this time by a horse named Euxton owned by Richard Barber. Not to be deterred, Mr Gleave did exactly as the previous year and ran the horse in the next race, obviously a believer in 'lighting does strike twice,' and sure enough it did! Miller of Mansfield, although relegated to third place in the first heat, proceeded to win the next two and take the prize money of £50.

The official results of the meeting were:

Wednesday 26th September 1827

A SWEEPSTAKES of 5 sovereigns each.
For horses not thoroughbred.

Mr Cato names	**Moses**	1	1
Mr Perks names	**The Counsellor**	2	2
Mr John Jesson names	**Julia**	3	dis

A MATCH for 50 sovereigns.

Mr Baker's	**Black pony**	1	1
Mr Vickers'	**Grey pony**	2	2

THE TOWN SUBSCRIPTION PLATE of 50 sovereigns each.
For three and four year old horses. Two mile heats.

Mr Giffard's b. c.	by Ambo	2	1	1
Mr Howard's br. c.	by Filho da Puta	1	2	3
Mr White's b. c.	**Granby**	4	3	2
Mr J. Beardsworth's b. c.	**Chesterfield**	3	4	dr
Mr Cooke's b. c.	**His Majesty**	dr	-	-

Thursday 27th September 1827

A GOLD CUP value 100 sovereigns, in specie.
For horses of all ages. Three miles and a distance.

Mr R. Barber names br. c.	**Euxton**	1
Mr Gleaves' b. h.	**Miller of Mansfield**	2

35

1820 – 1839

A SWEEPSTAKES of 10 sovereigns each with ten added.
For horses of all ages.

Mr Gleaves' b. h.	**Miller of Mansfield**	3	1	1
Mr White's	**Susan**	1	2	dr
Mr J. Beardsworth's	**Chesterfield**	2	dr	-

THE CORPORATION PLATE of 50 sovereigns.
For horses of all ages. Two mile heats.

Mr Giffard's b. c.	**by Ambo**	1	1
Lord Chesterfield's ch. m.	**by Young Grimaldi**	2	2
Mr J. Beardsworth's b. c.	**Loraine**	3	3

1828

The meeting for 1828 began on Wednesday September 24th, again, the race that appeared to be the most popular, and the one that proved the biggest talking point, was the Sweepstakes for none thoroughbreds. In recent years the amateur jockeys had provided entertainment for the people of Walsall without incident. This year saw a return to farce in the first heat when the rider of the certain winner, Caribert, forgot where the winning post was and pulled up to soon. This allowed the second horse, Optimus, to close up and force a dead-heat, making the heat void. The race began again, this time Caribert's rider making no mistakes to take the heat from Optimus. These two horses were now exhausted by their efforts and this didn't go un-noticed by Lord Anson whose un-named filly had yet to feature in the proceedings. When the next heat finished it was his Lordship that had 'pinched' the prize, his filly gaining an easy victory from Caribert and Optimus. There was another horse in the quartet that hasn't been mentioned, and that was a horse named Tom Moody, who had arrived at the course with a group of vociferous supporters from Burton-Upon-Trent who were convinced victory was theirs. The horse never featured until the fourth heat and by then it was too late, it must have been a long walk back to Burton for those men.

Walsall had waited many years for a race with Gold Cup status, this year they had two. The second of these two races was a new event, the Cavalry Gold Cup for horses belonging to the Walsall Troop of Yeomanry Cavalry, and worth one hundred guineas to the winner.

The first of the Gold Cup races was held on Wednesday afternoon with only three runners going to post. Two of the entries, Sampson and The Weaver were owned by Thomas Giffard of Chillington Hall, near Brewood. The horse that made the running was Edward Peel's Grimalkin, a winner the previous day. His over exhuberant efforts early in the race made him somewhat of a spent force. As the runners approached the judge's chair, it was Thomas Giffards pair, Sampson and The Weaver being left to battle it out. Unlike his namesake in the bible, Sampson's strength didn't desert him and won by about a length from The Weaver.

The Cavalry Gold Cup was the first event on the card for Thursday morning with five runners going to post. Like many heat races, the first event 'sorted the wheat from the chaff,' Mr T. F. Sharratt's chestnut mare Maria Darlington winning by half a length from Little Doctor owned by Mr Elkington. Sir Edward Scott's runner was unplaced in the first heat and bolted at the start of the second, finishing his owner's chance of Gold Cup glory. When the second heat began there were in effect, only three contenders, and very soon only one as Maria Darlington stamped her authority on the race winning easily this time from Mr S. Perk's, Slender Billy, with Little Doctor third.

In the *Guide to Walsall* published by William Henry Robinson in 1889, it states:-

'In 1828 the Gold Cup [Cavalry] was won by Maria Darlington, a chestnut mare, and the event was celebrated by Miss Foote, afterwards Countess of Harrington, singing the Little Jockey at the Walsall Theatre.'

William Lear the jockey, who hailed from Brewood, must have been a happy man. He won three of the five races on the card open to professional jockeys, including one on John Beardsworth's highly talented horse, Arachne, a winner at last years meeting.

The official results of the meeting were:

Wednesday 24th September 1828

A SWEEPSTAKES of 10 sovereigns each,
with 25 sovereigns added.

Mr E. Peel's b. f.	**Grimalkin** *(John Spring)*	1
Mr Rogers names a bl. c.	**Frederick**	2
Lord Warwick's ch. c.	**brother to Paul Jones**	3

A SWEEPSTAKES of 5 sovereigns each,
with ten sovereigns added by the Stand Committee.
For horses not thoroughbred.

Lord Anson's g. f.	**sister to Mayflower** *(Burton)*	r	r	1	1
Mr E. F. Meynell names	**Caribert**	0	1	2	3
Mr W. Foster's br. g.	**Optimus**	0	2	dr	-
Mr Hinchcliffe names	**Tom Moody**	r	r	r	2

THE TOWN SUBSCRIPTION PLATE of 50 sovereigns each.
For three and four year old horses. Two mile heats.

Mr Giffard's b. c.	**by Ambo**	2	1	1
Mr Howard's br. c.	**by Filho da Puta**	1	2	3
Mr White's b. c.	**Granby**	4	3	2
Mr J. Beardsworth's b. c.	**Chesterfield**	3	4	dr
Mr Cooke's b. c.	**His Majesty**	dr	-	-

A GOLD CUP value 100 sovereigns, in specie.
For horses of all ages. Three miles and a distance.

Mr Giffard's b. c.	**Sampson** *(William Lear)*	1
Mr Giffard's br. c.	**The Weaver**	2
Mr E. Peel's b. f.	**Grimalkin**	3

Thursday 25th September 1828

A CAVALRY GOLD CUP of 100 sovereigns.
For horses of the Walsall Troop of Yeomanry Cavalry.

Mr T. F. Sherratt's ch. m.	**Maria Darlington**	1	1
Mr Elkington's b. c.	**Little Doctor**	2	3
Sir Edward Scott's b. m.	**Rosalinda**	0	bolt
Mr S. Perks' b. m.	**Slender Billy**	0	2
Mr Wilkins' br. c.	**Cossack**	dis.	-

1820 - 1839

A SWEEPSTAKES of 10 sovereigns each, with 10 added.

Mr J. Beardsworth's b. f.	**Arachne** (W. Lear)	2	1	1
Mr E. Peel's b. m.	**Little Bo Peep**	1	2	2

Two horses drawn

A MATCH for 100 sovereigns. Two mile heats.

Mr Aston's b. m.	**Diana**	1	1
Mr Richard Evans' br. h.	**Sportsman**	2	2

THE CORPORATION PLATE of 50 sovereigns.
For horses of all ages. Two mile heats.

Mr Giffard's br. c.	**The Weaver** (William Lear)	1	1
Mr White's b. g.	**Granby**	2	2
Mr J. Beardsworth's b. f.	**Emily**	3	3

1829

Looking at the results for the meeting in 1829, which took place on Wednesday 23rd and Thursday 24th September, made encouraging reading with regard to the quality of many of the horses engaged.

The first race Wednesday was won by Mr Jackson's bay colt, Hazard, who had previously won a gruelling four, two mile heat Maiden race at the prestigious Chester meeting in early May. A couple of weeks later he was even money favourite for a race at Liverpool but was beaten into second place. The race at Walsall was a two-mile, single heat or 'dash' race, which produced an excellent race with Hazard, ridden by William Lear, holding off the nearest opposition by a neck only.

The Gold Cup Stakes proved to be a disappointment with Thomas Saunders bay mare, Sarah, having to go through the formalities of a walkover to take the prize. Not that the horse didn't deserve the race, she had already won in good company at Liverpool and Newton before coming to Walsall. There were three very good horses entered but all withdrew, last years winner of this race, Sampson was one. He had continued to improve, and earlier in the season had won at Chester and Ludlow. One of the other horses withdrawn was the mighty Independence, owned by John Beardsworth. By the end of July the horse had already run in seven races, winning two. He was a three year-old and was still learning his craft, in three of those events he had bolted, but it did show the spirit was there.

Reading down the list of horses and owners that were running at Walsall, it was somewhat reminiscent of the card at the Spring Meeting at Chester, with many of the horses being the ones that ran on Britain's oldest racecourse five months previously.

The Sweepstakes for the none thoroughbred horses was another excellent race, with the Birmingham Journal congratulating the runners on their terrific pace and stating 'it is scarcely possible a finer race could be run.' Lord Anson's un-named grey mare, a full sister to Mayflower and ridden by Captain Lamb, won the race by a head from the horse the Burtonians placed so much faith in two years ago, Tom Moody.

Another Chester runner, R. Turner's, Clinton, ridden by John Spring, won the Corporation Plate. The colt actually won the race on the Roodee, beating Sampson in the process, but was later disqualified on the grounds of crossing. This time John Spring made no mistakes, and after an exciting three heats, Clinton won the final one, and the race, by a head. Clinton's meeting wasn't over however; he turned out an hour or so later to pick up another prize in the easiest way possible, a walkover in the penultimate race.

Thomas Giffard's colt, Barrabas ridden by William Lear, won the final race at the meeting from Mr Tomes entry, The Burgess. Yet another runner at Chester four months earlier, Barrabas had finished second to the winner, Hazard, who had won the first race of the Walsall meeting.

The official results of the meeting were:

Wednesday 23rd September 1829

A SWEEPSTAKES of 10 sovereigns each, with 20 added.
For three year old colts. Twice round.

Mr Jackson's b. c.	**Hazard** (William Lear)	1
Mr Richards' b. c.	**Allerdale**	2
Mr E. Phillips ch. c.	**by Bobadil**	3
Mr J. Beardsworth's ch. f.	**by Tiresias**	4

A GOLD CUP SWEEPSTAKES in specie, by subscribers of 10 sovereigns each. Three miles and a distance.

Mr Saunders' b. m.	**Sarah**	walked over

A SWEEPSTAKES of 5 sovereigns each,
with 30 sovereigns added. Two mile heats.

Mr R. Turner's b. c.	**Clinton** (William Lear)	1	1
Mr Freemantle's br. f.	**Flora**	5	2
Mr Gleaves' b. h.	**Miller of Mansfield**	2	3
Mr J. Tomes' b. c.	**Foxcote**	3	4
Mr Russell's b. c.	**Macassar**	4	dr

A SWEEPSTAKES of 5 sovereigns each,
with 10 added by the Stand Committee.
For horses not thoroughbred. Two mile heats.

Lord Anson's gr. m.	**sister to Mayflower** (Lamb)	1	1
Mr Whitehurst's bl. g.	**Tom Moody**	0	2
Mr H. W. Hickes' ch. g.	**Tartar**	2	3
Mr Jackson's b. m.	**Antiope**	3	dr
Mr Measure's br. m.	**Revenge**	0	dr

Thursday 24th September 1829

THE CORPORATION PLATE of 50 sovereigns.
Two mile heats.

Mr R. Turner's b. c.	**Clinton** (John Spring)	5	1	1
Mr Richards' b. c.	**Allerdale**	1	2	2
Mr Giffard's b. h.	**The Weaver**	2	3	dr
Mr Jackson's br. m.	**Brenda**	3	4	dr
Mr Wakefield's br. m.	**Billingsgate**	4	dr	-

A SWEEPSTAKES of 25 sovereigns each, 15 forfeit.
For two year olds. Four furlongs.

Mr Massey's b. f.	**The Little Duchess** (J. Spring)	1
Mr Wadlow's ch. f.	**by the Grand Duke**	2
Mr J. Beardsworth's b. f.	**by Paulowitz**	3

A SWEEPSTAKES of 10 sovereigns each, with 20 added.
Two mile heats.

Mr R. Turner's b. c.	**Clinton**	walked over

1820 - 1839

A SWEEPSTAKES of 10 sovereigns each, with 20 added.
For three year-olds. One mile.

Mr Giffard's b. c.	**Barabbas,** 8st. 5lb. *(W. Lear)*		1
Mr J. Tomes' br. c.	**The Burgess,** 8st. 5lb.		2
Mr J. Beardsworth's ch. f.	**by Tiresias,** 8st. 2lb.		3

1830

The meeting opened on Wednesday 29th September with three Sweepstake races and the Gold Cup, whilst the programme for Thursday consisted of a further two Sweepstakes and the Corporation Plate. Included in the runners at the races this year was the finest horse ever to grace the Long Meadow, Independence, owned by John Beardsworth and trained by Thomas Flintoff at Hednesford.

Wednesday morning saw the Gold Cup open the proceedings with just two runners, a disappointing field for such a race. Undoubtedly one of the reasons for such a small field was the fact that Independence was running; from the original seven subscribers there was only one owner, Edward Yates, brave enough, or foolish enough, to take the big brown gelding on. Yates' horse, a three year-old filly called Lilla came to Walsall with a hundred percent record, having won at Much Wenlock and Stourbridge twice, earlier in the season. With that sort of form, Edward Yates must have been confident of his filly's chances, especially as she was to carry only six stone twelve pounds against Independence's weight of eight stones. The gelding arrived at Walsall from Hednesford with a big reputation that was fully justified, having won nine races from ten starts. He started the season with four straight wins and then mysteriously ran unplaced at Manchester, where he had won two days previously. Not surprisingly, at Walsall he started a red-hot favourite at two to one on, generous odds considering his form, which continued in this race when ridden by George Calloway. He won the one heat, three-mile event with ease. After winning at Walsall he contested three further races, one at Rugeley and two at Nottingham, winning them all, bringing his total for the season to thirteen wins from fourteen starts.

Lord Warwick, new to the races at Walsall, won the final event on the first day with Merman, his four year-old brown horse, who had won earlier in the season at Epsom's Derby meeting. Merman, with George Calloway up, carrying his Lordship's colours of brown, with white sleeves and cap, started as the 8/11 favourite and justified the confidence of his backer's by winning the race with ease after two heats.

Thursday's events opened as they had left off the previous day, with only the horse being different. This time it was the turn of his Lordship's un-named colt by Whalebone, again ridden by Calloway that took the prize, beating another un-named colt by Filho Da Puta owned by John Beardsworth.

The Corporation Plate, with five runners, proved to be the most competitive race of the meeting, taking four heats to decide the winner after the judge could not split Mr Giffard's, Lucy and Mr Charlton's, Kalmia in the first heat, declaring it void. Lucy won the second run but was beaten in the final two heats by Mr Morris', Zulima, a three year-old filly ridden by Henry Wadlow.

The final race of the meeting was a Sweepstakes race that had only one starter, Lord Warwick's Merman, which left George Calloway, the rider, the easiest of tasks to take the money.

It was almost a benefit meeting for Lord Warwick and his rider, Calloway, his Lordship taking three of the six prizes on offer, and the jockey riding four of the winners.

This was also the year that John Beardsworth's second horse to be named Birmingham triumphed in the St. Leger Stakes

The site of the racecourse in 2005 showing Bradford Street and The Cenotaph. The incline on Bradford Street, which proved to be a stern test for the runners as they set off, is still clearly visible today.

1820 - 1839

at Doncaster. Like Independence, Birmingham was another hard working horse, also trained by Flintoff at Hednesford, and between them they won a total of twenty-one races this season alone. Beardsworth did nothing by halves, least of all his betting, from his victory in the St. Leger, he won over £19,000.

The official results of the meeting were:

Wednesday 29rd September 1830

THE CUP STAKES of 10 sovereigns each.
Mares and geldings allowed 2lb. Three miles and a distance.

Mr J. Beardsworth's br. g.	**Independence,** 4 y-o, 8st.		
	(George Calloway)		1
Mr E. Yates' b. f.	**Lilla,** 3 y-o, 6st. 12lb.		2

2/1 on favourite, Independence.

A SWEEPSTAKES of 5 sovereigns each, with 10 added.
For horses not thoroughbred. Two mile heats.

Mr Hobson's br. h.	**Contraband,** 5 y-o, 12st.			
	(Henry Arthur)	2	1	1
Mr Brown's b. f.	**Daylight,** 4 y-o, 10st. 9lb.	1	2	3
Mr Burton's gr. g.	**Post Captain,** 4 y-o, 11st. 2lb.	3	3	2

6/4 against favourite, Contraband.

A SWEEPSTAKES of 5 sovereigns each,
with 30 added by the Stand Committee.
For horses of all ages. Two mile heats.

Lord Warwick's br. c.	**Merman,** 4 y-o, 8st. 9lb.		
	(George Calloway)	1	1
Mr J. Tomes' br. c.	**Port,** 3 y-o, 6st. 9lb.	3	2
Mr Applewhaite's ch. c.	**Zodiac,** 4 y-o, 8st. 9lb.	2	fell

Thursday 30th September 1830

THE CORPORATION PLATE of 50 sovereigns.
For horses of all ages. Two mile heats.

Mr Morris' b. f.	**Zulima,** 3 y-o, 6st. 10lb.				
	(Wadlow)	2	-	1	1
Mr Giffard's br. f.	**Lucy,** 4 y-o, 8st. 2lb.	-	1	2	2
Mr R. Turner's b. h.	**Clinton,** 5 y-o, 9st. 1lb.	-	2	4	dr
Mr J. Tomes' b. c.	**Foxcote,** 4 y-o, 8st. 7lb.	3	3	5	dr

A SWEEPSTAKES of 10 sovereigns each, with 20 added.
For horses of all ages. Twice round.

Lord Warwick's br. c.	**Merman,** 4 y-o, 8st. 4lb.	walked over

INDEPENDENCE – The horse

Independence was foaled in 1827, with a question mark about his sire. In all records his pedigree is described as 'by Filho Da Puta or Sherwood.' Looking at his racing record and stamina, it appears to be a certainty that his sire was Filho Da Puta, who won the stayer's classic, the St. Leger Stakes in 1815. It is great pity that the fact of his sire cannot be confirmed one way or the other, as Independence won thirty six and half races in his career, the half race being a dead heat, as this would have made him Filho Da Puta's most successful offspring. Filho', as he was known, was as good a stallion as he was a racehorse, and became a favourite sire of John Beardworths.

Independence's career on the racecourse began as early as 11th August 1828 in the Chillington Stakes at Wolverhampton, a race he won. Less than a month later, on 2nd September he turn out to race at Warwick but finished unplaced. The following season began with unplaced runs at Lichfield and Chester before he returned to winning ways at Ludlow in July.

As a three year-old, he was somewhat impetuous and in an effort to curb this, he was gelded during the winter of 1829/30. This was a deciding factor in turning him into the formidable racehorse he became, allowing him to focus on racing without being concerned if there were any fillies around.

One of the most important wins of the horse's career was in 1831 when he won the prestigious Chester Cup on the Roodee. John Beardsworth completed a double in this race the year after when his horse Colwick, another of Filho's offspring, won. Other successes for Independence that year came at Warwick winning two races before being taken to Doncaster where he registered another double. Further victories followed at the Holywell Hunt meeting in Cheshire, finally rounding off the trip with a visit to Manchester where he won again. The season began in mid March, and by the beginning of May of this year he had already won seven races. His form continued through into September when he again won the Gold Cup at Walsall for the second successive year, this time ridden by Sam Darling.

Many of his victories came when giving weight, and lots of it, to his opponents, but none more so than in 1832 when winning the Gold Cup at Nottingham. As at Walsall, Independence was ridden by George Calloway, carrying twelve stones, he only had one opponent, who carried eight stone three pounds, a difference of fifty-three pounds. That gives some idea of the horse's ability.

He continued his winning ways for the next two seasons and in 1834 won his third Gold Cup at Walsall in the easiest way possible, with a walk-over. But by 1835 the devastating form of previous years was fading, after all, he was now eight years of age. It was in 1835 he appeared at Walsall again for the final time in his life, unfortunately being beaten into second place by a horse some six years his junior and carrying thirty-one pounds less in weight. His appearances on the racecourse got less and less and when John Beardsworth died in 1835, Thomas Flintoff bought the horse from the executors. It was in Flintoffs name Independence ran his final race, the two mile Worcestershire Stakes at Worcester on 1st August 1837. Unfortunately he finished last of the four runners.

The story doesn't quite end there, in 1839 the second volume of the *Sporting Magazine* contained an article by one of their correspondents about the Hednesford Hills training grounds, detailing various trainers activities. The article gave praise to Thomas Flintoff's outstanding ability as trainer and in the remarks commented, *'Flintoff was to be seen riding around his yard and the Hills on his old hack, Independence, now thirteen years old.'*

1820 - 1839

1831

The first changes in land close to the racecourse took place in this year when the New Road or Bradford Street, as we know it today, was opened. The road cost £2,000 pounds to build and ran from the bottom of Park Street, alongside the left side of the racecourse. Prior to this building work, the land had just been open-fields and this is the first instance of the town beginning to grow around the racecourse.

By now everyone will have realised that Walsall Races was not just about horse racing but also a great social event – for the privileged few anyway. This year was no exception; contemporary reports state that John Gough of Perry Hall presented Richard Fletcher of the George Hotel with a fine buck for roasting, and to further the feast, Edward Littleton, M.P. and Sir Edward Scott, M.P. provided ample supplies of game from their estates.

The Steward's Ordinary was well attended as usual, and presided over by the Steward of the Races for the year, John Heeley who was also Mayor of Walsall.

The meeting opened with a Sweepstakes for three year-olds on Wednesday morning, which was won by Mr Morris' Blue Beard, beating just two opponents.

Mr Morris had obviously been enjoying the hospitality on offer a little too liberally and wasn't thinking too clearly. Approximately half an hour after the first race had ended, Blue Beard was declared to run in the Gold Cup against two opponents, one of them being Independence, who won the race for the second consecutive year. It could be argued that Morris knew of the oppositions record and worked on the assumption of someone has to be second. Blue Beard did finish second, relegating last year's runner-up, Lilla, to third place.

The opening race on Thursday was a new event called the Birmingham Stakes, no doubt instigated by John Beardsworth in honour of his horse of the same name that won the St. Leger the previous year. The race was run over two miles and a distance with just the one heat being required to declare the winner; the race attracted nineteen subscribers initially, with five declaring to run. Along with the entry fee, and then having to pay extra for declaring a horse to run at a certain stage, and also having to pay forfeit for withdrawing, all of these rather complex conditions made this the richest race ever run for at Walsall so far, at around £400. It was no great surprise to find that the winning owner was a certain Mr John Beardsworth, his horse Warwick, taking the prize, and in the process, no doubt raising a few eyebrows in the grandstand and the odd uncomplimentary remark from the remainder of the masses on the Long Meadow.

The second race saw the return of Lord Warwick whose horse, Water Witch beat three other contenders in the Sweepstakes race for horses of all ages. The jockey that rode the winner, his first at Walsall, was the fifteen year-old Charles Marlow, who was apprenticed to Thomas Saunders at Hednesford. He was later to become a famous jockey whose life ended in tragic circumstances.

The Corporation Plate on Thursday afternoon proved to be an endurance race with four heats being required to decide the winner. Mr Jones' bay gelding, King of Diamonds, eventually came out on top, winning two of the heats in possibly the most competitive race at the meeting.

The official results of the meeting were:

Wednesday 28th September 1831

**A SWEEPSTAKES of 25 sovereigns each, with 20 added.
Three year olds. Twice round.**

Mr Morris'	**Blue Beard,** 8st. 5lb. *(Wadlow)*	1
Mr E. Yates' gr. f.	**Sylph,** 8st. 3lb.	2
Mr J. Beardsworth's b. c.	**by Figaro,** 8st. 3lb.	3

**A GOLD CUP STAKES of 10 sovereigns each.
Mares and geldings allowed 2lb. Three miles and a distance.**

Mr J. Beardsworth's br. g.	**Independence,** 5 y-o, 8st. 7lb. *(Samuel Darling)*	1
Mr Morris'	**Blue Beard,** 3 y-o, 6st. 12lb.	2
Mr E. Yates' b. f.	**Lilla,** 4 y-o, 7st. 12lb.	3

Nine horses drawn.

**A SWEEPSTAKES of 5 sovereigns each, with 10 added.
For horses not thoroughbred. Two mile heats.**

Mr Hobson's b. c.	**Donnington,** 3 y-o, 9st. 12lb. *(William Lear)*	2	1	1
Mr H. Lamb's b.g.	**by York,** 4 y-o, 11st.	3	2	2
Mr Eld's	**brother to Atlas,** 5 y-o, 11st. 7lb.	4	3	dr
Mr Burton's b. f.	**sister to The Admiral,** 3 y-o, 9st. 5lb.	1	0	dr
Mr Barber names	**Tom Whittington,** 4 y-o, 10st. 9lb.	5	0	dr

Thursday 29th September 1831

**THE BIRMINGHAM STAKES of 20 sovereigns each,
with 25 added from the Race Fund.**

Mr Wilday names b. c.	**Warwick,** 3 y-o, 6st. 10lb. *(Lock)*	1
Mr T. F. Sherratt names	**Russell,** 5 y-o, 8st. 4lb.	2

Three horses drawn, 14 paid 5 sovereigns each.

**A SWEEPSTAKES of 10 sovereigns each, with 20 added.
For horses of all ages. Twice round.**

Lord Warwick's b. f.	**Water Witch,** 3 y-o, 6st. 10lb., *(Charles Marlow)*	1	1
Mr J. Beardsworth's	**Sir Walter,** 5 y-o, 8st. 13lb.	2	3
Mr E. Yates' gr. f.	**Sylph,** 3 y-o, 6st. 12lb.	3	2
Mr Jones' br. g.	**by King of Diamonds,**	fell	-

THE TWO YEAR OLD STAKES
did not fill and was cancelled.

**THE CORPORATION PLATE of 50 sovereigns.
For horses of all ages. Two mile heats.**

Mr Jones' br. g.	**by King of Diamonds,** 4 y-o, 8st. 5lb.	1	4	3	1
Mr E. Yates' b. m.	**Lilla,** 4 y-o, 8st. 5lb.	2	0	1	2
Mr Morris' b. m.	**Gazelle,** 5 y-o, 8st. 13lb.	3	0	2	dr
Mr J. Twamley's b.m.	**Sappyho,** 4 y-o, 8st. 2lb.	4	3	dr	-

1832

The meeting for 1832 was scheduled for Wednesday 26th and Thursday 27th September and announcements to that effect were published in the *Staffordshire Advertiser* and *Aris' Gazette*.

1820 - 1839

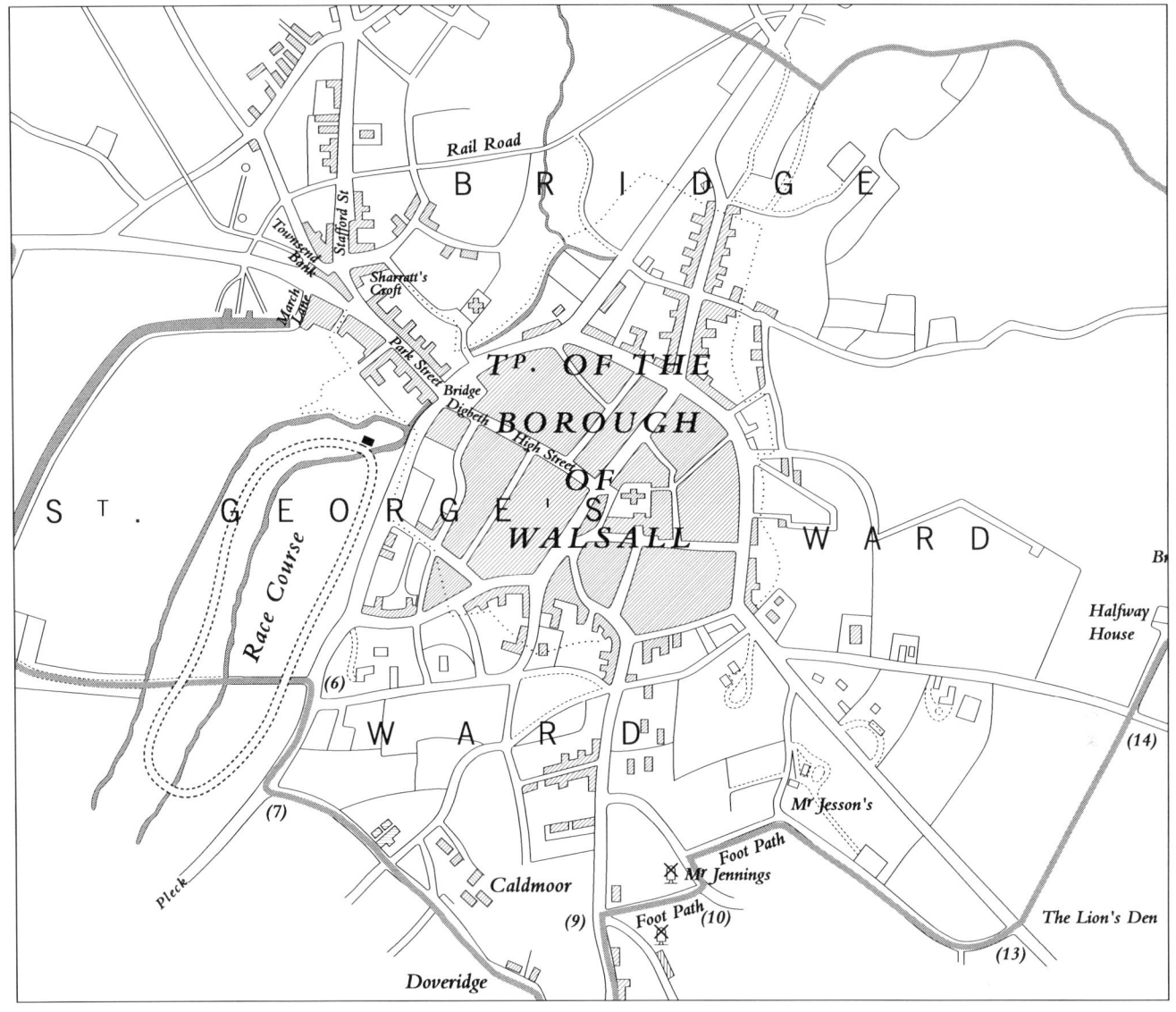

A redrawn section from an 1832 map showing Walsall at that time, some details have been omitted for the sake of clarity.

Everything was set for Walsall's annual sporting and over indulgence festival until cholera struck the Black Country area, causing the Races and the Fair to be cancelled. The towns of Bilston, Tipton, Sedgley and Dudley were the hardest hit but Walsall didn't escape the epidemic, reporting 346 cases, which resulted in 85 deaths.

1833

With the cholera epidemic now safely in the past, it was business as usual on the Long Meadow, in an effort to make up for lost time the meeting was brought forward a week to Thursday 19th and Friday 20th September.

The Gold Cup, which was run on Thursday afternoon proved to be an excellent race with five runners going to post. The favourite of these was John Beardsworth's brown horse, Wolverhampton, who had run several good races prior to arriving at Walsall, and gave his owner every chance of completing his hat trick in the race. Unfortunately two of the five runners had different ideas and relegated Wolverhampton to third place, victory going to another man well known in the locality, Sir Edward Scott. His horse Repentance, ridden by Henry Arthur, proved the better in a dour battle to the line fending off Mr Wightwick's horse, Manchester.

In the first race on Friday morning Charles Marlow rode his second winner at Walsall, partnering Lord Warwick's three year-old bay colt, Trepidation to victory in the Sweepstakes for horses of all ages.

The next race on the card, a Sweepstakes of three heats over two miles each, restricted to non-thoroughbred horses, the property of gentlemen resident in Walsall. This race had always proved popular in the past but this year the number of entries was down slightly to past years. It proved to be a good race giving the spectators some excitement when one of the four runners bolted before the start. After two of the three heats had been run, the race was over as Mr Hawkins' horse, Jerry, had won them both.

The races for two year-olds at Walsall were now a thing of the past as they hadn't appeared in the calendar of events for several years, and if they did, they didn't fill. No doubt, some enterprising man of Walsall would resurrect the event in the future as all other courses in the locality were running races for the juveniles.

This was a year when the reporting of the Races left

1820 – 1839

something to be desired regarding accuracy of horse ownership. The final official race of the meeting was a Handicap Sweepstakes of one mile over three heats and was won by John Tomes' horse Sir Gray. The horse had run in the Gold Cup, running in the name of Sir Thomas Boughey, likewise, Manchester, second in the Gold Cup was running for Mr Robinson on this occasion instead of Mr Wightwick. These discrepancies in ownership must be put down as errors in the reporting of the events.

The final paragraph from the *Staffordshire Advertiser* report states: –

'These races afforded excellent sport and gave great satisfaction to the numerous company assembled; every heat being most closely contested. The Steward's ordinary, at the George Hotel was very respectably attended, and consisted of a plentiful supply of venison and delicacies of every description, the whole reflecting much credit upon Mr Fletcher. At the ball in the Assembly Room, on Thursday night was Sir T.F.F. Boughey, Bart. and E.L. Charlton, Esq. (the stewards of the races,) with several highly respectable families in the town and neighbourhood, were present.

The Theatre, under the management of Mr Parker Cooke, of the Theatre Royal, Birmingham, was well attended each evening, and report speaks favourably of the company.'

In addition to the official race card there was further activity on the racecourse before and after the meeting. Late on Wednesday afternoon two matches were contested that attracted a considerable number of spectators to view the informal proceedings and again on Saturday afternoon it is reported a match was run – between three horses! One of the contenders was a horse called Mouse Trap, owned by Mr Farrington of Walsall that had come third in one of the official races on Friday. The informality of this gathering must have put him at ease as he won the race.

The official results of the meeting were:

Thursday 19th September 1833

A SWEEPSTAKES of 10 sovereigns each, with 20 added.
For horses not thoroughbred. Two mile heats.

Mr Foster's b. f.	by **Bizarre**, 3 y-o *(John Spring)*	1	1
Mr Wilson's b. c.	**Theodolite**, 3 y-o	2	dr
Mr Pickernell's b. g.	**Witley**, 4 y-o	dr	-

A GOLD CUP STAKES of 10 sovereigns each, in specie.
Three miles and a distance.

Sir E. D. Scott's ch. f.	**Repentance**, 3 y-o *(Henry Arthur junior)*	1
Mr S. Wightwick's b. h.	**Manchester**, 3 y-o	2
Mr J. Beardsworth's br. h.	**Wolverhampton**, 4 y-o	3
Sir T. F. Boughey's b. c.	by **Sir Gray**, 3 y-o	dr
Lord Warwick's b. c.	**Trepidation**, 3 y-o	dr

Friday 20th September 1833

A SWEEPSTAKES of 10 sovereigns each, with 20 added.
For horses of all ages. Two mile heats.

Lord Warwick's b. c.	**Trepidation**, 3 y-o, *(Charles Marlow)*	1	1
Sir T. F. Boughey's b. c.	by **Sir Gray**, 3 y-o	2	2
Col. Walhouse's b. c.	**Tom Brown**, 3 y-o	dr	-
Mr Pickernell's ch. f.	**Repentance**, 3 y-o	dr	-

A SWEEPSTAKES of 10 sovereigns each, with 10 added.
For horses not thoroughbred, the property of gentlemen resident in Walsall.
One mile heats, to start at the distance chair.

Mr Hawkins' br. h.	**Jerry**, aged, *(Jackson)*	1	1
Mr S. Perks' ch. h.	**Swing**, aged	2	3
Mr Farrington's b. h.	**Mouse Trap**, aged	3	2
Mr Moore's br. f.	**Donna Maria**, 4 y-o	bolted	

A HANDICAP SWEEPSTAKES of 10 sovereigns, with 20 added.
Heats, once round, to start at the distance chair.

Mr J. Tomes' b. c.	by **Sir Gray**, 3 y-o, *(J. Harris)*	2	1	1
Mr Wightwick's b. h.	**Manchester**, 3 y-o	1	2	2
Mr Bodenham's ch. c.	by **Young Phantom**, 4 y-o	3	dr	-

1834

In 1834 the meeting was extended to three days, beginning on the morning of Wednesday 24th September, with what should have been the principle race of the three days. But with the declaration by John Beardsworth to run Independence, no other contenders could be found and the grand horse took his final Gold Cup with a simple stroll past the winning post, quite fitting for the old campaigner in his twilight years.

The second race of the morning, the Sweepstakes for the half-bred horses attracted five runners but two withdrew leaving Captain Lamb's horse, Vivian, Mr Ongley's Donnington and the eventual winner, T. F. Sharratt's horse Buffalo to contest the race. During the first heat Donnington fell, and in the process brought down Vivian who was close behind. The latter was re-mounted and finished second. John Spring, the rider of Donnington wasn't so lucky, receiving serious injuries in the fall; the report fails to give details of what his injuries were.

The winner of the race was ridden by George Whitehouse, recording his first win at Walsall. Whitehouse was no stranger to Walsall, having been born in the Town End Bank area in 1815; he was apprenticed to Samuel Lord at Hednesford and lived there until his retirement from the saddle when he moved to Lichfield. Coincidentally, the jockey that rode the most winners at Walsall in its one hundred and twenty year history was Whitehouse, who topped the list, with fifteen victories.

It is not known if this was George Whitehouse's first appearance at the course, but if it was, he was determined to impress the spectators of his hometown, many of whom must have known him personally. At the end of the meeting he had ridden four of the six winners, three of them for John Beardsworth if the walkover with Independence is included. Welcome home George!

The final race at the meeting was the Cavalry Stakes for gentleman riders only. The man that was to become leading gentleman rider at Walsall, Mr Friend, also rode his first winner on the course when he partnered T. F. Sharratt's, Jack Hatch to victory.

Another note of interest for this year was the mention of the first ever hurdle race to be run at Walsall, on the Wednesday evening, unfortunately, no other details of the event were recorded. This inaugural event wasn't keenly contested with only two runners appearing. As far as is known, steeplechases

1820 - 1839

were never held on the Long Meadow, but races over the smaller obstacles became a regular part of the programme in later years.

Steeplechasing and hurdle races, commonly known as 'jump racing' originated in Ireland around 1752. In the early part of the nineteenth century there are reports of steeplechase matches taking place at various venues in England but it wasn't until 1810 that the first organised 'chase took place at Bedford over specially constructed fences. This branch of the sport, even though its origins came from the hunting field, where the nobility and gentry had their roots in regard to field sports, looked down their noses at this new form of sport as being rather crude. If jockeys that rode on the flat were supposedly rough men, the contemporary accounts of their colleagues who rode over 'the jumps' would have us believe they were driven to the course in cages, complete with armed escorts and shouldn't be left alone within a mile of women and children. Maybe a touch exaggerated, half-a-mile would probably be sufficient!

Earl Wilton (Thomas Egerton), who had runners at Walsall in the past and was keen gentleman rider over obstacles, was severely castigated by General William Dyott of Lichfield for associating himself with *'these commonest of stablemen.'* General Dyott may not have been to keen on this new sport, but for many others their distaste waned and they eventually became supporters of jump racing.

An engraving of Earl Wilton taking a tumble whilst riding in a steeplechase at Croxton Park with his chums, 'those commonest of stablemen'.

George Calloway, the jockey who was also an innkeeper at the Turf Tavern, Lichfield, had been riding at Walsall, without success this year, and was to experience the highs and lows of life in just over a week. The Wednesday prior to the meeting opening at Walsall, Calloway had won the St. Leger Stakes at Doncaster on Lord Westminster's famous horse, Touchstone. Ten days later, he was travelling from Lichfield to Walsall on the Quicksilver coach when it crashed and overturned, throwing him out onto the road and breaking his leg in the process. The long winter break obviously helped the healing process because five months later, at the beginning of April, he was back riding winners. More about this story and the ensuing court case that followed under Calloway's entry in Chapter Seven, The Jockeys.

The official results of the meeting were:

Wednesday 24th September 1834

A GOLD CUP SWEEPSTAKES in specie, by subscribers of 10 sovereigns each. Three miles and a distance.

Mr J. Beardsworth's br. g.	**Independence**	walked over

A SWEEPSTAKES of 10 sovereigns each, with 20 added. For horses not thoroughbred. Two mile heats.

Mr T. F. Sharratt's	**Buffalo**, 3 y-o *(George Whitehouse)*	1	1
Capt. Lamb's	**Vivian**, aged	2	2
Mr Ongley's b. h.	**Donnington**, 6 y-o	dis	-
Lord Lichfield's b. f.	**Nell Gwynn**	dis	-
Mr Webb's br. f.	**by Antelope**, 3 y-o	dis	-

A SWEEPSTAKES of 5 sovereigns each, with 25 sovereigns added. Heats, once round.

Mr J. Beardsworth's	**brother to Derby**, 3 y-o *(George Whitehouse)*	4	1	1
Mr J. Tomes' b. c.	**by Bedlamite**, 3 y-o	1	2	2
Mr Warren's b. f.	**Shalot**, 3 y-o	2	3	3
Mr E. Peel's, b. c.	**Rutland**, 3 y-o	3	dr	-
Mr Jones' c. f.	**by Pantaloon**, 3 y-o	fell	-	-
Mr Giffard's br. f.	**by Tramp**, 3 y-o	dis	-	-

Thursday 25th September 1834

THE MEMBER'S PLATE of 50 sovereigns. For horses of all ages. Two mile heats.

Mr J. Beardsworth's b. f.	**by Longwaist**, 3 y-o *(George Whitehouse)*	4	1	1
Mr Giffard's b. f.	**by Tramp**, 3 y-o	1	2	2
Mr J. Tomes b. c.	**by Bedlamite**, 3 y-o	2	4	4
General Yates' b. f.	**Juliana**, 3 y-o	5	3	3
Mr Evans' b. f.	**Shelah**, 3 y-o	3	dr	-
Mr Jones' c. f.	**by Pantaloon**, 3 y-o	dr	-	-
Mr E. Peel's	**Rutland**, 3 y-o	dr	-	-

A HANDICAP SWEEPSTAKES of 10 sovereigns each, with 20 added. One mile heats.

Mr Holloway's	**Coquet**, aged *(George Whitehouse)*	2	1	1
Mr Evans' b. f.	**Shelah**, 3 y-o	1	2	dr
Mr J. Beardsworth's br. f.	**by Longwaist**	dr	-	-

Friday 26th September 1834

A CAVALRY SWEEPSTAKES by subscription only. Two mile heats.

Mr T. F. Sharratt's ch. h.	**Jack Hatch** *(Mr Friend)*	2	1	1
Mr Brown's b. m.	**Lady Emma**	1	2	2
Mr Chawner's b. h.	**Mouse Trap**	3	3	3
Mr Hawkins' b. h.	**Jerry**	4	4	4
Mr Edwards' b. h.	**Duke**	fell	-	-

1820 – 1839

1835

A larger programme of events awaited the sportsmen of Walsall this year with eight races over the two days. Two races on the card were for non-thoroughbred horses but the quality of the thoroughbred horses contesting the remaining six races did not appear to be as good as the last few years. Examination of previous form for the horses engaged confirms this. Mr Haywood's brown colt, Lentolus had done little in eight previous races prior to Walsall; and he won three of the contests, including the Gold Cup.

John Beardsworth continued his success at the course by winning two races but even his runners were below his usual standards. His great horse Independence, now nine years old was trying to win his fourth Gold Cup, but could only finish second to Lentolus; this was down to his age and the huge difference in weights; two or three years ago, a horse of Independence's ability would have wiped the floor with opposition such as Lentolus. The entries for the Gold Cup generally were inferior to previous years. Two of the runners had only run once before and one was a half-bred horse not even listed in the *Racing Calendar* index.

The final race on Wednesday afternoon was won by John Beardsworth's, brother to Derby, beating four others, this race did offer some good sport however, with all three heats being eagerly contested by the runners. Sadly, John Beardsworth died in November of 1835, and brother to Derby was his last winner in the town that began his turf career eighteen years earlier, and whose racecourse he had supported so loyally ever since.

The Cavalry Stakes for non-thoroughbreds again proved popular with six runners contesting it, Walsall's leading gentleman rider, Mr Friend, won the race on his own horse, The Jewess, beating the other five runners with ease.

The final race of the meeting, the Member's Plate, was won by Mr Haywood's Lentolus, his third victory in two days, when he got home in the deciding second heat by a head from the un-named filly by Longwaist, owned by Beardsworth.

After the official races had ended, several matches took place over the course and it would appear that this practice was becoming normal as there had been reports of similar activity in previous years, unfortunately there are few details, if any, of this additional sport in any of the newspapers.

There was plenty of other entertainment on offer too, the *Staffordshire Advertiser* in its account of the proceedings, tells of the re-decoration of the theatre in The Square at the expense of Mr Parker Cooke himself. Appearing at the theatre was Miss Adelaide Cooke, 'a most versatile young lady of prodigious talent,' yes, Walsall has had a few of those over the years!

The report goes on to say that 'a fine buck was served each day at the George Hotel along with desserts of the first description, and wines of the finest flavour.' There was seemingly a much larger gathering of local nobility and gentry than in earlier years for the ordinaries and the ball in the evening. In addition, the officers of the 1st Dragoon Guards in full uniform were also present to enjoy the entertainment that went on until the early hours.

The official results of the meeting were:

Wednesday 23rd September 1835

A SWEEPSTAKES of 15 sovereigns each, with 20 added. For three year olds. Two miles.

Mr Haywood's br. c.	**Lentolus** (H. Arthur, sen.)	1
Mr Bower's b. c.	**Bucephelus**	2
Mr Fielding's br. f.	**Wolfruna**	dr
Mr Watson's bl. c.	**Lichfield**	dr

A HANDICAP SWEEPSTAKES of 10 sovereigns each, with 20 sovereigns added. Heats, twice round, starting at the distance chair.

Mr J. Beardsworth's	by **Longwaist**, 4 y-o, 8st. 2lb. (George Calloway)	4	1	1
Mr W. Foster's br. m.	**Nike**, 5 y-o, 9st.	1	2	dr
Mr Warren's b. f.	**Shalot**, 3 y-o	2	3	3
Mr Jones' ch. f.	**Emily**, 3 y-o, 7st.	2	dr	-
Mr J. Fryer's ch. c.	**Dr. Halley**, 3 y-o, 6st. 7lb.	3	dr	-

A CAVALRY SWEEPSTAKES, for horses bona fide property of Members of the Walsall Troop. Heats, once round

Mr Friend's br. m.	**The Jewess**, aged, 12st. (Owner)	1	1
Mr Sheward's b. m.	**Kate**, aged	2	2
Mr T. F. Sharratt's b. m.	**Lady Teazle**, 6 y-o	3	4
Mr Bealey's b. h.	**Woodley**, 6 y-o	4	fe
Mr Brown's b. m.	**Lady Emma**, aged	5	3
Mr Hawkins' bl. m.	**Sloe**, 5 y-o	6	5

A SWEEPSTAKES of 5 sovereigns each, with 25 added. One mile heats.

Mr J. Beardsworth's br. f.	**brother to Derby**, 4 y-o, 8st. 9lb. (George Calloway)	5	1	1
Mr Giffard's	**Miss Charlotte**, 5 y-o 8st. 10lb.	1	3	3
Mr Fielding's br. f.	**Wulfruna**, 3 y-o, 7st. 1lb.	4	2	2
Mr J. Tomes' b. g.	by **Bedlamite**, 4 y-o, 8st. 7lb.	2	4	4
Mr Mott's ch. f.	**Daffodil**, 4 y-o, 8st. 5lb.	3	dr	-

Thursday 24th September 1835

A SWEEPSTAKES of 15 sovereigns each, with 10 added. For two year olds. Four furlongs.

Mr B. King's	**Zora**, 7st. 12lb. (Hardy)	1
Mr E. Peel's b. c.	**Wingfield**, 8st. 1lb.	2
Mr J. Beardsworth's b. c.	by **Busted**, 8st. 1lb.	3

A SWEEPSTAKES of 10 sovereigns each, with 20 added. For horses not thoroughbred. Two mile heats.

Mr W. Foster's br. m.	**Nike**, 5 y-o, 10st. 7lb. (Lear)	1	1
Mr Ongley's	**Donnington**, aged, 11st. 3lb.	2	2
Capt. Lamb's	**Jack**, 3 y-o, 8st. 5lb.	3	dr

A GOLD CUP SWEEPSTAKES in specie, by subscribers of 10 sovereigns each. Three miles and a distance.

Mr Haywood's br. c.	**Lentolus**, 3 y-o, 6st. 10lb. (Henry Arthur, jun.)	1
Mr J. Beardsworth's br. g	**Independence**, aged, 8st. 13lb.	2

THE MEMBER'S PLATE of 50 sovereigns. For horses of all ages. Two mile heats.

Mr Haywood's br. g.	**Lentolus**, 3 y-o, 7st. 1lb. (Henry Arthur, jun.)	1	1
Mr J. Beardsworth's br. f.	by **Longwaist**, 4 y-o, 8st. 2lb.	4	2
Mr J. Tomes b. g.	by **Bedlamite**, 4 y-o, 8st. 5lb.	2	3
Mr Griffin's br. g.	**Chance**, 4 y-o, 8st.	3	4

Stewards: Sir Edward Scott and John Vaughan Barber
Clerk of the Races: John Newman

1820 - 1839

1836

Bad weather on both days marred this years racing, but it didn't deter the people of Walsall from gathering in there thousands to enjoy the annual sporting spectacle.

The George Hotel, now the premiere hostelry in the town, or so it seems, provided the wealthier members of the racing fraternity with excellent fare at the ordinaries and the evening ball. Presiding over the ordinaries was Captain Lamb, a well-known figure in the racing world at this time, who was Senior Steward at the meeting, John Vaughan Barber from Walsall, was the other Steward.

At the end of the meeting Captain Lamb must have thought his post of Senior Steward had been the kiss of death as far as his three runners were concerned. In the first race his un-named chestnut colt finished second, beaten by Edmund Peel's filly, Cantata, trained for Peel by his private trainer, Samuel Lord at Hednesford.

The fourth race, the Handicap Sweepstakes, must have been the biggest embarrassment to Captain Lamb, with only three runners in the race it is difficult to see how things could go wrong. The three runners were, John Tomes' gelding, Random, who was the favourite, Captain Lamb's colt, Count D'Orsay and Captain Bunney's un-named filly by Pantaloon. The two military men took the first two berths with the favourite third, and then the bombshell was dropped. A keen eyed observer made it known that all three horses had started from the wrong place and without authority. It must have been a bitter pill for Captain Lamb to swallow as Senior Steward when he had to disqualify his own horse, including the other two, and declare the race void. His luck was out on the second day too, his only runner, a half-bred brown filly by Memnon finished a poor third of the three runners in the morning's first race. It was still raining too!

The Gold Cup proved to be a disappointment with only Edmund Peel's horse, Tamworth, contesting the event and taking the prize after the formalities of the walkover had been completed. One reason for Tamworth not finding an opponent was possibly that other owners didn't fancy their chances against a very good horse who had won four of his seven previous races.

Hurdle racing was in vogue at this time and the Race Committee would have been keen to get a race into the programme after first introducing 'jump racing' two years ago. With no plans or maps to accurately show the racecourse at any period of its life it is difficult to understand how, and where, the hurdles would have been placed. Many of the larger, and wider courses could accommodate both flat and hurdle racing within the same track.

The only riders allowed in the race were amateurs, and first blood went to Mr H. Stanley, riding John Hawkins' horse, Lustre, beating two others in the two-mile event and jumping ten hurdles in all.

The final paragraph of the race report in the *Staffordshire Advertiser* was enough to give the serious gamblers of the town palpitations, it read: -

> *'The magistrates laudably prohibited all kinds of gambling at the races, and in consequence the marquees which had been erected were removed.'*

Lord George Bentinck, Senior Steward of the Jockey Club and the innovator of 'vanning'.

There are no details to say exactly who was deprived of the gambling facilities, but it is hard to believe the nobility and gentry would have suffered; racing for some of them, without the chance of a wager was unthinkable. In resorting to prohibition, the problem may have appeared to have been solved, but in reality, the good people of Walsall would have simply continued to lose their hard earned cash away from the prying eyes of the law.

It was in this year that the first reports of criminal activity were being reported on the racecourse as several pickpockets were caught in the act and arrested by the sharp-eyed constables on duty. This problem persisted at Walsall Races until its closure, when the nimble fingered of the town's population went back to plying their trade 'up the market,' or at Wolverhampton and Lichfield races!

It was in late July of this year that an advertisement ran in Aris's Gazette announcing what appears to be the inaugural race meeting at Bloxwich held on The Slang, see map on page 52. Meetings at Bloxwich ran for several years but only two were classed as 'official', the meetings in 1841 and 1842. An 'official meeting' was one whose results were recorded in the *Racing Calendar*. Further research has shown that meetings were also held at Bloxwich in 1838, 1839, 1840, 1841, 1842, 1845, 1847 and 1849.

1820 – 1839

A John Sturgess illustration of one of the wooden, horse driven vans used so effectively by Lord George Bentinck in 1836.

This year saw a great innovation introduced to the racing scene, the 'vanning' of horses to the racecourse, as travelling by rail was some years away. Although this form of transport probably didn't apply to Walsall Races for some time, if at all, it is worth explaining this simple procedure.

Lord George Bentinck, Senior Steward of the Jockey Club was the first to use the method, and to great advantage. The horse concerned was named Elis, and owned by Lord Lichfield whose horses were managed by Lord George who wasn't happy with the odds of 5/1 being offered against Elis winning the St. Leger Stakes at Doncaster. Lord George stated the horse would not run unless odds of 10/1 or more were on offer. At the last moment, when it was considered impossible for the horse to reach Doncaster in time by the usual method of walking, the bet was made, at much more agreeable odds. Lord George then put his master plan into action. He borrowed from Lord Chesterfield a large wooden van, used in the transportation of his Lordships show cattle. The horse, Elis, was loaded into this somewhat cumbersome vehicle and pulled from Danebury to Doncaster by four-post horses, arriving, much to the consternation of the betting ring, in plenty of time. The horse won, and so did Lord George and the horse's owner, Lord Lichfield, very handsomely apparently. Shortly after this innovation was introduced, every member of the turf of any note was having wooden vans built.

The official results of the meeting were:

Wednesday 28th September 1836

A SWEEPSTAKES of 15 sovereigns each, with 15 added. For two year olds. Four furlongs.

Mr E. Peel's b. f.	**Cantata,** 8st. 4lb. *(G. Calloway)*	1
Capt. Lamb's ch. c.	**by Winton,** 8st. 7lb.	2
Mr Giffard's b. f.	**by Cadland,** 8st. 4lb.	3

A GOLD CUP STAKES of 10 sovereigns each, in specie. Three miles and a distance.

| Mr E. Peel's ch. h. | **Tamworth,** 5 y-o, 8st. 9lb. *(G. Calloway)* | walked over |

A CAVALRY STAKES
For horses bona fide the property of Members of the Walsall Troop. Heats, one mile.

Mr Friend's b. g.	**Gauntlet,** aged, 12st. 7lb. *(Owner)*	1	1
Mr Sheward's br. m.	**?,** 6 y-o	2	2
Mr Danks' b. m.	**The Steamer,** aged	3	3
Mr J. H. Curtis's b. m.	**Cropthorne,** 4 y-o	4	4
Mr Shaw's b. g.	**Jerry,** aged	dis	-

A HANDICAP SWEEPSTAKES of 15 sovereigns each, with 20 added. Two miles.

Capt. Lamb's br. c.	**Count D'Orsay,** 3 y-o 7st. 7lb., *(Bradley)*	-
Capt. Bunney's b. f.	**by Pantaloon,** 3 y-o, 6st. 10lb.	-
Mr J. Tomes' b. g.	**Random,** 5 y-o, 8st. 11lb.	-

This race was declared void due to the horses starting from the wrong place.

Thursday 29th September 1836

A HANDICAP SWEEPSTAKES of 10 sovereigns, with 20 added. For horses not thoroughbred. Heats, twice round.

Mr Ongley's b. h.	**Donnington,** aged, 11st. 13lb. *(G. Calloway)*	2	1	1
Mr J. Newman's br. g.	**Smallhopes,** aged, 11st. 3lb.	1	2	3
Capt. Lamb's br. f.	**by Memnon,** 3 y-o, 8st. 5lb.	3	3	2

THE MEMBER'S PLATE of 50 sovereigns. Heats, twice round.

| Mr Fowler's br. c. | **Heron,** 3 y-o, 7st. 3lb. *(J. Dodgson)* | 1 | 1 |
| Mr Giffard's ch. g. | **Traveller,** aged, 9st. 5lb. | 2 | 2 |

A HURDLE RACE of 3 sovereigns each, with a purse added. For gentlemen riders only. Twice round with 10 hurdles to be jumped.

Mr John Hawkins' b. h.	**Lustre,** *(Mr H. Stanley)*	1
Mr John Bealey's b. h.	**Woodley**	2
Mr George Parker's br. h.	**The Pope**	3

1837

For the second successive year the weather was again poor, particularly on the first day, Wednesday 27th September, when it is reported that the company on the racecourse was less than in previous years.

A new handicap race the Barr Beacon Stakes, began the events with just two runners going to post after an initial entry of nine. The contest, if it can be called that, was won by Mr Critchley's four year-old bay colt, Wolverhampton, ridden by Walsall born jockey, George Whitehouse. This horse, Wolverhampton, should not be confused with the horse of the same name that was owned by the late John Beardsworth. To confuse matters further, the horse named Wolverhampton, previously owned by Beardsworth, ran in the hurdle race later in the day. The racing authorities today do not allow two or more horses to have the same name for obvious reasons.

Over the last year or so it has become noticeable that the races at Walsall consisting of multiple heats were becoming less. This was a general trend throughout the country, and in time, this type of race became obsolete. Of the seven races in the programme, only three were run in heats.

1820 – 1839

The hurdle race, another illustration by John Sturgess. Races of this type had been popular at Walsall since 1836 and remained so until the course closed in 1876.

The Sweepstakes race on Wednesday afternoon saw the final appearance on the Long Meadow of Independence, now a ten year-old and running for his lifelong trainer, Thomas Flintoff. The old fellow was beaten into second place by Thomas Walters' horse, King Cole a future Chester Cup winner, but not before he had won one of the three heats. The four runners in the race all came from training stables in the Hednesford area, as did three of the jockeys.

The weather on Thursday was somewhat better than the previous day, much to the appreciation of the town's folk who swelled the course to its more usual attendance. The contemporary newspaper reports states that the running was of a superior quality to the previous day.

The Hurdle Sweepstakes was run over two miles and a distance with ten hurdles to be negotiated. The winner, The Steamer, owned by John Hawkins' and ridden by Mr Stanley won the race easily from Mr Adams', The Count. Wolverhampton, now owned by Mr Halford, came third. The old horse Wolverhampton was never really in the race and when The Count stumbled on landing over a hurdle, the race was at the mercy of The Steamer.

Mr Critchley, and the race goers of Walsall, must have been impressed with the other horse named Wolverhampton, already the winner of one race on Wednesday; he had doubled his tally at the close of the meeting.

The first win on Thursday came in the two runner Gold Cup when he beat another previous winner from Wednesday, King Cole by a neck in a fine race to the line.

With little more than a half hour break, Wolverhampton turned out again to win the final race of the meeting, The Member's Plate, a two mile race over two heats, in which he was ridden by Henry Arthur junior.

The official results of the meeting were:

Wednesday 27th September 1837

THE BARR BEACON HANDICAP STAKES
of 20 sovereigns each, with 30 added.
Twice round and a distance.

Mr Critchley's b. c.	**Wolverhampton**, 4 y-o *(George Calloway)*	1
Mr J. Fowler's	**Mersey**, 4 y-o	2

Two horses drawn.

A SWEEPSTAKES of 10 sovereigns each, with 20 added.
Twice round and a distance.

Mr W. Foster's br. m.	**Nike**, aged *(George Calloway)*	1	1
Mr T. Ongley's b. h.	**Donnington**, aged	2	2

A SWEEPSTAKES of 5 sovereigns each, with 25 added.
Heats, one mile and a distance.

Mr T. Walter's br. c.	**King Cole**, 4 y-o *(Charles Marlow)*	1	4	1
Mr T. Flintoff's br. g.	**Independence**, aged	0	1	3
Mr E. Phillips' b. f.	**by Cadland**, 3 y-o	0	2	2
Mr E. Peel's br. c.	**Morrison**, 4 y-o	2	3	dr

A HURDLE SWEEPSTAKES of 3 sovereigns each,
with 50 added. For horses the property of gentlemen residing within six miles of Walsall. Two miles and a distance, ten hurdles.

Mr Danks' b. m.	**The Steamer**, aged, *(Mr Stanley)*	1
Mr Adams names b. h.	**The Count**, 5 y-o	2
Mr Critchley's br. h.	**Wolverhampton**, 4 y-o	3

Thursday 28th September 1837

A SWEEPSTAKES of 20 sovereigns.
For two year olds, the last half mile.

Mr T. Walters' b. c.	**by Shrigley**, *(Charles Marlow)*	1
Mr Alderson's br. f.	**by Emancipation**	2
Mr Sharratt's b. f.	**by Fungus**	3

A GOLD CUP STAKES in specie, by subscribers of 10 sovereigns each.
Three miles and a distance.

Mr Critchley's b. h.	**Wolverhampton**, 4 y-o, *(Henry Arthur, junior)*	1
Mr T. Walters' br. c.	**King Cole**, 4 y-o	2

THE MEMBER'S PLATE of 50 sovereigns each.
Heats, twice round, to start at the distance chair.

Mr Critchley's b. h.	**Wolverhampton**, 4 y-o, *(Henry Arthur, junior)*	1	1
Mr Collett's br. c.	**Conservative**, 3 y-o	2	2
Mr E. Painter's b. h.	**Matadore**, 5 y-o	5	3
Capt. Lamb's ch. c.	**Metal**, 3 y-o	3	dr
Mr W. Foster's b. m.	**Nike**, aged	4	dr

1838

In 1838 the meeting appears to have been given a miss as far as the reporting of the event goes. None of the local newspapers making any comment regarding the running, admittedly, the horses entered did appear to be inferior to those that had run in previous years.

Another reason that may account for the lack of publicity, apart from the quality of the racing, was that several other courses, relatively local to Walsall, had also held meetings, both before and after the events on the Long Meadow. The week before Walsall began, many of the trainers, particularly those from Hednesford, had entered many of their horses at the Shrewsbury meeting. On the Monday and Tuesday prior to Walsall, Uttoxeter and Oswestry had held one-day events, and four days after Walsall Races had ended there was a meeting at Birmingham. All of this competition obviously played a part in the entries and this was one year when it appears to have suffered more than in previous years.

1820 - 1839

This year there was no Gold Cup to be run for, and the race card consisted of just five events over the two days, which began on Wednesday 26th September. Of the five races listed, horses trained at Hednesford won four of them.

The Sweepstakes for non-thoroughbred horses was inferior to previous years, attracting just three runners; two of the horses, one of which was the winner, Captain Lamb's horse, Jack, were making their one and only appearance on a racecourse for the season.

The Barr Beacon Stakes had been the most heavily subscribed event; initially attracting eighteen entries, but only five runners went to post. The race was won by Mr Fowler's five year-old bay mare, Mersey, trained at Hednesford by Thomas Flintoff and ridden by John Dodgson.

The first race on Thursday was for two year-olds and run over half-a-mile. All three horses contesting the race were from Hednesford stables, the winner, May The First was trained by Thomas Walters and ridden by Robert Denman, second was Mr Fowler's, Concordia, with Edmund Peel's horse, Alzdorf, third.

The second race of the day, a Sweepstakes race for horses of all ages and run over one mile and a distance bought this years meeting to a close. The Walsall born jockey, George Whitehouse rode the winner, Edmund Peel's grey, Saul, another horse that had shown little ability in its races prior coming to Walsall.

In conclusion, this year appears to have been the poorest for quite sometime, in terms of quantity and quality of horses running, the Race Committee must have been aware of this and hopefully, 1839 would show a marked improvement in standards.

There was additional racing in the locality six months prior to the Walsall meeting. Two steeplechase meetings took place at Barr Beacon, a few miles to the east of Walsall, in March and April. The first meeting, known as the Barr Beacon Steeple Race, was run on Wednesday 28th March in glorious spring weather in front of a large gathering of spectators. The prize on offer was The Scott Cup (presumably in the name of Sir Edward Scott of nearby Great Barr Hall), to which was added a Sweepstakes of five sovereigns by the officers of the 5th Dragoon Guards. Eleven horses were entered but only seven actually ran, with two horses dominating both heats. The battle was between Mr Whittaker's bay gelding Spotless and Captain King's mare, Persiani, who could not get the better of the former in two heats and so had to settle for second place.

Nineteen days later the second meeting took place, this time in appalling weather. Torrential rain caused the meeting to be cancelled on the day it was scheduled, Monday 16th April, but twenty four hours later the meeting eventually got under way. Before a race had even been run the organisers had upset the staff of the *Staffordshire Advertiser* with its official title emblazoned on the race card, that of the 'Birmingham Steeple Races.' Unthinkable and unforgiveable was the attitude of the newspaper of the county, that a race meeting held in Staffordshire should be associated with Birmingham. The newspaper considered that if the towns of Walsall or West Bromwich were honourable enough not to title the meeting under their banner, why should Birmingham?

The meeting consisted of five races, four official races and a sweepstakes of £5 each 'run for by the gentlemen of West Bromwich.' The winners of two of the four steeplechases, Grayling and Tom Leedham were ridden by a famous rider of the day, Tom Olliver. In 1842, Olliver won the first of his three Grand Nationals on Gaylad, followed in 1843 on Vanguard and in 1853 on Peter Simple. It is reputed Olliver was so attached to his second 'National winner, Vanguard, that when the horse died he had a sofa made and it was covered with the horses skin.

This year saw the arrival in England of one of the great racehorses of the time, Harkaway, who came over from Ireland with his owner, Thomas Ferguson to capture many of the large prizes on offer. Throughout his stay in this country, Harkaway was based at Hednesford, due to its central location within the country it was ideal for travel to courses in all directions. No jockey came over from Ireland with the duo so George Calloway from Lichfield was picked by Ferguson to do the job.

One of the many races that Harkaway won was Her Majesty's Plate of one hundred guineas, run over four miles at Doncaster. The procedure and advantages of the 'vanning' of horses, talked about in earlier pages is no better illustrated for its efficiency than in Harkaway's journey to the course from Hednesford.

On Sunday, September 16th, Harkaway left Hednesford in his travelling van pulled by four post horses, along with his owner and jockey, for a race that was to be run twenty-four hours later.

Thanks to Lord George Bentinck's brilliant initiative of two-years earlier, three days had been taken off the journey to Doncaster. It was known to take four days to walk a horse from Hednesford to Doncaster and six days for the walk from Hednesford to York. This method of transporting horses was to be short lived however, railways were already becoming the favoured method for long distance travel and it wasn't too long before horses were travelling to meetings by this method.

The official results of the meeting were:

Wednesday 26th September 1838

A SWEEPSTAKES of 10 sovereigns each, with 20 added.
For horses not thoroughbred.
Heats, twice round, starting at the distance chair.

Capt. Lamb's br. h.	**Jack**, 6 y-o, 11st. 1lb. *(W. Saunders)*	1	1
Mr Stevenson's ch. h	**True Blue**, aged, 11st. 3lb.	2	2
Mr T. Ongley's b. h.	**Donnington**, aged, 11st. 3lb,	3	3

THE BARR BEACON HANDICAP STAKES
of 20 sovereigns each, with 30 added.
Twice round, starting at the distance chair.

Mr J. Fowler's b. m.	**Mersey**, 5 y-o, 7st. *(J. Dodgson)*	1
Mr James' b. f.	**by Cadland**, 4 y-o, 6st. 6lb.	2
Mr Moss' ch. f.	**Maid Marian**, 4 y-o, 7st.	3
Mr Critchley's b. c.	**His Grace**, 4 y-o, 6st. 10lb.	4
Mr E. Peel's gr. c.	**Saul**, 3y-o, 7st.	5

1820 - 1839

THE MEMBER'S PLATE of 50 sovereigns each.
Heats, twice round, to start at the distance chair.

Mr Wascoe's br. h.	**Swainby,** 5 y-o, 9st. 1lb.			
	(Livesey)	3	1	1
Lord Warwick's b. c.	**by Brutandorf,** 3 y-o, 7st.	1	2	dr
Capt. Lamb's b. h.	**Gardham,** 4 y-o, 8st. 2lb.	2	3	dr
Mr Critchley's b. c.	**His Grace,** 4 y-o, 8st. 7lb.	4	dis	-

Thursday 27th September 1838

A SWEEPSTAKES of 20 sovereigns.
For two year olds, the last half mile.

Mr T. Walters' b. c.	**May the First,** 8st. 7lb. *(Robert Denman)*	1
Mr Fowler's	**Concordia,** 8st. 4lb.	2
Mr E. Peel's	**Alzdorf,** 8st. 7lb.	3

A SWEEPSTAKES of 5 sovereigns each, with 25 added.
Heats, starting at the distance chair, once round.

Mr E. Peel's gr. c.	**Saul,** 3 y-o, 7st. 5lb. *(George Whitehouse)*	1
Mr Rowell's b. m.	**Theano,** 5 y-o, 9st. 1lb.	2
Lord Warwick's b. c.	**by Brutandorf,** 3 y-o, 7st. 3lb.	3

1839

By the announcement in the *Staffordshire Advertiser* for the Races in 1839, the Race Committee was aware that the meeting the previous year was a sub-standard affair and made great efforts to ensure this years event didn't go the same way. There were six races, three on each day, including a hurdle race, the final race on Wednesday afternoon.

Since the opening of Bradford Street in 1831 it was clear that the racecourse would be affected by these developments, and alterations of a minor nature had been going on for a few years. The press announcement included a paragraph relating to the course improvements, implying that work of a more severe nature had taken place; unfortunately no details are given as to what these were.

The only information available that gives some sort of clue as to the work being carried out comes from the diaries of Peter Potter. Since the land was first used as a racecourse it has been known that two watercourses crossed the land. The one stream did not interfere with the line of the course but the one known as the Mill Fleam certainly did. It ran to the left of the grandstand and exited the course around what is now Corporation Street West. Quite how the Race Committee overcame the problem in the early days is unknown for definite, possibly planks were laid across the void to allow the horses to cross, but by 1839 a permanent structure was in place. Entries from Peter Potter's diaries show that around this time brick arches were built over the Mill Fleam and also, the racecourse itself was diverted in front of the grandstand to allow a road to pass from Bradford Street, across the course to a new iron bridge. Without any accurate maps of the course being available, it is difficult to visualise what these alterations were and exactly how the course changed, other than that the run-in is flat, a full half-a-mile in length and almost straight.

To the stars of the show, the horses, the alterations to the course were immaterial, they ran wherever they were taken to.

The opening race was a Sweepstakes to be run over one mile and a distance; six horses went to the post with Mr Barrow's outstanding mare, Catharina taking the race from Ascanius. Mr Barrow didn't believe in keeping his horses in cotton wool, when the mare arrived at Walsall she had already run sixteen times, winning a quarter of those races. To give some idea of how hard the racehorses of this era worked, Catharina had previously run at Burnley, Clitheroe, Chester and Manchester in the north west to Tenbury Wells, and Kington in the south midlands, all the time being walked to these venues, the luxury of 'vanning,' beyond her owners reach. Towards the second half of the season, Mr Barrow always ran the horse twice at each meeting; if she won the first race invariably she lost the second she was entered in. At the end of the season, Barrow's equine servant had run twenty three times, winning on seven occasions and being placed in a further fourteen events, a record which bears testament to the horses stamina and ability. When the mare eventually retired at the age of eleven in 1841 she had won more races than any other horse in the history of British racing. Throughout her career, she won seventy nine races from one hundred and seventy-six starts, which meant she had won almost forty-five percent of the races entered.

The Barr Beacon Stakes, which was a handicap race over two-miles was won by probably the best horse to run at Walsall this year. The horse was King Cole, owned by Alderman William Copeland and trained at Hednesford by Thomas Walters, in whose name he was occasionally raced. King Cole first appeared at Walsall Races in 1837, and the following year he won the prestigious Chester Cup race at the spring meeting. The horse wasn't worked so hard as winner of the first race; this appearance was his tenth of the season from which he had won four races. King Cole was used to running in better company than his opposition on the Long Meadow and he was expected to make light work of his rivals, but he had to get it right first time, as this was a one-heat race.

Only three other runners, Gardham, Kitty Cockle and Prudence were at the post to take on King Cole, who was ridden by Charles Marlow from Hazel Slade near Hednesford. From the start all four kept well together but on the second circuit, approaching home, Kitty Cockle was leading with Prudence upsides, as the quartet closed on the post. Marlow, who had been riding a waiting race, made his move, and came in between the two to win by half a neck, with Gardham, a length behind in fourth place. There was no disputing the winner but the judge couldn't split the second and third, and gave a dead heat. The contemporary reports tell of how the spectators were thrilled to see such a race and loud applause and cheering greeted the horses and jockeys as they came in.

The following day, King Cole was out again to win the first race of the morning from Mr Barrow's brilliant mare, Catharina. Charlie Marlow rode a different race this time, winning the first two heats comfortably. King Cole's hat trick of wins was foiled in the race, or match as it was technically, for the Gold Cup, when he was beaten by Lord Warwick's filly, Petty Larceny ridden by local lad, George Whitehouse.

The meeting closed with the Tally-Ho Stakes, a race run over three heats of one mile for gentlemen riders only. The

1820 - 1839

prize money for this race was boosted by the then Mayor of Walsall, William Dixon, who added ten sovereigns to the fund. Five runners started the race with just the one thoroughbred horse, Kitty, winner of the hurdle race the day before, in the field of half-breeds. Good breeding in horses, as with people, doesn't always make a winner, as this race proved. Kitty was beaten into fourth place by her lesser-bred opponents. The race was won by Mr Higg's mare, Jenny Jones, ridden by Mr Boot, a new name to the list of gentleman rider's at Walsall.

The days racing finished shortly before six o'clock in the evening, plenty of time to enjoy the fare on offer at the George Hotel, if you could afford it. John Gough of Perry Barr, with his accustomed generosity sent a buck for roasting and Lord Hatherton and Sir Edward Scott supplied large quantities of game; as in many years past, Richard Fletcher, the host, put on a magnificent spread complete with delicious desserts and the finest of wines.

At the other end of the human spectrum, the press reports tell of the increased number of pickpockets in operation at both the Races and the Fair, with several being apprehended by the police. They were brought before the Magistrates on the Friday morning, the day after the Races.

The official results of the meeting were:

Wednesday 25th September 1839

A HURDLE SWEEPSTAKES of 5 sovereigns each, with 20 added. Heats, once round, with three leaps. To start at the distance chair.

Mr Adams' b. m.	**Kitty,** 4 y-o, 10st. 4lb. *(W. Saunders)*	1	1
Mr Barker's ch. g.	**Leopard,** aged	2	2
Capt. Lamb's b. h.	**Gardham,** 4 y-o, 8st. 2lb.	3	3

A SWEEPSTAKES of 5 sovereigns each, with 25 added. Heats, once round, starting at the distance chair.

Mr Barrow's b. m.	**Catharina,** aged 9st. 5lb. *(James Hopwood)*	1	6	1
Mr Moss' br. c.	**Ascanius,** 4 y-o, 7st. 13lb.	6	1	2
Capt. Lamb's br. c.	**Speed,** 3 y-o, 7st. 3lb.	3	4	3
Lord Warwick's b. c.	**Melodrama,** 4 y-o, 7st. 13lb.	2	2	dr
Mr Jackson's b. c.	**Wings,** 3 y-o, 7st. 3lb.	5	3	dr
Mr Parker's br. f.	**Rosetta,** 3 y-o, 6st. 7lb.	4	5	dr

THE BARR BEACON HANDICAP STAKES of 20 sovereigns each, with 30 added. Twice round, starting at the distance chair.

Mr Walter's br. h.	**King Cole,** 6 y-o, 9st. *(Charles Marlow)*	1
Mr Saunder's b. m.	**Kitty Cockle,** 5 y-o, 6st. 7lb.	2
Mr J. Fowler's br. f.	**Prudence,** 4 y-o, 7st.	3
Capt. Lamb's br. h.	**Gardham,** 5 y-o, 7st. 10lb.	4

Thursday 26th September 1839

THE MEMBERS PLATE of 50 sovereigns. Heats, twice round, to start at the distance chair.

Mr T. Walters' br. c.	**King Cole,** 6 y-o, 9st. 7lb. *(Charles Marlow)*	1	1
Mr Buckley's ch. c.	**Charley,** 3 y-o, 7st. 3lb.	3	2
Mr Barrow's b. m.	**Catherina,** aged, 9st. 5lb.	2	3

A GOLD CUP in specie, by subscription of 10 sovereigns each. Three miles and a distance.

Lord Warwick's ch. f.	**Petty Larceny,** 3 y-o, 6st. 9lb. *(George Whitehouse)*	1
Mr T. Walter's br. h.	**King Cole,** 6 y-o, 8st. 13lb.	2

THE TALLY-HO STAKES of 3 sovereigns each, with 10 added by W. Dixon, Mayor of Walsall. Gentlemen riders. Heats, once round, to start at the winning chair.

Mr Higgs's ch. m	**Jenny Jones,** 5 y-o, 10st. 11lb. *(Mr Boot)*	5	1	1
Mr W. Dixon's b. m.	**Protegée,** 5 y-o	1	4	3
Mr S. Perks' b. m.	**Maid of all Work,** 6 y-o	2	3	2
Mr Adams' b. m.	**Kitty,** 4 y-o	4	2	dr
Mr Timmins' bl. m.	**The Lady,** 5 y-o	3	5	dr.

WALSALL RACES

CHAPTER FOUR
1840 – 1859

1840

It was a busy scene that greeted the hardened racegoer who arrived early for start of the meeting on Wednesday 23rd September. The weather was again poor, the town experiencing torrential rain in the days leading up to the Fair and Races, and some effort was being made to clear the course of lying water. Inevitably, this had an effect on the spectators, whose numbers were reduced by the inclement weather on both days. With the weather deteriorating still further, it caused two races on Thursday being carried over to Friday afternoon.

The Barr Beacon Handicap Stakes opened the meeting with three horses declaring to run, but only two actually contesting the race. The winner, Mr Fowler's grey horse, The Friar, trained by Thomas Flintoff, arrived at Walsall with little to support his claim for the prize, running unplaced in all of his previous races. It was fortunate his sole opponent, a four year-old colt, Wings, was equally mediocre, slightly less equal on the day as he was beaten a length.

Edmund Peel's horse, Saul, had been improving since his first appearance on the Long Meadow two years previously, not much, but enough to get the better of the first race winner, The Friar, in the second event of the day. No doubt being asked to run twice within the hour, on heavy going, proved too much for The Friar. He was beaten into the runners-up spot, but he went down fighting, winning the first heat. Mr Peel's horse won the second heat, so it was all to play for in the final one, with Saul edging out his opponent by about a half-a-length. They were trained tough at Hednesford, The Friar ran around five miles in a couple of hours, on heavy ground too!

There was a small sting in the tail for the winner of the Hurdle Sweepstakes, the owner had to pay one sovereign for the upkeep of the hurdles. The first victim of this new rule was Thomas Wadlow who made the relatively short trip over from Shifnal with his mare, Mary Wood, who defeated the only other runner, Mr Friend's, Protegee, very easily.

The going was having an effect on the number of runners contesting the races on Thursday, and with the weather deteriorating further only two races were run before the days sport was abandoned.

The more well to do members of the crowd retiring to the George Hotel to dry out and enjoy the now legendary fare on offer in the evening, courtesy of Richard Fletcher. After the meal, sit down before a roaring fire with plenty of ale and wine flowing, the room filling with the aroma of tobacco from the churchwarden pipes; is there a better atmosphere on a wet September night to explain why your horse failed to live up to the boasts of the previous evening?

On Friday, the Races continued, beginning at two o'clock, with Joseph Bullock of the Royal Oak Inn, Ablewell Street, acting as Steward. There were two official races run, The Butcher's Stakes and the Sweepstakes for beaten horses, plus several matches. Quite a number of spectators gathered to watch the additional sport and it is a pity no one bothered to write down the results and forward them to the local press, because the outcome of the afternoon's events are not known.

The official results of the meeting were:

Wednesday 23th September 1840

THE BARR BEACON HANDICAP STAKES
of 20 sovereigns each, with 30 added.
Twice round, starting at the distance chair.

Mr T. Flintoff's gr. h.	**The Friar**, 5 y-o, 7st. 11lb. (George Calloway)		1
Mr Jackson's b. c.	**Wings**, 4 y-o, 7st. 2lb.		2
Mr J. V. Barber names	**Tubalcain**, 4 y-o, 7st. 11lb.		dr

A SWEEPSTAKES of 5 sovereigns each, with 25 added.
Heats, once round, starting at the distance chair.

Mr E. Peel's gr. h.	**Saul**, 5 y-o, 9st. 3lb. (George Whitehouse)	2	1	1
Mr T. Flintoff's gr. h.	**The Friar**, 5 y-o, 8st. 7lb.	1	2	2
Mr T. Lamb's ch. f.	**by Zingance**, 3 y-o, 6st. 9lb.	3	3	dr

A HURDLE SWEEPSTAKES of 5 sovereigns each, with 20 added.
Heats, once round, with three leaps.
To start at the distance chair. The winner to pay 1 sovereign towards the expenses of the hurdles.

Mr T. Wadlows' b. m.	**Mary Wood**, 6 y-o, 12st. 3lb. (Mr J. Wadlow)	1	1
Mr Friend's b. m.	**Protegée**, 6 y-o, 11st. 10lb.	2	2

1840 - 1859

Thursday 24th September 1840

A SWEEPSTAKES of 5 sovereigns each, with 25 added.
Heats, twice round, to start at the distance chair.

Mr T. Flintoff's br. m.	**Prudence,** 5 y-o, *(John Dodgson)*	1	1
Mr Barrow's b. m.	**Catherina,** aged,	2	2

THE TALLY-HO STAKES of 3 sovereigns each, with 15 added by the Innkeepers of Walsall. Gentlemen riders.
Heats, once round, to start at the winning chair.

Mr Lowe's b. m.	**Isabella,** 4 y-o, *(Mr Friend)*	1	1
Mr Walters' b. m.	**by Flexible,** 4 y-o	2	3
Mr Meeson's b. g.	**Deception,** aged	3	2

1841

It was only nine years since the Races had been cancelled for the first time in almost eighty years due to cholera, and 1841 saw a second cancellation in a decade. The *Staffordshire Advertiser* ran this paragraph in their columns, one week after the Races should have been held:-

'Walsall Michaelmas Fair, on Tuesday last, was very numerously attended. The quantity of onions exhibited was unusually large, and fetched 6d. and 7d. per bundle. Cheese 63s. to 65s. per cwt. The innkeepers had a considerable portion of business, but it ended with the fair, as the turf amusements, usually held on the two consecutive days to the fair, have been suspended. Holloway's establishment was the only place of amusement open, and the caterings of the proprietors for the public taste were well remunerated.'

Although the *Staffordshire Advertiser* couldn't throw any light as to why the meeting had been cancelled their rival publication could. On Thursday 14th October the *Staffordshire Gazette & County Standard* ran the following small article:-

'Walsall races, so many years the favourite resort of the lovers of the turf in this didtraict, have this year been discontinued, in consequence of the want of adequate funds.'

The trainers from Hednesford who were by now sending many of horses that ran at Walsall had plenty of other venues in the area to race their charges, with meetings at Brewood, Wolverhampton, Lichfield, Stafford, Stone, Uttoxeter, The Pottery (at Stoke) and Hednesford. As well as the official meetings, there were other places such as Burntwood and Bloxwich, where their horses ran.

1842

After the disappointment of last year's cancellation, in was a case of making up for lost time. The Walsall meeting was scheduled for its usual two days in late September but six weeks prior to that, Bloxwich was to hold its own race meeting under the Rules of Racing. There was a meeting at Bloxwich in 1841 that was run under official rules, but the *Racing Calendar* for that year shows no entry. The course on which the races were run is difficult to determine, all that is known is that the course was close to The Pinfold and on land known as The Slang. The details of the Bloxwich meeting are included along with the Walsall results at the end of this year's entry.

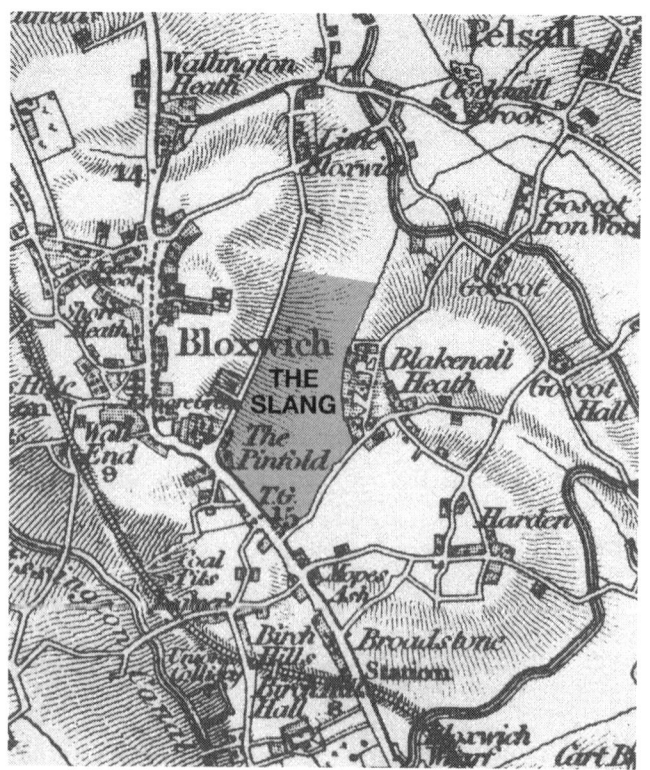

The area shaded in grey and titled The Slang is most probably the land on which Bloxwich Races were run.

Meanwhile, back at Walsall, the meeting opened on Wednesday 28th September with three races on the programme, and four for the following day. The gentlemen riders appeared to be taking centre stage from their professional colleagues as four of the seven races were confined to amateur riders.

The first race for two years on the Long Meadow was won by Mr Fowler's filly, Sunflower, trained by Thomas Flintoff and ridden by another resident of Hednesford, Robert Denman. Sunflower took the prize easily from Captain Crofton's horse, Muleteer. The horse that completed the trio of runners was a half-bred horse named Tresilian who didn't feature in the proceedings at all, being distanced in the first heat and then withdrawn.

Mr Friend was back to his winning ways, riding the winner of the Welter Sweepstakes for half-bred horses, and the first race for gentlemen riders only. Although a well-contested race by all five runners, the mount of Mr Friend, Isabella, came home first in both heats with the real battle coming for the places.

The best race of the meeting came in the first event on Thursday morning, a Sweepstakes race over one mile one furlong that took five heats to decide the winner. The *Staffordshire Advertiser* commented on this race with the following statement: -

'Persons conversant with the turf characterised this as the most splendid race, superior to any ever before run on Walsall course, and seldom surpassed on any other.'

Seven runners went to the post for the race and six of them played a part in the proceedings. Two of the runners had met in the first race on Wednesday morning, Sunflower and Muleteer. Although Sunflower won that race, Captain Crofton's horse, Muleteer, was the favourite as he came to Walsall with four consecutive wins under his belt. Captain

1840 - 1859

Crofton was a serving army officer and must have taken the horse with him wherever he was posted, as the horse's previous outings had been at Liverpool, Abergavenny, Plymouth and Exeter. First blood went to Muleteer who won the first heat with Sunflower way back in fourth spot. The second heat went to Mr Parrack's, Jolly Boy, with Sunflower third and Muleteer fourth. The third heat was very close to deciding the race in favour of Muleteer, but the judge declared a dead heat between him and Sunflower. With the event now turning into a marathon, it would appear the earlier heats had taken there toll on Muleteer's stamina as Sunflower won the fourth and fifth heats by a length both times. The spectators on the Long Meadow were thrilled to see such a competitive race and loud applause and cheering greeted the jockey, Charles Marlow as he returned to be weighed. As the heats continued, three of the horses were withdrawn at various stages of the race, but the remaining four ran over five and a half miles before a winner was declared in an event that must have taken at least two and half hours to complete.

That 'evil' of the new sporting generation was next on the card, the Hurdle race. This was won by Mr Boycott's oldstager, Donnington who had appeared many times at Walsall, running over hurdles and on the flat. He last ran on the flat the day before, finishing fourth, but the slower run hurdle races must have suited him because he ran a spirited race to fend off his four rivals in both heats.

The final two races of this year's meeting were for non-thoroughbred horses to be ridden by gentlemen only. With the Gold Cup now a thing of the past these races were becoming more frequent at the meeting. The runners for these two races, both Cavalry Stakes, were as motley a crew that ever descended on the Long Meadow. Of the eight runners, only two had run in any sort of official race before. The final race has an coincidental connection with events on the course almost forty years ago. Winner of the race was the mare, Mrs Spittle, and last was Wednesbury Lass. It may be remembered from earlier pages that a lady of that name, from Wednesbury, was killed on the course in 1803!

The report in the *Staffordshire Advertiser* thanks a Mr Kilner for providing excellent provision at the Stewards' ordinaries, which were held at the New Inn in Park Street instead of the George Hotel; this was the first time in many years that the latter hostelry hadn't featured in any of the events concerning the races. Mr J. Fowler, president of the Stewards' ordinaries announced during the proceedings that they, the Committee, would be supporting a new race for the following year, to be known as 'The Birmingham Stakes,' which had already attracted twenty subscriptions from the gentlemen present.

The official results of the meeting were:

Wednesday 28th September 1842

A SWEEPSTAKES of 5 sovereigns each, with 25 added by R. Scott, M.P. for the Borough.
Heats, twice round, starting at the distance chair.

Mr Fowler's ch. f.	**Sunflower,** 4 y-o, 8st. 3lb. *(Robert Denman)*	1	1
Capt. Crofton's b. h.	**Muleteer,** 5 y-o, 9st. 8lb.	2	2
Mr Shepherd's	**Tressilian** (half bred), 3 y-o	bolted	

A WELTER SWEEPSTAKES of 5 sovereigns each, with 20 added from the Race Fund. Gentlemen riders.
Heats once round, starting at the distance chair.

Mr Greaves'	**Isabella** (half bred), 5 y-o 11st. 7lb. *(Mr Friend)*	1	1
Mr Boycott's b. g.	**Donnington,** 6 y-o, 11st. 12lb.	4	2
Mr E. Davis' b. g.	**Brewood,** 4 y-o, 11st.	2	dr
Mr Parrack's	**Jolly Boy,** 4 y-o, 11st. 10lb.	3	dr

A MAIDEN STAKES of 3 sovereigns each, with 20 added by the Innkeepers and Publicans of Walsall.
Heats, once round and a distance.

Mr Woodhouse's ch. g.	**Caitliff,** 3 y-o, 6st. 5lb. *(Thomas Day, junior)*	1	1
Mr Tempest's ch. g.	**Forester,** aged, 8st. 8lb.	2	2

Thursday 29th September 1842

A SWEEPSTAKES of 5 sovereigns each, with 25 added by the proprietors of the grandstand.
Heats, once round and a distance.

Mr Fowler's ch. f.	**Sunflower,** 4 y-o, 8st. 7lb. *(Charles Marlow)*	4	3	0	1	1
Mr Parrack's	**Jolly Boy,** 4 y-o, 8st. 11lb.	6	1	4	3	2
Capt. Crofton's b. h.	**Muleteer,** 5 y0o, 9st. 7lb.	1	4	0	4	3
Mr E. Peel's br. g.	**Palaemon,** 4 y-o, 7st. 3lb.	3	2	3	2	dr
Mr Greaves'	**Isabella,** 6 y-o, 8st. 11lb.	5	5	5	dr	-
Mr Davis' b. g.	**Brewood,** 4 y-o, 8st. 7lb.	2	dr	-	-	-

A HURDLE SWEEPSTAKES of 3 sovereigns each, with 15 added. Heats, once round and a distance.

Mr Boycott's b. g.	**Donnington,** 6 y-o, 11st. 7lb. *(T. Davis)*	1	1
Mr Carter's bl. g.	**Negro,** 6 y-o, 11st. 7lb.	4	2
Mr Hotham's ch. h.	**Ace of Diamonds,** 5 y-o, 11st. 5lb.	2	3
Mr Lowndes' ch. g.	**Astrologer,** aged, 11st. 9lb.	3	4
Mr Tempest's ch. g.	**Forester,** aged	dis	-

A CAVALRY SWEEPSTAKES of 2 sovereigns each, with 10 added. Gentlemen riders. Heats, once round.

Mr Proffitt's bl. m.	**Providence,** 5 y-o, 11st. 7lb. *(Owner)*	1	1
Mr Smallwood's gr. m.	**Violante**	2	3
Mr Johnson's ch. m.	**Princess,** aged	3	2
Mr J. Newman's br. m.	**Un-named,** aged	4	4

A CAVALRY STAKES of 2 sovereigns each, with 10 added.
Heats, once round and a distance.

Mr Wallace names br. m.	**Mrs Spittle,** aged, 12st.	1	1
Mr Fowler names gr. h.	**Sneaker,** aged	2	2
Mr Pringle names br. h.	**Dusty,** aged	4	3
Mr Hughes' names b. m.	**Wednesbury Lass,** 4 y-o	3	4

The official results of the meeting at Bloxwich were:

Monday 8th August 1842

THE TRIAL STAKES of 2 sovereigns each, with 10 added. The winner to be sold for 40 sovereigns if demanded.
Heats, about one and a half miles.

Mr Doncaster's ch. m.	**Miss Ferguson,** 6 y-o, 9st. 11lb.	1	1
-	**St. Botolph,** 4 y-o, 9st. 2lb.		

Two others distanced after the first heat.

Bloxwich results continued overleaf

1840 - 1859

Bloxwich results continued,

THE HURDLE RACE of 2 sovereigns each, with 10 added.
Heats, thrice round with six leaps in each heat.

| Mr Channer's b.m. | **Kate Kearney,** aged, 11st. 7lb. | 1 1 |

Beating two others, both unknown.

Tuesday 9th August 1842

THE HURRY SCURRY STAKES of 1 sovereign each,
with 5 added. Heats, thrice round and a distance.

| Mr Doncaster's ch. m. | **Miss Ferguson,** 6 y-o |

Beating two others, both unknown.

A HANDICAP STAKES of 1 sovereigns each, with a purse added.
Heats, once round and a distance.

| Mr Harrison's b. m. | **Oakbranch,** 5 y-o, 10st. 7lb. |

Beating two others, both unknown

1843

The George Hotel wasn't out of the limelight for long. Whatever had happened the previous year to send everyone packing over to the New Inn was quickly forgotten, or resolved. It was business as usual as The George again hosted the Stewards' ordinaries, and John Gough presented another fine buck to mine host, Richard Fletcher, to help the proceedings along. The Stewards for the meeting were Robert Peel Esq. and Mr W. F. Fryer who also presided over the ordinaries, as was the custom.

Few members of the nobility were coming to Walsall these days for the Races, but one did manage it this year, Lord Milltown, who was on the course both days, staying overnight at the George. Where else?

The meeting, which began on Wednesday 27th September, and consisted of seven races over the two days, coincided with a very good spell of weather, making viewing for the large numbers that again gathered to watch the spectacle, very pleasant.

The Birmingham Stakes proved to be somewhat of an anticlimax, it being reduced to a match between Lord Milltown's filly, Birdeen and Mr Worthington's colt, Hooton. Both of the horses had been lightly raced and running in better quality races, without success. Birdeen had only run twice before at the headquarters of racing, Newmarket and Hooton had also run twice at Chester.

The race was a one-mile event, at the end of it, Hooton was the one no longer qualified to run in maiden races.

Another new race on this year's card was the grandly named Champagne Stakes, a race name more in keeping with Ascot or Epsom. Even in those days, Walsall has never appeared to be a champagne type of town, but the 'Mild Ale Stakes' doesn't have the same sophisticated ring about it as the Champagne Stakes. The reason behind the name was not what one would think either. Any other racecourse would present twelve bottles of champagne to the winner, but not at Walsall. The winner of the race had to present a dozen bottles of bubbly to the Race Committee for the Stewards ordinaries!

The winner of the race where you 'gave with one hand and received with the other' was Mr Woodhouse's gelding, Caitliff, ridden by John Walker. A gentleman rider that must have needed the spirit of his namesake when it came to handing over the champagne.

Lord Milltown wasn't having too good a time of it on the racecourse. He entered Birdeen for the Sweepstakes race on Thursday only to be beaten into second place in heat one and then withdrawing. The winner was Mr W. Fowler's gelding, Jack, who won the first and third heats with Tubalcain second, a horse that had been a fair animal in his day but age was taking its toll. The third horse was last year's dual winner, Sunflower, owned by Mr J. Fowler.

The gentlemen riders were now riding more winners at the meeting than the professional jockeys. Three of the four winners on Thursday being ridden by amateurs although only one race was confined to those of that status.

The official results of the meeting were:

Wednesday 27th September 1843

A SWEEPSTAKES of 10 sovereigns each, with 25 added.
Two year old course.

Mr A. W. Hill's br. c.	**Beaumont,** *(George Calloway)*	1
Mr Fowler's	**John Goldham**	2
Mr Raworth's br. c.	**Kilgram**	3
Mr Herbert's b. f.	**Joanna**	4
Mr T. Flintoff's ch. f.	**The Elbe**	5
Mr Copeland's ch. f.	**Ninety-One**	dis

THE BIRMINGHAM STAKES of 10 sovereigns each,
with 20 added from the Race Fund.

| Mr Worthington's | **Hooton,** *(William Arthur)* | 1 |
| Lord Milltown's | **Birdeen** | 2 |

THE CHAMPAGNE STAKES of 5 sovereigns each, with 20 added
by the Innkeepers and Publicans of Walsall.

Mr Woodhouse's ch. g.	**Caitliff,** *(Mr J. Walker)*	0	1	1
Mr Southby's b. g.	**Waterloo**	1	3	2
Mr Hall's b. g.	**Brewood**	2	4	3
Mr Price's ch. c.	**The Scavenger**	0	2	4

A CAVALRY STAKES of 3 sovereigns each, with 10 added from the Race Fund. Horses to be owned by Members of the Walsall Troop.

Mr Mills' br. m.	**Tixall Lass,** *(Mr Taylor)*	1	0	0	1
Mr Whitehouse's ch. m.	**Cayenne**	0	3	0	2
Mr Clarkson's bl. m.	**Providence**	0	0	0	3
Mr Bentley names br. h.	**The Major**	0	1	dr	-
Mr James' b. m.	**Lucy Long**	2	2	dr	-
Mr Wood's br. m.	**Fanny Elsler**	0	0	dr	-
Mr Proffitt's gr. m.	**Kitty**	dis	-	-	-

Thursday 28th September 1843

A SWEEPSTAKES of 5 sovereigns each, with 25 added by
R. Scott, M.P. for the Borough

Mr W. Fowler's br. g.	**Jack,** 4 y-o, *(Owner)*	1	2	1
Mr W. Jones' b. g.	**Tubalcain,** aged	5	1	2
Mr J. Fowler's ch. m.	**Sunflower,** 5 y-o	4	2	3
Lord Milltown's ch. f.	**Birdeen,** 3 y-o	2	dr	-
Mr T. Flintoff's ch. f.	**Countess of Lichfield,** 3 y-o	3	dr	-

1840 - 1859

THE STAND STAKES of 5 sovereigns each, with 15 added.

Mr Jones' br. c.	**Sweet William**, 3 y-o, *(W. Arthur)*	1	
Mr Woodhouse's ch. g.	**Caitliff**, 4 y-o	2	

A HURDLE SWEEPSTAKES of 5 sovereigns each, with 30 added.

Mr W. H. Turner's b. m.	**Ellen**, 6 y-o, *(Mr Turner)*	1	1
Mr Duncan's b. h.	**Wild Boy**, 5 y-o	3	2
Mr Jones' b. g.	**Milo**, aged	2	3

A HANDICAP STAKES of 3 sovereigns each, with 15 added.
For any horse entered at Walsall Races in 1843.

Mr James' b. m.	**Lucy Long**, *(Mr Friend)*	1	1
Mr Woodhouse's ch. g.	**Caitliff**, 4 y-o	2	dr

1844

For the second consecutive year, the Races were blessed with excellent weather for late September, which no doubt helped to swell the crowds eager for their annual turf amusements. Inevitably, large crowds attracted the criminal element of the town onto the racecourse, as the race report in The *Staffordshire Advertiser* concludes with the following statement: -

'As is usual at such times the light-fingered gentry were in many instances detected in making free with their neighbours pockets.'

Leaving the thieves and pickpockets to weave their way through the crowd, the real business of racing horses began on the morning of Wednesday 25th September with the Sweepstakes for two year-olds.

None of the four runners were that experienced on a racecourse, Edmund Peel's colt General Nott had never seen a racecourse until this appearance. None of the horses were phased by the event, Mr Skerratt's filly, Louisa Lowe winning from the slightly more experienced Salopian, owned by Mr A. W. Hill. William Copeland's filly, My Mary, was third with General Nott bringing up the rear. It was an excellent race with all four runners keeping well together until close home when the winner came through from third place to win by half-a-length.

It is interesting to note that two of the four runners featured in the *Sporting Magazine's* annual review of two-year olds for 1844. Both Louisa Lowe and My Mary were extremely well thought of by the magazine's wonderfully named correspondent, The Quiet and Easy Observer, who commented on their running at the Walsall meeting. My Mary, who was entered in the 1845 Oaks but didn't run, must have been an impressive filly as Copeland later sold her to Lord George Bentinck, no less. The filly was sent from Walter's stables at Hednesford to Mr Kent, one of his Lordship's trainers at Goodwood.

The second race for the Birmingham Stakes, proved to be an even better contest with all eight runners providing an excellent race for the turf aficionados of Walsall.

Had there been a prize for the most imaginatively named horse it would have surely gone to one of the runners in this race, Mr W. Becher's, Devil Among The Tailors. Where this name originated from is unknown and no clues are given by the horses parentage, his sire being, appropriately for Walsall, The Saddler, out of the mare, Fickle.

Unlike the runners in the previous race, the one thing none of these horses lacked was experience. Prior to arriving at Walsall, they had run in total of ninety races and the venues read like a gazetteer of England. Unusually for runners at Walsall, they all had some commendable form behind them, one in particular a five year-old horse named Counsellor. Of the sixteen races he had competed in, he had won nine of them, including a hurdle race.

When the race got under way, with all eight horses getting away cleanly, they kept together in a close group and maintained a strong gallop up the hill (Bradford Street) until disappearing from view. They were next seen along the flat run-in (on the railway side) with six of the eight still in a group. As the winning post neared, Counsellor, ridden by Tommy Sly, spared neither spur nor whip. He got his mount to the front, maintaining the advantage to the line and winning by a neck. The *Staffordshire Advertiser* summed up the race with its usual eloquence: -

'This race, it must be remarked, drew forth high encomiums from the vast assemblage, and would have done no small credit even to Doncaster'

After winning this event, Counsellor ran another four times, winning three of them and being unplaced in the prestigious Cambridgeshire Handicap, a race that is still run at Newmarket today.

The Walsall Stakes opened the programme on Thursday morning in what was a match between Devil Among The Tailors and Caitliff, winner of Wednesday's Champagne Stakes, who was running for the third time. Both horses set off at a fast pace with Caitliff taking the lead. Charles Marlow, rider of Devil Among The Tailors allowed him to maintain his advantage until about a furlong from the post when he pushed his mount hard to pass Caitliff and win by half a length.

Devil Among The Tailors work wasn't finished yet. Mr Becher turned him out for the next race, a Sweepstakes with money added by the M.P. for the Borough, Mr R. Scott. Five runners lined-up for the start, and after the first heat, the winner, Alderman Copeland's Assay fell lame after passing the post, his jockey dismounted and walked back to be weighed. The jockeys concern for the welfare of his mount cost him the heat as he had dismounted in an unauthorised area of the course. The horse that came second, Thomas Flintoff's, The Rhine, ridden by George Calloway was awarded the heat. With Assay now out of the contest, the remaining four horses began the final heat. As the quartet reached the top of the hill (opposite the site of the old General Hospital) one of the runners, Sands, bolted and was not seen for a while, eventually reappearing as the race was ending. This time The Rhine needed no assistance from the Stewards, coming home by half a length from another Hednesford trained horse, The Duke, running in the colours of John Fowler.

The meeting concluded with the Hurdle Sweepstakes, another race that became a match. Mr Halford's horse, Pickwick winning both heats easily from Mr Woolf's, Kitty. Pickwick was ridden by James Bradley, a jockey and trainer from Hednesford who was well known for training

1840 – 1859

steeplechasers and hurdlers. One of the jockeys employed by Bradley at Hednesford was William Archer, father of the legendary Victorian flat race jockey, Fred Archer.

The official results of the meeting were:

Wednesday 25th September 1844

A SWEEPSTAKES of 10 sovereigns each, with 25 added.
For two year olds.

Mr Skerratt's b. f.	**Louisa Lowe,** 8st. 2lb. *(Copeland)*	1
Mr A. W. Hill's b. c.	**Salopian,** 8st. 5lb	2
Ald. Copeland's ch. f.	**My Mary,** 8st. 2lb.	3
Mr E. Peel's b. c.	**General Nott,** 8st. 5lb.	4

THE BIRMINGHAM HANDICAP STAKES
of 10 sovereigns each, with 20 added
Twice round and a distance.

Mr T. Westley's ch. h.	**Counsellor,** 5 y-o, 8st. 4lb. *(T. Sly)*	1
Mr Worthington's	**Hooton,** 4 y-o, 7st. 10lb.	2
Mr G. Ongley's b. m.	**Fama,** 6 y-o, 7st.	3
Mr J. Ongley's ch. g.	**Roderick,** 5 y-o, 7st. 3lb.	4
Mr Becher's br. g.	**The Devil Among The Tailors,** 5 y-o, 7st. 3lb.	5
Mr Edmondstone's	**Ermengardis,** 6 y-o, 7st.	6
Mr Jones' ch.g.	**Caitliff,** 5 y-o, 6st. 13lb.	7
Mr Raworth's br. c.	**Kilgram,** 3 y-o, 6st.	8

THE CHAMPAGNE STAKES of 5 sovereigns each,
with 20 added by the Innkeepers and Publicans of Walsall. Gentlemen riders, the winner to give a dozen bottle of champagne to the Ordinary.
Heats, once round.

| Mr Jones' ch. g. | **Caitliff,** 5 y-o, 11st. 9lb., *(Mr Walker)* | 2 | 1 | 1 |
| Mr James names | **Ivanhoe,** 5 y-o 11st. 2lb., *(Mr Friend)* | 1 | 2 | 2 |

Thursday 26th September 1844

THE WALSALL STAKES of 7 sovereigns each, with 20 added.
The owner of the second to receive back his Stake.
Twice round and a distance.

| Mr W. Becher's | **The Devil Among The Tailors,** 5 y-o 8st. 4lb. *(Charles Marlow)* | 1 |
| Mr Jones' ch. g. | **Caitliff,** 5 y-o, 8st. 2lb. | 2 |

A HURDLE SWEEPSTAKES of 5 sovereigns each,
with 20 added.

| Mr Halford's | **Pickwick,** aged, 12st. 6lb. (J.Bradley) | 1 | 1 |
| Mr Woolf's | **Kitty,** aged, 11st. 13lb. | 2 | 2 |

A SWEEPSTAKES of 5 sovereigns each,
with 25 added by R. Scott, M.P. for the Borough.
Heats, once round and a distance.

Mr T. Flintoff's br. f.	**The Rhine,** 4 y-o, 8st. 7lb. *(George Calloway)*	2	1
Mr Copeland's	**Assay,** 3 y-o, 6st. 7lb.	1	dr
Mr W. Becher's br. g.	**The Devil Among The Tailors,** 5 y-o, 9st. 5lb.	0	2
Mr John Fowler's	**The Duke,** 5 y-o, 8st. 7lb.	3	3
Mr J. Gill's	**Sands,** 4 y-o, 7st. 13lb.	bolt	-

Assay, winner of the first heat, broke down and the rider did not weigh-in, the heat was awarded to The Rhine.

1845

As early as 1837 Walsall had been connected to the ever-expanding rail link of the Grand Junction Railway, the line only ran to Bescot where a small station had been erected. Passengers were conveyed to and from the town to the station in a horse drawn omnibus.

There were now plans to bring the railway directly into the town itself and the page in *The Staffordshire Advertiser* that contains the report of the proceedings on the Long Meadow for this year is surrounded by advertisements for the many railways being constructed throughout the region at this time. One advertisement for the South Staffordshire Junction Railway contains, as one of its selling points, the following statement '…*to the large and rapidly increasing town of Walsall.*' What better assurance for a potential investor in this revolutionary form of transport, with the town expanding due the industry it was now attracting, which meant more people to travel on the railway, good news for everyone, except the racecourse.

The two Stewards for the meeting this year were Viscount Newport and the Honourable E. R. Littleton, the only members of the nobility mentioned in this year's proceedings, and neither of them entered any horses.

Another contender for the most imaginatively named horse, Nix My Dolly, owned by Mr Hawkins, won the opening race of the meeting, the Birmingham Stakes. The horse was ridden by George Whitehouse who set off at a cracking pace in an attempt to build an unbeatable lead in the hope the horse would last until the post. The tactic worked, Nix My Dolly winning by a length from Mr Ongley's horse, Roderick.

An engraving from the 1845 period showing the outdoor weighing of jockeys. The jockey had to ride his horse into the area designated for weighing before he could dismount. Dismounting prior to this area was a breach of rules resulting in disqualification.

1840 - 1859

The Champagne Stakes was still being run for, with the same conditions, the owner of the winning horse must present twelve bottles of the finest champagne to the Race Committee. The 'unfortunate' winning owner and rider this year was William Shepherd, the trainer from Hednesford, whose horse, Glaucus won the first two heats with ease from Mr Parker's Ivanhoe and Mr Batson's gelding, The Bird.

Gentlemen riders were still being catered for with the Cavalry Stakes continuing its long association with the course. The winner was another with Hednesford connections, although it is not known where the horse was trained, the rider of The Major was William Saunders junior, son of the trainer Thomas. The Major, like the previous winner, made the job look easy, winning both heats comfortably.

Thursdays programme this year was minus the hurdle race that had always proved popular in the past with the spectators, if not with the owners, with few runners being attracted in previous races.

Opening the programme on Thursday morning was the Walsall Stakes, a handicap race over one and a half miles. George Whitehouse was reunited with Nix My Dolly who carried the top weight of the four runners at seven stone eleven pounds. At the start of the race the jockey riding T'Auld Squire had obviously watched the previous running of Nix My Dolly and adopted the same tactics by setting off at a rattling pace. Unfortunately his horse wasn't up to it and faded badly after a mile was run, allowing Whitehouse to take the lead and win by two lengths. A winner from the previous year, Thomas Flintoff's The Rhine, ridden by George Calloway, was second.

The final race was the Sweepstakes over two miles, which had twenty sovereigns added by the innkeepers and publicans of Walsall. With the profits that band of tradesmen made at this time of the year, it seems almost a paltry sum. The horse Glaucus, who won the Champagne Stakes on the Wednesday, proved that experience had not dampened his spirit as he won both heats with relative ease.

If the good people of Walsall hadn't had enough of horses, Batty and Whites Equestrian Establishment arrived in town with a Mr Bridges driving fourteen in hand. Their performances on Wednesday and Thursday evening were held on the bowling green of the Green Dragon Inn. A strange choice of venue for anything to do with horses.

If horses were the last things you wanted to see, there was always the theatre in The Square, which, although not mentioned in recent years as it had been in the past, was still attracting considerable audiences.

The official results of the meeting were:

Wednesday 24th September 1845

THE BIRMINGHAM HANDICAP STAKES
of 10 sovereigns each, with 20 added
Twice round and a distance.

Mr Charlton's	Nix My Dolly, 6 y-o (G. Whitehouse)	1
Mr J. Ongley's ch. g.	Roderick, 6 y-o	2
Mr Raworth's br. c.	Kilgram, 4 y-o	3
Mr Emery's	Princess Olga, 3 y-o	4

A MATCH for 50 sovereigns. Four furlongs.

Mr Osborne's	Merry Girl	walked over

THE CHAMPAGNE STAKES of 5 sovereigns each, with 20 added by the Innkeepers and Publicans of Walsall. Gentlemen riders, the winner to give a dozen bottles of champagne to the Ordinary.
Heats, once round and a distance.

Mr Sheppard's b. f.	by Glaucus, 3 y-o, (Owner)	1	1
Mr C. A. Parker's	Ivanhoe, 6 y-o	2	2
Mr Batson's br. g.	The Bird, 6 y-o	3	3

THE CAVALRY STAKES of 5 sovereigns each, with 20 added. Once round and a distance.

Mr Saunders names br. g.	The Major (Mr W. Saunders)	1	1
Mr Smallwood names	Maid of All Work	2	2
Mr Spencer names ch. m.	Hebe	3	3

Thursday 25th September 1845

THE WALSALL STAKES (Handicap) of 10 sovereigns each, with 20 added.
About one and a half miles, to start at the four furlong pole.

Mr Charlton's	Nix My Dolly (George Whitehouse)	1
Mr T. Flintoff's br. f.	The Rhine, 5 y-o	2
Mr Raworth's	Kilgram, 4 y-o	3
Mr W. Tempest names	T'Auld Squire, 4 y-o	4
Mr Taylor names	Princess Olga, 3 y-o	dis.

A SWEEPSTAKES of 5 sovereigns each, with 25 added by R. Scott, M.P. for the Borough.
Heats, once round and a distance.

Mr Raworth's b. c.	Idolator, 3 y-o, (James Bradley, jnr.)	1	1
Mr T. Flintoff's ch. f.	The Elbe, 4 y-o	2	dr

A SWEEPSTAKES of 5 sovereigns each, with 25 added by the Innkeepers and Publicans of Walsall.
Heats, once round and a distance.

Mr Sheppard's b. f.	by Glaucus, 3 y-o, (Styche)	1	1
Mr C. A. Parker's ch. f.	Whitelock, 4 y-o	3	2
Mr Raworth's	Kilgram, 4 y-o	2	dr

1846

An ominous first sentence in the opening paragraph of the race report greeted the readers of *The Staffordshire Advertiser*, it read: -

'The annual race meeting, at the Borough of Walsall, was celebrated on Wednesday and Thursday last, but was productive of very indifferent sport.' The Steward (Hon. E.R. Littleton) was present on both days, together with a numerous party of the local gentry, but in consequence of the unfortunate character of the weather there was a slight attendance of female loveliness. Mr J. Newman executed the duties of Clerk of the Course, and Mr W. H. Newman discharged the onerous task of judging the various contest in a very impartial manner. The course was somewhat heavy by the frequent showers of rain, but not so much as was first expected.'

If Walsall Races were indifferent, they had been for many years, as the report of the running appears to be the same as in previous years. Opening this year's meeting was the two year-old Sweepstakes race, which was in actual fact a match

1840 - 1859

between Edmund Peel's chestnut filly, Credential and a Mr Green's un-named black filly by Jereed. It wasn't much of a contest on the course and an even worse one from a betting point of view, Credential started at 1/8 on favourite. It would have been interesting to know what odds, if any were being given against Mr Green's filly winning. However, it all prove to be academic as the favourite won as she pleased, being eased coming to the line she still won by many lengths.

The Champagne Stakes was the only race of the day, with four runners attempting to give the Race Committee their twelve bottles of bubbly.

If the meeting had got off to a slow start from the spectators view, this event livened the proceedings. Designated to be decided after three heats, if necessary, this one went to four, thanks to a dead heat in the third.

Thomas Flintoff's four year-old bay mare, Reliance, ridden by Mr J. S. Walker won the race from Mr Raworth's colt, Engineer, ridden by Mr W. Friend. The report of the race from *The Staffordshire Advertiser* read as follows, with some additions that hopefully clarify certain points:-

5 to 4 on Reliance. First heat – Reliance got off with the lead, the Dick mare lying second to the turn near the stand, when she shot in front, and led up the hill to the Coal Pit Turn [where Corporation Street West is today] at a smart pace, Engineer filling third place, but evidently waiting for another heat. At the T.Y.C. post [two year-old course starting post] Reliance resumed her lead, and being challenged at the distance chair [240 yards from the post] by Kitty Wee, a pretty race home, the former winning by a neck only. Second heat – The Dick mare made the running to the top of the hill, where she was beat, and soon gave way to Engineer and Kitty Wee, made the latter assuming the lead after passing the Caldmore Lane [possibly Corporation Street]. The two raced home, and the colt won by a bare head. Third heat – Only Engineer and Reliance started. The mare who made severe play throughout, was only caught in the last two or three strides, and the judge gave it in a dead heat. Fourth heat – They got off at a regular 'jog trot' the mare leading, and continued in that way to the Coal Pit Sweep [Turn], when the speed was necessarily improved; Reliance, however, maintained her position, and won cleverly.'

One of the other conditions of the race was that the winner should be sold, if required, and the owner had to fix the price to sell on entering. The price the horse was to be sold at determined what weight allowance would be given. All of the four runners elected the price of £60 to be sold at, and were given a stone less in weight to carry. The more the owner thought his horse was worth, the less he got in weight allowance. Little wonder some of the races were walkovers and matches – the owners couldn't fathom out the rules and conditions!

On Thursday, Mr Peel continued where he had left off the previous day, by winning the Walsall Stakes, with his four year-old colt, General Nott, a previous winner on the course as a two year-old. General Nott, ridden by Charlie Marlow, led from start to finish, beating another Hednesford trained horse, Thomas Eskrett's, Exhort, the mount of the jockey, James Bradley, who was also a trainer.

The final race of the meeting was a Handicap Sweepstakes of just over a mile, once again, the Hednesford contingent were out in force. Edmund Peel's General Nott appeared for the second time that day, again ridden by Marlow. Thomas Flintoff entered The Rhine, another previous course winner, and ridden by his son, William and the final member of the trio being Mr Raworth's Idolater, the mount of James Bradley. The Rhine came out the winner of this one heat race and the race comments are provided by *The Staffordshire Advertiser*:-

'6 to 4 against General Nott. The Rhine got off with lead at a strong pace, the favourite lying second to the foot of the hill, [bottom of Bradford Street, near the junction with today's Midland Road] where he went in front, kept there until nearing the farm house [presumably Bodley's Farm] at which point the mare regained her place, and won a splendid race by a length.'

Although not all of the races have been included in the above comments, it was apparent that the Hednesford connection was now the most prominent factor at Walsall Races, as they were at all of the local racecourses. Of the seven races run, six of them were trained at 'Hedgford,' as the locals called it, and five of the winning jockeys were also based in the village.

Away from the Races, it is worth adding that this was the year the South Staffordshire Railway arrived in Walsall, the newly constructed line running alongside the racecourse.

The official results of the meeting were:

Wednesday 23rd September 1846

A SWEEPSTAKES of 10 sovereigns each, with 25 added.
For two year olds, four furlongs.

Mr E. Peel's ch. f.	**Credential,** 8st. 7lb. *(J. Dufflo)*	1
Mr Green's bl. f.	**Maid of the Mist,** 8st. 2lb. *(Flintoff)*	2

THE BIRMINGHAM HANDICAP STAKES of 10 sovereigns each, with 20 added.
Twice round and a distance.

Mr Collett's ch. c.	**Pal,** 3 y-o, 6st. 10lb. *(Jones)*	walked over

THE CHAMPAGNE STAKES of 5 sovereigns each, with 20 added.
The winner to give a dozen bottle of champagne to the Race Committee.
Heats, twice round and a distance.

Mr T. Flintoff's b. m.	**Reliance,** 4 y-o, 10st. 6lb. *(Mr J. S. Walker)*	1	0	0	1
Mr Raworth's b. c.	**Engineer,** 3 y-o, 9st. 2lb. *(Mr W. Friend)*	4	1	0	2
Mr Davis' b. m.	**Kitty Wee,** 4 y-o, 9st. 13lb. *(Owner)*	2	2	dr	-
Mr Green's bl. m	**Dick,** 4 y-o, 9st. 13lb. *(Mr Lord)*	3	0	dr	-

Thursday 24th September 1846

THE WALSALL STAKES (Handicap) of 10 sovereigns each, with 20 added.
About one and a half miles, to start at the four furlong pole.

Mr E. Peel's b. c.	**General Nott,** 4 y-o, 7st. 12lb. *(Charles Marlow)*	1
Mr T. Eskrett's br. h.	**Exhort,** 4 y-o, 7st. 10lb. *(James Bradley)*	2

1840 - 1859

A SWEEPSTAKES of 5 sovereigns each,
with 25 added by R. Scott, M.P. for the Borough.
Heats, once round and a distance.

Mr Baker's b. g.	**Redskin**, 4 y-o, 8st. 5lb. (James Bradley)	1	wo
Mr Vickers' b. m.	**Princess Olga**, 4 y-o, 7st. 13lb. (J. Dufflo)	2	dr
Mr Green's ch. m.	**by Dick**, 3 y-o, 6st. 9lb. (T. Jones)	3	dr

A SWEEPSTAKES of 5 sovereigns each, with 20 added by the
Innkeepers and Publicans of Walsall.
Once round and a distance.

Mr T. Flintoff's	**Princess Royal**, 4 y-o, 8st.4lb. (W. Flintoff)	2	1	wo
Mr T. Eskrett's br. h.	**Exhort**, 4 y-o, 8st. 7lb. (James Bradley)	1	2	dr

A HANDICAP SWEEPSTAKES of 3 sovereigns each, with 20 added.
Once round and a distance.

Mr T. Flintoff's br. m.	**The Rhine**, 6 y-o, 8st. 4lb. (W. Flintoff)	1
Mr E. Peel's b. h.	**General Nott**, 4 y-o, 8st. (Charles Marlow)	2
Mr J. Raworth's b. c.	**Idolator**, 4 y-o, 7st. 9lb. (James Bradley)	3

1847

The Races in 1847 opened on Wednesday 29th September with the now customary race for two year-olds. Walsall's own George Whitehouse was the victorious jockey on Mr S. L. Marsh's bay filly, Mother Carey's Chicken, another contender for the most imaginatively named horse competition.

The contemporary reports stating that is was a good race, with all three runners taking an active part in proceedings, with Whitehouse just getting his mount over the line in front of the other two.

The first race in the afternoon turned out to be a disappointment from a spectators point of view. The three horses declared to start entered the saddling enclosure and were tacked up ready to go when two of the owners decided to withdraw their charges for some unknown reason. Because of this decision, George Whitehouse was left with easiest of tasks to take the money.

For the second year running, the Champagne Stakes was the best race, certainly of the day, and possibly the meeting. Four heats were again required to decide the winner due to another dead heat. At the end of the marathon, the winner was Mr Turner's mare, Icicle, ridden by Mr Davenport, who eventually got the better of his four rivals, *The Staffordshire Advertiser* reported the race as follows:-

'In the first heat the four made a good start, Icicle taking the lead (which she did in every heat throughout the race) and keeping it to the other side of the hill, when she tailed off, and Maid of the Mist took her place, and run a good in with Piefinch and Daring close in her wane. The second heat was a severely contested one, the brown filly Mainbrace and Icicle running neck and neck for about the last two hundred yards home, which ended in a dead heat, and those two only started after for the remaining heats, the third being won by about two lengths, and the fourth by a neck. Of this race it may be truly said, the lovers of the turf could not help being gratified to the utmost, both with the running and the honesty displayed by the riders.'

The first race on the card on Thursday, the Walsall Stakes, was won by Edmund Peels' colt, General Nott, winner of the race last year. This year however, the colt didn't even have to break into a trot to claim the prize, as the sole entry, the formalities of a walk over were all that was necessary.

The best race on Thursday was the Sweepstakes of three sovereigns, run in three heats of just over a mile each. Only three runners contested the race, one of them being Maid of the Mist, who had such a tough race the previous day in the Champagne Stakes. The two other runners were Captain Knight's gelding, Jolly Beggar and Mr Critchley's filly, Atalanta. After the first heat it appeared that the Maid of the Mist was still feeling the effects of yesterday's running as she could only finish a poor last of the three runners. What ever the connections of the filly gave her, or did to her during the interval, it worked wonders. She won the next two heats beating Atalanta, in good style.

George Calloway, the now retired jockey, had his first runner at Walsall as a trainer in the Consolation Stakes, and was very nearly first time lucky. The mare that he ran was named Morality who was narrowly beaten to the line by another mare, Florine, ridden by Robert Denman.

The final race of the meeting was won by Mr Barton's Hector, who carried off the money in two events without really having to exert himself. On Wednesday he walked over in the Sweepstakes race and for this final event he ran against two others who he beat easily in the first heat. Seeing Hectors superiority, the two remaining owners withdrew their horses from the second heat.

The official results of the meeting were:

Wednesday 29th September 1847

A SWEEPSTAKES of 10 sovereigns each, with 25 added.
For two year olds, four furlongs.

Mr S. L. Marsh's b. f.	**Mother Carey's Chicken** (George Whitehouse)	1
Mr E. Lord jnr's b. f.	**by Bretby**	2
Mr W. H. Turner's b. f.	**Conquest**	3

THE BIRMINGHAM HANDICAP STAKES
of 10 sovereigns each, with 20 added from the Race Fund.
Twice round, to start at the distance chair.

Mr Fowler's	**Rhanthos**, 3 y-o (John Tasker)	1
Mr T. Eskrett's	**Exhort**, 5 y-o	2

A SWEEPSTAKES of 5 sovereigns each,
with 20 added by the tradesmen of Walsall.
Heats, twice round and a distance.

Mr Barton's	**Hector**, 5 y-o, (George Whitehouse)	wo

THE CHAMPAGNE STAKES of 5 sovereigns each, with 20 added. Gentlemen riders, the winner to give a dozen bottle of champagne to the Race Committee. Heats, twice round and a distance.

Mr Turner's b. m.	**Icicle**, 4 y-o, (Mr Davenport)	4	0	1	1
Mr Green's b. f.	**Maid of the Mist**, 3 y-o	1	0	2	2
Mr C. Hughes' b. f.	**Piefinch**, 3 y-o	2	4	dr	-
Mr Parker's br. c.	**Darling**, 3 y-o	3	3	dr	-

1840 – 1859

Thursday 30th September 1847

THE WALSALL STAKES (Handicap) of 10 sovereigns each, with 20 added.
About one and a half miles, to start at the four furlong pole.

Mr E. Peel's b. c.	**General Nott,** 5 y-o		wo

A SWEEPSTAKES of 3 sovereigns each, with 25 added by Hon. E. R. Littleton, M.P. for the Borough. Heats, once round and a distance.

MrGreen's b. f.	**Maid of the Mist,** 3 y-o, (John Tasker)	3	1	1
Mr Critchley's ch. f.	**Atalanta,** 3 y-o	1	2	2
Capt. Knight's ch. g.	**Jolly Beggar,** 6 y-o	2	3	3

THE CONSOLATION STAKES of 2 sovereigns each, with 15 added. Twice round, to start at the distance chair.

Mr Knowles' b. m.	**Florine,** 5 y-o, *(R. Denman)*	1
Mr G. Calloway's ch. m.	**Morality,** aged	2
Mr T. Walters' bf. f.	**Mainbrace,** 3 y-o	3
Mr C. Hughes' b. f.	**Piefinch,** 3 y-o	4
Mr Pearce's	**Foxbury,** aged	5

A SWEEPSTAKES of 3 sovereigns each, with 20 added by the Innkeepers and Publicans of Walsall. Heats, twice round and a distance.

Mr Barton's	**Hector,** 5 y-o, *(G. Whitehouse)*	1	1
Mr Turner's	**Icicle,** 4 y-o	2	dr

1848

The meeting in 1848 again consisted of six races, three on each day. In the second race on Wednesday, the Birmingham Stakes, a very young jockey rode his first ever winner on the Long Meadow and so launched what was to be a very successful and occasionally controversial career. The lad in question was John Wells, born in Sutton Coldfield in 1832 and apprenticed to Thomas Flintoff at Hednesford. The horse that he won on was Mr Fowler's Ribaldry, which was also the horse that gave Wells his first ride in public some months earlier at Northampton. In later life, as well as being champion jockey twice in 1853 and 1854, he also became very well known for his eccentric dress sense, being somewhat of a dandy, a fact not always appreciated by the rulers of racing.

A brown mare named Rebecca, owned by Mr Edwards, won two of the four Sweepstakes races run. The horse won the final race of the day on Wednesday for amateur riders only, beating four other opponents. Rebecca had to contest all three heats to get the verdict and covering a distance of over three miles. Less than twenty-four hours later the horse was out again contesting a race of virtually the same distance, and having to complete all of the heats to defeat the four opponents. The mare lost the first heat but then piled on the pressure, to win the final two heats easily.

The Consolation Stakes on Thursday proved to be a good race, even if it was a match. The two runners, Mr Green's mare, Clara, the odds on favourite versus Marlow, the horse, not the jockey. Marlow was owned by Edward Phillips, the horse breeder from Bushbury, whose horses were trained by Thomas Saunders at Hednesford. With just the one heat to decide the winner, Clara took off in the lead. She held the advantage until the last one-hundred and twenty yards, when Marlow, ridden by George Whitehouse, made a concerted effort to get his mount home. A severe struggle between the two saw the experience of Whitehouse pay off, as he managed to get his mount home by a head.

Marlow, like his namesake the jockey, was a tough fellow, and his owner thought he could stand the pace and entered him in the next race, the final event of the meeting. With just three other contestants, Mr Phillips must have been confident of his gelding's ability and stamina, to contest another race so close to the previous one, and this time over longer distance of two miles and possible three heats.

The earlier race had taken its toll on Marlow and the closest he could get to the winner of the first heat, Mr Lord's Clairvoyance, was second. Wisely, Phillips withdrew Marlow from the race after this, as did the owner of one of the other runners, Mind Your Own Business, realising they were beaten animals. The second heat between the two remaining runners, Marlow and Tally-Ho proved to be a close battle, so close the judge couldn't decide and declared a dead heat. The final heat began where the previous one had left off, and another dour battle ensued. Unfortunately Tally-Ho stumbled and fell leaving Marlow to come home alone. Tally-Ho and his jockey escaping injury in the fall, leaving the course with only their pride dented.

The official results of the meeting were:

Wednesday 27th September 1848

A SWEEPSTAKES of 5 sovereigns each, with 20 added.
For two year olds, four furlongs.

Mr Dyson's br. f.	**by Kremlin** *(George Whitehouse)*	1
Mr J. Hamp's b. f.	**Ferret**	2

THE BIRMINGHAM HANDICAP STAKES of 10 sovereigns each, with 20 added from the Race Fund. Twice round, to start at the distance chair.

Mr Fowler's	**Ribaldry** *(John Wells)*	1
Mr Felton names ch. f.	**by Lord Stafford**	2
Mr Phillips' b. g.	**Marlow**	3

A SWEEPSTAKES of 5 sovereigns each, with 20 added. Gentlemen riders. Heats, once round.

Mr Edward's	**Rebecca,** *(William Sharpe)*	1	4	1
Mr Shirley's br. m.	**Novelist**	3	1	2
Mr T. Davis' br. g.	**Jack**	2	3	dr
Mr J. Phillips' b. g.	**Tally-Ho** (half bred)	4	2	dr
Mr Fowler's	**Ranthus**	5	5	dr

Thursday 29th September 1848

A SWEEPSTAKES of 3 sovereigns each, with 25 added by Hon. E. R. Littleton, M.P. for the Borough. Heats, once round and a distance.

Mr Edward's	**Rebecca** *(William Sharpe)*	3	1	1
Mr Williams' b. f.	**Repulse**	2	3	2
Mr T. Flintoff's	**Princess Royal**	4	4	3
Mr E. Lord jnr's	**Clairvoyance**	1	2	4
Mr Hawkins'	**Jenny Wren**	5	dr	-

1840 - 1859

THE CONSOLATION STAKES of 2 sovereigns each,
with 15 added. Twice round, to start at the distance chair.

Mr Phillips' b. g.	Marlow (George Whitehouse)			1
Mr Green's b. m.	Clara			2

A SWEEPSTAKES of 3 sovereigns each,
with 20 added by the Innkeepers and Publicans of Walsall.
Heats, twice round and a distance.

Mr E. Lord jnr's	Clairvoyance (C. Edwards)	1	0	1
Mr Phillips' b. g.	Marlow	2	dr	-
Mr W. Mytton's b. g.	Mind Your Own Business	3	dr	-
Mr J. Phillips' b. g.	Tally-Ho (half bred)	4	0	f

1849

The meeting in 1849 was scheduled to take place on Wednesday 26th and Thursday 27th September but the efforts of the Race Committee were foiled for the second time in seventeen years by an outbreak of cholera.

An announcement was made by the Race Committee on September 12th and published in the next edition of *The Staffordshire Advertiser* that read: -

'The Walsall Race Committee hereby give notice, that in consequence of the fearful visitation of the Cholera in the neighbouring districts, and in compliancy with a Requisition from the Town Commissioners, the Races advertised to take place on the 26th and 27th instant, will be postponed.'

The races and wake at Brewood, which were due to take place a week before the Walsall event were also cancelled.

The outbreak originated in the Town End district of Walsall, an over-crowded area with people living in the most dreadful unsanitary conditions, the perfect breeding ground for cholera. With no hospital available to isolate the victims, they were taken to the sick ward of the workhouse, which only succeeded in spreading the disease there.

The official poster cancelling the event is shown below left and is reproduced by permission of Walsall Local History Centre.

The cholera outbreak arrived in the town very quickly as just twenty-three days before the Walsall meeting was called off a race meeting was held on The Slang in Bloxwich on 20th and 21st of August. Although the results of this meeting didn't appear in the *Racing Calendar* for that year. Exactly the same scenario happened two years earlier in 1847, a race card for that meeting exists but no mention of the fact in the *Racing Calendar*.

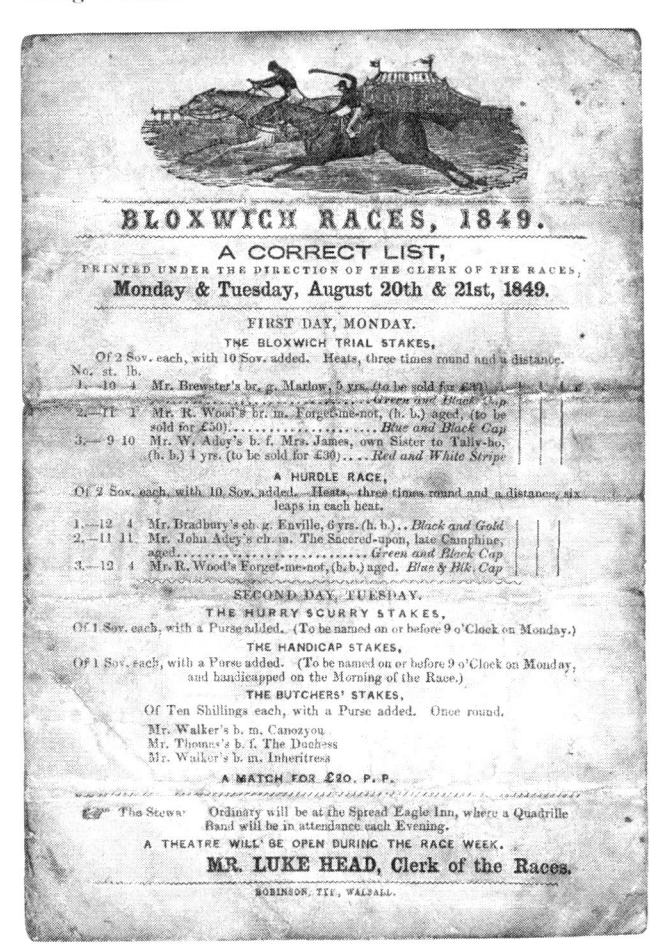

1850

In 1850 the Races were moved from the customary last Wednesday and Thursday in September to commence just over a week earlier on Monday 16th and Tuesday 17th. The reason behind the move was because the usual second day of the Races coincided with Birmingham Fair. In earlier years, people from the city and its surrounding districts made their way to Walsall for the annual Races. Now, with the introduction of the railways, plus the cheap fares they were offering, meant they were now coming in their multitudes, and the Walsall tradesmen didn't want to miss out on all the potential spending power.

Fine weather on both days helped swell the crowds and many booths were erected on and around the course by the

1840 – 1859

local victuallers who, *The Staffordshire Advertiser* assures us *'were kept very busy throughout both days.'*

The race programme officially consisted of six races, three on each day. Wednesday's card commenced with the running of the Innkeepers' Stakes, followed by the Members' Stakes. The days events closed with a hurdle race, back in the programme after an absence of six years. Thursday began with the running of the Welter Stakes, which was followed by the South Staffordshire Railway Stakes. The meeting closed with the Consolation Stakes for beaten horses. In reality, the meeting actually ran eight events, with two un-advertised contests being added to the proceedings. The first was a match that opened the meeting and the other, a handicap race that closed the proceedings for the year.

The first race of any note was the third on the card, the Members' Stakes, beginning in the early afternoon on Wednesday. The cost for entry was three sovereigns each, with twenty five sovereigns being added to the total by the Hon. E.R. Littleton, M.P. for the Borough, one of the few people of his class still supporting the races in Walsall. Just three runners arrived at the starting post, two of them already familiar to the ardent racegoers on the Long Meadow. The two horses were Marlow and Ribaldry, the latter being the horse that launched John Wells turf career, and both winners the last time the meeting was held in 1848. The other runner was the charge of Mr C. Briscoe, a gelding named Charlatan. It was Ribaldry that made the early running at what was described as a slow pace, Marlow, now two years older appeared to have lost his form and played little part in the race. With Ribaldry hacking along in front, partnered by George Whitehouse, Charlatan attempted a challenge on the leader but couldn't make up the lost ground and Ribaldry came home, hard held, to win very easily. This easy victory in the first heat was enough for the owners of the other two, they withdrew their horses, allowing Ribaldry to walk over and take the prize.

The best, and final race of the day, was the hurdle race, which went to four heats to determine a winner. The race was over a distance of one mile and a distance with three flights of hurdles to be jumped in each heat, the hurdles standing three feet six inches in height. The five runners were, Mr Land's Little Envy, Mr J. M. Taylor's Gipsy Lass, Mr Page's New Brighton, Mr Oakley's The Streamer and finally, Mr J. Cooke's Verax. The latter horse made the play at a strong pace, followed by New Brighton and The Streamer with Little Envy third; going up the hill, Verax increased the pace and led all the way round to win the heat in a canter. The jockey of Verax, thinking he had another circuit to go, went round the entire course again, with New Brighton following him until his jockey realised his mistake half way round and pulled up, adding a little farce to the ending of the first heat. This additional trip ended the challenge of Verax and his owner withdrew him from the race, no doubt with a few expletives thrown in the direction of the jockey. New Brighton was obviously not bothered by his additional exertions as he won the second heat from The Streamer by a length, pinching the heat as they approached the grandstand. The third heat began with New Brighton again making the running until the top of the hill when The Streamer took over and won cleverly from New Brighton. This race was now coming down to the survival of the fittest between The Streamer and New Brighton. Both Gipsy Lass and Little Envy were withdrawn from the final heat. The Streamer, ridden by Charlie Boyce, proved the fittest of the pair, making the entire running to win easily by three lengths.

In less than twenty-four hours, The Streamer came out again to win another four-heat race for the Welter Stakes, to be ridden by gentlemen riders on the flat. The Streamer certainly proved he was the fittest horse on the Long Meadow, covering over nine miles in his quest for victory in the two races; and he wasn't finished yet!

The South Staffordshire Railway Stakes was a none event, with just two runners entered, Mr Baly's mare Colycynthus and the locally owned mare, Mr Sharratt's Egret. For whatever reason, Mr Sharratt withdrew his mare leaving Colycynthus to take the money with a walkover. The jockey who was aboard Colycynthus was the rather eccentric John Chesswas, a native of Cheltenham, who had ideas well above his station for those days. He enjoyed nothing better than mingling with the nobility at every opportunity, much to their annoyance apparently. He must have had a difficult job in Walsall these days trying to find someone to mingle with after racing.

The race that closed the proceedings for another year was the Handicap Race, which saw The Streamer run again. Only four runners went to the post, three of them had contested previous races with the one 'fresh' horse amongst them. The Streamer, after some gallant performances behind him, found this one too much, and he could only finish second to the 'fresh' horse, Mr Choyce's May Day, ridden by an unknown boy.

The official results of the meeting were:

Monday 16th September 1850

A MATCH for 25 sovereigns. Once round.

Mr Griffiths'	**Ferret** *(Cleobury)*	1
Mr Gordon's	**Emily**	2

THE INNKEEPERS' STAKES of 3 sovereigns each, with 20 added. Heats, twice round.

Mr Choyce's ch. c.	**Bedford**	1
Mr Lewis' b. g.	**Hardwick**	2

THE MEMBERS' STAKES of 3 sovereigns each, with 25 added by the Hon. E. R. Littleton, M.P. for the Borough. Heats, once round.

Mr Fowlers's b. m.	**Ribaldry** *(George Whitehouse)*	1	1
Mr C. Briscoe's b. g.	**Charlatan**	2	dr
Mr Johnson's b. g.	**Marlow**	dis	-

A HURDLE RACE of 3 sovereigns each, with 20 added. Heats, once round, to start at the distance chair.

Mr Oakley's ch. m.	**The Streamer** *(C. Boyce)*	2	2	1	1
Mr Page's b. g.	**New Brighton**	3	1	2	2
Mr J. M. Taylor's b. m.	**Gipsy Lass**	4	dr	-	-
Mr J. Cooke's	**Verax**	1	dr	-	-
Mr Land's b. m.	**Little Envy**	5	3	3	dr

1840 – 1859

Tuesday 17th September 1850

THE WELTER STAKES of 3 sovereigns each,
with 20 added. Heats, once round and a distance.

Mr Oakley's ch. m.	**The Streamer** *(C. Boyce)*	0	1	4	1
Mr James' b. g.	**Lyme**	0	0	1	2
Mr J. Davies' f.	**Lily Dawson**	1	0	2	3
Mr Briscoe's b. g.	**Charlatan**	0	2	3	dr
Mr Johnson's b. g.	**Marlow**	5	dr	-	-

THE SOUTH STAFFORDSHIRE RAILWAY STAKES
of 3 sovereigns each, with 25 added by the Lessees of the South Staffordshire Railway. Twice round, starting at the distance chair.

Mr Baly's b. m.	**Colycynthus** *(John Chesswas)*	1
Mr Sharratt's b. m.	**Egret**	didn't finish

THE CONSOLATION STAKES of 2 sovereigns each, with 15 added.
Heats, once round, starting at the distance chair.

Mr Jones' b. f.	**Flirt** *(Arthur)*	2	1	1
Mr Lowe's b. g.	**Hardwick**	1	2	2

A HANDICAP STAKES of 2 sovereigns each,
with 25 added. Heats, once round and a distance.

Mr Choyce's	**May Day** *(a boy)*	1	1
Mr Oakley's ch. m.	**The Streamer**	2	dr
Mr Baly's b. m.	**Colycynthus**	3	dr

Stewards: John Fowler and Joseph Phillips.
Clerk of the Races: John Newman

1851

The advertisement for the Races appeared as normal in *The Staffordshire Advertiser*, ten days or so before the event was due to begin, giving no clue as to the discord that was going on behind the scenes. Serious disagreements of an unknown nature, involving members of the Race Committee had taken place, putting the meeting in jeopardy. Whatever the reasons behind the disagreements, they came to a head when the old Race Committee resigned. A new committee was immediately formed in an urgent effort to save the meeting, with the deposed members of the old Committee refusing to have anything to do with the new regime. John Newman, Clerk of the Course for almost thirty years obviously sided with the new members as he retained his position.

Dates for the meeting were announced as Wednesday 24th and Thursday 25th September, the threat from Birmingham Fair coinciding with the second day obviously being short-lived. The new Race Committee had even managed to arrange good weather for the opening day that brought out the spectators in their thousands.

The opening race of the meeting, the Innkeepers' Stakes was completed without incident, but the second race proved to be somewhat of a disaster. Five runners contested the Members' Stakes and in the first heat, whilst the runners were descending the hill at the far end of the course, disaster struck. Alfred Freeborne, the jockey of Mr Taft's un-named filly by Don John, mistook the course and went the wrong side of the one of the posts marking the course. Three of the others followed, Mr Fowler's filly, Silence, Mr Evan's filly,

> **WALSALL RACES** will take place on WEDNESDAY and THURSDAY, September 24th and 25th.
> JOHN FOWLER, Esq., } Stewards.
> JOHN WIGGAN, Esq., }
> FIRST DAY.
> The **INNKEEPERS' STAKES** of three sovs. each, with twenty sovs. added by the Innkeepers and Publicans of Walsall. Heats, twice round and a distance.
> The **MEMBER'S STAKES** of three sovs. each, with twenty-five sovs. added by the Honourable E. R. Littleton, M.P. for the borough. Heats, once round and a distance.
> A **HURDLE RACE** of three sovs. each, with twenty sovs. added. Heats, once round and a distance. Three leaps in each heat.
> SECOND DAY.
> The **WELTER STAKES** of three sovs. each, with twenty sovs. added. Heats, once round and a distance.
> The **TRADESMEN'S STAKES**, of three sovs. each, with twenty sovs. added by the Race Committee. Heats, once round. To start at the Distance Chair.
> The **CONSOLATION STAKES** of two sovs. each, with fifteen sovs. added. Heats, once round and a distance.
> The Stakes to close and name to the Clerk of the Races, at the Grand Stand, before eight o'clock in the evening of Monday, the 22nd of September. Nominations in writing, sealed up.
> J. NEWMAN, Clerk of the Races.

The advertisement from the Staffordshire Advertiser for the proceedings in 1851, giving no hint of the discord between the members of the Race Committee.

Palace Royal and Mr Hawkins' filly, The Nun. In the ensuing confusion, Silence and The Nun both fell, with the latter crashing into a ditch and breaking one of her legs. Due to the seriousness of her injury she became the first reported horse that had to be destroyed on the course in almost one hundred years of racing. The two riders involved in the incident escaped relatively unscathed, suffering from slight bruising only.

Due to the accident, the heat was declared null and void, with one runner now being dead and two of the remaining four being withdrawn. It left Silence, obviously not affected by the crash, and the un-named filly to finish the race. Silence made all of the running until turning into the straight at the far end of the course when the Don John filly went past her to win cleverly. After this defeat, Mr Fowler decided Silence had taken enough punishment and withdrew the filly, leaving the culprit who caused the accident to take the prize with a walk over.

Fortunately for the new Race Committee the Hurdle Race came off without incident, won by Mr Davis' gelding, Lysimachus ridden by amateur jockey, John Shaw Walker from Wolverhampton, whose clever riding won both heats in a canter from his two opponents.

The weather, which had been glorious on the first day, deteriorated overnight and was quite unfavourable when the runners came out for the first race. Public enemy number one, the sixteen year old Alfred Freeborne, stable boy cum jockey from Hednesford Lodge stables, won his third race of the meeting. He partnered Mr Choyce's colt, Bedford, to victory in the first race on Thursday morning, the Tradesmen's Stakes.

The Consolation Stakes run over one mile had five runners contesting, including Lysimachus and the accident prone Silence. The first heat went to Lysimachus, ridden this time by another stable boy cum jockey from Hednesford, William Doley. Starting for the second heat saw the field cut to four runners at the off, John Fowler, a Steward at the meeting and owner of Silence couldn't believe his eyes just after the start, when he saw 'lightning strike twice' at his unfortunate steed.

1840 - 1859

A mounted marshall, attempting to clear the course of over enthusiastic spectators collided with Silence, knocking down the filly, and the young lad riding her. The filly and rider were hurt in the fall, the rider particularly so, to the extent he had to be carried from the course. With Lysimachus unaware of the incident going on behind her continued on her way and won the heat and race by a length from J. R. Scott's Pansey.

Concluding the eventful meeting for this year saw the return of the Cavalry Stakes. One of the conditions of entry being that all horses must have completed at least four days permanent duty with the Q.O.R.Y.C. (presumably the Queen's Own Royal Yeomanry Company), and to be ridden by members of the troop. Again, five runners went to post with one horse, Red Rover, owned and ridden by Mr S. Slater winning both heats comfortably. The horse that came last in both heats was appropriately named, Useless!

The official results of the meeting were:

Wednesday 24th September 1851

THE INNKEEPERS' STAKES of 3 sovereigns each,
with 20 added. Heats, twice round.

Mr Choyce's ch. c.	**Bedford** *(Alfred Freeborne)*	1	1
Mr Owen's b. c.	**Conscript**	3	2
Mr Sharratt's br. m.	**Egret**	2	dr

THE MEMBERS' STAKES of 3 sovereigns each,
with 25 added by the Hon. E. R. Littleton, M.P. for the Borough.
Heats, once round.

Mr Taft's ch. f.	**by Don John** *(Alfred Freeborne)*	1	1
Mr Fowler's b. f.	**Silence**	2	dr
Mr Hawkins' b. f.	**The Nun**	fell	-
Mr Evans' ch. f.	**Palace Royal**	0	dr
Mr Sharratt's br. f.	**Helen**	0	dr

A HURDLE RACE of 3 sovereigns each, with 20 added.
Heats, once round.

Mr Davis' ch. g.	**Lysimachus** (h.b.) *(Mr Walker)*	1	1
Mr Lines' b. g.	**The Baron**	2	2
Mr Roberts' br. m.	**Pay Your Debts**	3	3

Thursday 25th September 1851

THE TRADESMEN'S STAKES of 3 sovereigns each,
with 20 added. Heats, once round.

Mr Choyce's ch. c.	**Bedford** *(Alfred Freeborne)*	2	1	1
Mr Johnson's	**Lady Jersey**	1	2	2
Mr C. Hall's	**The Bird of Paradise**	3	3	dr

THE CONSOLATION STAKES of 2 sovereigns each, with 15 added.
Heats, once round, starting at the distance chair.

Mr Davis' ch. g.	**Lysimachus** (h.b.) *(W. Doley)*	1	1
Mr J. R. Scott's b. f.	**Pansey**	3	2
Mr Fowler's b. f.	**Silence**	2	fell
Mr Houghton's br. f.	**Old Charlotte Hyde**	4	0
Mr Wales' ch. f.	**by Birdcatcher**	5	dr

A CAVALRY SWEEPSTAKES of 1 sovereigns each, with 8 added.
For horses that have done permanent duty or more in 1851 in the
Q. O. R. Y. C., to be ridden by members of the Troop. Heats, once round.

Mr Slater's	**Red Rover** *(Mr S. Slater)*	1	1
Mr Hands'	**Jenny Lind**	2	2
Mr Holder names	**Nancy**	4	3
Mr Trussler's	**Major**	3	4
Mr Hayes'	**Useless**	5	5

Stewards: John Fowler and John Wiggan.
Clerk of the Races: John Newman.

1852

Walsall Races in 1852 reverted to being run on Monday 20th and Tuesday 21st September, as they were in 1850. The new Race Committee was hoping there was no repetition of last year's unfortunate incidents on the course, incidents that were out of their control admittedly, but nevertheless reflected on their management of the proceedings.

The Staffordshire Advertiser reporting on the running, stated, that in their opinion, *'the races were below par, and anticipated a much greater amount of sport.'* They were of course correct in their observations; the runners indeed did appear to be a pretty poor lot.

The prospects were not looking good, even the weather did much to dampen the spirits of all but the most ardent supporter of the turf, with rain falling for most of the day. The tents and booths that had been erected by the victuallers and other tradesmen did brisk business as the race goers attempted to keep out the effects of the cold and rain.

The opening race, the Innkeeper's Stakes, was won by the horse that caused so much trouble last year, the filly by Don John, who won the event without a repeat of last year's turmoil.

The hurdle race was deleted from the programme and replaced with a new event, the Ladies Purse, which was cancelled as no horses entered for it.

The remaining three races on this wet Monday in late September attracted just nine runners, and amounted to some pretty unspectacular racing. Two of three races consisted of heats, but whoever won the first, took the race as the other owners gave up and withdrew their charges, allowing a walk over to complete the proceedings in an unsatisfactory manner.

This obvious waving of the white flag by the owners did not go un-noticed by the spectators either, even if they were in the beer tents. Many members of the public voiced their opinions loudly that the races had been 'arranged.' The new Race Committee suddenly found that organising and running a race meeting was not as easy as had first appeared.

Tuesday was another day - it could get better, and certainly the weather did, remaining fine, although cold throughout the day.

The Tradesmen's Stakes began the days racing and this time it was the judge that managed to foul things up. Just three runners arrived at the post for the start, all three of them participants in yesterdays events. The first heat was won

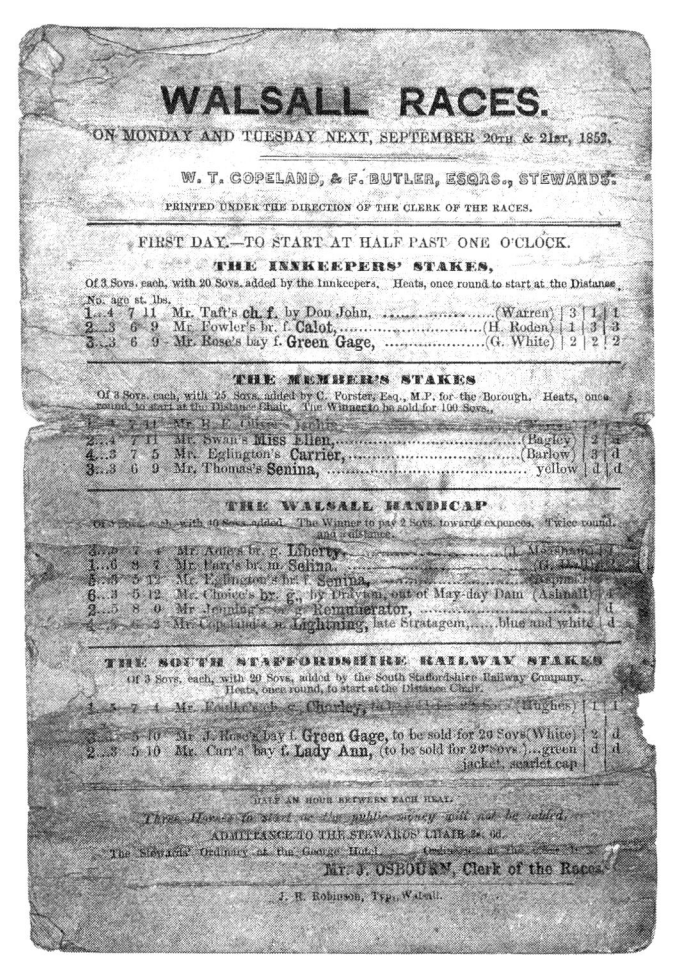

1840 – 1859

Both sides of a well-used race card from the meeting in 1852.

by Mr Swan's horse, Miss Helen from Mr Thomas' Senina second and John Adie's Liberty third. Liberty was withdrawn from the second heat, leaving Miss Helen and Senina to fight it out, the result proving to be in favour of the latter. In the third heat both horses contested the race with great spirit, with little difference between them as they approached the winning post. As they flashed past, the judge initially declared a dead-heat and then changed his mind, giving the verdict in favour of Miss Helen. After the previous day's accusations of the races being 'arranged,' this was not the way to appease the crowd. Not unsurprisingly, the spectators began to shout loudly again in the direction of the judge and the other officials in the grandstand.

Fortunately for the Race Committee, the next race on the card was run without incident and won rather easily in two heats by Mr J. Rose's Green Gage. The horse was later sold for £25 to comply with the race entry conditions.

To conclude the proceedings was the Yeomanry Cavalry Handicap for gentleman riders. Four horses were declared to run but only three went to the post. Mr Slater's Red Rover, winner of the same event last year had failed to arrive at the course. Victory in the first heat went to Mr Bayley's mare, Lady Bird, ridden by her owner, with Jenny Lind second and Stockwell third. As the horses were preparing for the second heat, Red Rover and his owner arrived and were allowed to take part. As the four runners neared the turn at Bradford Street, Mr Bayley allowed his mount to drift to far to the left, crossing another horse before running out of the course altogether. In his panic, the horse broke down a hurdle before diving into the brook, taking several spectators with him. Everyone involved in the unfortunate melee got away with a drenching and no injuries were sustained by any of the parties involved. The winner of the heat was Jenny Lind, Red Rover second and Stockwell third again.

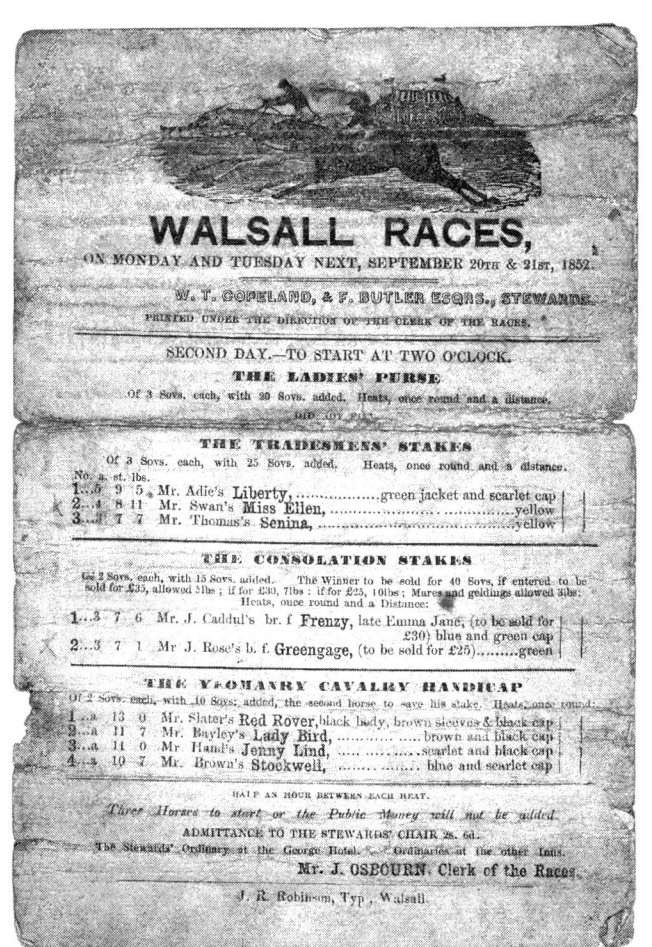

With many spectators' passions already high from previous dubious decisions, and fuelled by large amounts of alcohol, the last thing that was required was another controversial ruling from the Race Committee; unfortunately that is exactly what they got.

By the time Lady Bird, her rider and the other unfortunates had recovered from their aquatic expedition, the second heat was over, making the horse 'distanced.' The Rules of Racing at the time clearly state that any horse 'distanced' (at least two hundred and forty yards behind) is to take no further part in any future heats. Imagine the crowd's derision when Lady Bird was allowed to line up with the other starters for the third and final heat, even though she had obviously been distanced. The only explanation for this decision is that the other owners allowed Lady Bird to participate, but in the eyes of the crowd, this was cheating, which indeed it was. Finally, to really rub salt into the already large open wound, Lady Bird won the heat and consequently, the race. Uproar broke out on the Long Meadow amongst the spectators because of this bad decision. Fortunately the county police were already

1840 - 1859

on hand under the supervision of Inspector Price whose men quickly extinguished the ugly situation and prevented further trouble, on the racecourse at least.

For many years previously, both the Race Committee and the appointed Stewards had taken their positions very seriously, making sure the meeting complied with the Rules of Racing, the new Race Committee clearly had a lot to learn, and quickly.

The faces of any members of the old committee who were watching the events of the last two years must have been a picture. One immediately thinks of cats, complete with grins and from Cheshire!

The official results of the meeting were:

Monday 20th September 1852

THE INNKEEPERS' STAKES of 3 sovereigns each, with 20 added by the Innkeepers of Walsall. Heats, twice round.

Mr Taft's ch. f.	by Don John, 4 y-o, 7st. 11lb.			
	(Warren)	3	1	1
Mr Roses's b. f.	Green Gage, 3 y-o, 6st. 9lb.	2	2	2
Mr Fowler's br. f.	Calot, 3 y-o, 6st. 9lb.	1	3	3

THE WALSALL HANDICAP of 5 sovereigns each, with 40 added.

Mr J. Adie's br. g.	Liberty, 5 y-o, 7st. 4lb.	
	(J. Measham)	1
Mr Parr's br. m.	Selina, 6 y-o, 8st. 7lb.	2
Mr Eglington's	Senina, 3 y-o, 5st. 12lb.	3
Mr Choyce's br. g.	by Drayton, 3 y-o, 5st. 12lb.	4

THE MEMBERS' STAKES of 3 sovereigns each, with 25 added by C. Forster, M.P. for the Borough. Heats, once round. Winner to be sold for 100 sovs.

Mr R. E. Oliver's	Ischia, 4 y-o, 7st. 11lb.		
	(Warren)	1	1
Mr Swan's	Miss Helen, 4 y-o, 7st. 11lb.	2	dr
Mr Eglington's	Carrier, 3 y-o, 7st. 5lb.	3	dr

THE SOUTH STAFFORDSHIRE RAILWAY STAKES of 3 sovereigns each, with 20 added by the South Staffordshire Railway Company.

Mr Foulkes' ch. g.	Charley, 5 y-o, 7st. 4lb.		
	(David Hughes)	1	1
Mr J. Roses' b. f.	Green Gage, 3 y-o, 5st. 10lb.	2	dr

Tuesday 21st September 1852

THE TRADESMEN'S STAKES of 3 sovereigns each, with 25 added. Heats, once round.

Mr Swan's	Miss Helen, 4 y-o, 8st. 11lb.			
	(Bagley)	1	2	1
Mr Thomas'	Senina, 3 y-o, 7st. 7lb.	2	1	2
Mr J. Adie's	Liberty, 5 y-o, 9st. 5lb.	3	dr	-

THE CONSOLATION STAKES of 2 sovereigns each, with 15 added. Heats, once round, starting at the distance chair.

Mr J. Roses' b. f.	Green Gage, 3 y-o, 7st. 1lb.		
	(Harris)	1	1
Mr J. Caddul's br. f.	Frenzy, 3 y-o, 7st. 6lb.	2	2
Mr J. Adie's br. m.	Pay Your Debt's, aged, 9st.	3	dr

THE YEOMAN CAVALRY HANDICAP of 2 sovereigns each, with 10 added.

Mr Bayley's	Lady Bird, aged, 11st. 7lb.			
	(Owner)	1	4	1
Mr Hands'	Jenny Lind, aged, 11st.	2	1	2
Mr Slater's	Red Rover, aged, 13st.	4	2	3
Mr Brown's	Stockwell, aged, 10st. 7lb.	3	3	4

1853

Events of the last two years proves that Walsall Races was under the cosh from every angle. Already the residents of Bradford Street were making noises in the direction of anyone within earshot about the drunkenness, rowdyism and general bad behaviour that occurred during Race Week. Walsall was no longer the semi-rural town it was at the turn of the century, holding its quaint and fashionable little race meeting for the amusement of its citizens. Industry had taken over, and brought thousands of people into to the area to satisfy its thirst for manpower. It was a hard life for these men and their families, working and living in appalling conditions, the only escapism coming from the contents of a glass or tankard. With almost a year to think about it, the Race Committee had to get their act together if they wanted to win back the respect of the people and end the rumours of arranged races. One of the first moves they made in that direction was to appoint a new judge, one experienced in racing who knew the business well. The man hired for the job was the now retired jockey, George Calloway, a very experienced race rider and well-respected man, who was well known in the area. John Osbourne was appointed Clerk of the Course in place of local man, John Newman who had held the position for almost thirty years. The Steward picked to begin this new regime was Captain J. R. Scott.

During the course of researching this project, it came as a great surprise to discover that a second grandstand existed on the Long Meadow, and its building came about in this year, 1853. The building was described as a temporary structure, presumably of wood, and the idea behind this innovation was to create more revenue to support future events, which is exactly what it did. Another reason for its construction was, that it was much nearer to the winning post and gave a wider view of the racecourse than the permanent structure erected in 1809. As far as is known, there are no illustrations of any description in existence to show what it looked like, or exactly where it was situated. The building was described as being two tiered, with the upper tier for the viewing public, and the ground floor being used as a refreshment room.

The members of the new Race Committee may have had a baptism of fire in their first two years of existence, but this year, no one could criticise them for lack of effort. It was now down to the owners, trainers and jockeys.

Since the cancellation of the meeting in 1849, the days on which the meeting had been held had alternated between Monday and Tuesday and the more usual, Wednesday and Thursday. This year they reverted to the latter, the 28th and 29th September. Eight races were on the programme, four on each day. Initial signs were good, regarding entries and

1840 – 1859

although there were no world-beaters amongst them, they did appear to be a grade up from the previous years motley crew.

The Member's Stakes, run over one mile took some winning, with four heats being required, and some hard racing. After three heats had been run, it was stalemate with three different winners, Game Chicken, Athena Pallas and Gaffer Green. The deciding fourth heat was a match between Mr Samuel's, Gaffer Green and Robert Denman's Athena Pallas, as the other two owners withdrew their horses. Denman, the Hednesford based jockey was having his first runner at Walsall as a trainer with the horse, and must have thought he was in with a chance as Athena Pallas was carrying twelve pounds less in weight. The pace was slow, and the two kept together all the way round the course. Athena Pallas held a slight advantage until the distance pole, when the jockey of Gaffer Green pushed his mount on to win by half a length.

The Bradford Handicap, a two-mile, dash race, saw six runners line-up for starting. Two of the runners were half-bred horses, and one of them, Titterstone, had a reputation for beating his better bred rivals. Prior to the horses going out for the start, Mr Davis, owner of Titterstone, had refused an offer of £600 for his horse from an admirer who knew good horseflesh when he saw it. The horse was favourite to win the race, a task he would more than likely of accomplished had he not fallen in the early stages. When the stricken horse attempted to right itself, it trod on the chest of his jockey Bob Sly, inflicting some serious damage to the poor fellow's ribs.

With the main threat out of the way, Mr Roses' Sugar Candy won by a length, with Mr Owen's Timotheus, taking second place.

The second race on Thursday proved to be a non-event when one of last year's runners, Senina, reared up and refused to race. The horse had changed hands the previous year and was now under the care of the experienced Hednesford trainer, Samuel Lord, but not even his extensive knowledge could get the ill tempered beast to run. A compromise was reached when the other two owners decided not to race, and split the stake money equally between themselves.

Five runners started for the two mile Hatherton Handicap, including yesterday's faller Titterstone, ridden by his owner, Mr Davis, deputising for his injured jockey, Bob Sly. With three joint favourites, Titterstone, Sugar Candy, winner of yesterday's handicap, and Morning Star, the betting ring were taking their customary few chances. All five runners kept well together until the final turn for home when Titterstone, Sugar Candy and Liberty pulled away. At the line it was Sugar Candy that was declared the winner by half a length from Liberty, with Titterstone third.

Prior to the start of the final race of the meeting, the Consolation Stakes, the heavens opened and it continued to pour down throughout the running of the race. Kempson Walker of Wolverhampton, owner of the horse Eliza Hammond, saw his mare become the second victim of a fall at the meeting. The accident was attributed to the heavy rain that caused the mare to slip when leading the field, the unknown jockey escaping with a black eye. The winner of the heat was E. Taylor's Lady in Waiting, with the hard working Morning Star, second. The second and third heats saw a reversal in the places, when Luck's All, fourth in the first heat, came home an easy winner, beating Lady in Waiting both times. Luck's All was the first winner at Walsall for the Hednesford trainer, John Adie. The horse would not win for him again as he was sold to Mr Blood from Birmingham for £60 after some spirited bidding from other members of the racing fraternity.

As this meeting came to a close, there must have been a big sigh of relief from members of the Race Committee that there was no repetition of the previous years unsavoury behavour and their efforts to resurrect the meeting had succeeded, for this year anyway.

The official results of the meeting were:

Wednesday 28th September 1853

THE INNKEEPERS' STAKES of 3 sovereigns each, with 20 added by the Innkeepers of Walsall. Heats, twice round.

Mr Davis' b. g.	**Gay Lad**, 9st. *(R. Sly junior)*	1	1
Mr Wiggan's ch. g.	**Forester**, 9st.	3	2
Mr Shepherdson's	**Maid of Golborne**, 6st. 12lb.	2	dr

THE MEMBERS' STAKES of 3 sovereigns each, with 25 added by C. Forster, M.P. for the Borough. Heats, once round. Winner to be sold for 100 sovs.

Mr Samuel's ch. g.	**Gaffer Green**, 8st. 11lb. *(Giles)*	3	4	1	1
Mr Denman's	**Athena Pallas**, 7st. 13lb.	4	1	2	2
Mr Taylor's	**Game Chicken**, 7st. 1lb.	1	2	4	dr
Mr Lord's br. m.	**Senina**, 7st. 13lb.	2	3	3	dr

THE BRADFORD HANDICAP of 5 sovereigns each, with 50 added.

Mr Roses' br. g.	**Sugar Candy**, 7st. 6lb. *(Sharpe)*	1
Mr Owen's b. g.	**Timotheus**, 7st. 2lb.	2
Mr Merry's b. f.	**Mary Ann**, 8st. 10lb.	3
Mr Shepherdson's ch. f.	**by Ithuriel**, 7st. 13lb.	4
Mr Letsom's b. g.	**The Miner** (h b), 7st. 10lb.	5
Mr Davis' ch. g.	**Titterstone** (h b), 9st. 7lb.	fell

THE SADDLERS STAKES of 3 sovereigns each, with 20 added by the Saddlers of Walsall.

Mr Foulkes' ch. g.	**Charley**, 7st. 11lb. *(William Sharpe)*	1
Mr J. Adie's ch. g.	**Luck's All**, 7st. 11lb.	2
Mr Denman's	**Athena Pallas**, 7st. 13lb.	3

Thursday 29th September 1853

THE LADIES PURSE of 3 sovereigns each, with 20 added.

Mr Davis' b. g.	**Gay Lad**	1	1
Mr Taylor's	**Game Chicken**	3	2
Mr Brown's f.	**by Hornsea**	2	3

THE TRADESMEN'S STAKES of 3 sovereigns each, with 25 added. Heats, once round, starting at the distance chair.

Mr Davis' ch. g.	**Titterstone** (h b)	-
Mr Shepherdson's	**Maid of Golborne**	-
Mr Lord's	**Senina**	-

Senina refused to race and the stakes were divided between the other two.

1840 – 1859

THE HATHERTON HANDICAP of 3 sovereigns each, with 30 added.

Mr Roses's br. g.	Sugar Candy	1
Mr Shepherdson's	Liberty	2
Mr Davis' ch. g.	Titterstone (h b)	3
Mr Shepherdson's	by Ithuriel	4
Mr -	Morning Star	5

THE CONSOLATION STAKES of 2 sovereigns each, with 15 added.

Mr J. Adies's ch.g.	Luck's All	4	1	1
Mr G. Taylor's ch. f.	Lady in Waiting	1	2	2
Mr Foulkes' ch. g.	Charley	3	3	dr
Mr -	Morning Star	2	dr	-
Mr K. Walker's	Eliza Hammomnd	fell	-	-

1854

If the newspapers of the day are to be believed, it is astonishing how quickly the newly formed Race Committee has turned around the meeting from the near farce of two years ago. The report also makes a very obvious point of congratulating the Clerk of the Course, John Osbourne, the Judge, George Calloway and Clerk of the Scales, James Lynex for there excellent service and professional conduct in all matters.

Even the Stewards of the meeting for this year were a fair bit higher up the social ladder than in previous years, with Sir Edward Scott and the Earl of Uxbridge presiding. Sir Edward was there in person on the first day only, the Earl wasn't mentioned as being in attendance on either day!

The Staffordshire Advertiser reports that 30,000 spectators were present on the course for each days racing. If that figure is anywhere near correct, it does prove what an attraction horse racing, and all that accompanies it, was for the general public in the days when there was little other entertainment available on this scale.

The Stewards of today would certainly have had something to say about an incident in the first heat of the Innkeeper's Stakes. One of the horses, Mr Parkes' Syren, was knocked out of its stride by the eventual heat winner, Mr Shepppardson's un-named filly by Ithuriel at the last but one turn. There is no record of any objection being recorded so it must be assumed it was unintentional. In the second heat, Syren had a clear run, and won the heat, reversing the placing with the filly from the first heat. In the third heat the positions were reversed yet again, with the un-named filly getting home from Syren by half a neck.

The Bradford Handicap, of two miles, had a total of six runners, including two horses that ran at last years meeting, Mr Owen's, Timotheus and Mr G. Taylor's, Lady in Waiting. Also entered was a brown mare named Lancashire Lass, owned by Mr Handley. The horse came to Walsall with some pretty good form behind it, to the degree it was installed as favourite, even though it carried top weight. For the patient jockey with a good knowledge of pace, riding a waiting race was the way to win as many of the runners began a race at a ripping rate and come the end, had nothing left. The jockey of Timotheus, Walter White, was just such a patient fellow. He allowed the others to make the running and pounced as the winning post neared. Timotheus got home by a neck from Lancashire Lass with Lady in Waiting third, half a length separating the second and third.

The racing on Thursday, again consisted of four races, with the Railway Stakes opening the days sport. The race consisted of three heats of just over one mile each for the four runners, one of who had changed hands. Syren, second in Wednesday's opening race and the winner of the last race of the day, was sold after all his efforts to Mr Walker who was keen to try his new acquisition. Robert Denman was the jockey on Syren, both he and Walker must have been disappointed when the horse came in last of the four runners, beaten by Go Away. Miraculously, the interval between the heats worked its wonder, and Syren reversed the form with Go Away in the second heat. The final heat saw Syren triumph, but only just. She won by a neck from Lady in Waiting who was living up to her name and still waiting to win after three attempts at Walsall.

The two-mile Hatherton Handicap was won by Lancashire Lass, this time justifying her favouritism and winning the race in a canter from two rivals, after making every inch of the running.

Half an hour or so later, Lancashire Lass was out again for the two mile Tradesman's Plate, meeting her conqueror of the previous day, Timotheus. Mr Handley's mare must have been a very fit animal, as she trotted up to win as she pleased from two previous winners at the meeting. Timotheus was second and Mr Sheppardson's un-named filly by Ithuriel third, his other runner, Maid of Golborne was fourth and last of the quartet.

Closing the meeting for 1854 was the Consolation Stakes, run over a mile and a distance, and three heats. Lady in Waiting was still waiting at the end of the contest. She finished third this time to Mr Blood's, Grief who won two of the heats, winning the final one by five lengths. Second place went to Bulls' Eye with local owner, Mr Sharratt's gelding, Cream of the Valley in last place.

It is no wonder the Race Committee were pleased with the job George Calloway the judge was doing, he must have had eyes like a hawk to give some very close verdicts without hesitation, and in consequence, caused no controversies that led to wild accusations flying in every direction.

The official results of the meeting were:

Wednesday 27th September 1854

THE INNKEEPERS' STAKES of 3 sovereigns each, with 20 added by the Innkeepers of Walsall. Heats, once round.

Mr Shepherdson's	by Ithuriel, 8st. 4lb. *(T. Ashmall)*	1	2	1
Mr Parkes' br. m.	Syren, 8st. 2lb.	3	1	2
Mr J. F. Langley's	Katinka, 7st.	2	3	dr

THE MEMBERS' STAKES of 3 sovereigns each, with 25 added by C. Forster, M.P. for the Borough. Heats, once round. Winner to be sold for 100 sovs.

Mr J. Roses' ch. g.	Go Away, 6st. 7lb. *(John Walters)*	1	1
Mr Shepherdson's	Maid of Golborne, 8st. 4lb.	2	3
Mr T. Flintoff's b. f.	Wire, 6st. 7lb.	3	2

1840 – 1859

THE BRADFORD HANDICAP of 5 sovereigns each, with 50 added.

Mr Owen's b. g.	**Timotheus,** 7st. 4lb. *(W. White)*	1
Mr Handley's br. m.	**Lancashire Lass,** 8st. 13lb.	2
Mr G. Taylor's ch. f.	**Lady in Waiting,** 7st. 9lb.	3
Mr -	**Bright Phoebus**	4
Mr -	**Clio**	5
Mr -	**Bulls' Eye**	6

THE SADDLERS STAKES of 3 sovereigns each, with 20 added by the Saddlers of Walsall. One and half miles.

Mr Parkes' br. m.	**Syren,** 6st. 13lb. *(Thomas Cliff)*	1
Mr Blood's b. h.	**Grief,** 7st. 11lb.	2
Mr Rickard's b. m.	**Little Gipsy,** 7st. 6lb.	3
Mr Shepherdson's	**Liberty,** 7st. 11lb.	4

Thursday 28th September 1854

THE RAILWAY PLATE of 3 sovereigns each, with 20 added by the Lessees of the South Staffordshire Railway. Heats, once round and a distance.

Mr K. Walker's br. m.	**Syren,** 8st. 4lb. *(Robert Denman)*	4	1	1
Mr G. Taylor's ch. f.	**Lady in Waiting,** 8st. 9lb.	3	2	2
Mr J. Roses' ch. g.	**Go Away,** 6st. 12lb.	1	4	3
Mr J. Langley's b. f.	**Katinka,** 7st.	2	3	dr

THE HATHERTON HANDICAP of 3 sovereigns each, with 30 added. Two miles

Mr Handley's br. m.	**Lancashire Lass,** 8st. 12lb. *(Thorpe)*	1
Mr Shepherdson's	**by Ithuriel,** 8st. 1lb.	2
Mr K. Walker's br. h.	**Bulls' Eye,** 8st. 1lb.	3

THE TRADESMEN'S STAKES of 3 sovereigns each, with 25 added. Two miles.

Mr Handley's br. m.	**Lancashire Lass** *(Thorpe)*	1
Mr Owen's b. h.	**Timotheus** (hb)	2
Mr Shepherdson's c. f.	**by Ithuriel**	3
Mr Shepherdson's c.f.	**Maid of Golborne**	4

THE CONSOLATION STAKES of 2 sovereigns each, with 15 added. Heats, once round and a distance.

Mr Blood's b. h.	**Grief** *(John Walters)*	1	2	1
Mr Blakeway's br. h.	**Bulls' Eye**	4	1	2
Mr G. Taylor's ch. f.	**Lady in Waiting**	2	3	3
Mr Sharratt's br. g.	**Cream of the Valley**	3	4	4

1855

The meeting began on Wednesday 26th, continuing on Thursday 27th September with four races on each day. Thursday's sport was marred however by two walkovers.

To the intended racegoers of Walsall, it must have looked good to see the names of the Marquis of Anglesey and the Earl of Chesterfield at the top of the race card as Stewards. Unfortunately, that's all they were, names, neither of them attended!

There may have been few noblemen by birth at the meeting, but there was a real aristocrat of the turf riding at Walsall in this year, George Fordham. This year was also the

George Fordham, the best jockey ever to ride at Walsall. One of the 70 winners he rode in his first year as champion jockey in 1855 was at Walsall on Mr Leech's Cockspur. Fordham was champion thirteen times outright and joint champion with Charles Maidment in 1871.

first time Fordham became champion jockey, riding seventy winners. During his career he was champion fourteen times, including nine successive championships. Known as 'The Demon', Fordham became a genius in the saddle and unfortunately the people of Walsall never saw him at the peak of his career, as at the time he was just eighteen years of age, and still learning. His ability at this tender age was considerably greater than some of the other jockeys riding at Walsall, for all their experience and seniority.

Fordham's one and only winner at Walsall came in the final race on Wednesday afternoon, the Saddler's Stakes over one and a quarter miles, on Mr Leech's bay colt, Cockspur. Cockspur, the 4/6 on favourite beat his three other rivals easily in the second and third heats but in the first he could only come third. Like all jockeys, Fordham had to watch his weight, although this was never a major problem for him, being naturally small, which was just as well in this race, as Cockspur carried only 5 stones 13 pounds. The horse that won the first heat, William Saunders' filly, The Despised, was also carrying a light weight, 5 stone 10 pounds. As the horses were coming out onto the course for the first heat, The Despised bolted, eventually falling and throwing his jockey,

1840 – 1859

Prior, as well as injuring two of the bystanders. Neither filly nor jockey was any the worse for their fall as they went on to win from the 3/1 chance, Katinka.

Earlier in the day, two previous winners at last years meeting, Go Away and Timotheus appeared again to win their respective races. Go Away won the opening race of the meeting, the Bradford Handicap, by three lengths, and Timotheus, the one and a quarter mile Handicap race by a length and a half. Timotheus also appeared the following day to perform a walkover for the Tradesmen's Plate.

Another dual winner, in the proper sense this time, was Mr Andrew's, Little Davie, who won two heats of the three heats in the Innkeeper's Stakes with ease from his three rivals. On Thursday, he repeated the process with similar ease in the first race of the day, the Railway Stakes.

The final race at the meeting was the customary, in recent years anyway, Consolation Stakes, won by Cockspur, this time ridden by Prior, as George Fordham had seen Walsall – and left. Defeated in the first heat Cockspur came back in the second to win by a length and a half. Even in those days there were still jokers about, for the second time in a few years, another proud owner with a horse in the race named his mare Useless – one wonders why?

At the end of the race, Cockspur, was sold to Kempson Walker of Wolverhampton for 100 guineas, a bid of 75 guineas was made by a Mr Sparrow who was obviously a bad loser, he cried out that the sale was not bona fide and, as *The Staffordshire Advertiser* eloquently put it, *'some rather warm altercation ensued.'* There is no report of the constables being called so it must be assumed that the argument was settled in a gentlemanly manner.

The official results of the meeting were:

Wednesday 26th September 1855

THE BRADFORD HANDICAP of 10 sovereigns each, with 50 added. Two miles

Mr Walter's ch. g.	**Go Away,** 4 y-o, 7st. 12lb. *(A. Cowley)*	1
Mr Andrews' b. h.	**Little Davie,** 6 y-o, 8st. 12lb	2
Mr Batlow's b. c.	**Rocket,** 3 y-o, 6st. 12lb.	3

THE INNKEEPERS' STAKES of 3 sovereigns each, with 20 added by the Innkeepers of Walsall. Heats, once round.

Mr Andrews' b. h.	**Little Davie,** 6 y-o, 9st. 7lb. *(John Quinton)*	1	1
Mr Scaife's ch. m.	**Harriet,** 6 y-o, 9st. 4lb.	4	2
Mr J. Langley's br. m.	**Duet,** 3 y-o, 6st. 9lb.	2	dr
Mr J. Smith's br. c.	**Venture** (hb), 3 y-o, 6st. 12lb.	3	-

4/6 favourite, Little Davy.

A HANDICAP of 5 sovereigns each, with 25 added by C. Forster, M.P. for the Borough. One and a quarter miles.

Mr Owen's b. g.	**Timotheus** (hb), aged, 6st. 9lb. *(Walter White)*	1
Mr Moseley's b. g.	**Romeo,** 5 y-o, 7st. 8lb.	2
Mr Rogers' ch. m.	**Alma,** 6 y-o, 6st. 6lb.	3

4/7 favourite, Timotheus, 2/1 Romeo, 6/1 Alma.

THE SADDLERS STAKES of 3 sovereigns each, with 20 added by the Saddlers of Walsall. One and quarter miles.

Mr Leech's b. c.	**Cockspur,** 3 y-o, 5st. 13lb. *(George Fordham)*	3	1	1
Mr E. Preston's b. m.	**Katinka,** 4 y-o, 7st. 6lb.	2	2	dr
Mr Saunders' ch. f.	**The Despised,** 3 y-o, 5st. 10lb.	1	3	3
Mr Scaife's ch. m.	**Harriet,** 6 y-o, 7st. 11lb.	4	4	2

4/6 favourite, Cockspur, 3/1 Katinka.

Thursday 27th September 1855

THE RAILWAY STAKES of 3 sovereigns each, with 20 added by the Lessees of the South Staffordshire Railway. Heats, one mile.

Mr Andrews'	**Little Davie,** 6 y-o, 8st. 12lb. *(John Quinton)*	1	1
Mr J. Smith's br. c.	**Venture** (hb), 3 y-o, 6st. 12lb.	4	2
Mr Leech's b. c.	**Cockspur,** 3 y-o, 6st. 12lb.	2	dr
Mr Green's b. m.	**Tamyria,** 4 y-o, 7st. 11lb.	3	dr

THE HATHERTON HANDICAP of 7 sovereigns each, with 30 added. Two miles

Capt. Christie's ch. g.	**Little Tom,** 5 y-o, 7st. 10lb. *(W. Sharpe)*	1
Mr Batlowe's br. c.	**Rocket,** 3 y-o, 6st. 7lb.	2
Mr Robinson's br. h.	**Grief,** aged 6st. 9lb.	3

A HANDICAP of 5 sovereigns each, with 25 added by the Tradesmen's of Walsall. One and a quarter miles

Mr Owen's b. h.	**Timotheus** (h b)	walked over

THE CONSOLATION STAKES of 2 sovereigns each, with 15 added. Heats, one mile.

Mr Phillips' b. c.	**Cockspur,** 3 y-o, 7st. 6lb. *(Christopher Prior)*	3	1	wo
Mr Rogers' ch. m.	**Alma,** 6 y-o, 9st. 4lb.	1	3	dr
Mr Samwell's ch. m.	**Useless,** 3 y-o, 7st. 6lb.	2	2	dr
Mr Scaife's ch. m.	**Harriet,** 6 y-o, 10st.	4	dr	-

1856

The meeting began on Wednesday 24th September with four races, another five events due to be run on Thursday. Of the nine races, only two of them were run in heats, the remainder being single heat races. Many of the horses involved, particularly on the first day, had been running at Wolverhampton a couple of weeks previously, The Staffordshire Advertiser describing them as 'the nags that figured at Wolverhampton,' not the most charitable description of the horseflesh on parade.

As well as the large number of local inhabitants present on the racecourse, the South Staffordshire Railway brought many thousands of people to Walsall for the races. To cater for the large influx of people, the course itself was littered with refreshment stands of all kinds, which, The Staffordshire Advertiser remarks, 'they all appeared to receive extensive patronage.'

Just four runners contested the opening race, the Innkeepers Stakes. Three of the runners had names that

1840 - 1859

made them sound more like domestic pets than working racehorses, Cossey, Mary Ann and Blossom. The winner wasn't exempt from an unusual name either, that of Elastic. His owner, John Osborne was the famous Yorkshire trainer who arrived at Walsall with two horses. The long journey was worth it, he won three of the four races he entered.

The first attempt at getting the horses away resulted in a false start when two of them went prematurely. At the second time of asking, all four started with the 4/5 favourite Elastic taking the early lead and maintaining his advantage right to the line, winning by a neck from Thomas Flintoff's Blossom. The second favourite, at 2/1, Mary Ann, finished third with Cossey a bad fourth.

In two of the races, the Bradford Handicap and the mile and a quarter Handicap, a horse appeared that was pretty well known to the students of the turf at Walsall, Mr Owen's Timotheus. Previous years had given his owner some success, but age was now catching up with the old fellow and he could only finish a bad third in the Bradford Handicap. It appears Mr Owen had more optimism than common sense, after seeing the horse well beaten in his first race over two miles, less than an hour later Timotheus was asked to do it all again over the shorter distance with the same inevitable sad consequences.

In the final race of the day, the Saddler's Stakes, there was an objection lodged before the horses had even started. The race was run over one and a quarter miles, with added money of twenty sovereigns from the saddlers of Walsall. Only two horses were declared to run and the rules stated that unless a minimum of three went to post, the added money would not be given. The two jockeys weighed out and went to their respective mounts, Mr Joseph's Salmon and Mr Lane's Usurer. It was at this point the saddler's of the town decided to withdraw the twenty sovereigns, a decision that didn't go down too well with the parties concerned. After a lengthy discussion and a delay to the start, another storm in a teacup was resolved; the rule was ignored! This was one of the two races run in heats, with Salmon coming out the winner, in the first heat by a neck and winning as he pleased in the second.

The wonderfully named Neptune Henry Stagg, a Nottinghamshire lad based at one of the Hednesford training stables, rode the winner. Stagg competed in steeplechases as well as riding on the flat and rode in the Grand National and The Derby, unfortunately without success in either race.

Wednesday's events had been well attended, as usual, but Thursday, due to the heavy rain falling and also the day clashing with the Birmingham Fair, the attendances were well down in comparison.

In the second race of the day, a new event for two year-olds, the Committee Stakes over five furlongs, caused further controversy. Four runners contested the event, with the good young colt Master Bagot, owned by Mr Shutt, leading from start to finish to win by six lengths, a good margin for horses running at Walsall. An objection was immediately raised against the winner on the grounds of the wrong description of his pedigree, no one on the course would give a decision one way or the other, and the matter was passed to the Stewards of the meeting at Derby. The outcome of this blatant passing of the book is unknown.

Mr Osborne added two more winners to his list at the meeting when Elastic won the Hatherton Handicap and his other runner, Miss Tiff, won the Tradesmen's Handicap. In the former race, Elastic played nip and tuck with the even money favourite, Whalebone, on both circuits of the two-mile event before going ahead shortly before the line to win by a length. The Tradesmen's Handicap had the largest number of runners at Walsall for many years, if not the largest, with nine declared. It proved to be an excellent race, when the horses eventually began after a false start, with the runners all grouped together until the hill when three pulled away, Miss Tiff, St. Dunstan and Indian Queen. The three continued to stamp their authority on the race, increasing their lead and leaving the remainder of the field in their wake. On the straight run in, the three gave the crowd something to cheer about as there was nothing in it as they approached the post, the judge, George Calloway, must have had to call on all of his experience to get this one correct. The winner was declared as Miss Tiff by a short neck, a measure not used today, with St. Dunstan second and Indian Queen third.

The final race of the meeting, the Consolation Stakes for beaten horses, run in heats of one mile. The race was contested by another batch of homely named sorts, Dwarf, Betsy B, Cossey and Mabel, with Wednesday's well-beaten runner, Usurer, making up the numbers. Several false starts dogged this race too, when the runners finally did get away, Dwarf made the pace but in the latter stages, Usurer and Betsy B challenged. Dwarf found his second wind and fought back, beating off Betsy B but just failing to catch Usurer who won by a half a length. Whether Usurer was injured or the race just took too much out of him is not known, but he was withdrawn from the race, leaving Betsy B to win the second heat. At this point the race was in effect over when the owners of the remaining horses withdrew them from the final heat. With no opposition, this left Betsy B to walk over and take the prize money for her owner, Thomas Carr.

The official results of the meeting were:

Wednesday 24th September 1856

THE INNKEEPERS' STAKES of 3 sovereigns each, with 20 added by the Innkeepers of Walsall.

Mr Osborne's	**Elastic**	(William Bearpark)	1
Mr Flintoff's b. h.	**Blossom**	(Thomas Cliff jnr.)	2
Mr Knott's b. f.	**Mary Ann**	(J. Frost, snr)	3
Mr Morris'	**Cossey**	-	4

Elastic 5/4 fav., 2/1 against Mary Ann.

THE BRADFORD HANDICAP of 5 sovereigns each, with 50 added. Two miles

Mr Walter's	**Indian Queen**	(J. Walters)	1
Maj. Bringhurst's	**Fulbeck**	(Henry Hammond)	2
Mr Owen's	**Timotheus**	(J. Frost, snr)	3
Mr Stevens's	**Ethelbald**	(Christopher Prior)	4
Mr T. Carr's	**Betsy B**	(T. Challoner)	5

5/4 on the field.

1840 - 1859

A HANDICAP of 5 sovereigns each, with 25 added by C. Forster, M.P. for the Borough. One and a quarter miles.

Mr J. Davis'	Gay Lad	(Christopher Prior)	1
Mr J. Wilkes names	St. Dunstan	(J. Frost, snr.)	2
Mr J. Osborne's	Miss Tiff	(T. Challoner)	3
Mr Owen's	Timotheus	(E. White)	4

3/1 fav. St. Dunstan, 4/1 Gay Lad, 5/1 Timotheus.

THE SADDLERS STAKES of 3 sovereigns each, with 20 added by the Saddlers of Walsall. One and quarter miles.

| Mr Joseph's | Salmon | (Neptune Stagg) | 1 | 1 |
| Mr Lane's | Usurer | (Thomas Cliff jnr) | 2 | 2 |

Thursday 25th September 1856

THE RAILWAY STAKES of 3 sovereigns each, with 20 added by the Lessees of the South Staffordshire Railway. Heats, one mile.

| Mr Joseph's | Salmon, 6/4 fav. | (J. Frost, jnr.) | 1 |
| Mr Morris' | Cossey | (E. Jones) | 2 |

THE COMMITTEE STAKES of 5 sovereigns each, with 20 added. Five furlongs

Mr Shutt's gr. c.	Master Bagot	(James Knott)	1
Mr Smith's b. g.	Jack in the Box	(Walter White)	2
Mr Flintoff's	Echo	(Thomas Cliff jnr.)	3
Mr Peters'	Gun Boat	-	4

THE HATHERTON HANDICAP of 5 sovereigns each, with 30 added. Two miles.

Mr Osborne's	Elastic	(William Bearpark)	1
Mr J. Lynex's	His Piper	(J. Frost, snr.)	2
Mr E. Vickers names	Whalebone	(Thomas Cliff jnr.)	3

Evens fav. Whalebone, 2/1 against Elastic.

A HANDICAP of 5 sovereigns each, with 25 added. One and a quarter miles.

Mr Osborne's	Miss Tiff	(T. Challoner)	1
Mr J. Wilkes names	St. Dunstan	(J. Frost, jnr.)	2
Mr Thomas'	Indian Queen	(John Walters)	3
Mr J. Davis'	Gay Lad	-	4
Mr Richards'	Miss Hatch	-	5

THE CONSOLATION STAKES of 2 sovereigns each, with 15 added. Heats, one mile.

Mr Lane's	Usurer	(Thomas Cliff)	1	dr	-
Mr Wilkes'	Dwarf	(J. Frost, jnr.)	2	dr	-
Mr T. Carr's	Betsy B	(J. Frost snr.)	3	1	wo
Mr Morris'	Cossey	(J. Holmes)	4	2	dr
Mr Wilcox's	Mabel	(E. Jones)	5	3	dr

1857

1856 saw the publication of Walsall's first newspaper, the *Walsall Free Press and General Advertiser*; by 1857 they had lost no time in voicing their opinions regarding Walsall Races, the Fair and Wake. Most reports were of a condemnatory nature mixed with humerous and sarcastic comments, the majority of which were mostly true. It is all well and good to look at the events on the Long Meadow approximately one hundred and fifty years later through rose tinted spectacles, but the reality, one fears, was probably very different. It was the intention of the Walsall Free Press to lift the cultural activities in the town to a new level as they tried to educate the working people. In conjunction with the Temperance Movement, which they were obviously biased towards, to reduce the amount of beer-sodden wretches of both sexes staggering about the town.

In late September every year, Walsall was a very idle town, but at the same time an extremely busy one. Because of the Races, Fair and Wake, work stopped, the town was indeed idle, but the innkeepers, tradesmen and vendors of every description were busy plying their trades to satisfy the needs of the thousands gathered.

The sideshows that accompanied both events were in the majority tacky affairs that would make Blackpool look sophisticated; the wild beast show for example consisted of four monkeys and a dog! The act, which took place on a broken down stage in a canvas tent on the racecourse, comprised of the proprietor and his assistant, the canine star of the show, Growler, and a ladder. What the monkeys got up to during the show is left to the readers imagination. The owner balanced a small twenty-rung ladder on his chin and Growler would climb up it, and down the other side. The dog must have had a touch of stage fright; he ascended the ladder without any trouble, but couldn't, or wouldn't get over the top. After a good deal of coaxing from the assistant, the dog summed up the courage and went for it. Unfortunately, the dog lost his balance in the process and crashed down onto the owner's head, ladder and all. The showmen beat a hasty retreat to the rear of the tent, taking the monkeys, dog and ladder with them, leaving the amazed multitude to reach their own conclusions as to whether the performance was exactly as was intended.

The *Walsall Free Press* may well condemn the people for not supporting the Mechanic's Institution, the School of Design or the Floral and Horticultural Society. Analysing the activities of the latter organisation, it was very difficult for a foundry worker living in one room in a filthy court in Lower Rushall Street with his wife and six children to take an active interest in growing petunias. It was much easier to sit on your backside, drinking and waiting for the races and fair to come around again.

The newspaper commented in their August 15th edition: -
'We hear, and believe our information to be correct, that the annual Walsall Races are no more; - that the effort to get up this pitiable attempt at horse racing, so very difficult for some years to the few interested in the same, has altogether failed this year, and that not withstanding the success of last year, for it was said that our last races were most successful, they are now doomed.'

As much as the newspaper wished for the demise of the Races, their information was incorrect, as the meeting clung on perilously to life for a further nineteen years.

The meeting began on Wednesday 23rd September in fine weather. Throughout the morning trains from Wolverhampton, Birmingham and Dudley discharged their human cargo onto to the platforms of Walsall Station. From there the multitude made their way down Park Street to the Long Meadow, all willing to gamble a few pennies in the hope of making a few pounds.

1840 - 1859

The words of the *Walsall Free Press* had fallen on deaf ears, a report in *The Staffordshire Advertiser* tells of crowds much larger than in previous years with the race entries fewer due to the race meetings being held at Leicester and Warwick.

The opening race, the Bradford Handicap over two miles, saw the even money favourite, Redemption beaten into third place by the 6/4 chance, Laudamia, owned by Mr Olding and ridden by James Frost. The horse that finished second, Heads Or Tails, trained by Thomas Cliff at Hednesford, made all of the running, with the favourite never really in with a chance, nearing home James Frost pushed Laudamia on hard to get home by a head.

In the second race, the Innkeeper's Stakes over one and a quarter miles, saw last years impressive winner of the two year-old races, Master Bagot, reappear. Again just three runners contested the race, and all from Hednesford training stables, William Saunders' Master Bagot, Thomas Flintoff's Echo and Mr Cope's Mary Lovell. The latter horse bolting at the bottom of the hill and loosing many lengths in the process. From this point on it became a match between the other two, Echo lead for most of the way before jockey Knight, riding the even money favourite Master Bagot got to work, going past Echo in the latter stages to win by a length and a half.

Another horse well known at Walsall was Timotheus, appearing for the third consecutive year in the Handicap race over a mile and a quarter. After success on the course in 1855, Timotheus had disappointed the previous year, looking for all the world as though his form had deserted him for good. At the end of the meeting, his owner, Mr Owen must have been very pleased as his horse carried off three of the eight prizes on offer, including this race, where he beat his two opponents by a length.

In the final race of the day, the Saddler's Stakes, one of the trainers became public enemy number one as far as the crowd were concerned. It was in fact a match, not a race, between a previous runner earlier in the day, Mary Lovell and Thomas Flintoff's Oyster Girl. Both horses kept well together all the way round the course, fighting out an exciting finish, which saw Mary Lovell and James Frost triumph by a neck. There had been some exciting finishes of the races so far this year and the crowd anticipated another one when the second heat was run between these two, they were to be disappointed. For whatever reason, Flintoff withdrew his seemingly perfectly fit horse from the proceedings, leaving Mary Lovell to walkover to claim the prize. The crowd were not impressed by Flintoff's decision and made their feelings known with loud shouts of an uncomplimentary nature in the general direction of the trainer.

Thursday saw a reduction in the attendances on the Long Meadow, due to the dual combination of slightly inclement weather and the Birmingham Fair.

The days racing began with a Handicap race over a mile and quarter, four runners contesting the event, the largest field of the meeting. William Saunders' ran Master Bagot again and Thomas Flintoff ran his two previous runners, Echo and Blight, the fourth horse being Mr Olding's, Laudamia, winner of the first race on Wednesday. The betting showed, rather surprisingly, no bias toward any of the runners, all being quoted at 6/4. Generous odds when one considers the performance of Master Bagot in his earlier race. Backers of the horse must have been pleased when he retained his previous form against his old adversaries and came home, only just, by half a neck from Echo, with Blight third.

The jockey of Master Bagot was Joseph Kendall, a top rider on the flat and over fences. In 1861 he won the Grand National on Jealousy. Kendall had the dubious distinction of being one of the few people to be warned off twice by the Jockey Club, once as a jockey and again some years later as a trainer, as a result of a race run, appropriately enough, at Walsall. In 1858, as if to prove his versatility, he rode the winner of the French Derby on a horse called Ventre St. Gris at Chantilly. A far cry from the Long Meadow.

The jockey Walter White finished the meeting on a high note, riding the last three winners on the card. His first came in the race for two year-olds, the Hatherton Stakes over five furlongs, riding the outsider of the three runners, Lady of Tamworth for Mr Spencer. His last two winners came on the same horse, Timotheus, winning his second and third races of the meeting in the Railway Stakes and the Consolation Handicap.

Although the fields were small, nothing unusual for the Walsall meeting, the horses appeared to be well matched in ability and gave some excellent racing with closely contested finishes.

The final comment regarding the meeting for this year is left to a quote from the *Walsall Free Press:* -

'On the whole, however, we certainly were surprised to see so many take an interest in the sport, knowing that there was a feeling of doubt some months ago whether the Races, like nearly everything else in Walsall, would not this year prove a failure. To those interested in these things, and to the Committee whose energies have overcome the difficulties which once seemed to surround them, these results must be very satisfactory.'

The official results of the meeting were:

Wednesday 23rd September 1857

THE BRADFORD HANDICAP of 5 sovereigns each, with 50 added. Two miles

Mr Olding's	**Laudamia,** 3 y-o, 7st.	(J. Frost, jnr.)	1
Mr T. Cliff's	**Heads or Tails,** 3 y-o, 6st.	(Willis)	2
Mr Gulliver's	**Redemption,** 5 y-o, 8st. 7lb.	(Yates)	3

Evens fav. Redemption, 6/4 Laudamia, 2/1 Heads or Tails.

THE INNKEEPERS' STAKES of 3 sovereigns each, with 20 added by the Innkeepers of Walsall. One and a quarter miles.

Mr W. Saunders'	**Master Bagot,** 3 y-o, 7st. 3lb.	(Knight)	1
Mr T. Flintoff's	**Echo,** 3 y-o, 6st. 9lb.	(James Griffiths)	2
Mr Cope's	**Mary Lovell,** 5 y-o, 8st. 4lb.	(Denman)	3

Evens fav. Master Bagot

A HANDICAP of 5 sovereigns each, with 25 added by C. Forster, M.P. for the Borough. One and a quarter miles.

Mr Owen's	**Timotheus,** aged, 7st. 9lb.	(James Griffiths)	1
Mr Wilkinson's	**Blight,** 6 y-o, 8st. 7lb.	(E. Jones)	2
Mr Phillips'	**Lord Berkeley,** 3 y-o, 7st. 11lb.	(Thomas)	3

1840 - 1859

**THE SADDLERS STAKES of 3 sovereigns each,
with 20 added by the Saddlers of Walsall.
One and quarter miles.**

Mr Cope's	**Mary Lovell,** 5 y-o, 7st. 4lb.	*(J. Frost)*	1	1
Mr T. Flintoff's	**Oyster Girl,** 4 y-o, 6st. 13lb.	*(T. Cliff)*	2	dr

Thursday 24th September 1857

**A HANDICAP of 5 sovereigns each,
with 20 added. One and a quarter miles.**

Mr W. Saunders'	**Master Bagot,** 3 y-o, 7st. 13lb.	*(Kendall)*	1
Mr T. Flintoff's	**Echo,** 3 y-o, 7st. 1lb.	*(James Griffiths)*	2
Mr T. Flintoff's	**Blight,** 6 y-o, 8st. 7lb.	*(E. Jones)*	3
Mr Olding's	**Laudamia,** 3 y-o, 8st. 4lb.	*(Frost)*	4

**THE HATHERTON STAKES of 5 sovereigns each,
with 30 added. Two-year olds. Five furlongs.**

Mr Spencer's	**Lady of Tamworth,** 8st. 3lb.	*(W. White)*	1
Mr Moseley's	**Geneva,** 8st.	*(W. Sharpe)*	2
Mr Spencer's	**Knight of Tourney,** 8st. 7lb.	*(E. Jones)*	3

Evens fav. Geneva, 6/4 against Knight of Tourney.

THE HATHERTON HANDICAP of 5 sovereigns each, with 25 added.
Did not fill - cancelled

**THE RAILWAY STAKES of 3 sovereigns each, with 20 added by the Lessees
of the South Staffordshire Railway.
One and quarter miles.**

Mr Owen's	**Timotheus,** aged, 8st. 11lb.	*(W. White)*	1
Mr T. Flintoff's	**Blight,** 6 y-o, 8st. 12lb.	*(E. Jones)*	2
Mr T. Cliff's	**Grillade,** 5 y-o, 8st. 4lb.	*(W. Sharpe)*	3

Grillade, 5/4 fav., 2/1 Timotheus.

**THE CONSOLATION STAKES of 2 sovereigns each,
with 15 added. Heats, one mile.**

Mr Owen's	**Timotheus,** aged, 9st. 4lb.	*(W. White)*	1	1
Mr T. Cliff's	**Grillade,** 5 y-o, 9st. 6lb.	*(W. Sharpe)*	2	2

1858

Last year the *Walsall Free Press* reported that the Races were doomed; they were a year out with their prediction, due to a funding crisis, the meeting was cancelled. The Race Committee, or at least some of its more ardent supporters, decided Walsall would not be deprived of it Races and hastily arranged hack races to be held in the Paddock area of the town. Unfortunately, no details or the exact location of this impromptu meeting is known other than it was held over two days, as the official events were.

The Fair, Wake and hack races were held three weeks later than usual and for the second consecutive year, the *Walsall Free Press* were convinced this was to be the last year of the Races. A report in the paper from Saturday 23rd October tells of the tolling of the little bell on top the grandstand, stating: -

'... and whose dull sound reminded one of the passing bell, and a passing bell undoubtedly it was, for amid the flags with which the grandstand was decorated, and drooped like weeds around the belfry, the little bell we allude to was ringing out the death knell of The Races, and proclaiming that these, like all sublimary things, had run their course. The very turf, thanks to Mr Deeley, was covered with a black funeral pall and seemed to grieve over its departed glory. But let us hope they have only gone to make way for sports of a less questionable and rational kind. Races were originally established for improving the breed of horses, and that attained, they have served their purpose, and it is to be hoped will be succeeded by entertainments better calculated to improve the morals and intellects of men. By way of taking a step in this direction, the temperance people got up a very nice little entertainment in St. Matthew's Hall, to which there was free admission, and where the company spent a very agreeable evening.'

Whilst the attempts of the Temperance Movement, supported by the newspaper, must be applauded in their combined efforts to improve the moral and social climate of the town, it does make one wonder just how many foundry workers, limestone miners and labourers from the insanitary, cramped hovels of Town End Bank and Hell's Hole attended this soiree on Church Hill?

1859

It must have been a great disappointment for the editorial staff of the *Walsall Free Press* to find that all three of the town's demonic activities, as they put it, the Wake, Fair and Races were back on course this year. The two events prior to the Races littered the town from High Street to The Bridge, from there to the racecourse with shooting galleries, fly-boats, roundabouts, nut stalls, ginger bread vendors, a lady of porcine appearance, boxing booths, displays of fine-art production and every type of mechanical invention – and of course, drink. All of ones senses were invaded in this week of over indulgence in Walsall, the ears in particular. On The Bridge bagpipes were playing, the noise of thundering gongs, shouting children as they swung to and fro in the swing boats, the crack of rifle shots, the lowing of cattle, the neighing of horses, the braying of asses and the bawling of stentorian lunged showmen inviting you to boost their profits. Pick pockets, prostitutes, rogues and vagabonds mingled with the innocents, relieving them of hard earned cash in whatever way they could to fund their fetid lives. Meanwhile, on top of the hill, at St. Matthew's Church, the Temperance Society were holding a *'nice little social party where songs and recitations were delivered,'* in the words of the newspaper. For the majority of the town's population, their interests lay firmly at the bottom of the hill!

Whilst it is very obvious the *Walsall Free Press* were dismissive of the events taking place in the town at this time they nevertheless reported all three events in great detail, interspersed with negative remarks throughout. A classic example of their 'pat on the back, kick in the teeth' style of journalism is illustrated in the following quote from their columns regarding the Races: -

'Chagrined at their disappointment last year, the patrons and supporters of the turf this year doubled their diligence, and by perseverance worthy of a better cause, succeeded in raising the requisite funds; but be the prizes what they may, there is one

1840 - 1859

thing that will always militate against Walsall Races being of a first class character, and that is the unsuitable nature of the race course, which is such as few would be inclined to risk a first class animal upon. Be that as it may, arrangements were made for races coming off with more than the ordinary éclat, and according to the necessary preparations – such as levelling and staking of the course – was gone about with the greatest alacrity. On Tuesday several of the horses arrived by train, and that night was indeed a busy one for a while. In the morning the field, from the number and variety of booths, presented no bad idea of an encampment on a small scale. In addition the grandstand was furbished up a bit for the occasion, there were other stands erected contiguous to the judge's chair where for a trifle, sitting accommodation could be procured. The arrangements completed, all seemed to give promise of a glorious day; but alas! The authority in the weather office being no patrons of this kind of amusement, did their best to spoil the sport. Wednesday last, the morning was all that could be desired, and the sun shone out with than ordinary brilliancy; but shortly after noon the sky was overcast, and the rain began to fall pretty heavily, and continued to do so with but little intermission till between five and six o'clock. Not withstanding this drawback, the concourse of spectators upon the racecourse was very large, and the victuallers did a good stroke of business, perhaps more than they would have done had the weather been more favourable, for many, who would in all probability have remained outside, entered the tents for sake of shelter between the races.'

A new Clerk of the Course had taken over from John Osbourne, John Sheldon from Birmingham. Whether Osbourne was a casualty of the failure to secure a meeting last year, or, that he had 'had enough of it' is not known.

The Race Committee had certainly been industrious in organising this years meeting, with ten races on the card over the two days, it was the largest number of events in the history of the Races. Unfortunately, the Bradford Handicap was a walk over and on Thursday, the Consolation Stakes did not fill and was cancelled.

Walsall as a town, and the Races, had changed dramatically since the early years of the nineteenth century, but one thing remained the same, the racehorse trainers continued to work their horses just as hard as they did thirty or forty years ago.

On the first day, Wednesday 28th September, the four runners in the opening race, the Innkeeper's Stakes, had run a total of forty-five races between them, winning just seven. The lightest raced of the quartet, Lansquenet, owned and trained by Thomas Cliff at Hednesford, proved to be the fittest, coming home by a length from Mr Rich's, Adelaide.

The first day proved to be almost a benefit day for Thomas Cliff who won three of the four races, his second victory came in the Stand Stakes, run in two heats over one and a quarter miles and won by his three year-old filly, Stir Pudding, from two rivals. None of the trio had ever won before, making Stir Pudding the best of three rather mediocre runners, the betting showed she was the strongest too, starting as 1/4 favourite, she won both heats with ease.

Lansquenet won her second race of the day in the afternoon when she took the Member's Handicap Plate over one mile and a quarter, by eight lengths. The jockey that rode the filly in her second race was a little fellow named Henry Taylor, a well known lightweight of the day, he went to scale at just 5 stone 9 pounds, a few weeks previously he had won on a horse at Lichfield carrying the amazing weight of 4 stone 10 pounds.

Thursday saw an improvement in the weather, but come rain or shine, Thomas Cliff kept on saddling winners. His first of the day was in the second race, the Hatherton Handicap over two miles. The colt that won this one was another three year-old named Lustre, probably the best one of Cliff's runners at the meeting. Prior to Walsall, the colt had run eleven times and won five of his races over distances ranging from half a mile to a mile and a half. The longer distance and the five pounds overweight his jockey, Gardner, had to put up didn't make much difference to the outcome as the two other runners were pretty mediocre and were beaten easily.

The final winner for Cliff was in the penultimate race, the Tradesmen's Sweepstakes for two year-olds over five furlongs. Alderman Copeland, a lifelong turf supporter and subscriber to Walsall Races for many years entered his chestnut filly, Lady Grosvenor who started red-hot favourite at 4/1 on. Thomas Cliff's runner was also a filly, named The Creeper, who had won a quarter of her twelve previous races. Lady Grosvenor had won twice from ten starts, the other runner was a definite no-hoper, Guerilla, previous form suggesting a walkover would have been a challenge. It appeared to be a foregone conclusion if the betting was anything to go by, but no one accounted for Lady Grosvenor bolting shortly after the start. That must have brought thousands of loud voices into play from the crowd, suggesting foul play was rearing its head on the Long Meadow again. With the favourite out of the way, The Creeper could have done exactly what her name suggests, and crept home, Guerilla still couldn't have caught her

The meeting closed with the charitably named race, the Beaten Horse Handicap Stakes over a mile and a quarter. Only two runners contested this final event, Mr Tittensor's English Rose and Mr Martin's The Deer. English Rose, on previous form, was slightly the better of the two and that is how it turned out, little Henry Taylor making all the right moves to bring English Rose home to win easily.

Much to the dismay of some people in the town and the *Walsall Free Press* newspaper, the Races had survived for another year. However, it was becoming a case of 'the lid was on the coffin,' and certain people within the town were getting the nails ready and polishing the hammer!

The official results of the meeting were:

Wednesday 28th September 1859

THE INNKEEPERS' STAKES of 3 sovereigns each, with 20 added by the Innkeepers of Walsall. One and a quarter miles.

Mr T. Cliff's	**Lansquenet,** 3 y-o, 6st. 12lb.	*(Gardiner)*	1
Mr Rich's b. f.	**Adelaide,** 3 y-o, 7st.	*(Matley)*	2
Mr Copeland's br. f.	**Woman in Black,** 3 y-o, 6st. 9lb.	*(Standing)*	3
Mr Howse's br. g	**Pactolus,** 4 y-o, 7st. 12lb.	*(James)*	4

1840 – 1859

THE BRADFORD HANDICAP of 5 sovereigns each,
with 40 added. Two miles

Mr J. Gilbey's	**Flash in the Pan,** 3 y-o, 6st. 10lb.	wo

THE STAND STAKES of 3 sovereigns each,
with 20 added by the proprietors of the Stand.
Winner to be sold for at auction for 60 sovs.
One and a quarter miles.

Mr T. Cliff's ch. f.	**Stir Pudding,** 3 y-o, 5st. 10lb.	(Henry Taylor)	1	1
Mr Martin's ch. c.	**The Deer,** 3 y-o, 6st. 6lb.	(James)	2	2
Mr Wootton's b. f.	**Astarte,** 3 y-o, 7st. 3lb.	(Gardiner)	dis	-

The winner was bought in for 35 guineas.

THE MEMBER'S PLATE (HANDICAP) of 5 sovereigns each,
with 25 added by C. Forster, M.P.
One and a quarter miles.

Mr T. Cliff's b. f.	**Lansquenet,** 3 y-o, 5st. 9lb.	(Taylor)	1
Mr J. Tittensor's b. f.	English Rose, 4 y-o, 6st. 7lb.	(James)	2
Mr T. Cliff's	Cast Off, 3 y-o, 6st. 7lb.	(Gardiner)	3

Thursday 27th September 1859

THE RAILWAY PLATE HANDICAP of 3 sovereigns each, with 20 added by the
South Staffordshire Railway Company.
One and a quarter miles.

Mr Howse's	**Pactolus,** 4 y-o, 9st. 9lb.	(Palmer)	1
Mr Martin's ch. c.	**The Deer,** 3 y-o, 7st. 10lb.	(James)	2
Capt. Verner's	**Martello,** 3 y-o, 8st. 12lb.	(Wilberforce)	3

THE HATHERTON HANDICAP of 5 sovereigns each,
with 25 added. Two miles.

Mr T. Cliff's b. c.	**Lustre,** 3 y-o, 7st. 10lb.	(Gardiner)	1
Mr J. Gilbey's b. c.	**Flash in the Pan,** 3 y-o, 7st. 7lb.	(Spencer)	2
Mr S. Barratt's	**Commodore,** 3 y-o, 6st. 10lb.	(James)	3

A HANDICAP SWEEPSTAKES of 2 sovereigns each, with 10 added and a
purse for cavalry horses. Gentlemen riders. Six furlongs.

Mr J. Davy's b. g.	**Harry of Hereford,** aged 13st.	(Owner)	1
Mr W. Newman's	**Scroggins,** 4 y-o, 12st.	(Owner)	2
Mr Chambley's	**Tommy,** 4 y-o, 11st. 10lb.	(Owner)	3

A SWEEPSTAKES of 3 sovereigns each, with 25 added by the Tradesmen of
Walsall. Five furlongs, for two year olds.

Mr T. Cliff's br. f.	**The Creeper,** 8st. 8lb.	(Gardiner)	1
Mr Nicholson's ch. g.	**Guerilla,** 8st. 4lb.	(Britton)	2
Mr Copeland's ch. f.	**Lady Grosvenor,** 8st. 8lb.	(Wilberforce)	3

A HANDICAP SWEEPSTAKES of 3 sovereigns each, with 15 added, for the
beaten horses. One and a quarter miles.

Mr Tittensor's	**English Rose,** 4 y-o, 7st.	(Henry Taylor)	1
Mr Martin's	**The Deer,** 3 y-o, 6st. 6lb.	(James)	2

WALSALL RACES

CHAPTER FIVE
1860 - 1879

1860

For the last three years the Walsall Free Press had voiced their displeasure about the Races, Wake and Fair. This year, the editorial onslaught continued on two fronts only. For whatever reason, the Races were excluded from criticism. The reverse could almost be said upon reading their opening paragraph, which read: -

'The racing this year at Walsall exhibited a decided tendency towards a continued improvement of this truly British sport.'

In comparison to previous years reports, this was a glowing appraisal of the Race Committee's effort in the organisation and management of the meeting.

The programme, which began on Wednesday 26th September, consisted of ten races over the two days. Only one race proved to be a casualty and that was the final race of the meeting, the Innkeeper's Stakes, which became a walkover. There was slight increase in the number of horses competing for the prizes at this year's meeting, even though there was no increase in the prize money.

The Trial Stakes over one mile began the proceedings. Six owners subscribed to the event with five horses going to post. The race took two heats to decide the winner as a dead heat was declared by the judge, George Calloway, between Greenwich Fair and Lady Bird. In the run-off, Lady Bird made all of the running up to the distance pole when Greenwich Fair took up the running. Surprisingly, Lady Bird fought back and an exciting battle to the line ensued, with Greenwich Fair, ridden by A. Sadler, getting the verdict by a short neck.

For the first time, the meeting supported two races for two year-olds. On Wednesday there was the Two Year-Old Stakes, and on Thursday, the Hatherton Nursery Handicap, both races over six furlongs. Two races, and the same colt won both events, Mr Price's Biddy Nutts, ridden by A. Sadler. Second place in each race was also taken by the same horse, Archeress, owned by Mr Newland. These two were the stars of the juveniles this year, leaving their three remaining rivals in each race a long way down the course.

Another dual winner, but this time on the same day, was Mr A. Williams' Rara Avis who won the Tradesmen's Plate and The Stand Handicap on Wednesday. In the first of the two victories, Rara Avis, a 5/1 chance, lead from start to finish and was never headed. She won by half a length, surprising everyone, including the odds-on favourite, Emblem. In the second race involving Rara Avis, the betting ring were not being so generous with the odds, offering 6/4 against this time. The favouritism was justified, Rara Avis getting home by a head from the game little two year-old, Biddy Nutts, who surprised the remaining five runners with his ability against older horses. Today, two year-olds are only allowed to run against horses of their own age, but at this time they were allowed to compete against older horses.

In the opening event on Thursday, a one mile Handicap Plate, it is stated in the race reports that the runners must start from the old grandstand. This implies that the temporary grandstand built several years ago was not as temporary as everyone thought. From a researchers point of view, this statement gives a clue as to the positioning of the winning post, which up till now has never been known. The map on page 6 illustrates the approximate placement of the winning post. However, the emphasis must be placed on the word approximate. This information allows the various starting points around the course to be estimated.

Only three horses lined up for the start of the race, and it was another of Thomas Cliff's runners that came in first, the even money favourite, Nosegay, with Mr Byrns's runner, Catherine in second place at 6/4. The horse that made up the trio, Boniface, was beaten off in the early stages and eventually distanced. The yellow and blue colours of Cliff's had become a familiar site on the Long Meadow in recent years, but before this victory could be recorded, the owner trainer had to survive an objection from the second horse on the grounds of crossing which was, fortunately for Cliff, overruled.

The final two races of the meeting went to the same owner, Mr Thomas, but with different horses, both had run the day before, coming second in their respective races. Emblem was the winner of the Bradford Handicap, which proved to be a closely contested race by all five runners. Thomas Cliff's winner from last year, Lustre, was installed as 6/4 favourite with Emblem at 2/1, Miss Eleanor at 7/2 and the remaining two runners at 6/1. Throughout the mile and a quarter

1860 - 1879

trip, all five kept in close touch with each other, the lead changing several time, but nearing home, Emblem and jockey Moorhouse came through to win by a length, with only five lengths separating first and last.

The Member's Plate had just three runners, Lady Bird, second in Greenwich Fair's race yesterday, Mr Wright's Lazy Lass and Mr Randall's Boniface. As far as the betting ring was concerned, there was no contest as Lady Bird started as 4/6 favourite, with no odds quoted for the opposition. Lady Bird was receiving weight from her rivals, twenty pounds in the case of Lazy Lass, and so was expected to win with ease. Shortly after starting, the race became a match when Boniface fell. A good match it turned out to be too. Lady Bird won, but only by a neck, the jockey of Lazy Lass, Gardner, felt his mount was impeded by the winner, and lodged an objection on the grounds of crossing. The Stewards, or those acting on their behalf, quickly overruled the objection and Mr Thomas won his second race of the meeting within an hour.

Once again the Races had survived for another year, and the *Walsall Free Press* closed their report on the event with praise for everyone concerned with the organising of the meeting, and the local police for the excellent manner in which they kept order. The Race Committee needed all the friends they could get, and if the town's newspaper was one of them, all the better.

The official results of the meeting were:

Wednesday 26th September 1860

THE TRIAL STAKES of 3 sovereigns each, with 20 added. Optional selling weights. One mile.

Mr Price's	*Greenwich Fair, 5 y-o, 9st.	(A. Sadler)	1	1
Mr Thomas'	*Ladybird, 3 y-o, 8st.	(Madden)	1	2
Mr Edwin's	Alchymist, 3 y-o, 8st. 3lb.	(W. White)	3	-
Mr Coverdale's	Griffin, 4 y-o, 8st. 12lb.	(Harrison)	4	-
Mr Lincoln's	Jeanette, 2 y-o, 6st.	(Williamson)	5	-

* Greenwich Fair and Ladybird dead-heat, with the former winning the run-off.
Betting: 4/5 fav. Greenwich Fair, 5/2 Ladybird, 4/1 Jeanette.

THE TWO YEAR-OLD STAKES of 5 sovereigns each, with 25 added. Six furlongs.

Mr Price's	Biddy Nutts, 7st. 12lb.	(A. Sadler)	1
Mr Newland's	Archeress, 8st. 1lb.	(Thorpe)	2
Mr J. Dickins'	f. by Tadmor, 7st. 12lb.	(Madden)	3
Mr Coverdale's	Corfu, 8st. 5lb.	(Harrison)	f

Betting: 4/7 fav. Archeress, 5/2 Biddy Nutts and the Tadmor filly.

THE TRADESMEN'S PLATE of 60 sovereigns added to a Handicap Sweepstakes of 5 sovs. each. One and a quarter miles.

Mr Williams'	Rara Avis, 4 y-o, 6st. 10lb.	(Matley)	1
Mr J. Saville's	Emblem, 4 y-o, 6st. 13lb.	(Madden)	2
Mr T. Cliff's	Cast Off, 4 y-o, 7st. 2lb.	(Gardiner)	3
Mr Gulliver's	Miss Eleanor, 4 y-o, 7st. 11lb.	(Sadler)	4
Mr Byrne's	Wee Willie, aged, 6st. 6lb.	(Taylor)	5

Betting: Evens fav. Emblem, 5/2 Miss Eleanor, 4/1 Cast Off

THE RAILWAY HANDICAP of 3 sovereigns each, with 20 added. Six furlongs.

Mr Coverdale's	Griffin, 4 y-o, 8st.	(Harrison)	1
Mr Byrne's	Wee Willie, aged 7st. 6lb.	(Sadler)	2
Mr Lincoln's	Necklace, 2 y-o, 5st. 7lb.	(Williamson)	3

Betting: 2/5 fav. Griffin.

THE STAND HANDICAP of 3 sovereigns each, with 20 added. One mile.

Mr Williams'	Rara Avis, 4 y-o, 8st. 3lb.	(Madden)	1
Mr Price's	Biddy Nutts, 2 y-o, 6st. 1lb.	(Page)	2
Mr J. Adie's	Thornhill, 5 y-o, 8st. 2lb.	(Moorhouse)	3
Mr Byrne's	Catherine, 4 y-o, 7st. 12lb.	(Thorpe)	4
Mr J. Clarke's	Maid of Lyme, 3 y-o, 6st. 13lb.	(Matley)	5
Mr Lincoln's	Jeanette, 2 y-o, 5st. 8lb.	(Williamson)	6

Betting: 6/4 fav. Rara Avis, 3/1 Catherine and Thornhill, 4/1 Biddy Nutts.

Thursday 27th September 1860

A HANDICAP PLATE of 2 sovereigns each, with 20 added. One mile, starting at the Old Grandstand.

Mr T. Cliff's	Nosegay, 4 y-o, 6st. 10lb.	(Williamson)	1
Mr Byrne's	Catherine, 4 y-o, 7st. 6lb.	(A. Sadler)	2
Mr Randall's	Boniface, 3 y-o, 5st. 7lb.	(Page)	3

Betting: Evens fav. Nosegay, 6/4 Catherine.

THE HATHERTON NURSERY HANDICAP of 3 sovereigns each, with 25 added. For two year olds, six furlongs.

Mr Price's	Biddy Nutts, 7st. 5lb.	(A. Sadler)	1
Mr Newland's	Archeress, 7st. 5lb.	(Page)	2
Mr Newland's	Astarte, 8st. 7lb.	(Thorpe)	3
Mr Copeland's	Shugborough, 7st. 9lb.	(Farmer)	4
Mr Saunders'	Corona, 7st. 4lb.	(Huby)	5

Betting: 6/4 fav. Biddy Nutts, 2/1 Corona, 4/1 Shugborough and Archeress.

THE BRADFORD HANDICAP of 3 sovereigns each, with 25 added. One and quarter miles.

Mr Thomas'	Emblem, 4 y-o, 8st. 1lb.	(Moorhouse)	1
Mr Gulliver's	Miss Eleanor, 4 y-o, 8st.	(Harrison)	2
Mr Whitehouse's	Quiver, 3 y-o, 7st.	(Page)	3
Mr T. Cliff's	Lustre, 4 y-o, 7st. 12lb.	(Gardiner)	4
Mr Price's	Greenwich Fair, 5 y-o, 9st.	(A. Sadler)	5

Betting: 6/4 fav. Lustre, 2/1 Emblem, 7/2 Miss Eleanor, 6/1 any other.

THE MEMBER'S PLATE of 5 sovereigns each, with 25 added. One mile.

Mr Thomas'	Lady Bird, 3 y-o, 6st.	(Thomas)	1
Mr Wright's	Lazy Lass, aged, 7st. 4lb.	(Gardiner)	2
Mr Randall's	Boniface, 3 y-o, 7st.	(A. Sadler)	3

Betting 1/2 fav. Lady Bird.

THE INNKEEPER'S PLATE of 5 sovereigns each, with 25 added. One mile.

Mr Coverdale's	Griffin, 4 y-o,	(Harrison)	wo

1860 - 1879

1861

The Race Committee, after their baptism of fire ten years ago with the odd faux par, had learnt a lot in the those years. Already they had won over the local paper and now word was spreading. The *Birmingham Daily Post* was throwing praise their way, but not before criticising the Races prior to 1860. The opening lines of their report begin: -

'The leather-flapping character that attached itself to Walsall Races up to 1860 has been amply redeemed by Mr John Sheldon [the new Clerk of the Course], and from the amount of patronage that was bestowed upon his efforts yesterday despite the unfavourable weather, the meeting bids to be one of the best in the midland counties.'

George Calloway had resigned his post of judge after last year's meeting and his replacement was John Swindell, hopefully, the name didn't reflect his character.

Even the stewards at this years meeting were of a higher profile than many years previous, with Lord Alexander Paget, Lord Berkeley Paget and Captain Hawkesley. Whether any of these gentlemen actually attended the proceedings is another matter!

As the majority of the races were now run as today, in just one heat. The racing was confined to the afternoon, with a forty-five minute break, approximately, in between each contest. It will also be noticed by this time, the races had become much shorter than in previous years, long gone are the three and four mile triple heat races.

An incentive that was introduced this year, which was bound to please the owners, and increase the entries, was the money added to the races rose by almost £100. Also, to cater for the anticipated increase in spectators, the enclosures around the grandstand were enlarged to accommodate them. Little was apparently done in the way of improvements to the course, the place where it was really needed. Many booths and tents were erected in middle of the course with another encampment at the top of the hill in Bradford Street.

The Races began on Wednesday 25th September, the morning had been fine, but shortly after noon the storm clouds rolled in, literally. A tremendous thunderstorm descended over the town, the rain coming down in torrents, thunder and lightning playing havoc with the nerves of the highly strung thoroughbreds, on or around the course. The lower parts of the course (the railway side) being covered with large pools of water, and with all the people tramping about, it soon became a quagmire. At the start of the first race, the storm had passed over and the rain had abated somewhat, but continued to fall for the rest of the day. In a situation like that today, the meeting would be abandoned. But in those days, especially in the Walsall of 1861, unless you wanted a full-scale riot on your hands, it was better to let events run their muddy course, and so they did.

First race on the card was appropriately named for the conditions underfoot, the Trial Stakes over one mile. Four runners arrived at the start and were dispatched at the first attempt. At the second turn beyond the hill, the horses continued straight on across the meadows towards the railway instead of sweeping round to the right for the winning post. All four horses, jockeys and all, finished up in the sewer brook, this unexpected and disgusting plunge bath doing little for the appearance of neither man nor beast. First to extricate himself from the brook was Bavard, owned by Ben Land and ridden by George Clement. The jockey remounted and headed towards the winning post with the others following. Imagine their dismay on arriving at the post to be told by the Stewards that the race was void because none of the runners had followed the correct course, and the race was to be run again. The shock of the events at the far end of the course had now got to Clement - he was so shaken up he had to give up his ride and was replaced by jockey Sait. It was turning into a bad day for poor Clement. Already drenched from the rain, and then finishing up in something very unhealthy, he had to give up what turned out to be a winning ride. After the restart, Bavard made all of the running to win by a length from the favourite, Mr Bates' Rajah Brooke ridden by Walter White, in third place was Thomas Carr's Maid of Peru. The only horse seemingly affected by the earlier mishap was Camperdown who didn't fancy going through that again and bolted.

In the second race of the day, the Town Plate over three quarters of a mile, Bavard ran again. His win in the first race wasn't expected and the betting for this race reflected the fact he wasn't fancied this time either. Six horses started with Mr Bates' Cumberland the 5/4 favourite and Mr Adkins' two year-old, Doritta second choice at 2/1. The two fancied horses set off in front with the others a short distance behind. At the top of the hill Bavard took up the running followed by Doritta. It was as if the clock had been turned back, Bavard, ridden by another jockey, Beesley, refused to turn right and carried on towards the railway again, this time only Doritta followed. The horse in third place, Holdersyke took up the running right to the line, winning in a canter from Fairy Knowe with the favourite, Cumberland third. The story behind Bavard's dislike of the railway turn can only be surmised. Three times he had run the course, with different jockeys each time, and only once had he completed the trip. Some horses will run quite happily with other horses in front of them only to virtually stop when they hit the front. There is another explanation of course, there was a train coming and he simply took fright!

In the final race on this wet afternoon, the Stand Handicap over one mile, proved to be the best of the day. It was won by a horse owned and trained by another generation of the Wadlow family from Shifnal. This time it was son of Thomas Wadlow, Thomas junior that took the spoils with his four year-old, Diadem. Just four runners contested the race, with Mr Wood's Caliban the even money favourite and Diadem second choice. These two proving far superior to the other runners, Mr Land's Cheesecake and Mr Thompson's Sherwood, who were soon some way behind the favourites. At the post, Mr Swindell, the judge, was called upon for his first really close finish of his new appointment, deciding he couldn't favour either of the two, he declared a dead heat. Today, if a dead heat is called the money is split, but in those days they had to have a winner and so a run-off was required. Caliban's odds shortened even further, 4/5 for this one, with evens given for Diadem, the jockey on the latter

1860 - 1879

> **PUBLIC ANNOUNCEMENTS.**
>
> **LONDON AND NORTH-WESTERN RAILWAY.**
>
> **WALSALL FAIR AND RACES,**
> September 24, 25, and 26.
>
> WALSALL FAIR is held on TUESDAY NEXT, and the RACES on WEDNESDAY and THURSDAY NEXT.
> For the convenience of Passengers from Birmingham, &c., attending the above, TWO CHEAP TRAINS will be run, as under:—
>
> **FARES TO WALSALL AND BACK.**
>
> | | A.M. | NOON. | Cov. Cars. |
> |---|---|---|---|
> | Leave Birmingham | 10 30 | 12 0 | |
> | Bloomsbury | 10 35 | 12 5 | 1s. |
> | Aston | 10 40 | 12 10 | |
> | Perry Barr | 10 45 | 12 15 | |
> | Reach Walsall about | 11 0 | 12 30 | |
>
> Passengers can return from Walsall by Ordinary Trains at 6 20, 7 50, or by a Special Train at 8 30 p.m.
>
> By Order.
>
> Birmingham, September 5, 1861.

An advertisement from Aris's Gazette in September 1861 showing the timetable and fares of trains to the Races and Fair from Birmingham.

horse allowing Caliban to make the pace. Throughout the race, Diadem's jockey, Whiteley, kept in close touch and made his move shortly before the post, winning by half a length.

What began as a pretty dismal afternoon, finished up with some excellent racing, despite the heavy conditions. The crowd were wet, but happy, and those making the 'book' were ecstatic, not one favourite won all afternoon.

Weather wise, Thursday couldn't have been more of a contrast, the sun shone brightly virtually all day and although the going remained heavy, it still gave some excellent racing to the thousands of spectators. The day coincided with the Birmingham Onion Fair, but despite this, special trains were run from New Street Station to bring the 'Brummagem' contingent of the crowd to Walsall.

The Scurry Handicap of half a mile was the first race on the card with eight runners, quite a field for Walsall. The 2/1 favourite, Duplicity had a show of temperament exactly when you don't need such antics, immediately after the start. As the flag dropped the horse reared up and turned round, facing the opposite direction to the remainder of the field. With the favourite out of the way, the seven remaining runners made their way around the course. Included in the field was the previous days 'troublemaker' Bavard, who managed to get round the railway turn and head for the winning post. Bavard left yesterdays tantrums behind and fought out a very close finish with the eventual winner, Mr Rigby's Lord of the Tees. A winner from last year, Greenwich Fair, was a length further back in third place. It is interesting to note that the jockey of Bavard was Sait, the jockey that rode him when he won the first race on Wednesday, and the only rider of the three that were tried on him that managed to get the horse around the course. A further observation regarding this horse was in the running of the Member's Plate later in the afternoon - due to his lightweight Beesley rode him, as jockey Sait couldn't do the 5 stone 12 pounds required. With only four runners in the race, Bavard came in a very bad third and last! The fourth member of the quartet was none other than Duplicity, who again refused to start after being backed heavily for the second time, to become the 4/6 favourite. By today's standards, his owner, Mr Land would have at least been required to explain the horse's behaviour to the Stewards, but there is no mention of this in the race reports.

Four of the five runners in the Innkeeper's Plate also ran in the Town Plate the previous day, and the result was almost the same. The runners were, Doritta, Fairy Knowe, Holdersyke, an unnamed gelding and one newcomer, Mr Windsor's Jetty Bon, the favourite at 4/6 was Holdersyke. No dramatics marred the start and all five got away cleanly with Holdersyke making the early pace from Jetty Bon and Doritta. Holdersyke's jockey, Matthews, rode a clever race, kicking on each time one of the others came to challenge. At the winning post the favourite held on to win by a length from the Doritta, with Fairy Knowe a further length behind in third.

The closing race of the meeting was the Hatherton Nursery Handicap over six furlongs, with another fair sized field of eight horses. The outcome of this race was another victory for a previous winner, John Lands' Dunoon who came in at 6/1. Anyone shrewd enough to back him did well, as he won on Wednesday at 5/1.

There must have been something spooking the horses at the railway turn, probably trains. The even money favourite, Mr Murphy's Leonora, bolted whilst negotiating the turn. Dunoon surprised many people by recording his second win of the meeting with ease, coming home by a length and a half from Fairy Knowe, who did well to finish second after having run only an hour before. The horse that finished last but one, Agneta, was ridden by Walsall born jockey George Whitehouse, having what is believed to be his final ride on his home course before retiring.

Even though Walsall was only a small provincial racecourse it was known in Ireland as the *Belfast Mercury* published the results from Thursday's meeting in its pages on Friday 27th September.

The official results of the meeting were:

Wednesday 25th September 1861

THE TRIAL STAKES of 3 sovereigns each, with 20 added. Optional selling weights. One mile.

Mr B. Land's	Bavard, 3 y-o, 8st. 12lb.	(Sait)	1
Mr Bates'	Rajah Brooke, 4 y-o, 8st. 7lb.	(W. White)	2
Mr T. Carr's	Maid of Peru, 3 y-o, 7st. 9lb.	(J. Frost)	3
Mr Wood's	Camperdown, 2 y-o, 6st.	(E. Taylor)	4
Mr Lincoln's	Jeanette, 2 y-o, 6st.	(Williamson)	5

Betting: Evens fav. Rajah Brooke, 2/1 Maid of Peru.

THE TOWN PLATE of 3 sovereigns each, with 20 added. Six furlongs.

Mr Price's	Holdersyke, 3 y-o, 6st. 10lb.	(Thomas)	1
Mr Wood's	Fairy Knowe, 2 y-o, 5st. 7lb.	(E. Taylor)	2
Mr Bates'	Cumberland, 4 y-o, 8st. 10lb.	(Ogden)	3
Mr Johnson's	by Incense, 4 y-o, 8st.	(J. Frost)	4
Mr B. Land's	Bavard, 3 y-o, 6st. 7lb.	(Beasley)	5
Mr Adkins'	Dorritta, 2 y-o, 5st. 13lb.	(Whiteley)	6

Betting: 5/4 fav. Cumberland, 2/1 Dorritta, 3/1 Holdersyke.

1860 – 1879

THE TRADESMEN'S PLATE of 100 sovereigns added to a Handicap
Sweepstakes of 5 sovs. each. One and a half miles.

Mr T. Hunt's	**Bradfield**, 4 y-o, 6st. 10lb.	*(Thomas)*	1
Mr Wright's	**Twinkle**, 3 y-o, 5st. 9lb.	*(H. Taylor)*	2
Mr B. Land's	**Yorkshire Grey**, aged, 7st. 7lb.	*(J. Frost)*	3
Mr Price's	**Greenwich Fair**, 6 y-o, 7st. 7lb.	*(Matthews)*	4
Mr Wadlow's	**Diadem**, 4 y-o, 6st. 12lb.	*(Whiteley)*	5
Mr Wood's	**Caliban**, 3 y-o, 5st. 7lb.	*(E. Taylor)*	6

Betting: 5/4 fav. Twinkle, 3/1 Caliban, 4/1 Yorkshire Grey and Greenwich Fair, 5/1 Bradfield.

THE TWO YEAR OLD STAKES of 5 sovereigns each,
with 25 added. Six furlongs.

Mr John Land's	**Dunoon**, 8st. 1lb.	*(Sait)*	1
Mr Rigby's	**Strawberry Leaf**, 7st. 11lb.	*(Chapman)*	2
Mr Hopwood's	**Charles Fox**, 7st. 11lb.	*(Ogden)*	3
Mr Adkins'	**Dorritta**, 8st. 1lb.	*(W. White)*	4
Capt. Bernard's	**Paroquet**, 7st. 7lb.	*(Thomas)*	5

Betting: 6/4 joint favs. Paroquet and Charles Fox, 3/1 Strawberry Leaf, 5/1 Dunoon.

THE STAND HANDICAP of 3 sovereigns each,
with 20 added. One mile.

Mr Wadlow's	***Diadem**, 4 y-o, 7st. 5lb.	*(Whiteley)*	1
Mr Wood's	***Caliban**, 3 y-o, 6st.	*(E. Taylor)*	2
Mr B. Land's	**Cheesecake**, 4 y-o, 7st.	*(Beasley)*	3
Mr Thompson's	**Sherwood**, 3 y-o, 6st. 3lb.	*(H. Taylor)*	4

* Diadem and Caliban dead heat, the former winning the run-off
Betting: Evens fav. Caliban, 6/4 Diadem.

Thursday 26th September 1861

THE SCURRY HANDICAP of 25 sovereigns.
One mile, starting at the Old Grandstand.

Mr Rigby's	**Lord of the Tees**, 6st. 12lb.	*(Chapman)*	1
Mr B. Land's	**Bavard**, 3 y-o, 7st. 13lb.	*(Sait)*	2
Mr Sparrow's	**Greenwich Fair**, 8st. 13lb.	*(W. White)*	3
Mr B. Land's	**Cheesecake**, 4 y-o, 8st. 7lb.	*(Gammage)*	4
Mr T. Carr's	**Eheu**, 4 y-o, 8st. 5lb.	*(Comery)*	5
Mr Lincoln's	**Duplicity**, 3 y-o, 7st. 12lb.	*(H. Taylor)*	6
Mr T. Carr's	**Breechloader**, 3 y-o, 7st. 8lb.	*(J. Frost)*	7
Capt. Bernard's	**Paroquet**, 2 y-o, 6st.	*(Thomas)*	8

Betting: 2/1 fav. Duplicity, 3/1 Bavard, 5/1 Paroquet.

THE BRADFORD HANDICAP of 3 sovereigns each,
with 25 added. One and quarter miles.

Mr Wright's	**Twinkle**, 3 y-o, 5st. 9lb.	*(H. Taylor)*	1
Mr Wadlow's	**Diadem**, 4 y-o, 7st. 6lb.	*(Whiteley)*	2
Mr Wood's	**Caliban**, 3 y-o, 5st. 7lb.	*(E. Taylor)*	3
Mr B. Land's	**Yorkshire Grey**, aged, 7st. 7lb.	*(Sait)*	4

Betting: 1/2 fav. Twinkle, 3/1 Yorkshire Grey.

THE INNKEEPER'S PLATE of 30 sovereigns.
For horses of all ages. Six furlongs.

Mr Price's	**Holdersyke**, 3 y-o, 7st. 7lb.	*(Matthews)*	1
Mr Adkins'	**Dorritta**, 2 y-o, 5st. 7lb.	*(Whiteley)*	2
Mr Wood's	**Fairy Knowe**, 2 y-o, 5st. 7lb.	*(E. Taylor)*	3
Mr Windsor's	**Jetty Bon**, 2 y-o, 5st. 7lb.	*(Ward)*	4
Mr Johnson's	**by Incense**, 4 y-o, 8st. 6lb.	*(J. Frost)*	5

Betting: 6/4 fav. Holdersyke.

THE MEMBER'S PLATE (Handicap) of 5 sovereigns each, with 25 added. One
mile and a quarter.

Mr T. Carr's	**Eheu**, 4 y-o, 6st. 12lb.	*(Whiteley)*	1
Mr Wood's	**Caliban**, 3 y-o, 5st. 7lb.	*(E. Taylor)*	2
Mr B. Land's	**Bavard**, 3 y-o, 5st. 12lb.	*(Beasley)*	3
Mr Lincoln's	**Duplicity**, 3 y-o, 5st. 9lb.	*(H. Taylor)*	4

Betting: 4/6 fav. Duplicity.

THE HATHERTON NURSERY HANDICAP
of 3 sovereigns each, with 30 added.
For two year olds, six furlongs.

Mr John Land's	**Dunoon**, 7st. 12lb.	*(Sait)*	1
Mr Wood's	**Fairy Knowe**, 7st.	*(E. Taylor)*	2
Mr Thorpe's	**colt by Vanilla**, 7st. 6lb.	*(Whiteley)*	3
Mr Murphy's	**Leonora**, 7st. 12lb.	*(H. Taylor)*	4
Mr Wadlow's	**Pot Pourri**, 7st. 13lb.	*(W. White)*	5
Mr Phillips'	**Bay of Tunis**, 7st. 7lb.	*(Thomas)*	6
Mr Godfrey's	**Agneta**, 7st. 6lb.	*(George Whitehouse)*	7
Mr Rigby's	**Strawberry Leaf**, 7st. 3lb.	*(Chapman)*	8

Betting: Evens fav. Leonora, 5/1 Strawberry Leaf and Pot Pourri.

1862

After the success of last year's meeting it was inconceivable to think that Walsall would be deprived of its races, but that is what happened. The Race Committee had always relied on the trade's people of the town to support their cause by subscribing to the event. This year, their donations were sadly lacking and so the Committee had no alternative but to cancel the meeting. The cattle and sheep grazing on the Lammas Lands were permitted undisturbed pasture for this year.

One man in the town, William Mendicott, licensee of the Spring Cottage public house in Holtshill Lane, wasn't prepared to see Walsall go without its race meeting for the second time in four years. He set to work and succeeded in getting prize money together for another hack race meeting on a field in the Paddock. The ground was very uneven and the racing anything but first class but it amused the large number of spectators gathered to witness the events, which didn't pass without incident. No records are available of the running, but the press did report that one horse descending a hill on the far side of the course fell, the rider being severely bruised. The second day saw another faller, this time the rider, named Lord, wasn't so lucky as he broke his leg.

Although the hack races proved an excellent substitute for the race hungry fans of Walsall, the Fair became the principle attraction of the week, bringing with it the usual problems. In Lichfield Street the pedestrians and residents were up in arms at the large amount of cattle, which were allowed to roam around prior to being sold. Congestion had been a problem for many years, and the Council had made provision for a passage to be kept clear allowing horses and carriages etc to pass through unhindered.

Due to the activities at Paddock, the streets during the afternoon were quieter than usual, but as evening advanced, the crowds began to filter back into town. Many of them congregated in High Street and Park Street, both thoroughfares having an ample number of taverns and inns where they could

1860 - 1879

quench their thirst and visit the mass of stalls. The quacks were there selling medicinal compounds that would cure everything from gout to fleabites, constipation and baldness, it would even put the family dog back on its feet. One of these sweet talking gentlemen quoted the following little ditty to his enthralled audience in the hope they would buy a bottle or two:

'Men snatched from their grave as they were dropping in,
Their lungs coughed up, their bones pierced through their skin,
Men who spent all upon physicians' fees,
Who never slept nor had a moment's ease,
Are now as roaches sound, and all as brisk as bees.'

Another vendor was selling the 'servant's friend,' a wonderful cement that would render broken crockery stronger than new. Another voice cried out above the throng, 'cheap babies for sale,' much to the derision of some of the crowd, but fortunately they were only artistic imitations of the real thing. On the corner of Park Street and Bradford Street a photographic artist had pitched his tent, offering a true and correct likeness of your loved one for a moderate fee. In the vicinity of the grandstand, Bennett and Patches Theatrical Company were performing hourly to enthralled audiences. On the racecourse itself, Edmund's Menagerie had set up their show of performing leopards, elephants and other wild animal. They proudly displayed the only gorilla that had ever been brought into this country alive. Many other showmen had made this claim in the past, only for the 'gorilla' to be some drunk down on his luck, dressed in an animal suit, giving a poor impersonation of this magnificent animal. For the lucky ones that paid to see this spectacle they could go to bed knowing they had seen the real thing, at last. Next door to the menagerie was a caravan with a 'grand display of living wonders and scientific curiosities,' while in another; an exhibition of performing birds did their bit to entertain those members of the public willing to part with a halfpenny for the experience.

1863

To make sure there was no repetition of the previous years disappointment, the Race Committee held a series of meetings in the summer of 1863 regarding the intended forthcoming event in September.

Needless to say, the *Walsall Free Press* had something to say on the matter, whilst they make it obvious they disagree with the horse races in Walsall, they nevertheless report on the proceedings fairly, putting their prejudices aside. How many newspapers can say that today?

Their report mentions the resurrection of the meeting with the following statement: -

'The races, which were to considered to have been numbered with the things of the past, were, phoenix like, called into existence from their own ashes. The long train of carriages containing the nobility and gentry of the district, who, in former years, patronised the meeting were no longer visible. The Grandstand too has become a shattered fabric, the dilapidated condition of which compared with its former gay appearance reminded one forcibly of the career of the fast fraternity – flashy in youth, seedy in old age. As to the races themselves, a horserace alongside a railway is, therefore as comical a sight as a tournament alongside a battery of Armstrong guns. The original argument in favour of races is demolished, and the institutions must be judged of as an amusement, and in this respect it really is questionable whether, all things considered, they are worth the money spent on them. But a truce to moralising for the present, let us take the races as an established fact, and describe them.'

The summer meetings of the Race Committee bore their fruit on Wednesday 23rd and Thursday 24th September, after much hard work in securing the necessary finance required.

Ten races were on the card with a slightly unbalanced feel about the programme; only four races were run on the first day, while six were scheduled for Thursday.

The weather was initially bright on Wednesday morning but as the time of the first race came closer, the skies darkened and a good shower soaked the course. Many spectators dived for cover in the many tents surrounding the course. This gave the local pickpockets plenty of opportunity to swell their illegal earnings. One who fell foul to the parasites of society was the town surveyor, Mr Clark, who was relieved of his favourite old pocket watch.

The shower was the only bad weather of the day, the remainder of the day being bright. Just as well, no one wanted a repetition of the first race two years ago, no matter how humorous it appeared to the onlookers.

As was usual, the numbers of runners at the meeting were few, with only two or three of them looking anything more than mediocre.

After a disappointing first race for the Trial Stakes, which was actually a match as there were only two runners. Mr Wallace's experienced colt Sir Watkin, defeated Thomas Cliff's previously un-raced two year-old, Wyrley, but only just, winning by a neck.

The Tradesmen's Plate over a mile and a half was the first real race, and that only had four runners to enflame the passions of the ardent turf enthusiasts of Walsall. The favourite of the quartet, as far as the bookmakers were concerned, was William Hart's Middlewatch, the horse with the least ability on past form, winning just once from eight attempts. Two of the other runners, True Heart and The Pony had each won four of their previous races from ten starts. Making up the field was a previous course winner in 1860, Lady Bird, only lightly raced when she arrived at the Long Meadow having run just three times and winning once, at Lichfield. Previous form meant nothing, as average as Middlewatch appeared, he won in a canter by a couple of lengths, with Lady Bird second. The race should have only have had three runners as the owner of The Pony, Captain Moss, withdrew his horse at Weatherby's in London but the message never reached the trainer in time and the horse ran. Communications between Walsall and London were not at their best at this time. Captain Moss also withdrew another of his runners, Portland, but he also ran, coming second to Thomas Hunt's Jacob in the Member's Plate Handicap later in the afternoon.

1860 - 1879

Wednesday's card must have been a disappointment to the Race Committee as three of the four events on the programme were matches. The Two Year-Old Stakes over six furlongs had only two runners, with victory going to Thomas Hunt's un-named colt by Teddington, who inflicted the second defeat of the day on Thomas Cliff's colt Wyrley.

Thursday's proceedings began with the first race over hurdles for twelve years, when the Handicap Hurdle Race was run over two miles and six flights of hurdles. Jacob, the horse that won Wednesday's final flat race, showed his versatility by winning this one too. In second place was the same horse that had been beaten by Jacob yesterday, Portland, this time a legitimate runner for Captain Moss.

The following race, the Nursery Handicap over six furlongs was probably the most exciting race of the day, if not the meeting. With heat races now a thing of the past, this race brought about their resurrection. The race finished in a dead-heat between Mr Deveraux's Highland Mary and Mr Doyle's Jewel. To decide the matter a second heat was run, with victory going to Highland Mary by half a length. The jockey of the runner-up is shown in the *Racing Calendar* as Marlow, this is thought to be Charles Marlow from Hazel Slade, who rode many years ago at Walsall as a young man. The years in between had been both kind and cruel to the little man, winning the Derby and St. Leger in 1849 on The Flying Dutchman and achieving much success in many other races. His career began to falter after breaking his leg badly in The Oaks of 1855 when the horse he was riding, Nettle, fell. The horse was owned by Rugeley's infamous son, Dr. William Palmer, and trained at Hednesford by William Saunders, Marlow's brother-in-law.

The horse that finished third in the race, Rattler, was owned by Lord Anglesey. This was the first time for many years that a member of the nobility had run a horse at Walsall. As much as the Race Committee wished for the return of such high profile owners, it was not to be, the glory days, few that they were, had long gone.

The Innkeeper's Plate, over six furlongs, saw a pair of two year-olds go to the post, Thomas Cliff's bay colt, Wyrley and Mr Orme's un-named colt by Teddington. The pair had met the previous day with the Teddington colt coming out on top. This time, at the third time of asking, Wyrley reversed the places and won very easily in a canter by ten lengths.

In the final race of the meeting, the Scurry Handicap over four furlongs, saw the largest field of the meeting go to the post with six runners. The horse installed as evens favourite, Rowena, seemed an unusual choice, having only raced once before in the season, and coming in last at that. The best horse on previous form was Captain Moss' The Pony, but the field also consisted of two other course winners, Sir Watkin and the un-named Teddington colt. Of the two remaining runners, Lady Bird and London, the former appeared better qualified as a potential winner. Prior to this race, all of the favourites but one had won, this time the backers got it wrong, Rowena came in fourth of the six, the race going to the outsider, William Saunders' London who won by three lengths from The Pony with Sir Watkin two lengths further behind.

The official results of the meeting were:

Wednesday 23rd September 1863

THE TRIAL STAKES of 3 sovereigns each, with 10 added. One mile. (6subs).

| Mr Wallace's | Sir Watkin, 2 y-o, 5st. 13lb. | (W. Britton) | 1 |
| Mr T. Cliff's | Wyrley, 2 y-o, 5st. 8lb. | (Job Toon) | 2 |

Betting: 4/6 fav. Sir Watkin.

THE TRADESMEN'S PLATE of 50 sovereigns added to a Handicap Sweepstakes of 5 sovs. each. One and a half miles. (21 subs).

Mr W. Hart's	Middlewatch, 3 y-o, 6st. 12lb.	(H. Taylor)	1
Mr Dickins'	Lady Bird, 5 y-o, 7st. 8lb.	(Gurry)	2
Mr T. Hunt's	True Heart, 3 y-o, 6st. 9lb.	(Hulme)	3
Capt. Moss'	The Pony, 3 y-o, 6st. 11lb.	(E. Taylor)	4

Betting: 6/4 fav. Middlewatch, 5/2 Lady Bird, 3/1 True Heart.

THE TWO YEAR OLD STAKES of 5 sovereigns each, with 15 added. Six furlongs. (4 subs).

| Mr Orme's | by Teddington, 7st. 11lb. | (Neale) | 1 |
| Mr Cliff's | Wyrley, 8st. | (Henry Taylor) | 2 |

Betting: 4/7 fav. the winner.

THE MEMBER'S PLATE (Handicap) of 5 sovereigns each, with 25 added. One mile and a quarter. (15 subs)

| Mr T. Hunt's | Jacob, 6 y-o, 7st. 6lb. | (Neale) | 1 |
| Capt. Moss' | Portland, 6 y-o, 6st. 13lb. | (E. Taylor) | 2 |

Betting: 1/2 fav. the winner.

Thursday 24th September 1863

A HANDICAP HURDLE RACE of 3 sovereigns each, with 20 added. Two miles over six hurdles. (4 subs).

Mr T. Hunt's	Jacob, 6 y-o, 11st. 7lb.	(Knott)	1
Capt. Moss'	Portland, 6 y-o, 10st.	(A Thorpe)	2
Mr F. Jacob's	Nereus, aged, 10st. 2lb.	(G. Holman)	3
Mr S. Lloyd's	Foster's Captain, aged 9st. 5lb.	(Page)	4

Betting: Evens fav. Jacob, 2/1 Nereus.

THE NURSERY HANDICAP of 3 sovereigns each, with 30 added. For two year olds, six furlongs. (4 subs).

Mr Devereux's	*Highland Mary, 6st. 8lb.	(Williamson)	1
Mr Doyle's	*Jewel, 7st. 2lb.	(Marlow)	1
Lord Anglesey's	Rattler, 7st. 2lb.	(Neptune Stagg)	3
Mr J. A. Hind's	Drumhead, 7st. 10lb.	(D. Lomas)	4

Dead heat with Highland Mary winning the run-off.
Betting: Evens fav. Highland Mary, 5/4 Jewel.

THE BRADFORD HANDICAP of 3 sovereigns each, with 50 added. One mile. (21 subs).

Mr Lincoln's	Tourist, 3 y-o, 7st. 12lb.	(Henry Taylor)	1
Mr Wallace's	Golden Drop, 3 y-o, 7st.	(Connor)	2
Mr W. Hart's	Middlewatch, 3 y-o, 7st. 4lb.	(Williamson)	3
Lord Anglesey's	Cadeau, 3 y-o, 6st. 6lb.	(Neptune Stagg)	4

Betting: 4/6 fav. Tourist, 7/2 Golden Drop, 4/1 any other.

THE INNKEEPER'S PLATE of 20 sovereigns. For horses of all ages. Six furlongs.

| Mr T. Cliff's | Wyrley, 2 y-o, 5st. 7lb. | (Samuel Kenyon) | 1 |
| Mr Orme's c. | by Teddington, 2 y-o, 5st. 10lb. | (Hulme) | 2 |

Betting: 4/5 fav. the Teddington colt.

1860 - 1879

THE STAFFORDSHIRE YEOMANRY CAVALRY PLATE,
a sweepstakes of 1 sovereign each, with 10 added.
For horses the property of and ridden by members of the Corp.
Two miles.

Mr Davey's	**Lawyer,** 5 y-o, 11st. 10lb.	(Owner)	1
Mr Jones'	**The Brewer,** 7 11st. 10lb.	(Capt. Chawner)	2

THE SCURRY HANDICAP of 25 sovereigns.
Four furlongs.

Mr Saunders'	**London,** 2 y-o, 6st. 2lb.	(Hulme)	1
Capt. Moss'	**The Pony,** 3 y-o, 7st. 2lb.	(E. Taylor)	2
Mr Wallace's	**Sir Watkin,** 2 y-o, 6st. 10lb.	(W. Britton)	3
Mr Lincoln's	**Rowena,** 3 y-o, 7st. 8lb.	(Henry Taylor)	4
Mr Dickins'	**Lady Bird,** 5 y-o, 8st. 6lb.	(Gurry)	5
Mr Lincoln's	**Duplicity,** 3 y-o, 7st. 12lb.	(H. Taylor)	6
Mr Orme's colt	**by Teddington,** 2 y-o, 6st. 7lb.	(Marlow)	7

Betting: Evens fav. Rowena, 2/1 The Pony.

1864

The *Walsall Free Press,* as usual, painted a vivid picture in words regarding the happenings at the Fair and Races. Their article published in the October 1st edition of the paper tells of how, in recent years, the amount of stalls had grown in number. In years gone by the stalls occupied just High Street and Digbeth, now, they stretched up Park Street and almost all the way along Station Street, and from the grandstand up the length of Bradford Street. The Fair wasn't suppose to begin officially until twelve noon on Monday, by law, but by the time St. Matthew's Church bell chimed its opening chorus, much business had been done already. As in past recordings of the Fair, all sorts of entertainment awaited the eager crowds, for the young there were the numerous 'suck' stalls, toy vans, swing-boats, roundabouts and exhibitions of natural curiosities which included the 'fat boy' and the 'learned pig,' but could it pick a winner?

Between the Fair and Races there was no more than a brief interlude in the festivities. The revellers forgot about sleep and went straight to the racecourse to await the days sport. On Wednesday 28th September, the opening day, the weather was all that could be desired, consequently, huge crowds gathered. Bradford Street, up to the crest of the hill was densely crowded with people, standing row upon row, descending the incline to the middle of the course. The betting ring, with its three tier system, saw the 'second' and 'third class' fraternity set up directly in front of the judge's chair. The 'first class,' occupied an area close to the 'inner circle' near the grandstand, with large amounts of money, and property, being won and lost over the two days. Interspersed with all of this were more than a fair share of stalls serving drink to suit all palates, shooting galleries, Bennett and Patches Theatre Company plus a considerable number of fruit and confectionery stalls.

The entries for the races this year were huge in comparison to previous years with a total of one hundred and thirty one contesting the ten races over the two days. As has been said previously, a large entry does not necessarily mean large fields, and the fields were greatly reduced by the time the racing got under way.

Opening the meeting was the All-Aged Plate run over six furlongs with seven runners contesting the race. If the connoisseurs of the turf had read the form correctly, there was only going to be one winner. The horse concerned was Blue Mantle, a four year-old bay colt, owned by Captain Douglas Lane. The horse's credentials were impeccable, as a two-year old he won the New Stakes at Ascot in 1862. Although he had run ten races and won only one prior to coming to Walsall, it is where he had been running the races that makes one realise he was well above average for a Long Meadow 'nag.' The courses included Newmarket, Epsom, Ascot, Doncaster, York and Goodwood, running in some very high profile races and not being disgraced in any of them. In the Prince of Wales' Stakes at Newmarket he finished fourth of twenty-four high class horses and in the Stewards' Cup at Goodwood, he came in sixth of the thirty-nine runners. There was nothing else in the field at Walsall that could hold a candle to Blue Mantle. The ideal handicap would have been to have him pulling a cart, and a fully laden one at that. The betting didn't reflect the horse's superiority however, as the very generous odds of 4/6 were given about him. The second favourite was an un-named black mare by Osbaldeston who was having her first run of the season, also being odds-on at 4/7, with the rest of the field at 6/1. At the start, Blue Mantle made off and was never headed, winning by three lengths in a canter from two Hednesford trained horses, Thomas Eskrett's Robert Macaire and Thomas Cliff's Osbaldeston mare, the second favourite. The weight the winner carried was forty-six pounds more than the second horse, not quite a laden cart, but close. An hour and a half later, Blue Mantle turned out again for the Tradesmen's Plate over one and a half miles. This time with only one other horse brave enough to take him on, Mr Stirk's Zorah. He had run in the previous race, finishing last of three, so his chances didn't look too good. Starting as 1/10 favourite, Blue Mantle walked it, although the official margin was given as a length, he won as he pleased, this time giving his rival thirty eight pounds in weight. An interesting observation concerning this race is that the entries were the largest of any of the events on the race card, attracting twenty-four initially. Word obviously spread quickly that a horse of some quality was running, the other owners must have been falling over themselves to get their horses scratched from the race.

After watching a horse the calibre of Blue Mantle, it was back to earth for the remainder of the days programme. Mr R. Young's Rosebud who had triumphed in the three horse race for the Trial Stakes, ran again in the Member's Stakes, but this time having no effect on his two rivals. The race, which had three runners, was won by Sea Boy who defeated another odds-on favourite, Rifle, owned by Mr Lincoln. His colours of white jacket and black cap were becoming quite familiar, and successful at Walsall.

The last official race of the day was the Hednesford Handicap Plate over six furlongs, which was won by another horse with an army officer as an owner, Captain Handley's Ossian. Of the five runners in the race, three of them were two year olds, one of them, Wicket coming second. Mr Fellow's, the owner of Wicket, didn't believe in lightly racing his novices, this was the sixteenth race for the young colt who won just

1860 - 1879

one of the races contested. Ossian, who carried 8 stone 12 pounds, was another horse giving his rivals huge amounts of weight. Nearest to him in the weights was the fourth horse, Thomas Cliff's Lizard, who carried 6 stone 8 pounds.

On the second day of the meeting the weather was still holding out as the runners for the Handicap Hurdle Race went out onto the course. Initially eighteen had entered for the race but disappointingly, only two lined-up for the start. The winner was another of Mr Lincoln's horses, Ross, successful in five of his previous fifteen races. He started as the 1/5 favourite against a horse named Blight who ran as his name suggested, badly.

The next two races were won by horses trained at Hednesford. In the Nursery Handicap for two year-olds, Thomas Eskrett saw his colt, Edinburgh, defeat yet another odds-on favourite, Captain Handley's Saloon by two lengths. The following race, the Bradford Handicap, was won by Thomas Cliff's three year-old, Wildman, starting at 1/2 favourite, but he didn't have things all his own way. The favourite lead for all the race, but on the line he was caught by Mr Lincoln's Rifle, the judge declaring a dead-heat. In the run off, Wildman's price had shortened to odds of 1/3, justifying everyone's confidence in him, he won by a length.

The Race Committee saved the best until last, at least, the race with the most runners, nine in total. This included the best horse to grace the Long Meadow since Independence, thirty years previously, Blue Mantle. The race was the Scurry Handicap over five furlongs, confidence in Captain Lane's horse wasn't as strong as the previous day, as he started the 5/4 against favourite. The reason for these generous odds was the massive amount of weight the handicapper decided he must give his rivals, such was his superiority.

Today, such vast differences in weight are not allowed, the favourite was set to carry 10 stone 7 pounds, and the horse that finished last, Robert Macaire was carrying just 5 stone 10 pounds, a deficit of 4 stone 7 pounds. As good as Blue Mantle, was he couldn't concede so much weight to his rivals and was beaten into third place. The winner was previous course winner, Lady Maud, ridden by Neptune Stagg, with Thomas Smith's, Oulton Lowe, third. To the winner, the favourite gave fifty-two pounds and to the second horse, forty-seven pounds, all that weight difference and he was less than a length behind.

It had been quite a meeting for those involved in the betting ring, of the ten races, all but one had an odds on favourite, of those, seven had won.

The official results of the meeting were:

Wednesday 28rd September 1864

THE ALL AGE PLATE of 25 sovereigns each. Six furlongs.

Capt. Lane's	**Blue Mantle,** 4 y-o, 9st. 7lb.	(Connor)	1
Mr T. Eskrett's	**Robert Macaire,** 2 y-o, 6st. 3lb.	(Ward)	2
Mr T. Cliff's m.	**by Osbaldeston,** 5 y-o, 8st. 3lb.	(H. Taylor)	3
Mr R. Law's	**Lucy Long,** 2 y-o, 6st.	(Samuel Kenyon)	4
Mr Murray's	**Kathleen,** 2 y-o, 6st.	(Brown)	5
Mr Wallace's	**Kingmaker,** 2 y-o, 6st. 3lb.	(Britton)	6
Mr J. Page's	**Startler,** 4 y-o, 8st.	(Bendy)	7

Betting: 4/6 fav. Blue Mantle, 7/4 T. Cliff's mare, 6/1 any other.

THE TRIAL STAKES of 3 sovereigns each, with 20 added. One mile.

Mr R. Young's	***Rosebud,** 3 y-o, 7st. 9lb.	(Matley)	1
Capt. Little's	***Lady Maud,** 3 y-o, 7st. 6lb.	(E. Taylor)	1
Mr Stirk's	**Zorah,** 3 y-o, 7st. 6lb.	(Coslett)	3
Capt. Moss's	**The Pony,** 3 y-o, 6st. 11lb.	(Taylor)	4

*Rosebud and Lady Maud dead heat, Rosebud later walked over.
Betting: 1/2 fav. Lady Maud, 2/1 Rosebud.

THE TRADESMEN'S PLATE of 25 sovereigns added to a Handicap of 5 sovereigns each. One mile and a quarter. (24 subs)

Capt. Lane's	**Blue Mantle,** 4 y-o, 8st. 12lb.	(Connor)	1
Mr Stirk's	**Zorah,** 3 y-o, 6st. 2lb.	(Sopp)	2

Betting: 1/10 fav. the winner.

THE MEMBER'S PLATE (Handicap) of 5 sovereigns each, with 25 added. One mile and a quarter. (15 subs)

Capt. Handley's	**Sea Boy,** 3 y-o, 7st. 7lb.	(Henry Taylor)	1
Mr Lincoln's	**Rifle,** 3 y-o, 7st. 2lb.	(Samuel Kenyon)	2
Mr R. Young's	**Rosebud,** 3 y-o, 7st. 10lb	(Matley)	3

Betting: 4/5 fav. Rifle, 6/4 Sea Boy.

THE HEDNESFORD HANDICAP PLATE of 25 sovereigns, for horses of all ages. Six furlongs.

Capt. Handley's	**Ossian,** 4 y-o, 8st. 12lb.	(E. Taylor)	1
Mr W. Fellows'	**Wicket,** 2 y-o, 6st.	(Gregory)	2
Mr R. Law's	**Lucy Long,** 2 y-o, 6st. 3lb.	(S. Kenyon)	3
Mr T. Cliff's	**Lizard,** 2 y-o, 6st. 8lb.	(Job Toon)	4
Mr Page's	**Sensation,** 3 y-o, 6st. 4lb.	(Bendy)	5

Betting: 1/2 fav. Ossian, 3/1 Wicket, 4/1 Sensation.

Thursday 29th September 1864

A HANDICAP HURDLE RACE of 3 sovereigns each, with 20 added. Two miles over six hurdles. (4 subs).

Mr Lincoln's	**Ross,** 5 y-o, 10st. 12lb.	(J. Knott)	1
Mr Yardley's	**Blight,** 3 y-o, 9st. 2lb.	(E. Pratt)	2

Betting: 1/5 fav. Ross.

THE NURSERY HANDICAP of 3 sovereigns each, with 30 added. For two year olds, six furlongs. (6 subs).

Mr T. Eskrett's	**Edinburgh,** 7st. 13lb.	(Ward)	1
Capt. Handley's	**Saloon,** 8st. 13lb.	(Henry Taylor)	2
Mr Bird's	**colt out of Wire,** 6st. 12lb.	(Job Toon)	3
Lord Uxbridge's	**Cockrow,** 8st.	(Neale)	4
Mr W. Fellows'	**Wicket,** 6st. 13lb.	(Gregory)	5
Mr Goodlass'	**colt out of Pass Card,** 7st. 8lb.	(N. Stagg)	6

Betting: 4/6 fav. Saloon, 5/2 Edinburgh 5/1 any other.

THE BRADFORD HANDICAP of 5 sovereigns each, with 50 added. One mile. (19 subs).

Mr T. Cliff's	***Wildman,** 3 y-o, 7st. 10lb.	(Henry Taylor)	1
Mr Lincoln's	***Rifle,** 3 y-o, 6st. 13lb.	(Samuel Kenyon)	2
Capt. Handley's	**Sea Boy,** 3 y-o, 7st. 11lb.	(Job Toon)	3
Lord Anglesey's	**Cadeau,** 3 y-o, 6st. 6lb.	(Neptune Stagg)	4

* Wildman and Rifle, dead heat, Wildman winning the run-off.
Betting: 1/2 fav. Wildman.

1860 – 1879

THE HUNTER'S STAKES of 25 sovereigns.
For horses of all ages. One mile and a half.

| Capt. Handley's | Sea Boy, 3 y-o, 10st. 10lb. | (Mr Wood) | 1 |

Beating five other runners not listed.

THE SCURRY HANDICAP PLATE of 25 sovereigns.
For horses of all ages. Five furlongs.

Mr Drury's	Lady Maud, 3 y-o, 6st. 11lb.	(N. Stagg)	1
Mr T. Smith's	Oulton Lowe, 3 y-o, 7st. 2lb.	(Brown)	2
Capt. D. Lane's	Blue Mantle, 4 y-o, 10st. 7lb.	(Connor)	3
Mr Backhouse's	Barter, 4 y-o, 9st.	(E. Taylor)	4
Mr T. Cliff's	m. by Osbaldeston, 5 y-o, 8st.	(H. Taylor)	5
Mr Cherrington's	Jewel, 3 y-o, 6st. 10lb.	(Job Toon)	6
Mr Goodlass'	c. out of Pass Card, 2 y-o, 6st.	(Martin)	7
Mr W. Fellows'	Wicket, 2 y-o, 5st. 10lb.	(Samuel Kenyon)	8
Mr T. Eskrett's	Robert Macaire, 2 y-o, 5sr. 10lb.	(Ward)	9

Betting: 4/5 fav. Blue Mantle, 5/2 Lady Maud.

1865

In recent years, the weather had been kind to the Races, and this year was no exception, the *Walsall Free Press* describing it as *'the thermometer stood some degrees above blood heat, and the sky was of that pure cerulean blue peculiar to more southern climes.'*

Whilst the Races, even in bad weather never appeared to suffer from a lack of spectators, horses maybe, but fine weather brought out the populace in their thousands, and not only from Walsall. Excursions by train were still running from Birmingham and Wolverhampton specially for the event. The large crowds meant more pickpockets attempting to make an easy living. On the first day, two of the light-fingered fraternity from Wolverhampton were apprehended and sentenced to 21 days in prison for their trouble.

The old grandstand was showing its age by now, although a little rickety and shabby, it nevertheless gave one of the best views over the course and was always well patronised.

We tend to think today that corporate hospitality is a relatively modern phenomenon. The victuallers of old Walsall were using a similar practice one hundred and forty years ago. As well as erecting tents to serve drinks and refreshments, they also erected temporary wooden stands along side. The keen racegoer could hire a seat for the duration of the Races, with drinks available at the click of your fingers. The price for seats being determined by how close, or far, from the action the stand was positioned. The benefit of this was that you could leave your seat to place a few wagers and check out the look of your fancy, knowing that you had a seat when the time for the race came around.

The programme consisted of six races on Wednesday and five the following day, starting with the Trial Stakes at two o'clock on the first day. This race was won by a horse that had won at last years' meeting, Mr Stewart's, Rosebud, who defeated his two rivals easily. The odds-on favourite, Humphrey couldn't get on terms with the winner at any time during the race, and the third horse, Thomas Cliff's, Flattery, flattered no one by coming in last.

The interval between races at was approximately forty-five minutes, and at two forty-five, the four runners assembled for the start of the six-furlong Hednesford Plate. Included in the line-up was Captain Lane's good thing, Blue Mantle, although a year older, the handicapper was doing the horse few favours by continuing to give him big weights to haul around. Unusually, Blue Mantle wasn't the favourite, this honour going to Thomas Cliff's, Alice Lee at 4/6, the remaining two runners hadn't a chance according to the betting. The race itself proved slightly different however, all four runners contested the event well, making a very exciting race, but in the end, the 'ring' was proved correct, with Alice Lee getting home by half a length from a hard driven Blue Mantle, ridden as last year by Connor.

Another odds-on favourite started for the Tradesmen's Plate over a mile and a half, this time the horse was one of Lord Westmorland's, a three year-old named Orloff who started at 4/5. This was another good race with all five runners keeping close together for the circuit and a half of the course. At the line, it was defeat again for an odds-on favourite, beaten into third place by Gamecock with Mr Lynex's mare, Queen of Trumps second.

For the first time in many years, a race especially for half-bred horses was back in the programme. The race was titled, The Staffordshire Volunteers, Yeomanry and Militia Plate, was run over two miles. The conditions of entry were that each horse must be owned and ridden by a member of the corps, in whose possession the horse must have been since June 1st 1865. The entries for the race were large, the runners unfortunately were few. Only three lined up, with yet another 'hotshot' odds-on favourite, Captain Harrison's horse, The Colonel. Favourites are there to be beaten and that's what happened. He was beaten easily into second place by the 4/1 chance, Dewdrop, the property of Mr Shereary.

In the final race of the day, the All-Aged Plate, Alice Lee defeated a pair of two year-olds, Mr Pegg's, Voivode and William Saunders, Clatford, with considerable ease.

The weather remained perfect for the continuation of the meeting on Thursday; every one concerned with the organisation of the event hoped the racing could do it justice. As far as the newspapers were concerned, it may as well have been a one day meeting as none of them reported the afternoons racing. Fortunately, from a research point of view, the *Racing Calendar* came to the rescue with its usual comprehensive coverage.

The afternoon's sport began at two o'clock with the five furlong Scurry Plate, won by Mr Pegg's Voivode, with Sea Boy, a course winner the previous day in a match and a winner last year, second.

Still included in the card was the Bradford Handicap that had been included in the programme for many years, not surprisingly, considering the land was owned by his Lordship. The winner of the event, Gamecock, who also won the previous day made it a profitable double for his owner, Mr Bilham.

The final race of the day was the popular Handicap Hurdle Race, run over two miles, with six flights of hurdles to be negotiated. Mr Powell's horse, Humphrey, second in the opening race of the meeting, showed his versatility over hurdles by finishing runner-up to another flat performer, Wicket, owned by William Fellows.

1860 - 1879

As was mentioned previously, reporting for the meeting of 1865 was poor, but the *Staffordshire Advertiser* stated that during the proceedings, two horses had fallen, without injury to horse or rider, due to an awkward curve in the course. Unfortunately, no other details are known.

The official results of the meeting were:

Wednesday 27rd September 1865

THE HEDNESFORD HANDICAP PLATE of 25 sovereigns, for horses of all ages. Six furlongs.

Mr T. Cliff's	Alice Lee, 4 y-o, 7st. 11lb.	(S. Kenyon)	1
Capt. D. Lane's	Blue Mantle, 5 y-o, 9st. 3lb.	(E. Sharpe)	2
Mr Merrick's	Perfect Lady, 6 y-o, 6st. 7lb.	(Ward)	3
Mr Crook's	f. by Knight of Kars, 2 y-o, 5st. 7lb.	-	4

Betting: 4/5 fav. Alice Lee, 5/4 Blue Mantle.

THE TRIAL STAKES of 3 sovereigns each, with 20 added. One mile.

Mr Rickard's	Rosebud, 4 y-o, 8st. 10lb.	(Matley)	1
Mr Powell's	Humphrey, 6 y-o, 8st. 13lb.	(E. Taylor)	2
Mr T. Cliff's	Flattery, 6 y-o, 8st. 3lb.	(Gardener)	3

THE TRADESMEN'S PLATE of 25 sovereigns added to a Handicap of 5 sovereigns each. One mile and a quarter. (24 subs)

Mr Bilham's	Gamecock, aged, 7st. 10lb.	(Ward)	1
Mr W. Copeland's	Queen of Trumps, 4 y-o, 7st. 2lb.	(Neale)	2
Ld. Westmoreland's	Orloff, 3 y-o, 6st. 5lb.	(S. Kenyon)	3
Mr Robertson's	Danaus, 4 y-o, 7st. 9lb.	(F. Barnes)	4
Mr Roper's	King Tom, 4 y-o, 7st. 5lb.	(N. Stagg)	5

Betting: 4/5 fav. Orloff, 5/2 Gamecock, 3/1 Queen of Trumps.

THE STAFFORDSHIRE VOLUNTEER, YEOMANRY AND MILITIA PLATE of 2 sovereigns each, with 20 added. For half-bred horses the property of Members of the Corps. Two miles.

Mr Shereary's	Dewdrop	-	1
Capt. Harrison's	The Colonel	-	2
Mr Barrett's	Dick	-	3

Betting: 4/6 fav. The Colonel, 4/1 Dewdrop.

THE MEMBER'S PLATE (Handicap) of 5 sovereigns each, with 25 added. One mile and a quarter. (15 subs)

Mr T. Cliff's	Sea Boy, 4 y-o, 8st. 6lb.	(Gardener)	1
Mr Merrick's	Perfect Lady, 6 y-o, 7st. 3lb.	(Ward)	2

Betting: 1/3 fav. Sea Boy.

THE ALL AGED PLATE of 25 sovereigns each, Six furlongs. 5 ran.

Mr T. Cliff's	Alice Lee, 4 y-o, 9st. 4lb.	(Gardener)	1
Mr T. Pegg's ch. f.	by Voivode, 2 y-o, 6st. 7lb.	(Munton)	2
Mr J. Saunders'	Clatford, 2 y-o, 6st. 3lb.	(Dowley)	-

Thursday 28th September 1865

THE SCURRY HANDICAP PLATE of 25 sovereigns. For horses of all ages. Five furlongs. 5 ran.

Mr T. Pegg's ch. f.	by Voivode, 2 y-o, 5st. 10lb.	(F. Barnes)	1
Mr T. Cliff's	Sea Boy, 4 y-o, 8st.	(S. Kenyon)	2
Mr Mott's	Eola, 4 y-o, 7st. 7lb.	(Gregory)	3

THE HUNTER'S PLATE of 25 sovereigns. For horses of all ages. One mile and a half. (12 subs.) 9 ran.

Mr Jones'	Truant, aged, 12st.	(Mr Edmunds)	1
Mr -	Overtone, 5 y-o, 12st. 7lb.	-	2

THE BRADFORD HANDICAP of 5 sovereigns each, with 30 added. One mile. (19 subs).

Mr Bilham's	Gamecock, aged, 7st. 8lb.	(Ward)	1
Mr T. Stevens'	Fisherman's Daughter, 4 y-o, 7st. 7lb.	-	2
Mr R. Herbert's	Danaus, 4 y-o, 7st. 6lb.	(F. Barnes)	3
Mr Copeland's	Queen of Trumps, 4 y-o, 6st. 11lb.	(Neale)	4

THE NURSERY HANDICAP of 3 sovereigns each, with 30 added. For two year olds, six furlongs. (18 subs).

Mr Godfrey's	Longboat, 7st. 8lb.	(Neptune Stagg)	1
Mr Wadlow's	King of Spades, 7st. 2lb.	(Jamieson)	2
Mr D. George's	Wallet, 7st. 9lb.	(Britton)	-
Mr Thompson's	Cantharides, 7st. 2lb.	(S. Kenyon)	-

A HANDICAP HURDLE RACE of 3 sovereigns each, with 25 added. Two miles over six hurdles. (17 subs).

Mr Archers'	Wicket, 3 y-o, 9st.	(Gregory)	1
Mr Powell's	Humphrey, 6 y-o, 10st. 1lb.	(E. Taylor)	2

1866

In 1866, the only newspaper in the locality, the *Walsall Free Press,* had been on the streets of the town for ten years; in the early days of its publication, it regularly ran articles condemning the Races. In recent years, their attitude had mellowed considerably and they reported the events without any real derogatory remarks. This year, they aimed their condemnation at three booths situated near the original grandstand who were encouraging the youth of Walsall to take part in the noble art of pugilism – or as they put it, *'the fistic sciences.'* For the cost of one penny, Professor Posh Price, and two other 'professors', would initiate the young lads in the art of self-defence. The newspaper was outraged by this exploitation that encouraged the youngsters to fight, as if they needed encouragement, and felt the authorities should do everything in their power to put a stop to these *'disgraceful exhibitions.'*

The Races was just one of the ways people liked to enjoy themselves and this year they had eleven races to look forward to during the two days. The weather was dry on both days, but overcast on Wednesday with similar weather on Thursday but interspersed with bright sunny spells. The attendance for the first day was exceptional with many thousands congregating on or around the Long Meadow. On the second day the fair at Birmingham was responsible for a reduction in the attendance.

The sport commenced at two o'clock on Wednesday afternoon with the six furlongs Hednesford Plate, with six runners lining up. The race was won by E. W. Taylor's, Volhynia from Thomas Cliff's course winner from the previous year, Alice Lee, with J. Bilham's Acolyte, in third place.

Forty five minutes later the race with the snappy title of The Staffordshire Volunteer, Yeomanry and Militia Plate for half-bred horses was getting under way with four runners, all ridden by amateur riders. Everything went well with regard to the

1860 - 1879

race itself with Mr Plimmer's Reveller taking the spoils from Mr Webb's Carbine, second and Mr Aston's Miss Elcot third.

In an effort to see the finish of the race, the spectators gathered on the upper floor of a temporary stand, situated near the railway footbridge known as Stemmer Steps, rushed to the side of the construction nearest the winning post, with disastrous results. The weight of spectators, focused in a relatively small area, caused one of the wooden beams supporting the gallery to collapse, spilling around twenty occupants into the refreshment room below. A similar occurrence happened at Tamworth in 1865 and at Wolverhampton only a few weeks earlier, with much more serious consequences. George Pitt, licensee of The Woolpack Inn, owned the stand and his wife was one of those injured, although not seriously. Suffering from cuts and bruises to the head and shoulders, after treatment she returned to her duties in the evening. Two young men, one named Roden, employed by Mr Price, and Alfred Green, employed by Baggott and Love, both drapers assistants of High Street received leg injuries and concussion. Both were taken by cab to the Cottage Hospital for treatment. A Mrs. Westley of Stafford Street was possibly the most seriously injured. An occupant of the bar at the time of the collapse, she was severely bruised on the arms, shoulders and neck. If that wasn't bad enough, she was scalded on her legs when a boiling teakettle was overturned in the melee. Another casualty was William Taylor of Wolverhampton Street who sustained injuries to his back and hands, many other people were injured, obviously not seriously, and walked away before their injuries could be ascertained.

The stand was erected by a Mr Jones of Tantarra Street and he was warned by the Borough Surveyor earlier in the day that the middle part of the stand was considered insecure and requested that it should be strengthened. Mr Pitt, the owner, made a similar request just before the first race. Unfortunately, nothing was done, resulting in the accident, which may well have been much worse than it actually was, for all concerned.

The incident was widely reported in many newspapers with articles about the accident appearing in the *Belfast Mercury*, the *London Standard* and the *Dundee Advertiser* and many more.

By the following day, all temporary stands had been inspected by the Borough Surveyor, with a card attached to the stand declaring its safety. A Mr. W. J. Griffiths, the owner of a stand on the course placed an advertisement in the *Birmingham Daily Post* the following day declaring, *'The Alhambra is the only Stand on the Course that has been pronounced safe by the Borough Surveyor'*.

Today, the meeting would have been abandoned, but in those days, it was on with the show.

Thomas Eskrett, the Hednesford trainer won two of the remaining events, the All-Aged Plate and the Member's Plate with his horse, Edinburgh. In the former event the horse defeated an off form Alice Lee, who came second, and in the latter event took the prize money by default. The actual winner, Mr J. Bilham's Gamecock was found to be carrying two pounds overweight and was disqualified.

The Tradesmen's Plate was won by Thomas Wadlow's The Drone, defeating five other runners with some ease. The horse was ridden by Walter White, a native of Berwick-Upon-Tweed but now based at Wadlow's stable. The Wadlow family, from Shifnal in Shropshire had been supporters of Walsall Races for many years and had several winners on the course. The family is still connected with racing today, particularly in the training of point-to-pointers.

Eight runners lined up for the one-mile Trial Stakes, with another of Wadlow's horses, a filly by Vedette Basquinier, just failing to get up at the post and finishing second to Mr Halford's Foreign Stamp.

First race of the day on Thursday was the Nursery Free Handicap run over six furlongs, the thirteen entries being reduced to three runners. The even money favourite, Mr Halford's Recompense, was beaten a short head in a very close finish by Colenso, owned by Mr Turner, the third horse was Mr Barber's Alicia.

The Bradford Plate over one mile was delayed by many false starts. When the four runners eventually got away, it was Mr Bilham who was successful with his horse Gamecock, the 5/4 favourite. In second place, a length behind the winner was The Drone, with Mr Godfrey's horse, Longboat, third.

Always a spectacle, the Handicap Hurdle Race was a popular race with the spectators. This year it proved to be almost a runaway victory for William Saunders' horse, the 2/1 chance, Jacob, winner of the race in 1863. Many lengths behind was the second horse, Vision, with Sandford third and the joint 2/1 favourite, Foreign Stamp, a long way behind.

The final race of the meeting was the Hunter's Plate to be run over one and a half miles and to be ridden by gentlemen, farmers, tradesmen and professional jockeys; the latter had to carry six pounds excess for their additional competence. Only four runners contested the race, with Gamecock the evens favourite and 3/1 against any of the others. These were, Vision, second in the hurdle race, Humphrey and Yeatsall. The horse that won was the 'fresh' animal, Vision, the only one who didn't run the course twice due to a false start. Humphrey and Yeatsall completed the course in its entirety but Gamecock pulled up with only part of the course covered. When the time came to restart, three quarters of the field were spent forces, which left Vision, ridden by his owner, Mr Hobson, to take the win by just over a length from Gamecock.

The official results of the meeting were:

Wednesday 26th September 1866
THE HEDNESFORD HANDICAP PLATE of 25 sovereigns, for horses of all ages. Six furlongs.

Mr E. W. Taylor's	**Volhynia**, 3 y-o, 7st. 7lb.	*(H. Jackson)*	1
Mr T. Cliff's	**Alice Lee**, 5 y-o, 9st.	*(H. Taylor)*	2
Mr J. Bilham's	**Acolyte**, 5 y-o, 7st. 4lb.	*(Ward)*	3
Mr Rickards'	**Havannah**, 3 y-o, 7st. 2lb.	*(Bench)*	4
Mr J. Tittensor's	**Lady Constance**, 3 y-o, 6st. 4lb.	*(Carver)*	5
Mr W. Halford's	**Izzie**, 2 y-o, 6st. 4lb.	*(Job Toon)*	6

THE STAFFORDSHIRE VOLUNTEER, YEOMANRY AND MILITIA PLATE of 2 sovereigns each, with 20 added. For half-bred horses the property of Members of the Corps. Two miles.

Mr Plimmer's	**Reveller**, aged, 12st.	*(Owner)*	1
Mr Webb's	**Carbine**, 5 y-o, 12st.	-	2
Mr Aston's	**Miss Elcot**, 5 y-o, 12st.	-	3
Mr Shervyn's	**Dew Drop**, 5 y-o, 12st.	-	4

1860 - 1879

THE ALL AGE PLATE of 25 sovereigns each.
Six furlongs.

Mr T. Eskrett's	**Edinburgh,** 4 y-o, 9st. 8lb.	*(Payne)*	1
Mr T. Cliff's	**Alice Lee,** 5 y-o, 9st. 12lb.	*(H. Taylor)*	2
Mr Clarke's	**Bedford,** 2 y-o, 7st.	*(Job Toon)*	3
Mr Halford's	**Izzie,** 2 y-o, 7st.	*(Matthews)*	4

Six ran.

THE TRADESMEN'S PLATE of 40 sovereigns added
to a Handicap of 5 sovereigns each.
One and a half miles. (24 subs)

Mr Wadlow's	**The Drone,** 3 y-o, 6st. 6lb.	*(Amis)*	1
Mr Parry names	**Wave,** 3 y-o, 6st. 7lb.	*(Carver)*	2
Mr Badham's	**Gamecock,** aged, 7st. 7lb.	*(Ward)*	3
Mr Meeson's	**Charming Woman,** a. 7st. 12lb.	*(Taylor)*	4
Mr E. W. Taylor's	**Volhynia,** 3 y-o, 7st.	*(H. Jackson)*	5
Mr Godfrey's	**Longboat,** 3 y-o, 6st.	*(Shettle)*	6

THE TRIAL STAKES of 3 sovereigns each, with 20 added.
One mile. 8 ran.

Mr Halford's	**Foreign Stamp,** 3 y-o, 7st. 7lb.	*(Doolan)*	1
Mr Wadlow's	**f. by Vedette,** 3 y-o, 7st. 11lb.	*(Tomlinson)*	2
Mr Pemberton's	**Sparkle,** 3 y-o, 7st. 8lb.	*(Ward)*	3
Mr J. Wright's	**Humphrey,** aged, 8st. 12lb.	*(H. Taylor)*	4

THE MEMBER'S PLATE (Handicap) of 3 sovereigns each, with 25 added.
One mile and a quarter. (15 subs)

| Mr T. Eskrett's | **Edinburgh,** 4 y-o, 8st. 7lb. | *(Payne)* | 1 |
| Mr Bilham's | **Gamecock,** aged 8st. 2lb. | *(Ward)* | 2 |

Two ran. Gamecock came in first but was disqualified for carrying overweight.

Thursday 27th September 1866

THE NURSERY HANDICAP of 3 sovereigns each,
with 30 added. For two year olds, six furlongs.

Mr Turner's	**Colenso,** 7st. 7lb.	*(Jackson)*	1
Mr Halford's	**Recompense,** 7st. 10lb	*(Doolan)*	2
Mr Barber's	**Alicia,** 7st. 7lb.	*(Ward)*	3

Betting: Evens fav. Recompense, 2/1 Colenso.

THE BRADFORD HANDICAP PLATE of 5 sovereigns each, with 40 added.
One mile.

Mr Bilham's	**Gamecock,** aged, 7st. 9lb.	*(Ward)*	1
Mr Wadlow's	**The Drone,** 3 y-o, 6st. 7lb.	*(Amiss)*	2
Mr Godfrey's	**Longboat,** 3 y-o, 6st. 2lb.	*(Shettles)*	3
Mr Herance's	**Honeymoon,** 2 y-o, 7st. 4lb.	*(Paling)*	4

A HURDLE RACE FREE HANDICAP of 3 sovereigns each, with 20 added. Two
miles over six hurdles.

Mr Saunders'	**Jacob,** aged, 10st. 5lb.	*(James Knott)*	1
Mr F. Hobson's	**Vision,** 6 y-o, 10st.	*(Owner)*	2
Mr Topham's	**Sandford,** 6 y-o, 9st. 10lb.	*(E. Taylor)*	3
Mr J. Bilham's	**Acolyte,** 5 y-o, 10st. 2lb.	*(Morrell)*	4
Mr Powell's	**Humphrey,** 6 y-o, 8st. 12lb.	*(E. Taylor)*	5
Mr Halford's	**Foreign Stamp,** 3 y-o, 8st. 10lb.	*(Doolan)*	6

Betting: 2/1 favs. Jacob and Foreign Stamp, 3/1 Acolyte.

THE SCURRY HANDICAP PLATE of 25 sovereigns.
For horses of all ages. Five furlongs.

Mr E. W. Taylor's	**Volhynia,** 3 y-o, 8st. 2lb.	*(H. Jackson)*	1
Mr Rickards'	**Havannah,** 3 y-o, 7st. 8lb.	*(Bench)*	2
Mr Dutton's	**filly by Verdette,** 3 y-o, 7st.	*(Amiss)*	3
Mr F. Hobson's	**Bishopton,** 4 y-o, 8st. 4lb.	*(Mullinger)*	4
Lord Bateman's	**Anchorite,** 2 y-o, 6st. 12lb.	*(J. Fox)*	5
Lord Wilton's	**c. by Romulus,** 2 y-o, 6st. 12lb.	*(Jamieson)*	6

Betting: Evens fav. Volhynia, 4/1 Havannah, 7/1 any other.

THE HUNTER'S PLATE of 25 sovereigns.
For horses of all ages. One mile and a half. (12 subs.)

Mr Hobson's	**Vision,** 6 y-o, 11st. 10lb.	*(Owner)*	1
Mr Bilham's	**Gamecock,** aged, 11st. 10lb.	*(Cobham)*	2
Mr Wright's	**Humphrey,** aged, 11st. 10lb.	*(Owner)*	3
Mr Arthur's	**Yeatsall,** 4 y-o, 11st. 5lb.	*(Owner)*	4

1867

The *Walsall Free Press* had been much more tolerant of the activities in recent years, gone was the high moral tone examining the rights and wrongs of the events, replaced by descriptive reports of the town in Victorian times. Their report states: –

'High Street, Digbeth, Bradford Street, as far as the grandstand and Park Street, were lined with stalls containing every variety of fruit, confectionery and toys. There were also large supplies of hot potatoes and cooling beverages, and no lack of cheap Johns', shooting galleries, wheels of fortune, roundabouts and swing boats. There were also a few donkeys' on hire, either by the hour or the journey, and the owner seemed to be doing a good trade, as the poor animals appeared to be kept going all afternoon. On the Bridge was a booth in which Professor Bosco and his 'second sighted lady' were giving entertainments to crowded audiences at a penny a head. Near to the grandstand, Mander's Menagerie and Bennett and Patch's Theatre were erected and appeared to draw good audiences. Alongside the former was another exhibition in which the principal object of attraction was a learned pony. Notwithstanding the attendance was scarcely so large as at the Midsummer Fair, the town was pretty well thronged during the day, and all passed off quietly.'

Specifically for the Races, they penned this small comment included in their columns: –

'The weather being all that could be desired, the meeting was one of the most successful held in Walsall for several years past, so far as attendance was concerned. As usual, there was a heterogeneous assemblage of adventurers on the course, who most assiduously plied their various callings, and many of them no doubt netted considerable sums.'

At two o'clock on the afternoon of Wednesday September 25th, the first race, the All-Aged Plate got under way with only three runners. The six furlong race developed into a match in reality, included in the field was a two year-old named Harleston. The youngster couldn't keep pace with the two more experienced rivals and previous course winners, Thomas Eskrett's Edinburgh and E. W. Taylor's Volhynia. The race finished in favour of the 7/4 favourite Edinburgh, who

1860 - 1879

beat Volhynia by a length with Harleston, a very bad third.

The Hunter's Stakes was again proving popular with the owners, as it had done in years past, attracting what was in effect a cavalry charge for Walsall, with ten runners. It must have been a difficult job attempting to pick a winner from this lot, who were at best, mediocre, not even the Racing Calendar bothered to publish all of the details regarding the race. From a punters point of view, it must have been worth investing a penny with the gentleman who owned the 'learned pony' to see what his equine mastermind thought. As in all races, there has to be a winner, and it was a chestnut gelding, Plum Cake, owned by Mr J. Yates and ridden by Mr Dabbs.

The third race of the afternoon, the Hednesford Plate was won by Verity, trained by Thomas Cliff. The horse was ridden by his sixteen year-old apprentice Job Toon, riding his first winner at Walsall, and putting up two pounds overweight. Toon became a successful jockey and trainer, winning the Irish Derby with Innishowen in 1875. In later years, he became a publican in Walsall and died at the age of forty-five in 1896.

Only four runners contested the race with Verity starting as the 6/4 favourite, Volhynia was quoted at 7/4. The quartet kept close together throughout the six-furlong trip with Verity fighting out the finish with Mr Green's Quirina. The former got home by half a length with Volhynia third and Mr J. Trevor's Lady Lucan fourth.

In the mile and a half mile, Tradesmen's (Handicap) Plate only three runners went to the post, and the betting ring made no secret of their choice, Mr Eastwood's chestnut colt, Rejoinder at 4/6. His two rivals were J. Wright's Lord Bagot at 4/1 and Thomas Wadlow's, The Drone at 6/4. The race was well contested race with the favourite trailing for most of the way. Close to the finish, he removed the worried looks from the faces of his backers when he overhauled Lord Bagot to win by length, with The Drone a further six lengths behind, third.

Six runners contested the last race The Member's Welter Handicap run over one mile and a quarter. Gentlemen, or amateur riders were allowed to compete alongside their professional colleagues in this race. Any owner who engaged a fully-fledged jockey had a price to pay in the form of a six-pound penalty. Only two of the owners elected for this option, Thomas Cliff had Henry Taylor riding his horse, Troubador (3/1) and Mr T. Gough chose Walter White for his entry, Duchess of York. The betting ring obviously agreed with the pairing and installed the latter as 5/4 favourite. It is difficult to see why the spectators on the Long Meadow poured their hard earned cash onto this particular selection, the horse had only run four times prior to coming to Walsall and had not featured in any of them. The only thing the Duchess had in her favour was that White was riding her, but he needed to be a magician, not a jockey. Two of the other runners, Verdi and Quirina had much more form behind them, but were quoted as 5/1 and 8/1 respectively. Troubador was having his first run of the season, and again, the choice of jockey was the only reason he was second favourite. The two remaining horses, Young Lord and Foreign Stamp were better qualified as possible winners than the favourite, even though both were ridden by amateurs. The contemporary reports unfortunately tell nothing of the actual running of the race, but the results show the Duchess of York could only finish fifth of the six runners. Quirina was the winner, landing a nice gamble for her owner Mr Green and jockey, Mr Hobson, with a starting price of 8/1. This was the longest priced winner at Walsall so far. Troubador justified being second favourite, finishing only half a length behind the winner, with Verdi taking third place for her owner, Mr Wilkinson. This race proved to be the most exciting one from a betting point of view, with, one would imagine, a select few on the Long Meadow making a considerable sum from the victory.

Young Job Toon opened his account at Walsall by riding his first winner at the course on Wednesday. In the first race on Thursday, the Nursery Handicap, he doubled his tally on J. Halford's horse, Snuff. The race had only five runners, who can at best be classified as mediocre. Between them they had only run in twenty races, with one, Lady Love, recording a single victory from nine previous starts. Toon's mount started at 6/4 favourite and won by a length from Thomas Eskrett's Arigill, in third place was Chateau Margaux, the property of Mr Aston; unfortunately, the horse didn't have the same qualities as the wine it took its name from.

The Open Hunter's Plate had the same conditions as the Hunter Stakes of the previous day, with regard to the riding of the horses. No one was fooled today by Walter White being put up as jockey on yesterday's failed favourite, Duchess of York, contesting the race with four others, all ridden by amateurs. Mr Wright's Lord Bagot was the favourite at 5/4, Mr F. G. Hobson's Patience at 2/1 and Captain Heath's Dayrell quoted at 4/1. The Duchess and Verdi being the outsiders at 6/1. In this race the backers had got it right, Lord Bagot came home a four length winner from Verdi, with Patience, a further ten lengths behind.

Forty-five minutes later Lord Bagot was out the course again in the one-mile Bradford Handicap Plate. It was a virtual re-run of yesterdays Tradesmen's Plate, with the winner and runner-up, again facing each other, completing the trio was Thomas Cliff's Troubadour. Rejoinder started as 4/6 favourite with Lord Bagot at 4/1, it was name your own price on Troubadour. Once again the betting ring knew their business, Rejoinder beat Lord Bagot by two lengths, with the outsider ten lengths behind.

The penultimate race on the card was the popular Handicap Hurdle Race over two miles and six flights of hurdles. Of the five runners, Quirina, the 8/1 winner from Wednesday, was the form horse in the pack, but could she jump? The betting ring thought so and installed her as 6/4 favourite. The only other horse in the field that had won a race was Mr J. Smith's Prenez Garde, and this glimpse of ability saw her a firm second favourite at 2/1. The remaining three runners, Imogene (6/1), Jolly Jack (8/1) and Bird of Passage (3/1) had accounted for only six appearances on a racecourse between them prior to this race and on form, it looked as if they may struggle. At the end of the two-mile trip, it was Quirina who was struggling in an attempt to get on terms with Bird of Passage. At the line the filly was still three lengths adrift of Bird of Passage who won the race for the Hednesford trainer, William Saunders.

1860 - 1879

To conclude the proceedings on the Long Meadow for 1867 was the five-furlong Scurry Handicap. Six of the nine runners had run in previous races at the meeting, from these only Laura, winner of the Trial Stakes, had any winning form to recommend her. Volhynia was having her third run of the meeting finishing second both times, so these two looked to have the best chance against the three fresh horses entered. The three remaining runners were Mr Warrington's filly by Gunboat, two wins from nine previous races, Mr J. Smiths' The Squire, also two wins but from sixteen attempts and finally Mr T. Stevens' Betlow Lass, a two year-old who had won her only previous race. The betting was quite open for a race at Walsall. The Squire was installed as favourite at 2/1; these were generous odds, giving further indication that it was a pretty open race. The second fancy in the betting was the filly by Gunboat at 3/1 and Laura, 5/1; Volhynia was quoted at 10/1 and 12/1 for the remainder. With only a short distance to cover it was imperative to get a good start when the flag dropped and Volhynia did exactly that. She lead from start to finish beating the Gunboat filly by a length with Duchess of York, who had failed so obviously in previous races, third.

Quirina, who was the longest priced winner at Walsall at 8/1, saw her record stand for twenty-four hours before it was broken by E. W. Taylor's Volhynia, whose starting price was 10/1.

As this meeting closed, the Race Committee could only breath a sigh of relief there was no repetition of last year's disaster when the stand collapsed. The racing may have been slightly below par as far as quality of the runners was concerned, but no doubt the meeting was a great success as far as the majority of people in the town were concerned.

The official results of the meeting were:

Wednesday 25th September 1867

THE ALL AGE PLATE of 25 sovereigns each.
Six furlongs.

Mr T. Eskrett's	Edinburgh, 5 y-o, 9st. 12lb.	(J. Adams)	1
Mr E. Taylor's	Volhynia, 4 y-o, 9st. 5lb.	(T. Pegg)	2
Mr W. Davies'	Harleston, 2 y-o, 7st.	(Job Toon)	3

Betting: 7/4 fav. Edinburgh, 2/1 Volhynia.

THE HUNTER'S PLATE of 25 sovereigns.
For horses of all ages. One mile and a half. (12 subs.)

Mr J. Yates'	Plum Cake, 4 y-o, 11st. 2lb.	(Mr Dabbs)	1
Mr F. Hobson's	Patience, aged, 10st. 2lb.	(Owner)	2
Mr -	Harbinger, aged, 12st.	(Parkes)	3
Mr -	Imogene, 6 y-o, 10st. 11lb.	(Page)	4
Mr -	Lady Eryx, aged, 10st. 12lb.	(Owner)	5
Mr -	Trivet, 3 y-o, 9st. 8lb.	(Tomlinson)	6

Four others ran, not listed.

THE HEDNESFORD HANDICAP PLATE of 25 sovereigns,
for horses of all ages. Six furlongs.

Mr T. Cliff's	Verity, 3 y-o, 6st. 5lb.	(Job Toon)	1
Mr Green's	Quirina, 4 y-o, 7st.	(Sanderson)	2
Mr E. Taylor's	Volhynia, 4 y-o, 7st. 6lb.	(Studdart)	3
Mr J. Trevor's	Lady Lucan, 4 y-o, 6st. 11lb.	(J. Fox)	4

Betting: 6/4 fav. Verity, 7/4 Volhynia.

THE TRADESMEN'S PLATE of 40 sovereigns added
to a Handicap of 5 sovereigns each.
One and a half miles. (24 subs)

Mr Eastwood's	Rejoinder, 3 y-o, 7st.	(W. Handley)	1
Mr J. Wright's	Lord Bagot, 3 y-o, 6st.	(W. Bissell)	2
Mr Wadlow's	The Drone, 4 y-o, 6st. 12lb.	(J. Fox)	3

Betting: 4/6 fav. Rejoinder, 6/4 The Drone, 4/1 Lord Bagot.

THE TRIAL STAKES of 3 sovereigns each, with 20 added. One mile.

Mr T. Stephens'	Laura, 3 y-o, 8st. 4lb.	(Edward Payne)	1
Mr Reynolds'	Hoe d'ye Do, 2 y-o, 5st. 11lb.	(W. Bissell)	2
Mr T. Cliff's	Knight of St. George, 3 y-o, 8st. 9lb.	(Henry Taylor)	3
Mr J. Wright's	Captain, 3 y-o, 8st.	(Kelly)	4

Betting: 4/6 fav. Laura, 2/1 Knight of St. George.

THE MEMBER'S WELTER HANDICAP of 3 sovereigns each,
with 25 added. One mile and a quarter. (15 subs)

Mr Green's	Quirina, 4 y-o, 10st. 2lb.	(Mr F. G. Hobson)	1
Mr T. Cliff's	Troubadour, 5 y-o, 11st. 4lb.	(H. Taylor)	2
Mr Wilkinson's	Verdi, 3 y-o, 9st. 8lb.	(Mr Spence)	3
Mr T. Percival's	Young Lord, 3 y-o, 10st.	(Mr Brockton)	4
Mr T. Gough's	Duchess of York, 3 y-o, 9st. 13lb.	(Walter White)	5
Mr J. Halford's	Foreign Stamp, 4 y-o, 10st. 2lb.	(Owner)	6

Betting: 5/4 Duchess of York, 3/1 Troubadour, 5/1 Verdi, 8/1 Quirina.

Thursday 26th September 1867

THE NURSERY HANDICAP of 3 sovereigns each,
with 25 added. For two year olds, six furlongs.

Mr J. Halford's	Snuff, 6st. 6lb.	(Job Toon)	1
Mr T. Eskrett's	Arigill, 6st. 3lb.	(W. Handley)	2
Mr Aston's	Chateau Margaux, 7st. 6lb.	(C. Darling)	3
Mr J. G. Archer's	Lady Love, 7st. 3lb.	(Studdart)	4
Mr Davies'	Harleston, 8st. 8lb.	(Payne)	5

Betting: 6/4 fav. Snuff, 5/2 Chateau Margaux, 3/1 Arigill, 6/1 any others.

AN OPEN HUNTER'S PLATE of 25 sovereigns.
One and a half miles.

Mr J. Wright's	Lord Bagot, 3 y-o, 10st. 3lb.	(Mr Halford)	1
Mr Wilkinson's	Verdi, 3 y-o, 10st. 1lb.	(Mr Spence)	2
Mr F. Hobson's	Patience, aged, 10st. 2lb.	(Owner)	3
Mr T. Gough's	Duchess of York, 3 y-o, 10st. 2lb.	(W. White)	4
Capt. Heath's	Dayrell, 5 y-o, 12st.	(Mr Reynolds)	5

Betting: 5/4 fav Lord Bagot, 5/2 Patience, 4/1 Dayrell.

THE BRADFORD HANDICAP PLATE of 5 sovereigns each, with 40 added. One mile.

Mr Eastwood's	Rejoinder, 3 y-o, 7st. 5lb.	(W. Handley)	1
Mr J. Wright's	Lord Bagot, 3 y-o, 6st. 10lb.	(J. Fox)	2
Mr T. Cliff's	Troubadour, 5 y-o, 6st. 13lb.	(J. Toon)	3

Betting: 2/5 fav. Rejoinder, 4/1 Lord Bagot.

A HURDLE RACE FREE HANDICAP of 3 sovereigns each, with 20 added. Two miles over six hurdles.

Mr Saunders'	Bird of Passage, 6y-o, 9st. 5lb.	(Tomlinson)	1
Mr Green's	Quirina, 4 y-o, 9st. 5lb.	(Mr Hobson)	2
Mr Raworth's	Jolly Jack, 4 y-o, 9st. 2lb.	(Matley)	3
Mr J. Smith's	Prenez Garde, 4 y-o, 9st. 8lb.	(Hopkins)	4
Mr Powell's	Humphrey, 6 y-o, 8st. 12lb.	(E. Taylor)	5
Mr Whittington's	Imogene, 6 y-o, 10st. 4lb.	(Walter White)	6

Betting: 6/4 fav. Quirina, 2/1 Prenez Garde, 3/1 Bird of Passage.

1860 - 1879

THE SCURRY HANDICAP PLATE of 25 sovereigns.
For horses of all ages. Five furlongs.

Mr E. Taylor's	**Volhynia,** 4 y-o, 7st. 12lb.	(Stoddart)	1
Mr Warrington's	**f. by Gunboat,** 3 y-o, 7st. 9lb.	(Job Toon)	2
Mr T. Gough's	**Duchess of York,** 3y-o, 6st. 7lb.	(Handley)	3
Mr J. Smith's	**The Squire,** 4 y-o, 7st. 12lb.	(Howarth)	4
Mr T. Stevens's	**Laura,** 3 y-o, 7st. 10lb.	(C. Darling)	5
Mr J. Trevor's	**Lady Lucan,** 4 y-o, 7st. 2lb.	(J. Fox)	6
Mr C. Percival's	**Young Lord,** 3 y-o, 7st. 2lb.	(Sanderson)	7
Mr T. Stevens's	**Betlow Lass,** 2 y-o, 6st. 4lb.	(J. Clark)	8
Mr T. Bratton's	**How d'ye Do,** 2 y-o, 5st. 10lb.	(W. Bissell)	9

Betting: 2/1 fav. The Squire, 3/1 Gunboat filly, 5/1 Laura, 10/1 Volhynia, 12/1 any other.

1868

It was now twelve years since the *Walsall Free Press* had predicted the Races were a thing of the past, but they continued on their merry way regardless. This was thanks to an obviously dedicated and determined Race Committee headed by Abel Grove, licensee of the Nag's Head in Upper Rushall Street. Officials at the racecourse during this time were, Mr Johnson, handicapper, Mr Sheldon from Birmingham remained as Clerk of the Course, and Mr Swindell continued in his roll as judge, and finally, Mr Elliott, with the unenviable job of starter. *The Sportsman* newspaper also reported of improvements to the course in the form of all of the bends being fenced in.

The weather for this year's meeting remained good, ensuring the Long Meadow would again be overflowing with spectators. Both days saw large crowds from the town itself, swelled further by the trains bringing in more race goers from the outlying districts.

The races for the two-day programme varied little from previous years, the Member's Welter Handicap opened the meeting at two o'clock on Wednesday 23rd September. The race, over a mile and a quarter, had just four runners, Lord Bagot, a course winner last year, looked to have the best form of the quartet. The betting proved otherwise however, with Thomas Wadlow's Jezebel the clear market choice at 4/5. Two other runners, Mr Skelton's Greenhorn, and Mr Thorp's Frolicsome completed the field. At the start it was Greenhorn who was the one frolicking, he showed a fit of temper and spun round as Mr Elliott dropped the flag. From that point on it was a three horse race with Jezebel, partnered by Walter White, leading as they passed the judge's chair for the first time. Jezebel continued to dominate, and as the trio approached the judge's chair for the final time, he was six lengths clear, with Frolicsome second and Lord Bagot, third. Greenhorn must have looked a forlorn animal, walking back with his embarrassed jockey, amateur rider, Mr Shakespeare. The horse definitely didn't want to run as he wouldn't pass the winning post and was declared 'distanced' by the judge.

The Trial Stakes proved to be just that for Mr Shakespeare, again. Riding Greenhorn for the second time in the afternoon, he hoped his luck would change, as there was only one other competitor, William Bagot's Arigill. Greenhorn's tantrum in the first race had put backers off him and Arigill started odds-on at 1/3. As the flag dropped Greenhorn whipped round again, refusing to start, leaving Arigill to come home alone in a canter. With the gallery shouting various coarse comments in the direction of Mr Shakespeare and Greenhorn, his rider must have felt like throwing himself in the nearby sewer brook.

In the Tradesmen's Plate, a touch of comedy again prevailed at the start. This time with the winner of the first race, Jezebel. Only three runners lined up, including Thomas Eskrett's previous course winner, Edinburgh, everyone's favourite at 4/6, and Mr J. Wright's Gordian Knot, the outsider of the trio at 5/1. At the start it was the favourite that got away first, leading by a length from Gordian Knot. Shortly after the start, Jezebel threw her jockey, Fox, and continued rider less down the course. As the pair passed the stands on the first circuit, Edinburgh led by a length, but increased the lead as the race progressed, eventually winning in a canter by ten lengths.

The Hednesford Plate, a handicap race over six furlongs had the largest field at the meeting with six runners. Three of the runners were three year-olds and two were aged. The final horse that made up the field was a two year-old named Barcelona owned by Captain Douglas Lane of Blue Mantle fame. The favourite for the race, but only just, was Wynnstay at 6/4 with Ada Penelope second choice at 2/1. All six started at the first time of asking and Ada Penelope set off at a cracking pace, Job Toon, her jockey applying the 'catch me if you can' tactics. Toon dictated the running from start to finish and came home one and a half lengths clear of the favourite with Barcelona third.

In the All-Aged Plate over six furlongs, Edinburgh showed his class by winning for the second time in a couple of hours, and giving his opponents at least two stones in weight. He won easily from Jessie Flower with an un-named filly by Bit of Gold a very bad third. In all of the races so far, some of the runners appear to have taken exception to Mr Elliott, the starter. Although none refused to start in this race, there was a considerable delay due to several false starts. False starts were a fact of life and delayed a great many races. In one of the races for the Derby, there was no less than thirty-four attempts to get the runners away.

The final race of the day was the Hunter's Plate run over two miles, with another small field of three runners. Mr Bowles's Cabman, Mr G. Spafford's Hazard and a previous runner, Lord Bagot. All three horses were ridden by their owners, with the betting ring favouring Lord Bagot who started at 4/5, Hazard at 6/4 against and Cabman the outsider at 7/1. On leaving the enclosure, Lord Bagot and his rider were swamped by the crowd who for some unknown reason wanted a closer look at the favourite. This adulation didn't deter the horse from the job in hand however. Cabman took up the running in the early stages with Lord Bagot a length behind, turning into the home straight on the final circuit, Hazard who had been content to remain at the rear made a sudden effort, passing the other two with ease to win by a length from Cabman. The ease which the winner went past Lord Bagot, was to good to be true and it was found that the favourite had broken down very badly. The *Walsall Free Press* in their reporting of the race made a strange comment regarding the second horse, Cabman, they stated, *'a dashing race followed between Mr Spafford's horse and the despised outsider, Cabman,'* quite what the horse or Mr Bowles had done to warrant this comment, other than to beat the favourite, is unknown.

1860 - 1879

On Thursday, that good little jockey, Walter White, must have thought it was his benefit day come the close of the meeting, winning three of the five races on the card.

In the Bradford Plate, he was back on board Jezebel, with only two other runners competing, Arigill and the temperamental horse, Greenhorn. The backers in the ring must also have known of the skills of White, as his mount was an incredibly short price of 1/5 favourite, with Arigill at 3/1 and Greenhorn, 10/1. Greenhorn was up to his old tricks again, refusing to start until the other two were ten lengths or so in front, whereupon the horse finally started after them. He continued for three hundred yards down the course when he threw his jockey and bolted into the crowd. It was a close race between the other two, both keeping together until approaching the winning post. At this point the favourite, much to the delight of his backers, pulled away to win by one and a half lengths.

White's second winner came in the following race, the five-furlong Scurry Handicap, riding Batonnier for his master, Thomas Wadlow. There was little to choose between the four runners, all of them appearing to be nothing more than mediocre, and that is being charitable. The abilities of the runners may have been in question, but their spirit couldn't be criticised as they made a good race of it. All four keeping close together until the turn into the home straight where Fanny took up the running followed by Batonnier. As they neared the post, White pushed Batonnier, the 4/5 favourite, on to pass Fanny almost at the post, winning by half a length, with Ransom a close third.

His third winner of the day, and fourth of the meeting came in the penultimate race, the Open Hunter's Plate, over a mile and a half. The three runners were, Charles Fletton's Ada, White's mount, Mr Spafford's Hazard and Mr Taylor's half-bred, Snowdrop. Starting a 1/4 favourite, White elected, or had been instructed to drop the filly out if it in the early stages. Snowdrop made the running at a fast pace, soon holding a commanding lead, with Hazard chasing and Ada still last. As the trio climbed the hill on the second circuit, Snowdrop's lead began to diminish and soon the half-bred was beaten. Hazard took up the running turning into the straight but White got to work on Ada who passed her rivals close home to win by a length. Her jockey showing the two amateur riders how the job should be done.

The last race of the day, and the meeting, was the popular Handicap Hurdle Race. Usually this race had a fair turn out of runners, but on this occasion, it was a match between Mr Raworth's Jolly Jack ridden by Mr Halford and Mr Martin's Sorceress ridden by a professional jockey, Brady. Both horses set off at a fast pace jumping the first two flights simultaneously, on rounding a sharp bend the horses cannoned into each other with the result that Jolly Jack came to grief, rendering Mr Halford unconscious. Sorceress continued on her way unchallenged to win in a trot. Mr Halford, on being restored to consciousness wasn't too impressed with his professional colleague and lodged an objection on the grounds Brady intentionally fouled him. For the first time in several years, the Stewards were called upon to adjudicate, with the both officials, J. B. McLean and W. W. Bagot, agreeing the clash was accidental, allowing Sorceress to keep the race.

The official results of the meeting were:

Wednesday 23rd September 1868

THE MEMBER'S WELTER HANDICAP of 3 sovereigns each, with 25 added. One mile and a quarter. (15 subs)

Mr T. Wadlow's	Jezabel, 5 y-o, 10st. 11lb.	(Walter White)	1
Mr Thorpe's	Frolicsome, 3 y-o, 9st. 4lb.	(Britton)	2
Mr J. Wright's	Lord Bagot, 4 y-o, 11st. 7lb.	(Mr Halford)	3
Mr Skelton's	Greenhorn, 4 y-o, 10st. 3lb.	(Mr Shakespeare)	4

Betting: 4/5 fav. Jezabel, 3/1 Lord Bagot, 5/1 Greenhorn.

THE TRIAL STAKES of 3 sovereigns each, with 20 added. One mile.

Mr W. Bagot's	Arigill, 3 y-o, 8st.	(Handley)	1
Mr Skelton's	Greenhorn, 4 y-o, 8st. 13lb.		
	(carried 9st. 6lb.)	(Mr Shakespeare)	-

Betting: 1/3 fav. Arigill, Greenhorn bolted, fav. came in alone.

THE TRADESMEN'S PLATE of 40 sovereigns added to a Handicap of 5 sovereigns each. One and a half miles. (24 subs)

Mr Eskrett's	Edinburgh, 6 y-o, 8st. 12lb.	(Britton)	1
Mr J. Wright's	Gordian Knot, aged, 7st. 10lb.	(J. Toon)	2
Mr Wadlow's	Jezabel, 5 y-o, 7st. 3lb.	(J. Fox)	3

Betting: 4/6 fav. Edinburgh, 2/1 Jezabel, 5/1 Gordian Knot.

THE HEDNESFORD PLATE (H'cap) of 25 sovereigns each. For all ages. Six furlongs.

Mr C. Fletton's	Ada, 3 y-o, 7st. 3lb.	(Job Toon)	1
Mr E. Buckley's	Wynnstay, aged, 8st. 12lb.	(Britton)	2
Capt. D. Lane's	Barcelona, 2 y-o, 6st.	(W. West)	3
Mr W. P. Harley's	Fanny, 3 y-o, 7st. 4lb.	(James Gradwell)	4
Mr Marshall's	Ransom, 3 y-o, 7st. 2lb.	(Handley)	5
Mr J. Wright's	Gordian Knot, aged, 9st.	(Walter White)	6

Betting: 6/4 Wynnstay, 2/1 Ada, 3/1 Fanny & Barcelona, 6/1 bar.

THE ALL-AGED PLATE of 25 sovereigns. Six furlongs.

Mr Eskrett's	Edinburgh, 6 y-o, 9st. 12lb.	(Britton)	1
Mr Jones'	Jessie Flower, 4 y-o, 7st. 12lb.	(Peppler)	2
Mr Rickard's	b. f. by King of Trumps,		
	2 y-o, 6st. 4lb.	(James Gradwell)	3
Mr Cartwright's	b. f. by Knight of Kars,		
	2 y-o, 6st. 11lb.	(Paley)	4

Betting: 1/2 Edinburgh, 7/4 Jessie Flower, 6/1 bar.

A HUNTERS' STAKES of 2 sovereigns each, with 20 added. Two miles.

Mr Spafford's	Hazard, 3 y-o, 9st. 12lb.	(Mr G. Spafford)	1
Mr Bowles'	Cabman, 5 y-o, 10st. 9lb.	(Owner)	2
Mr J. Wright's	Lord Bagot, 4 y-o, 12st. 1lb.	(Owner)	3

Betting: 4/5 fav. Lord Bagot, 6/4 Hazard, 7/1 Cabman.

Thursday 24th September 1868

THE NURSERY HANDICAP of 3 sovereigns each, with 20 added. For two year olds, six furlongs.

| Mr Raworth's | Masquer, 8st. 2lb. | (Doolan) | 1 |
| Mr T. Eskrett's | Emily, 7st. 4lb. | (C. Taylor) | 2 |

Betting: 1/4 fav. Masquer.

1860 - 1879

THE BRADFORD HANDICAP PLATE of 5 sovereigns each, with 40 added. One mile.

Mr Wadlow's	**Jezabel,** 5 y-o, 8st. 7lb.	*(Walter White)*	1
Mr Bagot's	**Arigill,** 3 y-o, 7st. 3lb.	*(Handley)*	2
Mr Skelton's	**Greenhorn,** 4 y-o, 7st. 4lb.	*(E. Howarth)*	3

Betting: 1/5 fav. Jezabel, 3/1 Arigill, 10/1 Greenhorn.

THE SCURRY HANDICAP PLATE of 25 sovereigns. For horses of all ages. Five furlongs.

Mr George na.	**Batonnier,** 3 y-o, 8st. 7lb.	*(W. White)*	1
Mr W. P. Harley's	**Fanny,** 3 y-o, 7st. 9lb.	*(James Gradwell)*	2
Mr Copeland's	**St. Valentine,** 3y-o, 7st. 7lb.	*(Job Toon)*	3
Mr Marshall's	**Ransom,** 3 y-o, 7st. 7lb.	*(Handley)*	4

Betting: 4/5 fav. Batonnier, 6/4 Fanny, 7/4 St. Valentine.

AN OPEN HUNTER'S PLATE of 25 sovereigns. One and a half miles.

Mr C. Fletton's	**Ada,** 3 y-o, 10st. 11lb.	*(Walter White)*	1
Mr Spafford's	**Hazard,** 3 y-o, 9st. 5lb.	*(Owner)*	2
Mr Taylor's	**Snowdrop** (h-b), 4 y-o, 10st.	*(Mr Masters)*	3

Betting: 1/4 fav. Ada, 3/1 Hazard, 10/1 Snowdrop.

A HURDLE RACE FREE HANDICAP of 3 sovereigns each, with 20 added. Two miles over six hurdles.

Mr Martin's	**Sorceress,** 4 y-o.	*(Brady)*	1
Mr Raworth's	**Jolly Jack,** 4 y-o.	*(Mr Halford)*	2

1869

The Races in 1869 had a slight change to their usual schedule, being held on Tuesday 28th and Wednesday 29th September, with six races on each day. On the first day, fields were smaller than usual due to several horses en route to Walsall being detained at Chesterfield. The weather leading up to the Races had been very wet, with the inevitable result of heavy going, which lead to one or two intended runners being withdrawn.

The two opening races could only produce two runners for each event. The first real race was the Hednesford Handicap Plate with six runners, none of them previous runners at Walsall. Appearing at the course for the first time since his dunking in the sewer brook in 1861 was the jockey George Clement from Wiltshire, still riding but also training horses now. He entered and rode his own horse, Venetia, quoted at 3/1 in the betting. Thomas Wadlow's entry Ben Block was the even money favourite, with Mr Arthur's Clarionette another 3/1 chance. The three remaining runners, Bouquet, Titulus and Tetaphor all quoted at 4/1. Several false starts marred the proceedings, but when they eventually got off it was a fairly even break with all six grouped closely together. Nearing the post Bouquet edged to the front keeping his advantage to the line and winning by half a length. Second place went to the favourite with Clarionette in third. In last place was Clement's horse Venetia, obviously taking it slowly until he accustomed himself to the course again.

Although the Welter Handicap was in fact only a match, it nevertheless managed to cause some controversy with the two runners. The betting ring declared this was yet another predictable result, with all in favour of Thomas Wadlow's Ada Penelope who started odds-on at 1/2, and was to be ridden by the amateur rider, Mr Spafford. The other horse running was Mr Dyer's Gulnare ridden by Payne, a professional jockey, who knew a few tricks if things weren't going his way. Although Ada Penelope won by a length, complaints were aimed at Payne from Mr Spafford who accused him of 'pulling-in.' Payne, and those connected with the horse, justified their actions by saying Payne was reining-in when all hope of winning had been lost. The Stewards, Captain Lewis and J. R. McLean accepted the explanation and took no further action against Payne.

In the last race of the afternoon, the Hunter's Stakes had six declared runners to start the two-mile event. On virtually every race in recent years, the favourite was nearly always odds-on, such was the predictability of racing on the Long Meadow, but of course, the favourites didn't always win. Mr Spafford, who was making a name for himself on the racecourses in the area, entered his horse, Sir Walter. The backers liked what they saw, backing him down to 1/2 favourite, with the other runners at 5/1 and upwards. When the race began, the field kept together, with the favourite holding a slight lead on the first circuit, followed by Pablo and Bold Davie. As the runners turned for home along the straight, Pablo went on from Sir Walter, with Mr Russell's Beautiful Spring gaining on the front-runners. Mr Spafford, seeing the danger urged his mount on, with Gregory, the jockey of Beautiful Spring doing the same. The pair fought a good race to the line with the latter horse beating the favourite by a short neck. Third place went to an un-named half-bred horse, the property of Mr Ashley.

Thursday's card began with the Open Hunter's Plate. These races had become increasingly popular in recent years, possibly because half-bred horses could run in them and they boosted the number of entries. Six were declared for this one, with Ada Penelope starting as odds-on favourite, with 3/1 against a horse named Charlotte and 4/1 against any of the others. One of these was Venetia, owned and ridden by George Clement. The jockeys confidence was back, as was Venetia's form, who won easily from Beautiful Spring, with Ada Penelope finishing third.

The best contest of the day came in the third race, the Bradford Handicap Plate over one mile, with seven runners. The backers in the ring fancied Mr Dyer's Gulnare, backing him down to even money favourite, with odds from 2/1 up to 10/1 being offered against the others. Venetia who won earlier, couldn't attract much attention, her price closing at 4/1. After a good start, the runners remained grouped together, the lead changing several times throughout. Approaching the post, 10/1 chance King's Daughter was in the ruck along with Venetia, the favourite Gulnare and Veda. John Swindell, the judge had a hard job splitting the quartet but he favoured Mr Dobson's King's Daughter by a head from Venetia, Gulnare third, a neck behind. A good race for all concerned, especially anyone who had been shrewd enough to back the winner.

The Handicap Hurdle Race had always been a popular event in years past, but this year only attracted four runners including Sir Walter and Gulnare, the latter being ridden by Walter White. Of the other two runners, only one was given

1860 - 1879

a chance, Mr Grant's Sea Breeze. The remaining horse, Mr Williams' Sir Andrew had the distinction of being quoted the longest odds against winning in the history of the Races at 50/1. The backers couldn't decide who had the best chance between Sir Walter and Gulnare and so they started as joint favourites at evens. The bookmakers knew their business regarding the 50/1 shot, from the start he remained in the rear throughout the race. On the second circuit, Sea Breeze split the favourites but only for a while. Nearing the end Gulnare rallied and went on to challenge Sir Walter, ridden by his owner, Mr Spafford, but the pair ran on to win by a length.

Either Mr Dyer or Walter White were not happy with the outcome of the race and objected to Mr Spafford's victory. Before Spafford had weighed in, he was seen to touch his weights, the ultimate sin. The argument went on long and hard, and at the time of the race report being filed, a decision by the Stewards still hadn't been made.

Eight horses contested the five-furlong Scurry Handicap, which was won by Thomas Wadlow and Walter White with Parma, the 2/1 against favourite. Parma led virtually from start to finish, taking the race by a length from Mr Taylor's Snuff and Mr Hendon's Titulus, third.

The twelfth and final race of the meeting was resurrected from the past, the Beaten Horse Handicap. Qualification for this event was simple, your horse must have run at the meeting and not have won a race. Although many horses qualified only five went to post in attempt to recover their losses, and one final chance of glory. As far as the betting was concerned, all five runners started a 7/4 against, so the bookmakers weren't giving much away. Victory went to Mr Taylor's Snuff, ridden by George Clement

This last race of the meeting was also the last race of the decade. The following year, the Races entered their thirteenth and final decade.

The official results of the meeting were:

Tuesday 28rd September 1869

THE ALL AGED (HANDICAP) PLATE
of 25 sovereigns each. Six furlongs.

Mr Robinson's	Edna, 3 y-o, 8st. 9lb.	(Kennedy)	1
Mr Walter's	Dollie, 3 y-o, 7st. 9lb.	(Clark)	2

Betting: 4/5 fav. Edna.

THE TRADESMEN'S PLATE of 40 sovereigns added to a Handicap of 5 sovereigns each. One and a quarter miles.

Mr T. Wadlow's	Ada Penelope, 4 y-o, 7st. 3lb.	(J. Fox)	1
Mr Robinson's	Edna, 3 y-o, 6st. 8lb.	(F. Lynham)	2

Betting: 1/3 fav. Ada Penelope.

THE HEDNESFORD HANDICAP PLATE
of 25 sovereigns, for horses of all ages. Six furlongs.

Mr W. Baggott's	Bouquet, 3 y-o, 6st. 12lb.	(J. Humphreys)	1
Mr T. Wadlow's	Ben Block, 3 y-o, 7st. 2lb.	(J. Fox)	2
Mr Arthur's	Clarionette, 3 y-o, 7st. 12lb.	(Clark)	3
Mr Clement's	Venetia, 3 y-o, 7st. 6lb.	(Owner)	4
Mr Hendon's	Titulus, 2 y-o, 5st. 9lb.	(Jones)	5
Mr Robinson's	Metaphor, 2 y-o, 5st. 7lb.	(F. Lynham)	6

Betting: Evens fav. Ben Block, 3/1 Clarionette and Venetia.

THE WELTER HANDICAP of 5 sovereigns each,
with 25 added. To be ridden by gentlemen, farmers or tradesmen, professionals, 6lb. extra. One mile and a quarter.

Mr T. Wadlow's	Ada Penelope, 4 y-o, 11st. 4lb.	(Spafford)	1
Mr Dyer's	Gulnare, 5 y-o, 11st. 5lb.	(Payne)	2

Betting: 1/2 fav. Ada Penelope.

THE TRIAL STAKES of 3 sovereigns each, with 20 added. Six furlongs.

Mr T. Stevens'	Barcelona, 3 y-o, 7st. 7lb.	(Clark)	1
Mr Clement's	Venetia, 3 y-o, 7st. 7lb.	(Owner)	2
Mr Arthur's	Clarionette, 3 y-o, 7st. 7lb.	(J. Fox)	3
Mr Taylor's	Snuff, 4 y-o, 8st. 2lb.	(A. Hunt)	4

Betting: Evens fav. Clarionette, 2/1 Barcelona, 3/1 bar two.

THE HUNTER'S STAKES of 2 sovereigns each, with 20 added.
For hunters that have not been in a training stable since 1st January 1869.
Two miles.

Mr W. Russell's	Beautiful Spring, 3 y-o,	(William Gregory)	1
Mr Spafford's	Sir Walter, 5 y-o,	(Mr G. Spafford)	2
Mr Ashley's m.	by Old Calabar, 3 y-o,	(W. Hoystead)	3
Mr -	Pablo	(Read)	-
Mr -	Freeman	(Peacock)	-
Mr -	Bold Davie	(Mr Breece)	-

Betting: 1/2 fav. Sir Walter, 5/1 Beautiful Spring.

Wednesday 29th September 1869

AN OPEN HUNTER'S PLATE of 25 sovereigns.
One and a half miles.

Mr Clement's	Venetia, 3 y-o,	(Owner)	1
Mr Russell's	Beautiful Spring, 3 y-o,	(W. Gregory)	2
Mr T. Wadlow's	Ada Penelope, 4 y-o, 10st.	(Mr Spafford)	3
Mr -	Charlotte, 3 y-o, 10st. 7lb.	(Mr A. Dabbs)	-
Mr -	Chassepot, 3 y-o, 10st. 5lb.	(Matley)	-
Mr -	Bold Davie, aged, 10st. 4lb.	(Mr E. Rhys)	-

Betting: 4/5 fav Ada, 3/1 Charlotte, 3/1 any other.

THE MEMBER'S PLATE of 25 sovereigns added to a Nursery Free Handicap of 3 sovs each, for two year olds, six furlongs.

Mr Stamford's	Rosamond, 6st.	(J. Fox)	1
Mr J. Shore's	The Lawyer, 6st.	(Edwards)	2
Mr H. Weaver's	Octavia, 6st. 9lb.	(James Gradwell)	3
Mr J. Shield's	colt by Caractacus, 7st.	(John Deakin)	4

Betting: 4/5 fav. Rosamond.

A HURDLE RACE (FREE HANDICAP) of 3 sovereigns each, with 20 added.
Two miles over six hurdles.

Mr Spafford's	Sir Walter, 5 y-o, 11st. 7lb.	(Mr Spafford)	1
Mr Dyer's	Gulnare, 5 y-o, 11st.	(Walter White)	2
Mr Grant's	Sea Breeze, 3 y-o, 10st.	(Darrill)	3
Mr Williams'	Sir Andrew, 3 y-o, 10st. 3lb.	(Robinson)	4

THE BRADFORD HANDICAP PLATE of 5 sovereigns each, with 40 added.
One mile.

Mr Dobson's	King's Daughter, 5 y-o, 7st. 10lb.	(James Gradwell)	1
Mr Clement's	Venetia, 3 y-o, 6st. 6lb.	(John Deakin)	2
Mr Dyer's	Gulnare, 5 y-o, 7st. 1lb.	(Clark)	3
Mr W. Fletcher's	Veda, 4 y-o, 8st. 1lb.	(Count)	-
Mr T. Wadlow's	Ampleforth, 3 y-o, 7st. 3lb.	(J. Fox)	-
Mr W. Baggott's	Bouquet, 3 y-o, 6st. 12lb.	(J. Humphreys)	-
Mr Robinson's	Edna, 3 y-o, 6st. 13lb.	(F. Lynham)	-

Betting: Evens fav. Gulnare, 2/1 Veda, 4/1 Venetia, 10/1 King's Daughter

1860 – 1879

THE SCURRY HANDICAP PLATE of 25 sovereigns.
For horses of all ages. Five furlongs.

Mr T. Wadlow's	**Parma**, 5 y-o, 8st. 12lb.	(Walter White)	1
Mr Taylor's	**Snuff**, 4 y-o, 8st. 10lb.	(George Clements)	2
Mr Hendon's	**Titulus**, 2 y-o, 6st.	(F. Lynham)	3
Mr J. Barber's	**Pantaloon**, aged, 8st. 7lb.	(James Gradwell)	-
Mr Arthur's	**Clarionette**, 3 y-o, 8st. 4lb.	(Payne)	-
Mr J. Smith's	**Whirlwind**, 3 y-o, 7st. 8lb.	(Heraud)	-
Mr Walter's	**Dollie**, 3 y-o, 6st. 8lb.	(Clark)	-
Mr Stamford's	**Rosamond**, 2 y-o, 6st. 7lb.	(J. Fox)	-

Betting: 2/1 fav. Parma, 3/1 Whirlwind, 10/1 Titulus.

THE BEATEN HANDICAP of 1 sovereign each, with 10 added,
for beaten horses at this meeting. Once round.

Mr Taylor's	**Snuff**, 4 y-o, 9st.	(George Clements)	1
Mr Arthur's	**Charlotte**, 3 y-o, 7st.	(J. Humphreys)	2
Mr J. Smith's	**Whirlwind**, 3 y-o, 7st. 9lb.	(Heraud)	3
Mr Arthur's	**Clarionette**, 3 y-o, 8st. 6lb.	(Matley)	-
Mr Walter's	**Dollie**, 3 y-o, 7st.	(Clark)	-

Betting: 7/4 the field.

Stewards: Captain H. Lewis and J. R. McClean.

1870

In 1870, the Races were held a week later than usual, on Monday 3rd and Tuesday 4th October. This was due to an Agricultural Meeting taking place in the town on the dates usually reserved for the meeting.

The *Walsall Free Press* published the following article describing the events for the year: –

'Favoured with splendid weather the patrons of 'The Turf' had the satisfaction of seeing on Monday and Tuesday, assembled on the course a much larger concourse of people than has been seen in Walsall for a length of time; indeed, the course was so crowded as to make moving about not only uncomfortable, but really difficult; and from the indiscriminate manner in which those dangerous affairs – the cocoa-nut alleys – were placed about the course several accidents occurred, and the only wonder is that more did not happen. But, however crowded the outer course, the 'inner circle' was not so well filled as we have seen it – an unmistakable proof that horse-racing is rapidly declining. If every course is as poorly patronised by amateur turfites as ours was, the professionals, who cannot very well exist by preying upon each other, must find considerable difficulty in finding victims to prey upon, and must soon discover that their occupation is gone. We were pleased to see fewer of those betting men outside the 'ring,' who pick up the shillings and half-crowns of the operative classes and the unthinking youths who frequent the course. We think some little credit is due to the police, who notwithstanding the mammoth crowd – as one of the sporting correspondents designated the gathering assembled, tolerably good order was preserved.'

Although the tone of the currents reports from the newspaper is much different to that of ten years ago, there is an element of wishful thinking about their comments. In a perfect world, their views would not be required, but Walsall, like the world, was not perfect. No amount of moralising articles was going to change attitudes towards how people lived their lives. As long as there were races in Walsall, the working people would enjoy them.

This year there were twelve races, six on each day, *The Walsall Observer* in their reports stated the fields were smaller than in the past. This doesn't appear to be the case, the runners on Monday seem to be more than usual, with Tuesday about the same. Two races for hunters were again on the programme and the race for beaten horses had reverted to its original name, first used in the late 1700s, The Consolation Stakes.

The training stables at Hednesford had supplied a high percentage of the runners, and winners, at Walsall for a great many years. By 1870, the Hednesford training grounds were on the decline, the once rural community was now covered with coalmines, the producing fuel for the coal hungry industries in the Black Country.

As the names of Hednesford trainers became less and less on the race card, other familiar names were replacing them. Men like Thomas Wadlow from Shifnal, was now sending many horses to try their luck at Walsall. This year he wasted no time, winning the opening race, the six furlongs Hednesford Handicap Plate. His horse, Lady of Croome, was one of only three runners contesting the race, starting odds-on at 4/6, she justified the faith of the betting ring, trotting up to win by a couple of lengths, as she pleased. Last year Wadlow's jockey Walter White rode four winners, this year it was the turn of another of his riders, Fox, to enjoy the spotlight, riding two winners on the first day.

In the Trial Stakes of five furlongs, Fox was back on Lady of Croome, this time quoted as second favourite at 7/4 against with Mr Cassidy's Pulchra, favoured by the majority at 6/4. The six horses were heading out to the starting post when Mr Brown's two year-old, Elton, threw his jockey, Stafford. The jockey re-mounted and headed for the start, again something spooked the youngster and this time he bolted with Stafford clinging on to his uncontrollable mount for dear life. Coming round the turn by the grandstand, close to today's junction with Caldmore Road, Stafford saw a policeman crossing the course. To avoid colliding with him, the jockey made one final attempt to stop the runaway, this caused the horse to fall, throwing the jockey into the crowd at some force. Stafford smashed into one of the unfortunate spectators, a wagoner named John Masters who was also carrying a small child. Both jockey and child were relatively unscathed, but badly shaken, Masters wasn't so lucky, he was taken to the Cottage Hospital with an injured arm and broken ribs. Hopefully, he got to meet Sister Dora personally, for his trouble. Another report of the incident is that the horse jumped into the crowd. It is more feasible that the first account is nearer the truth, if less dramatic, a frightened horse will usual run away from the thing that spooked them, not into it.

When the pandemonium had subsided, the horse race got under way, minus one runner. The race was won by Lady of Croome ridden by Fox, the duo recording their second win of the day. Pulchra, the favourite finished second, three lengths behind the winner, with E. W. Taylor's Florence in third place. One of the conditions of the race was each runner had to nominate a price at which the animal would be sold if required. Wadlow put the princely sum of thirty pounds on his horses head, resulting in the sale of the horse to Mr J. Wright.

1860 - 1879

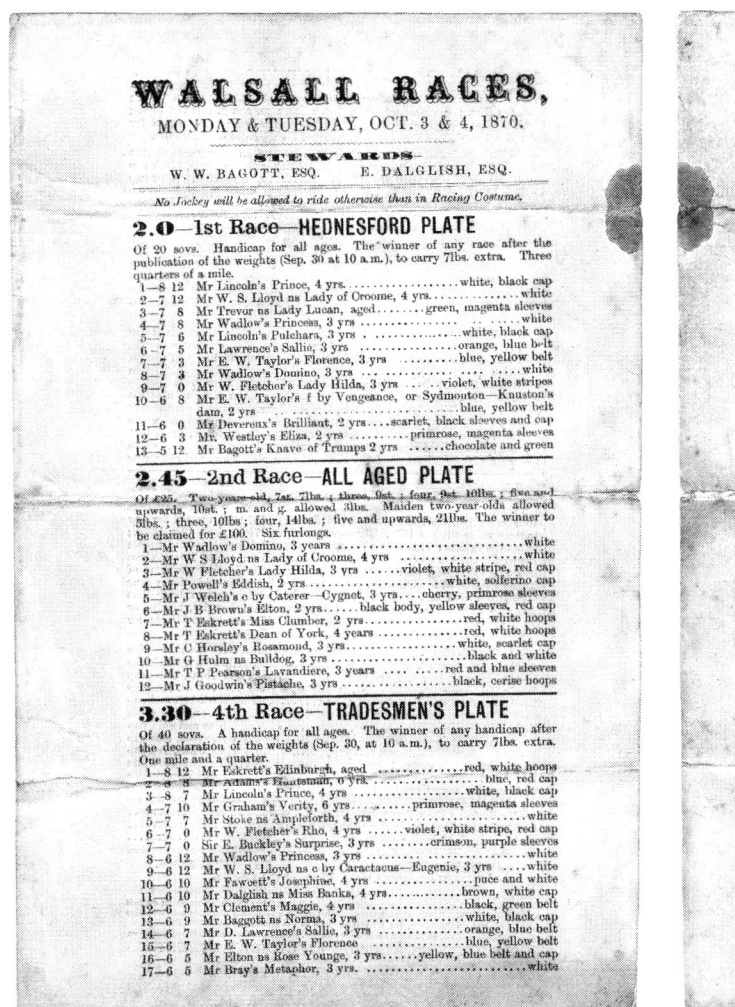

The racecard for Monday 3rd October 1870, complete with a printer's error that shows two fourth races, the 3.30 and the 4.00. (Reproduced by kind permission of Gary Burgess).

Mr Wright, the purchaser of Lady of Croome, recouped his loses on the sale, and made a bit too, when his unfancied horse Bulldog won the All-Aged Plate at 10/1. Five runners contested the race, with Bulldog and Mr C. Horsley's Rosamund not attracting much attention in the betting. The main attraction was Thomas Wadlow's three year-old, Domino, who started as favourite at 6/4 against. The jockey of Bulldog, Wheeldon rode a clever race, allowing the others to set the pace, he brought his mount through as the runners neared the post and won easily by two lengths.

To end the day's sport, the Hunter's Stakes was the last on the card and with eight runners was the largest field of the day. The favourite for the race was Thomas Wilkinson's Extra Number, who started odds-on at 4/6. Second choice of the backers was a runner of George Clements, Robert Laundrie at 4/1. At the end of the race the favourite could only finish third to J. Poinon's horse, Hawk, who surprised everyone by flying home by four lengths at 8/1, beating one of the previous runners, Florence. Hawk was possibly not fancied because of the weight he was set to carry, 11 stone 9 pounds. The horse must have had some ability to win by the margin he did, conceding 43 pounds to Florence.

A couple of hours before racing began on the second day, the constables on duty at the course had a serious assault to deal with. It concerned one of the stall holders and a local bully who was well known to the police. With the course thronged with spectators and many of the stalls doing brisk business, Robert Wright of Dudley Street, decided to steal some cocoa-nuts from one of the 'Aunt Sally' stalls. The stall was owned by a poor itinerant family who made a meagre living the best way they could. The victims of the assault were George and Isabella Powell and their young daughter, Eliza. It was she who attempted to stop Wright from stealing the cocoa-nuts. Wright indecently assaulted the daughter before turning his attentions to her parents who were trying to protect their child. Several other members of the crowd began assisting Wright in his assault on the adults, before smashing up their stall. The mother was knocked to the ground and dragged around for some distance, the father receiving similar treatment. Fortunately, the reputation of the town was saved when several people gave information to the police, which led to the apprehension of Wright. His attempts to resist arrest became extremely violent, but he was eventually taken to the Police Station after being 'subdued.' The police fought fire with fire in those days. On being charged with the assault, Wright protested his innocence, but previous form in humans is much more reliable than that of racehorses. The Bench found Wright guilty on all charges and sentenced him to six

1860 – 1879

months imprisonment, with the Mayor of Walsall stating; -

'The accused seemed to think that because the prosecutors (the Powells) were poor defenceless people, he could do what he liked with them, but the more poor and defenceless they were, the more they needed the protection of the Magistrates. A worse offence than that the prisoner committed it would be impossible to find.'

An unusual sentiment by today's standards, the Bench sympathising with the victims!

Having seen the worst Walsall could offer on show in the morning, the proceedings in the afternoon restored ones faith in human nature by the charitable actions of one man.

The first race on the card on Tuesday was the six-furlong race, the Member's Nursery Handicap for two year-olds. The effects of this race had lasting repercussions for Mr J. Brown, owner of the horse that caused the incident the previous day, Elton. Lining up with just two opponents, William Saunders' Bandsman and Mr Powell's Eddish, the trio got away with Elton making the pace. As the horse neared the Congregational Chapel in Bradford Street he decided to do things his own way again and bolted. In his panic he jumped a wall onto a footpath on Wednesbury Road, on landing he fell heavily, injuring himself. The young lad riding him, Edward Hunter of Walhouse Street, realising he couldn't restrain his mount, leapt off as the horse jumped the wall, falling backwards onto the perimeter of the racecourse field. He was carried to the Cottage Hospital unconscious with severe cuts on his head, he was thought to be in some danger initially, but by Thursday, his condition had improved.

While all of this pandemonium was going on one side of the course, the two remaining runners had a horse race to finish on the other side. The result came out in favour of Eddish who beat the backer's choice, Bandsman by a length.

Mr Brown, Elton's owner, was distraught at the thought of the damage his horse had done to several people on the course, to such an extent he vowed to give up horse racing there and then. He kept to his word that very afternoon by selling Elton for a nominal sum to some poor unfortunate who no doubt thought he 'nu 'ow t'andle th'oss.' Brown visited Edward Hunter in hospital and insisted on paying all the expenses that occurred in restoring the unfortunate lad back to health. Brown asked Hunter to give up the turf and he would find him a good job as a groom in a gentleman's establishment. Whilst at the hospital, Brown also enquired as to the health of John Masters, the first victim of Elton's temperament, and vowed to do something for him also.

The Open Hunter's Plate, run over one and a half miles, had just four runners including Thomas Eskrett's splendidly named Dean of York. The three others in the race were, Bulldog, a winner from the previous day, who started as the 5/4 favourite, and Florence at 4/1, completing the field was Mr Goodwin's Pistache ridden by his owner. The latter, second choice in the betting ring at 5/2 justified his followers confidence, winning the race easily by three lengths from Florence, with the Dean of York third. Bulldog proved to be a disappointing favourite, being beaten convincingly by the others and finished last.

The Handicap Hurdle Race proved, for the second consecutive year, not to have much in the way of spectacle or excitement, with three modest runners. The race was actually a match as J. Wright's horse Bulldog was only started as a technicality to secure the added money in the race. After cantering a short distance, the horse was stopped and returned to the paddock, his job done. The race itself turned out to be a procession, the 1/3 favourite, Mr Barber's Miss Banks winning as she pleased from J. Wright's other horse William, sounding, and running like the family pet.

This second day of the meeting had been a poor one regarding the sport on offer to the public, with just two races left, the downward slide continued. The Bradford Handicap Plate had three runners who attempted to make some sort of a race of it, but one horse dominated. This was the favourite, Rose Young who started at 1/2 on. The mare won cantering in at her own pace, with Mr Lincoln's Prince second, eventually, Florence who had run one race to many was third.

The final event was a match, was between J. Wright's new acquisition, Lady of Croome, and J. Welch's un-named colt by Cygnet. The backers went for Wrights horse in a big way, backing her down to 2/5, implying the opposition had little chance. Someone should have told Mr Welch's horse and his jockey Vinell the plan, because at the line the Cygnet colt won by three-quarters of a length.

There were reports of several accidents to spectators both on and off the racecourse. One form of entertainment that was giving cause for concern with its high number of casualties was the seemingly innocent, 'Aunt Sally' or cocoa-nut shy. Just one of the incidents that occurred was to ten year-old John Massey of Ryecroft Street. He was taken to the Cottage Hospital for treatment to a severely cut lip, sustained when a wayward stick intended for the cocoa-nuts missed its target and struck him. Many other reports of a similar nature were also reported by the local newspapers, with the *Walsall Free Press* insisting that these dangerous stalls were removed from areas densely populated by the public in an effort to avoid future accidents.

Concluding this years racing activities, a small article printed in *The Walsall Observer* the week before the Races were held proves the Race Committee had the meeting for 1871 almost secured, it read: -

'Walsall Races – The Committee for carrying out the above are making an active canvass for subscriptions in support of the races, and, from the success they have already made, together with the promises they have received from local patrons of the turf, anticipate having a meeting equal, if not superior, to those of previous years.'

The official results of the meeting were:

Monday 3rd October 1870

THE HEDNESFORD HANDICAP PLATE
of 20 sovereigns, for horses of all ages. Six furlongs.

Mr T. Wadlow's	**Lady of Croome**, 4 y-o, 7st. 12lb.	(J. Fox)	1
Mr Taylor's	f. by Vengeance, 2 y-o, 6st. 8lb.	(Lake)	2
Mr Lawrence's	Sallie, 3 y-o, 7st. 5lb.	(W. Bissell)	3

Betting: 4/6 fav. Lady of Croome, 2/1 Sallie.

1860 - 1879

THE ALL AGED (HANDICAP) PLATE
of 25 sovereigns each. Six furlongs.

Mr J. Wright's	**Bulldog,** 3 y-o, 8st. 4lb.	*(Wheeldon)*	1
Mr T. Wadlow's	**Domino,** 3 y-o, 8st. 11lb.	*(J. Fox)*	2
Mr J. Welch's	**c. by Caterer,** 3 y-o, 8st. 11lb.	*(J. Vinell)*	3
Mr Powell's	**Eddish,** 2 y-o, 7st. 7lb.	*(W. Bissell)*	4
Mr C. Horsley's	**Rosamond,** 3 y-o, 8st. 11lb.	*(J. Matley)*	5

Betting: 6/4 fav. Domino, 2/1 Eddish, 5/2 colt, 10/1 others.

THE TRADESMEN'S PLATE of 40 sovereigns added
to a Handicap of 5 sovereigns each.
One and a quarter miles.

| Mr G. Clement's | **Maggie,** 4 y-o, 6st. 9lb. | *(Connor)* | 1 |
| Mr Robinson's | **Edna,** 3 y-o, 6st. 8lb. | *(F. Lynham)* | 2 |

Betting: 1/3 fav. Ada Penelope.

THE TRIAL STAKES of 3 sovereigns each, with 20 added. Six furlongs.

Mr T. Wadlow's	**Lady of Croome,** 4 y-o, 8st. 12lb.	*(J. Fox)*	1
Mr Cassidy's	**Pulchra,** 3 y-o, 8st. 4lb.	*(Samuel Kenyon)*	2
Mr Taylor's	**Florence,** 3 y-o, 7st. 13lb.	*(A. Hunt)*	3
Mr Brown's	**Elton,** 2 y-o, 6st. 11lb.	*(Stafford)*	bol

Betting: 6/4 fav. Pulchra, 7/4 Lady of Croome.

THE WELTER HANDICAP of 5 sovereigns each, with 15 added.
One mile and a quarter.

| Mr J. Welch's | **c. by Caterer,** 3 y-o, 10st. 2lb. | *(Wellan)* | 1 |
| Mr G. Clement's | **Maggie,** 4 y-o, 10st. 3lb. | *(Owner)* | 2 |

Betting: 2/5 fav. Maggie.

THE HUNTER'S STAKES of 2 sovereigns each, with 20 added.
Two miles.

Mr J. Poinon's	**Hawk,** 5 y-o, 11st. 9lb.	*(Owner)*	1
Mr E. Taylor's	**Florence,** 3 y-o, 8st. 7lb.	*(Cox)*	2
Mr Wilkinson's	**Cavendish,** 3 y-o, 10st. 2lb.	*(Crawshaw)*	3
Mr Emmitt's	**David,** 4 y-o, 11st. 1lb.	*(Mr H. M. Rudd)*	4
Mr G. Clement's	**Robert Laundrie,** 4 y-o, 11st. 10lb	*(S. Huntley)*	5
Mr W. Smith's	**Elegance,** 4 y-o, 9st. 10lb.	*(Mr F. Smith)*	6
Mr C. Horsley's	**Rosamond,** 3 y--o, 9st. 9lb.	*(J. Matley)*	7
Mr J. Wright's	**William,** 5 y-o, 10st. 2lb.	*(Job Toon)*	8

Betting: 4/5 fav. Cavendish, 4/1 Robert Laundrie, 6/1 William, 8/1 Hawk.

Tuesday 4th October 1870

THE MEMBER'S NURSERY HANDICAP of 3 sovereigns each, with 25 added.
Six furlongs.

Mr Powell's	**Eddish,** 7st. 10lb.	*(W. Bissell)*	1
Mr Saunders'	**Bandsman,** 7st. 4lb.	*(Thomas Osborne)*	2
Mr Brown's	**Elton,** 7st.	*(Hunter)*	bol

Betting: 5/4 fav. Bandsman, 6/4 Eddish, 3/1 Elton.

AN OPEN HUNTER'S PLATE of 25 sovereigns.
One and a half miles.

Mr Goodwin's	**Pistache,** 3 y-o, 10st. 5lb.	*(Owner)*	1
Mr Taylor's	**Florence,** 3 y-o, 9st. 3lb.	*(A. Hunt)*	2
Mr T. Eskrett's	**Dean of York,** 4 y-o, 9st. 13lb.	*(Eskrett, jnr)*	3
Mr J. Wright's	**Bulldog,** 3 y-o, 10st. 3lb.	*(J. Matley)*	-

Betting: 5/4 fav. Bulldog, 5/2 Pistache, 4/1 Florence, 100/15 Dean of York.

THE SCURRY HANDICAP PLATE of 25 sovereigns.
For horses of all ages. Five furlongs.

Mr Willis's	**Sallie,** 3 y-o, 8st. 7lb.	*(Samuel Kenyon)*	1
Mr Lincoln's	**Pulchra,** 3 y-o, 7st. 10lb.	*(W. Bissell)*	2
Mr Taylor's filly	**by Vengeance,** 2 y-o, 7st. 4lb.	*(Lake)*	3
Mr T. Wadlow's	**Lady of Croome**	*(J. Matley)*	-
Mr -	**Thunderclap**	*(Turner)*	-
Mr -	**gelding by Cygnet**	*(J. Vinell)*	-
Mr -	**Syren**	*(W. Edwards)*	-

Betting: 5/4 fav. Sallie, 3/1 Cygnet gelding, 7/1 any other.

A HURDLE RACE (FREE HANDICAP) of 3 sovereigns each, with 20 added.
Two miles over five hurdles.

Mr Barber's	**Miss Banks** 4 y-o, 11st.	*(Thorpe)*	1
Mr J. Wright's	**William,** 5 y-o, 11st. 4lb.	*(Mr A. Dabbs)*	2
Mr J. Wright's	**Bulldog,** 3 y-o, 10st. 5lb.	*(J. Matley)*	3

Betting: 1/3 fav. Miss Banks.

THE BRADFORD HANDICAP PLATE of 5 sovereigns each, with 40 added.
One mile.

Mr Elton named	**Rose Young,** 3 y-o, 6st. 6lb.	*(G. Ashworth)*	1
Mr Lincoln's	**Prince,** 4 y-o, 8st. 7lb.	*(Samuel Kenyon)*	2
Mr Taylor's	**Florence,** 3 y-o, 6st. 8lb.	*(Lake)*	3

Betting: 1/2 fav. Rose Young.

THE CONSOLATION HANDICAP of 1 sovereign each, with 10 added.
Six furlongs.

| Mr J. Welch's | **gelding by Cygnet,** 3 y-o, 8st. | *(J. Vinell)* | 1 |
| Mr J. Wright's | **Lady of Croome,** 4 y-o, 8st. 12lb. | *(Matley)* | 2 |

Betting: 2/5 fav. Lady of Croome.

1871

The Race Committee's confidence in announcing they had secured sufficient funds for this years meeting to go ahead may have been somewhat premature, as the opening paragraph of the race report in the *Walsall Free Press* shows what a close call it was: -

'Up to within a few weeks of the time a general impression prevailed in the town that there would be no races this year. But just at the last moment, as it were, a vigorous effort was made by the patrons of the turf, and the result was that once more there was a meeting on the Walsall course, although — owing to the delay in commencing the arrangements — the races could not be held in the wake week.'

The reason for the meeting being put in jeopardy at such a late stage was due to a statement issued to all Clerks of the Course from the Jockey Club and printed along with the race announcements in *The Walsall Observer* of September 16th.

A liberal response was forthcoming this year, but for how much longer? It was apparent financing the meeting was becoming an increasing problem for the Committee members, and this instruction from the Jockey Club was the last thing that was needed.

The week before the Races were due to take place, the weather in the area was terrible, day after day, the rain came down in torrents. Even the annual auction of the sites for the erection of the tents and booths was affected by it. The

1860 - 1879

> **Public Notices.**
>
> ## WALSALL RACES.
>
> THESE RACES are fixed to take place on MONDAY and TUESDAY, OCTOBER 2nd and 3rd, 1871.
>
> The new rule adopted at Newmarket for more Money to be added, will cause the above Races to cost considerably more than formerly, and unless therefore there is a liberal response to the Canvassers they cannot be carried out.
>
> By order of the Committee,
> A. GROVE,
> Chairman.
>
> September 8th, 1871.

The announcement in the Walsall Observer for the 1871 meeting.

meeting was held on the course itself, presumably to show bidders exactly what they were getting for their money. When the day came it was pouring down, resulting, according to the Committee's accounts, in them being £50 down on sales.

The Friday and Saturday preceding the meeting, rain continued to fall in torrents, to the point where the lower parts of the course, the railway side, were completely flooded. The fire brigade were called in to pump the lying water away, working all day Saturday and Sunday in an effort to ensure the meeting went ahead. Come Monday, all was set fair, although threatening. The rain held off until half way through the programme when it began to drizzle, continuing to the end of the meeting. The firemen had worked a minor miracle and cleared the flooded course, but it remained extremely heavy underfoot, some said, the worst going in living memory.

Before the first race had been run, the 'Aunt Sally's' were claiming their first victims, several children were taken to the Cottage Hospital with injuries resulting from flying sticks. Again the Walsall Free Press condemned the sighting of them in the hope something would be done.

The race programme consisted of ten races, three of them over hurdles, with two events being taken from the card in an effort to boost the prize fund for the remaining races, and so comply with the orders from the Jockey Club.

The first mud-lover to pass the post was Mr Lincoln's three year-old, Ushant, ridden to victory by Job Toon in the All-Aged Stakes over six furlongs. Mr Lincoln was eager to get his hands on the increased prize money, which appeared little different than in previous years, as he owned two of the five runners. His second entry being a two year-old colt, White Rose, who, to his credit in all the mud, finished in third place. Splitting Lincoln's horses was one of Thomas Wadlow's charges, Polyglot, a couple of lengths behind the winner.

In the Tradesmen's Handicap Plate, the jockeys of all four runners were guilty of jumping the start, and not realising the starter had declared the fact. The four horses completed the entire seven furlongs of the race before the jockeys realised they had to do it all again. The condition of the horses on their return from the first race must have spoken volumes to anyone intending to back any of them. The odds were turn upside down, Mr Stevens' Magdala was the one everyone went for, making him 4/6 favourite. Mr Lawrence's Rose Young was at 3/1, the remaining two runners, Wadlow's Woerth and Mr Brown's Astonishment both being quoted at 4/1. At the second time of asking, the race began, with the clever backers in the crowd who were on Magdala, grateful for the dress rehearsal earlier, as the horse came home an easy winner from Rose Young, and Woerth.

Thomas Wadlow, who usually had at least one winner at the meeting, saw his two year-old filly, Rosa, win the five furlong Trial Selling Stakes. Lady of Croome, one of his old horses, sold the previous year after victory in the same race came in second. To comply with the conditions of the race, the mud-loving youngster was sold to Mr Bancroft for 30 guineas. It is good to know that even in 1871 the ill-treatment of horses would not be tolerated. Finishing last in the Trial Stakes was a three year-old named Gruelthorpe owned by George Willan of Gorgate Hall near Dereham, Norfolk. Two weeks after the colt had run at Walsall, Willan was charged with ill-treatment of the animal who ran in a match at Leicester Races. The prosecution was brought by Inspector Choyce of the Society for the Prevention of Cruelty to Animals who was determined to obtain a prosecution after Mrs Willan bet him £10 he would not get one!

The first of the three hurdle races to be run was the Maiden Hurdle Plate, run over a mile and a half, jumping six flights of hurdles en route. Five runners contested the race, which was won by Eddish, a course winner on the flat at last years meeting, now showing his prowess over hurdles. In second place was Jessie some lengths in front of the tiring third horse, Hawk. The favourite, Madeline at 6/4 couldn't handle the heavy ground, and finished a long way behind, accompanied by one of the other runners, the 8/1 chance, Goldhanger. Since Eddish's victory last year the horse had changed hands and was now under the ownership of Mr Gilliver who had to endure a Stewards enquiry. Several of the other owners objected to Gilliver's description of the horse, but the Stewards saw no reason for the objection and allowed Eddish to keep the race.

Closing the day's muddy sport was the six furlong Hednesford Handicap, won by the winner of the first race, Ushant. This was a horse that could obviously run on heavy going judging by his earlier victory and the backers were not slow in realising this, installing him as the even money favourite.

With the going remaining heavy at the start of Tuesday's card, the horses that contested the Hunter's Hurdle Race Stakes over the longer distance of two miles with eight flights to negotiate would have to be real mud-pluggers. The backers found one in Mr Howard's Cruiskeen. Initially, the even money favourite was a horse called Cotton, but confidence in him suddenly waned and the backers lost faith rapidly as he finished third choice in the ring. Of the four runners, Cruiskeen, ridden by Gregory, was the only one who could run in mud. He made it look easy, coming home in a canter, a very easy winner. The remaining three runners arriving at the winning post as soon as their tired legs allowed them.

Ushant, already winner of two races, made it a treble for his owner Mr Lincoln, when winning the Scurry Handicap over

1860 – 1879

five furlongs, ridden again by Job Toon. Four horses should have started for the race and although the jockey Fletcher had weighed out, his mount, Gruelthorpe wasn't saddled up in time and missed out on the event. Ushant won by two lengths from Lady of Croome who was still having problems trying to win for her new owner, six lengths further back was Euphemia in third place.

In the third and final hurdle race of the meeting, the Hurdle Plate, five horses attempted the mile and a half trip in ground that by now must have been very badly cut-up. This relatively short race was to become a real test of stamina. Cruiskeen, after his easy win the previous day, rather surprisingly, wasn't really fancied by the gamblers of Walsall, who only gave him a 5/1 chance of winning. The favourite at 4/6 was another previous course winner on the flat, Rose Young, now owned by Mr Lawrence. He justified everyone's faith in him, winning by a length and a half from Cruiskeen, with William Saunders' Corfu, back in third place.

Two horses previously owned by Thomas Wadlow claimed first and second spots in the All-Aged Selling Stakes for their new owners. Lady of Croome still couldn't get her nose in front and win a race for new owner Mr J. Wright. Failing this time, four lengths behind the winner Rosa, bought by Mr Bancroft from Wadlow when the mare won the seller the previous day. During this race one of the runners, Salamanca, ridden by seventeen year-old Frederick Newcombe, slipped up shortly after the start. Newcombe who was knocked unconscious in the fall and initially, there was great concern for his welfare. He remained unconscious until Thursday of that week, but was later reported to be progressing well at the Cottage Hospital.

The meeting had been fortunate so far to have just the one accident on the course, given the bad state of the ground. The final race of the meeting, the Bradford Handicap Plate, doubled the tally. The jockey concerned was Thomas Skelton who was riding the favourite, Mr Ranny's Mintyus. Shortly after the start, probably around the same place Salamanca came to grief, Skelton's mount fell. The other two runners, Rose Young (2/1) and Mr Lincoln's Fair Maid of Kent (3/1) were left to finish the race, with the latter horse pulling away from her opponent to win by four lengths. Both Thomas Skelton and his mount were uninjured by the fall, and gamely the jockey re-mounted to finish the race.

Unfavourable weather or not, one man who would remember the meeting for all the right reasons was Mr Lincoln. Two of his four runners, Ushant, with three wins and Fair Maid of Kent with her single victory meant he had won forty percent of the races on the card.

The official results of the meeting were:

Monday 2nd October 1871

THE ALL AGED PLATE of 25 sovereigns each.
The winner to be claimed for 100 sovs. Six furlongs.

Mr Lincoln's	**Ushant,** 3 y-o, 8st. 11lb.		*(Job Toon)*	1
Mr T. Wadlow's	**Polyglot,** 3 y-o, 8st. 11lb.		*(A. Deakin)*	2
Mr Lincoln's	**White Rose,** 2 y-o, 7st. 4lb.		*(W. Bissell)*	3
Mr Bancroft's	**Stilts,** 2 y-o, 7st. 4lb.		*(J. Fox)*	4
Mr Robinson's	**Salamanca,** 2 y-o, 6st. 3lb.		*(R. Fletcher)*	5

Betting: Evens fav. Ushant, 7/2 Stilts, 4/1 Polyglot. No claim for the winner.

THE TRADESMEN'S PLATE of 50 sovereigns added
to a Handicap of 5 sovereigns each. Seven furlongs.

Mr Stevens'	**Magdala,** 3 y-o, 7st.	*(Thomas Skelton)*	1
Mr Lawrence's	**Rose Young,** 4 y-o, 8st.	*(George Ashworth)*	2
Mr T. Wadlow's	**Woerth,** 3 y-o, 6st. 7lb.	*(Richard Fletcher)*	3
Mr Brown's	**Astonishment,** 3 y-o, 6st.	*(F. Newcombe)*	4

Betting: 5/4 fav. Rose Young, 6/4 Magdala, 5/1 Woerth.
After false start: 6/4 fav. Magdala, 3/1 Rose Young, 4/1 Woerth.

THE TRIAL STAKES of 3 sovereigns each, with 20 added. Five furlongs.

Mr T. Wadlow's	**Rosa,** 2 y-o, 6st. 9lb.	*(Thomas Skelton)*	1
Mr J. Wright's	**Lady of Croome,** 5 y-o, 8st. 11lb.	*(J. Fox)*	2
Mr Lincoln's	**Pulchrior,** 3 y-o, 8st. 11lb.	*(Job Toon)*	3
Mr Willan's	**Gruelthorpe,** 3 y-o, 8st. 11lb.	*(J. Crickmere)*	4

Betting: 4/6 fav. Rosa, 4/1 Gruelthorpe, 10/1 others.

A MAIDEN HURDLE PLATE of 25 sovereigns.
One and a half miles over six hurdles.

Mr Gilliver's	**Eddish,** 3 y-o, 10st. 7lb.	*(T. Dixon)*	1
Mr Broughton's	**Jessie,** aged, 12st. 2lb.	*(Owner)*	2
Mr Hepburn's	**Hawk,** 6 y-o, 12st. 2lb.	*(Martin)*	3
Mr -	**Madeline**	*(W. Gregory)*	-
Mr -	**Goldhanger**	*(J. Tomlinson)*	-

Betting: 6/4 fav. Madeline, 3/1 Eddish, 4/1 Hawk, 8/1 bar.

THE HEDNESFORD HANDICAP PLATE
of 2 sovereigns each, with 20 added. Six furlongs.

Mr Lincoln's	**Ushant,** 3 y-o, 7st. 6lb.	*(W. Bissell)*	1
Mr Ranny's	**Mintyus,** 3 y-o, 6st. 9lb.	*(Thomas.Skelton)*	2
Mr Lawrence's	**Rose Young,** 4 y-o, 7st.	*(G. Ashworth)*	3
Mr Gilliver's	**Eddish,** 3 y-o, 6st. 2lb.	*(Ross)*	4

Betting: Evens fav. Ushant, 6/4 Mintyus, 5/1 Rose Young.

Tuesday 3rd October 1871

THE HUNTER'S HURDLE RACE STAKES
of 2 sovereigns each, with 20 added.
Two miles with eight flights of hurdles.

Mr Horwood's	**Cruiskeen,** 4 y-o, 11st. 10lb.	*(W. Gregory)*	1
Mr Broughton's	**Jessie,** aged, 11st. 4lb.	*(Owner)*	2
Mr Hepburn's	**Hawk,** 6 y-o, 11st. 6lb.	*(Mr J. Poinons)*	3
Mr Angle's	**Cotton,** 4 y-o, 10st. 8lb.	*(Mr T. Newton)*	4

Betting: 4/6 fav. Cruiskeen, 3/1 Jessie, 7/2 Cotton.

THE SCURRY HANDICAP PLATE of 1 sovereign each, with 20 added.
For horses of all ages. Five furlongs.

Mr Lincoln's	**Ushant,** 3 y-o, 9st.	*(Job Toon)*	1
Mr J. Wright's	**Lady of Croome,** 5 y-o, 7st. 12lb.	*(J. Fox)*	2
Mr Robinson's	**Euphemia,** 3 y-o, 8st.	*(Thomas Skelton)*	3

Betting: 1/2 fav. Ushant, 3/1 Lady of Croome.

THE HURDLE PLATE of 30 sovereigns.
One and a half miles over six flights of hurdles.

Mr Lawrence's	**Rose Young,** 4 y-o, 10st. 12lb.	*(S. Kenyon)*	1
Mr Horwood's	**Cruiskeen,** 4 y-o, 11st. 9lb.	*(W. Gregory)*	2
Mr Saunders'	**Corfu,** 4 y-o, 10st. 12lb.	*(J. Adams)*	3
Mr -	**Marriage**	*(Tomlinson)*	-
Mr -	**Sorceress**	*(Brady)*	-

Betting: 4/5 fav. Rose Young, 7/2 Corfu, 4/1 Marriage.

1860 – 1879

THE ALL-AGED SELLING STAKES of 1 sovereigns each, with 25 added. Five furlongs.

Mr Bancroft's	**Rosa,** 2 y-o, 6st. 9lb.	*(Thomas Skelton)*	1
Mr J. Wright's	**Lady of Croome,** 5 y-o, 8st. 1lb.	*(J. Fox)*	2
Mr Lincoln's	**Pulchrior,** 3 y-o, 8st. 1lb.	*(Job Toon)*	3
Mr Robinson's	**Salamanca**	*(Newcombe)*	-
Mr Willan's	**Gruelthorpe**	*(Gough)*	-

Betting: 4/5 fav. Rosa, 7/4 Pulchrior, 4/1 any other.

THE BRADFORD HANDICAP PLATE of 50 sovereigns. One mile.

Mr Lincoln's	**Fair Maid of Kent,** 3 y-o, 6st. 1lb.	*(George Ashworth)*	1
Mr Lawrence's	**Rose Young,** 4 y-o, 6st. 13lb.	*(Fletcher)*	2
Mr Ranny's	**Mintyus,** 3 y-o, 6st. 10lb.	*(Thomas Skelton)*	3

Betting: 4/6 fav. Mintyus, 2/1 Rose Young, 3/1 the winner.

1872

Through the winter of 1871/72 the Race Committee must have been an unhappy group of men. With their accounts showing a deficit, the writing was on the wall for the meeting in the following September.

> WALSALL RACES, 1871.—Receipts, £413 10s. 3d.; Deficiency, £40 14s. 3d.— £454 4s. 6d. Sum total paid for races, £454 4s. 6d. Audited by A. D. Aulton, accountant.
> The above is the sum paid for last year's races; Mr. Aulton has audited the accounts, and certified them correct. A MEETING will be held on WEDNESDAY NEXT, the 14th inst., at Mr. Beebee's, the Old Still Inn, Digbeth, at Eight o'clock, when all persons interested in the continuance of the races this year will please attend. It will be seen from the above that a considerable deficiency exists in the accounts of the past year, owing to the great disadvantage under which the races were held, making it evident that unless a good effort is quickly made the races cannot be held this year.
> On behalf of the Committee,
> ABEL R. GROVE, late Chairman.

Early in the year the Committee must have known they were fighting a losing battle regarding the meeting, but deferred any official announcement until August. Following the announcement above from the *Walsall Observer*, another was published a week later in the same newspaper which read; -

'The deficit referred to above came about last year when the numbers of stalls and booths sold was below the number required to ensure financial security, the knock on effect resulted in the cancellation of this years meeting.'

At the top of the next column is a picture of the Old Still Inn c.1910 where the meeting to save the 1872 fixture took place. Described in 1925 as very old property but in a reasonable state of repair it was finally closed in April 1959 and demolished later that same month. It was reputed to be the premises where Dr. Samuel Johnson waited for his coach when returning to Lichfield. Next to the Old Still another famous Walsall landmark can be seen, Dance's Dining Rooms on the corner of Lower Hall Lane and Digbeth. A little further down towards The Bridge is the entrance to the Victorian Arcade with Buxton & Bonnett sign showing.

1873

The Race Committee had worked hard to ensure Walsall had its annual race meeting this year, after the disappointment of 1872. The deficit was cleared, and with money raised from the subscriptions, the Races were once again back on a sound financial footing, for the time being. The one major change that did occur was the moving of the race days forward to August, the reason behind this change is unknown.

Once again the weather was unfavourable. Despite this natural setback, and the fact the dates clashed with Bloxwich Wakes, the attendance was very large on both days. The quality of the horses running was said to be well above the average, and consequently, the races produced some exciting finishes.

The programme consisted of six races each day, beginning on Monday 18th and continuing on Tuesday 19th August. At the last running of the Races in 1871, the programme had been padded out with three hurdle races for hunters. This year, there was one on each day, for thoroughbreds only. Consequently, the standard of horses running was somewhat higher. There was only one race specifically for hunter's and that was the final race of the programme, the Welter Plate.

Over the two days racing, three riders were injured when their mounts came to grief. Which races these were, and who the jockeys and horses involved were, is unknown due to the briefness of the newspaper reports. A groom leading one of the runners around the parade ring on Monday was kicked in the face by his charge, resulting in a serious injury to the unfortunate lad. Medical attention was on hand immediately from Dr. Drewry who was standing close by the incident.

The opening race was the Trial Selling Stakes over five furlongs, with eight runners. H. Taylor, keen to get in the winners enclosure, had two runners in the race, Pansey at 2/1, and Raby the evens favourite. Much to the annoyance of the other owners, Pansey won and Raby was third, splitting the pair was Mr Poinan's horse, Orthodox.

1860 – 1879

For the first time in many years a Knight of the Realm had a runner at Walsall. A winning one at that. Sir Edward Buckley entered his horse, Witch (4/1) in the 2-45pm race, the Tradesmen's Handicap Plate. The horse was trained at Hednesford by James Hopwood and ridden by his son, James junior, his first winner at Walsall.

Thomas Wadlow usually had at least one winner at the meeting. This year he opened his account with victory in the third race, a new five-furlong event named the Artisan's Plate. The horse, Siluria, started as even money favourite, beating a dual winner from two years ago, Mr Lincoln's, Ushant, with E. W. Taylor's horse, Reform, third.

Another new race on the programme was the Lilliputian Plate, so named because it was a race for Galloway ponies. These pony races had proved popular at other courses with both owners and spectators alike, the race was over one mile with five starters. The winner of this inaugural event was P. Burniston's Honeydew who came in at 3/1, beating Game Hen, a pony owned by a man almost perfectly named for the occasion, Mr Gilliver. Third was Royal Lad, owned and ridden by Mr Tomlinson. The surprising thing about this race was the weights the ponies had to carry, considering they should not exceed fifteen hands high. The winner carried 10stone 13 pounds and Royal Lad had the huge weight of 11 stone 7 pounds to contend with, similar burdens to those carried by horses in the hurdle races.

Jockey Thomas Skelton rode his second winner of the day, the 4/6 favourite, Mayoress, in the All-Aged Handicap Stakes. Skelton rode under both codes of racing and in 1886 rode Old Joe to victory in the Grand National. In the short time he rode at Walsall, he did make an impression, finishing as the jockey who rode the second highest number of winners on the course to George Whitehouse.

To end the first days sport was the first of the hurdle races, the Maiden Hurdle Plate, which got under way shortly before five o'clock. As the five runners were making their way to the start, one of them got a little excited and kicked out in panic, unfortunately striking a youth named Alfred Stokes, a brush maker from the Caldmore area. Although not badly injured, he was taken to the Cottage Hospital for treatment. The winning horse, Venom, was owned by E. W. Taylor who took the prize money, no doubt also collecting from the betting ring as the horse finished with a good starting price for those days, 6/1. Second place went to Lillyput, with Sir George Chetwynd's Faust, third. After the race had ended, J. T. Raworth, owner of Lillyput placed an objection to the winner on the grounds of crossing. Everyone looked to the Stewards for their opinion, unfortunately no one could find either of the gentlemen concerned to ask their opinion. The result was allowed to stand, for the time being. The following Tuesday, at a meeting of the Race Committee, the members agreed to allow the original result to stand, probably because no one could remember what had exactly happened!

Monday's card closed with a hurdle race and Tuesday's opened with one. The Handicap Hurdle Race, over one and a half miles jumping six flights in the process. Only three runners started and unusually not one of those who competed the previous day started in this one. Mr H. Taylor was back in the winner's enclosure when his horse, a brother to Hannah triumphed from Mr Melsom's Kitty and in third place, a previous course winner, Ushant.

Thomas Wadlow got his second winner of the meeting when Siluria won again in the disappointing Bradford Handicap Plate. This was a match in fact, the winner only having one opponent, Lothair owned by the chairman of the Race Committee, Abel Grove.

Mr Lincoln's Ushant, who came third and last in the hurdle race earlier, was put back to flat racing in the penultimate race of the day, the Town Welter Handicap Plate, with some effect too. Six runners lined up for the start of the six-furlong trip, and the exertions in the hurdle race proved not to have concerned Ushant in anyway. The horse winning under the guidance of Job Toon.

The final race, or match, the Welter Plate was the only race specifically for hunters this year. At previous meetings these races had always proved popular and attracted a fair few runners. This year was the exception, and disappointingly only two runners started for the two-mile event. By the time this race came round many people had drifted away from the racecourse as the race was of little interest to anyone other than the two owner riders. First past the post was Rosalita, believed to be the favourite, with Mr J. Tyler's Naughty Boy following up.

While the racing was taking place, people were still getting injured on the racecourse, with the wayward sticks from the 'Aunt Sally' stalls flying in every direction. Children and adults were continuing to fall like nine-pins. Even watching horse racing could be a dangerous business. Many accidents occurred in the most innocent of ways - a young lady named Jane Mills from Hall Lane apparently slipped on the damp grass or caught her foot under one of the tent pegs and fell, breaking her leg in the process.

The official results of the meeting were:

Monday 18th August 1873

THE TRIAL STAKES of 3 sovereigns each, with 20 added. Five furlongs.

Mr Taylor's	**Pansy**, 8st. 9lb.	*(John Deakin)*	1
Mr Poinon's	**Orthodox**, 6st. 12lb.	*(Ross)*	2
Mr Taylor's	**Raby**, 8st. 12lb.	*(Faulkner)*	3

Eight ran.

THE TRADESMEN'S PLATE of 50 sovereigns added to a Handicap of 5 sovereigns each. Five furlongs.

Sir E. Buckley's	**Witch**, 4 y-o, 7st. 6lb.	*(James Hopwood)*	1
Mr Heartfield's	**Harbinger**, 3 y-o, 6st. 10lb.	*(Glover)*	2
Mr Taylor's	**Venom**, 5 y-o, 7st. 6lb.	*(James Orbell)*	3

Six ran.

THE ARTISAN'S PLATE (HANDICAP) of 50 sovereigns. Five furlongs.

Mr T. Wadlow's	**Siluria**, 3 y-o, 7st. 5lb.	*(Thomas Skelton)*	1
Mr Lincoln's	**Ushant**, 5 y-o, 7st. 12lb.	*(T. Wheldon)*	2
Mr Taylor's	**Reform**, 5 y-o, 7st. 12lb.	*(Walker)*	3

Eight ran.

1860 - 1879

THE LILLIPUTIAN PLATE of 20 sovereigns.
For Galloway ponies not exceeding 15 hands. One mile.

Mr Burniston's	**Honeydew,** 10st. 13lb.	(J. Dixon)	1
Mr Gilliver's	**Game Hen,** 11st.	(Madeley)	2
Mr Tomlinson's	**Royal Lad,** 11st. 7lb.	(Owner)	3

Five ran.

THE ALL-AGED STAKES of 2 sovereigns each.
Weight for age. Five furlongs.

Mr Robinson's	**Mayoress,** 6 y-o, 9st. 11lb.	(T. Skelton)	1
Mr J. Garner's	**Parliamentary,** 6 y-o, 8st. 4lb.	(Hunt)	2
Mr H. Taylor's	**Hertford,** 3 y-o, 8st. 4lb.	(Walker)	3

Eight ran.

A MAIDEN HURDLE PLATE of 30 sovereigns.
One and a half miles over six flights of hurdles.

Mr E. Taylor's	**Venom,** 5 y-o, 11st.	(Hunt)	1
Mr J. Raworth's	**Lillyput,** 4 y-o, 10st. 7lb.	(J. Fox)	2
Sir G. Chetwynd's	**Faust,** 4 y-o, 10st. 7lb.	(J. Tomlinson)	3

Five ran.

Tuesday 19th August 1873

THE HURDLE HANDICAP PLATE of 30 sovereigns.
One and a half miles over six flights of hurdles.

Mr H. Taylor's	**br. to Hannah,** 4 y-o, 10st. 9lb.	(Wardle)	1
Mr Melsom's	**Kitty,** aged, 10st. 2lb.	(Caitlin)	2
Mr Cockin's	**Ushant,** 5 y-o, 11st. 3lb.	(Job Toon)	3

Three ran.

THE BRADFORD HANDICAP PLATE of 50 sovereigns. Six furlongs.

Mr T. Wadlow's,	**Siluria,** 3 y-o, 7st. 12lb.	(Thomas Skelton)	1
Mr A. Groves'	**Lothair,** 3 y-o, 6st. 10lb.	(McEwan)	2

Two ran.

THE ALL-AGED SELLING STAKES of 3 sovereigns each, with 25 added.
Five furlongs.

Mr Taylor's	**Pansey,** 9st.	(John Deakin)	1
Mr Fenwick's	**Premier Argonaut,** 8st. 11lb.	(J. Fox)	2
Mr Poinon's	**Theresa,** 6st. 8lb.	(Glover)	3

Three ran.

THE SCURRY HANDICAP PLATE of 2 sovereigns each, with 20 added.
For horses of all ages. Five furlongs.

Mr Turner's	**Nightshade,** 6st. 10lb.	(Thomas Glover)	1
Mr R. Garner's	**Parliamentary,** 8st. 10lb.	(Hunt)	2
Mr Jennen's	**Salesman,** 8st. 13lb.	(H. Bunn)	3

Three ran.

THE TOWN WELTER HANDICAP PLATE of 50 sovereigns. Six furlongs.

Mr Cockin's	**Ushant,** 5 y-o, 10st. 11lb.	(Job Toon)	1
Mr Turner's	**Nightshade,** 3 y-o, 9st. 12lb.	(T Glover)	2
Mr -	**Lady Ongley,** 4 y-o, 9st. 11lb.	(J. Fox)	3

Six ran.

THE WELTER PLATE of 19 guineas for hunters.
Weight for age. Two miles on the flat.

Mr -	**Rosalita,** 11st. 4lb.	(Owner)	1
Mr J. Tyler's	**Naughty Boy,** 11st. 4lb.	(Owner)	2

Two ran.

1874

Again the Race Committee had risen to the occasion to ensure the Races went ahead as usual. No one, then or now, can possibly criticise Abel Grove and the other members for their lack of endeavour, and their commitment to the cause should be applauded.

The *Walsall Free Press* sum up the events on the Long Meadow perfectly in the opening paragraph of their report on the Races of 1874: -

'The patrons of the turf, like the lovers of cricket, have been exceedingly fortunate in the selection of time for their favourite sports; for the weather was all that could be desired on Monday and Tuesday last – the two days set apart for the races – and the result was that each day a vast concourse of spectators assembled on the course and in the surrounding thoroughfares, and it is questionable whether the assembly was surpassed by even the monster muster at Wolverhampton. Some assert that the gathering was the largest that has taken place in the Midlands; but whether it was the largest or not, the spectacle presented by the dense masses of people who crowded the crest of the hill, and filled the valley to the north and west of the Mill Fleam was picturesque and exciting, and such as was likely to be long remembered. Before the racing commenced there was a good deal of gambling going on, but both the 'dice dodge' and the 'umbrella' and 'bag men' were put a stop to by the police. One 'welsher' was caught and made to disgorge before he left the ring, in order to avoid being lynched.'

The *Walsall Observer* also did their bit in praise of the proceedings, commenting: -

'...in the principle races larger fields showed at the post than even those at Wolverhampton and other local races in the vicinity, where higher stakes were offered. Among the entries were horses from many well-known stables, and with one or two exceptions the running was above the average. Mr Hebblethwaite, the respected chief of the Walsall Post Office, with characteristic forethought, put down a telegraph wire direct to the grandstand, thereby affording the means for the transmission of telegraphic messages direct from the ground, which proved of great public convenience, with no less than 194 messages being dispatched on Monday. Mr Grove, as chairman of the committee, was most energetic in his efforts and deserves the thanks of everyone desirous of seeing these annual gatherings perpetuated in the town. Most of the members of the committee as well as the stewards also worked well to secure success, and should not be lost sight of in our mode of commendation. The Stewards on the occasion were Captain J. M. Browne, Lieutenant Charles Forster and F. Villiers Forster Esq.'

It is difficult to believe after reading the above comments of praise, and the fact that the Races were still extremely popular, that within two years they would be history.

The entries for the events were indeed large. The local newspapers published a list of entries for six of the twelve races and the total was ninety-eight horses. Inevitably, only a relatively small number of those horses made it onto the course. Large entries meant the prize fund for the races was boosted as each owner had to pay a fee to enter each horse. The added money from tradesmen etc. in the town amounted

1860 – 1879

to almost £500, this sum being divided amongst the individual races and added to the fund for the designated events.

In the opening race on August 24th, the Walsall Plate, a handicap race run over five furlongs, the total prize money amounted to approximately £120. Of the twenty-two entries, only seven made it to the start, Thomas Stevens's Cranbourne was top weight and the most fancied by the backers at 6/4. The weight burden is the most obvious reason for his defeat, as he could only finish third to Mr Eykes's Rhapsody (4/1), with an un-named filly by Hermit owned by Mr Ison in third place. The running of the race didn't suit many of the horses in the field. The jockey of Rhapsody, John Deakin set off as he meant to go on – fast, winning as he pleased with a length and a half to spare. The horse that finished in fifth place, Ironsides, was ridden by Charles Loates, the eldest of four brothers from Derby who all became jockeys. The younger two of the four, Sam and Tom, were to become champion jockeys in later years.

The jockey Deakin triumphed again in the All-Aged Plate riding with very similar tactics as he did when winning the first race, by playing a game of 'catch me if you can.' Riding Mr J. Robinson's aged horse, Mayoress, he set off in front, building up a lead, then giving his mount a breather before asking her to go on again. The other jockeys hadn't cottoned on to this tactic, and Deakin's mount won easily, this time by eight lengths.

The Maiden Hurdle Race was disappointing from the number of runners that turned out. Only four going to the post, but thanks to the spectators, the race turned out to be anything but dull. As far as the backers were concerned, the result was predictable, Thomas Wadlow's horse Relief would walk it, consequently backing it heavily to 4/6 favourite. Two other runners were quoted at 5/2, Lucerne and Lady Ravensden with Mr Marsden's Catty at 10/1. At the start Lucerne made the pace followed by Relief and Lady Ravensden. After a third of the race had been covered, the horses were confronted by large numbers of spectators spilling onto the course. In the confusion, Relief was knocked down and the jockey of Lady Ravensden, William Daniels, thought it advisable to pull his mare up. Lucerne avoided the danger but was hampered, allowing the 10/1 outsider Catty to pass her and go on at leisure to win by over thirty lengths. The rider of the runner-up, Mr Gilpin lodged an objection to Catty on the grounds of crossing but the Stewards allowed the result to stand.

The Trial Selling Stakes ended with a touch of farce about it too, provided you hadn't backed the horse concerned. Five runners started and the betting ring saw it as a pretty open race, with odds ranging from 3/1 to 4/1, favouring at the post Mr Russell's Lady Lyon at 3/1. The horse making the early running was Bird of Prey ridden by Hammond. He led his four rivals to within yards of the winning post when he began pulling his mount up, mistaking the winning post. In the process, one might say, snatching defeat from the jaws of victory. His two nearest rivals, Lady Lyon and the 4/1 chance Hilarity went past the slowing horse, with the latter just getting the official judges verdict by three-quarters of a length. Bird of Prey and Hammond finished an embarrassed third.

On the second day, The Staffordshire Advertiser reported that the crowd was larger than on the first day, making it one of the most successful meetings ever as far as attendances were concerned. As with any large group of people, especially where drink is freely available, trouble can erupt at any time, and it did so on several occasions throughout the day, the police and race officials having difficulty in keeping the course clear and maintaining control. Many pickpockets were also in attendance and this inflamed the masses even further, as the crowd, who didn't require a judge and jury to claim their justice, set upon any person suspected of the offence, guilty or not.

Thomas Wadlow rarely returned from Walsall Races without some of the prize money in his pocket. His winner in the Innkeeper's Handicap Plate made sure it didn't happen this year. A horse who was already familiar with the course, Siluria, won the race as the 4/7 favourite. The victory also meant that the jockey, John Deakin, resplendent in the all white colours of the Wadlow family, had now ridden three winners at the meeting.

For once, Thomas Wadlow had just the single winner to against his name when he left Walsall that night. Relief, his horse that was knocked down, came out for the Hurdle Handicap Plate and was installed as even money favourite by the backers. He ran a stinker of a race and never featured at all, finishing fourth of the six runners. In the following race, the Bradford Handicap Plate, Siluria was saddled-up again, but was never fancied in the betting ring and started as the dual outsider at 6/1, which was strange considering the horses earlier win. As the three front runners, headed by Non Compos, bred, owned and trained by ex-jockey Neptune Stagg, turned into the straight, all three ran out negotiating the bend. This left Siluria and Raby Castle in the lead, the latter pulling away to win as he pleased by twenty lengths. The three remaining runners eventually recovered their stride, with Mr Walker's Industrious finishing third.

The best race of the day and possibly the meeting was the five furlong Member's Selling Stakes. Although the race only had four runners, there was less than a length separating the quartet at the winning post. The favourite was Lady Lyon at 6/4 with Hilarity, the second choice at 9/4. The two remaining horses, Minnie Warren and Seclusion both at 3/1. Hilarity and Seclusion vied for the lead until close home when the favourite challenged the pair with Minnie Warren close up. All four jockeys rode a driving finish with Hilarity repeating the earlier victory over Lady Lyon by a neck. Seclusion was a head further behind and Minnie Warren beaten half a length in last place. The winner was sold for 50 guineas to Kempson Walker.

In the penultimate race, the Town Welter Handicap Plate saw to old adversaries line up again, Mr Stevens's Cranbourne and Mr Eykes's Rhapsody, the latter winning the opening race of the meeting, with the former finishing third. Cranbourne on that occasion was the favourite and the backers saw no reason to change their opinions of the horse, installing him at 4/7, with Rhapsody at the generous price of 4/1. The two remaining runners were Mr Prime's Lady Hanson, and Mr Lawrence's The Shah. The race itself proved to be an anti-climax. As the flag was dropped, Rhapsody whipped round

1860 - 1879

and was left by the other three. Cranbourne made the pace and continued to lead the remaining two runners right to the line, winning by a length from The Shah and Lady Hanson.

With one race remaining on the programme, the Hunter's Selling Plate over two miles, attracted just three runners and ended the proceedings on a sour and highly suspicious note. Mr Marsden's previous runner and winner at 10/1, Catty, Mr Amey's horse Over and Charlotta owned by Mr C. Marsdon. It was almost as though the betting ring dictated the outcome of the race, Over was at first backed to 4/6 favourite, when a sudden rush of money deposed him as favourite, installing Catty in his place with the incredibly short odds of 1/4. It was no surprise to find that Catty romped home with the utmost ease from Charlotta with Over a very bad third. The Stewards of the meeting were not happy with what they saw and summoned the owner and rider of Over, Mr Amey's, to explain what the Stewards saw as suspicious riding. The answers given by the rider did not satisfy the Stewards and they announced that the case would be reported to the Grand National Hunt Committee, the arm of the Jockey Club that supervised 'jump' racing. The outcome of the referral of the case to the powers that be is not known, but given the suspicious nature of both the fluctuation in the betting, and the riding of Over, the odds did not look to be in favour of anyone connected with the horse.

The official results of the meeting were:

Monday 24th August 1874

THE WALSALL PLATE (HANDICAP) of 50 sovereigns.
Five furlongs, straight.

Mr Eyke's	**Rhapsody,** 5 y-o, 8st. 7lb.	*(John Deakin)*	1
Mr Ison's	**filly by Hermit,** 3 y-o, 7st. 2lb.	*(Ross)*	2
Mr Stevens's jnr.	**Cranbourne,** 5 y-o, 9st. 5lb.	*(E. Payne)*	3
Mr Marston's	**Ironsides**	*(Charles Loates)*	-
Mr Boylan's	**Seclusion**	*(McEwen)*	-
Mr J. Breedin's	**Tocher**	*(Thomas Skelton)*	-
Mr Gomm's	**Ranee**	*(J. Frost)*	-

Betting: 6/4 fav. Cranbourne, 4/1 Rhapsody, 5/1 Hermit filly.

THE TRADESMEN'S PLATE of 50 sovereigns added
to a Handicap of 3 sovereigns each. One mile.

Mr Robinson's	**Raby Castle,** 5 y-o, 8st. 2lb.	*(Th. Skelton)*	1
Capt. Ley names	**Anchorite,** 3 y-o, 7st. 4lb.	*(Ross)*	2
Mr Bradbury's	**Baby,** 5 y-o, 7st. 12lb.	*(Charles Loates)*	3
Mr Prime's	**Lady Hanson,** 4 y-o, 6st. 7lb.	*(McEwen)*	4

Betting: 5/4 fav. Anchorite, 6/4 Raby Castle.

THE ALL-AGED PLATE of 50 sovereigns. Five furlongs.

Mr Robinson's	**Mayoress,** aged, 9st.	*(John Deakin)*	1
Mr Stevens'	**St. Patrick,** 3 y-o, 9st.	*(E. Payne)*	2
Mr Ison's filly	**by Hermit,** 3 y-o, 8st. 1lb.	*(Ross)*	3
Mr T. Drake's	**Pilgrim**	*(H. Wyatt)*	-
Mr Richards'	**Frugality**	*(Barnard)*	-

Betting: Evens fav. St. Patrick, 5/4 Mayoress.

A MAIDEN HURDLE RACE of 30 sovereigns, for horses that have never won a hurdle race.
One and a half miles over six flights of hurdles.

Mr Marsden's	**Catty,** aged, 11st. 3lb.	*(Mr Tait)*	1
Mr Sparrow's	**Lucerne,** 3 y-o, 10st. 7lb.	*(Mr Gilpin)*	2
Mr -	**Relief**	*(John Deakin)*	-
Mr -	**Lady Ravensden**	*(William Daniels)*	-

Betting: 4/6 Relief, 9/4 Lucerne, 5/2 Lady Ravensden, 10/1 Catty.

THE TRIAL SELLING STAKES of 5 sovereigns, with 30 added.
Five furlongs.

Mr Walker's	**Hilarity,** 3 y-o, 8st. 11lb.	*(Th. Skelton)*	1
Mr Russell's	**Lady Lyon,** 3 y-o, 8st. 9lb.	*(Jonas Jarvis)*	2
Mr Slinn's	**Bird of Prey,** 3 y-o, 8st. 4lb.	*(Hammond)*	3
Mr N. Stagg's	**Nil Desperandum,** 2 y-o, 6st. 4lb.	*(J. Frost)*	4
Mr Stevens'	**Ma Chere,** 2 y-o, 6st. 4lb.	*(John Deakin)*	5

Betting: 3/1 favs. Lady Lyon and Nil Desperandum, 7/2 Ma Chere, 4/1 bar

A HUNTERS STAKES of 30 sovereigns each, added to a sweepstakes of
2 sovs. Gentlemen riders only. Two miles.

Mr Amyes's	**Over,** 6 y-o, 12st. 4lb.	*(Owner)*	1
Mr Glover's	**Tom Pinder,** 5 y-o, 11st. 4lb	*(Hon. Douglas Sandilands)*	2
Mr Marsden's	**Charlotta,** aged, 13st. 2lb.	*(Mr Tait)*	3

Betting: 1/3 fav. Over.

Tuesday 25th August 1874

THE INNKEEPER'S HANDICAP PLATE of 50 sovereigns.
Five furlongs.

Mr T. Wadlow's	**Siluria,** 4 y-o, 8st. 12lb.	*(John Deakin)*	1
Mr Marston's	**Ironsides,** 4 y-o, 7st. 2lb.	*(Jonas Jarvis)*	2
Mr Gomm's	**Ranee,** 3 y-o, 7st. 5lb.	*(Ross)*	3
Mr Walker's	**Tommy,** 5 y-o, 7st. 10lb.	*(Fletcher)*	4

Betting: 4/7 fav. Siluria, 3/1 Ranee, 5/1 Ironsides.

THE HURDLE HANDICAP PLATE of 40 sovereigns.
One and a half miles over six flights of hurdles.

Mr S. Melsom's	**Kitty,** aged, 11st. 1lb.	*(Purcell)*	1
Mr Bradbury's	**Baby,** 5 y-o, 11st. 7lb.	*(William Daniels)*	2
Mr Marston's	**Ironsides,** 4 y-o, 11st. 5lb.	*(J. Fox)*	3
Mr T. Wadlow's	**Relief,** 4 y-o, 11st. 2lb.	*(A. Deakin)*	4
Mr Marsden's	**Catty,** aged, 11st.	*(Mr Tait)*	5
Mr Adams'	**Batchelor,** 4 y-o, 11st. 1lb.	*(Owner)*	6

Betting: Evens fav. Relief, 3/1 Batchelor, 4/1 Baby.

THE BRADFORD PLATE (HANDICAP) of 3 sovereigns each,
with 50 added. Six furlongs.

Mr Robinson's	**Raby Castle,** 5 y-o, 9st. 1lb.	*(Th. Skelton)*	1
Mr T. Wadlow's	**Siluria,** 4 y-o, 9st. 1lb.	*(John Deakin)*	2
Mr Walker's	**Industrious,** 3 y-o, 7st. 9lb.	*(Charles Loates)*	3
Mr J. Breedin's	**Tocher**	*(Thomas Skelton)*	-
Mr Lawrence's	**The Shah**	*(Fletcher)*	-
Mr N. Stagg's	**Non Compos**	*(Ross)*	-

Betting: 5/2 fav. The Shah, 3/1 Raby Castle, 5/1 Industrious.

THE SCURRY HANDICAP PLATE of 2 sovereigns each, with 20 added.
For horses of all ages. Five furlongs.

Mr Turner's	**Nightshade,** 6st. 10lb.	*(Thomas Glover)*	1
Mr R. Garner's	**Parliamentary,** 8st. 10lb.	*(Hunt)*	2
Mr Jennen's	**Salesman,** 8st. 13lb.	*(H. Bunn)*	3

1860 - 1879

THE MEMBER'S SELLING STAKES of 5 sovereigns each, with 30 added.
Five furlongs.

Mr Batson's	**Hilarity,** 3 y-o, 8st. 7lb.	*(J. Fox)*	1
Mr Russell's	**Lady Lyon,** 4 y-o, 8st. 7lb.	*(Charles Loates)*	2
Mr Boylan's	**Seclusion,** 4 y-o, 8st. 7lb.	*(McEwen)*	3
Mr Walker's	**Minnie Warren,** 3 y-o, 8st. 11lb.	*(Skelton)*	4

Betting: 6/4 fav. Lady Lyon, 9/4 Hilarity, 3/1 Minnie Warren.

THE TOWN WELTER HANDICAP PLATE
of 50 sovereigns. Six furlongs.

Mr Stevens' jnr.	**Cranbourne,** 5 y-o, 12st.	*(E. Payne)*	1
Mr Lawrence's	**The Shah,** 3 y-o, 9st. 11lb.	*(Th. Skelton)*	2
Mr Prime's	**Lady Hanson,** 4 y-o, 9st. 5lb.	*(Job Toon)*	3
Mr Eyke's	**Rhapsody,** 5 y-o, 11st. 9lb.	*(John Deakin)*	4

Betting: 4/7 fav. Cranbourne, 5/2 The Shah, 4/1 Rhapsody.

THE HUNTERS SELLING PLATE of 30 sovereigns, added to a sweepstakes of
5 sovs. Gentlemen riders only. Two miles.

Mr Marsden's	**Catty,** aged, 12st. 10lb.	*(Mr J. Goodwin)*	1
Mr C. Marsden's	**Charlotta,** aged 12st.	*(Hon. D. Sandilands)*	2
Mr Amey's	**Over,** 6 y-o, 12st. 3lb.	*(Owner)*	3

Betting: 1/4 fav. Catty, 6/4 Over.

1875

Up until a few years ago, the demise of Walsall Races appeared to be as predictable as many of the races run on the Long Meadow. Thanks to one man, Abel Grove, licensee of the Nag's Head in Upper Rushall Street, they were allowed to continue for a few more years. Although Grove, chairman of the Race Committee, had assistance to ensure the Races continued, he was the major driving force behind the venture.

The Races took place in this year on Monday 16th and Tuesday 17th August, and as was now usual, the event was completely separate from the Wake and Fair, an event it had accompanied for well over a hundred years. The weather, particularly on the first day was glorious, with very high temperatures. On Tuesday, although cooler and somewhat threatening it remained dry all day. Because of the excellent weather, the attendance was huge, with movement anywhere in the vicinity of the racecourse proving difficult.

Betting on horse racing had always caused controversy. Many attempts to stop it had proved impossible, like all vices, it doesn't go away, just moves away from the eyes of the law. Betting shops first came on the scene around 1850, and in London at this time there was reputed to be four hundred illegal shops of this nature. This practice wasn't restricted to London, the shops were rife throughout the land. They were usually set up in a tobacconists or barbers premises, many were insolvent and downright dishonest, being in business for only a few days before the occupants did a 'moonlight,' along with the punters cash stuffed in their pockets. One of the most famous shops was Dwyer & Co., of London. In 1851 they took a large amount of money from punters betting on the outcome of that year's Chester Cup, the foremost handicap of the day. When the favourite won, alarm bells began to ring at Dwyer's. They had taken a huge amount money on the favourite, and inconsequence, stood to lose many times the amount. The morning after the race, their premises in St. Martin's Lane was empty, stripped of all movable fittings, leaving an empty shell of old cigar shop and over £25,000 owing. Although there are no details of similar shops in Walsall, there is every probability that similar activities took place in the town.

A Betting Act had been passed through Parliament in an attempt to stop the practice, but as Daniel O'Donnell put it, *'there was no Act of Parliament that a coach and six couldn't be driven through.'* He was of course correct.

As the first race at this years meeting began to get underway, betting was as brisk as ever on the Long Meadow. The gamblers not even bothering to take hide their vice, much to the consternation of Chief Superintendent Cater of the Police. The shouts of 'two to one, bar one etc.' was still to be heard around the course and men with red hats, green hats, hats with a large brim, hats with no brim were doing brisk business for all to see, including Mr Cater. The police chief was furious at this flagrant disregard for the law and sent his men to intervene in the illegal transactions, with unforeseen consequences. The starter, thinking it was the signal that the course was clear, dispatched the runners who proceeded to run straight into the crowds still on the course. Sensibly, many dived for cover and finished up in the sewer brook alongside the railway.

The betting at the meeting continued, despite the Act of Parliament and a very determined Mr Cater.

Nine horses lined up for the start of the Trial Selling Stakes over the straight five furlongs. It appeared, from the betting, to be quite an open race, with the joint favourites, Tears and Louisa quoted at 3/1, with Eveleen and Flourish at 5/1 and Circumlocution and Keepsake at 6/1. Soon after the start, Mr J. T. Raworth's Eveleen, confidently ridden by Job Toon, headed for the rails and made the pace, followed by Keepsake, Tears, Louisa, Flourish and Circumlocution. At the distance pole, Flourish came through the other horses but couldn't reach Eveleen, being beaten a length and a half with Mr Batson's Keepsake third. The jockey of Keepsake, Fox, objected to Flourish on the grounds that some of his saddle cloths had been lost in the race. They were later handed back to the jockey for the weigh-in, a flouting of the Jockey Club Rules. The Stewards disqualified Flourish and awarded the second place to Keepsake.

The next two races on the card, the Tradesmen's Plate and the Walsall Plate were mediocre, predictable affairs. Both races had just four runners and the odds-on favourites in each case taking their victories at leisure.

In the Hunter's Plate, a two mile flat race run under the rules of the Grand National Hunt Committee and to be ridden by amateur riders only. It was won by the favourite, Mr Cobden's Kemptown and ridden by Mr Trewent. The horse was never out of the first three, although the lead changed several times between, Kemptown, Ballerat (6/1) and Venus (5/2), finishing in that order.

The final race of the day was the Maiden Hurdle Race and Thomas Wadlow's only winner of the meeting came in this race. The horse with everyone's money on it was Kempson Walker's five year-old Thornton, backed down to 6/4, but he

1860 - 1879

never started the race. The *Walsall Observer* reported that the horse *'staked himself so badly on one of the hurdles, he was unable to go post'*. With the favourite withdrawn, the second choice in the betting, Wadlow's Blue Ribbon (2/1) was driven through the remaining three horses close home by Davis his jockey, to win by two lengths.

Overnight the weather deteriorated, leaving an overcast, but fresher day to enjoy the sport on offer. It opened with another hurdle race, the Handicap Hurdle Plate, six jumps being included in the mile and a half trip. The two joint favourites of the six runners at 5/2 were Stanton and Stella, but they played little part in the finish. This was another race where the jockey simply rode his horse flat out, hoping his mount wouldn't 'blow-up,' but the opposition would. The horse that set out in front was E. Dalgleish's Neptune, ridden by Wheeldon, whose plan worked perfectly. No one could catch him and he won in a canter by ten lengths.

The next two races were disappointing affairs, both having runaway winners. The result of the second of the two races, the Bradford Handicap being so predictable, betting was suspended. This no doubt giving Chief Superintendent Cater much pleasure.

The Member's Selling Plate, with five runners was quite a competitive race as all the runners remained close together throughout the race. The Walsall solicitor, J. B. Oerton owned the favourite, Lucerne, who started at 4/6, with the remaining runners all at 3/1. Even the bookmakers thought they were all pretty well matched. Kempson Walker's two year-old, Claude Duval made the early pace holding a slight lead over the favourite, followed by Keepsake and Pretty Bird. At the distance pole all five closed up together with a frantic dash for the line. Thomas Skelton, Lucerne's jockey, pushed his mount on with all his strength, getting the favourite home by a neck from Mr Batson's Keepsake. The early pacemaker, Claude Duval just holding on to third place.

Selling races had become popular in recent years at the meeting, which was bad news. Horses that run in races of this nature are not usually known for their ability. At the end of the Member's Selling Plate, Mr Batson, second with Keepsake, liked the look of Lucerne and bought him from Mr Oerton for 76 guineas.

As the meeting drew to a close, the racing was becoming as predictable as ever. Of the six races run during the afternoon, the favourites had won five. The favourite in yet another hunters race, the Second Hunters Plate was Cash Box at 4/6. Only four ran and Cash Box set off for home a half a mile from the winning post to take the prize unchallenged. In the following race, the Town Welter Handicap Plate, J. Shepherd's Emmeline, even money favourite, lead from start to finish in the six furlong event to win by two lengths. Second was J. T. Raworth's Sylvanus (5/2) with another of Mr Batson's runners, Nancy back in third place.

Again, four runners went to post for the final race, the five furlong Innkeeper's Handicap Plate. This too finished as a procession for the favourite, Mr Cockin's Rattener at 5/4. At the start Rattener slipped her opponents and ran at a storming pace driven on by jockey Ashworth. She won as she pleased although the trio behind were closing they presented no real challenge. The minor berths were taken up by Kempson Walker's Woodcut (3/1) with the winner of the previous race, Emmeline back in third spot. After this final race, an objection was lodged by some eagle-eyed observer on the grounds that the race was started before the official time. At the time of filing the race report, the outcome remained in abeyance, a fact that remains one hundred and twenty nine years later.

The official results of the meeting were:

Monday 16th August 1875

THE ALL-AGED PLATE of 50 sovereigns. Five furlongs.

| Mr J. Batson's | Bras de Fer, 5 y-o, 10st. | (J. Fox) | 1 |
| Mr F. Pryor's | c. by The Rake, 2 y-o, 7st. 2lb. | (H. Wyatt) | 2 |

Betting: 1/5 fav. Bras de Fer.

THE TRIAL SELLING STAKES of 5 sovereigns, with 30 added.
Five furlongs, straight.

| Mr J. Raworth's | Eveleen, 4 y-o, 8st. 2lb. | (Job Toon) | 1 |
| Mr J. Batson's | Keepsake, 3 y-o, 8st. 11lb. | (J. Fox) | 2 |

Eight ran. Betting: 6/1 the winner.

THE TRADESMEN'S PLATE of 5 sovereigns each,
with 50 added. One mile.

Mr W. Mytton's	Martini, 5 y-o, 7st. 2lb.	(Thomas Glover)	1
Mr W. Walker's	Industrious, 4 y-o, 8st. 12lb.	(H. Macksey)	2
Mr J. Raworth's	Sylvanus, 5 y-o, 7st. 5lb.	(Downs)	3

Four ran. Betting: 5/6 fav. Martini, 7/4 Industrious.

THE WALSALL PLATE (HANDICAP) of 50 sovereigns.
Five furlongs, straight.

Mr Shepherd's	Lille, 3 y-o, 7st. 1lb.	(Thomas Glover)	1
Mr C. Ison's	Pretty Bird, 4 y-o, 8st.	(Ross)	2
Mr J. Oerton's	Lucerne, 5 y-o, 8st. 12lb.	(J. Fox)	3
Mr T. Wadlow's	Blue Ribbon	(T. Skelton)	4

Four ran. Betting: 5/4 fav. Lille, 5/2 Blue Ribbon, 4/1 the others.

A HUNTERS PLATE of 19 guineas. For hunters duly qualified under the Grand
National Hunt Rules. Gentlemen riders only. Two miles.

Mr Cobden's	Kemptown, 5 y-o, 12st.	(Mr Trewent)	1
Mr Chapman's	Ballerat, 4 y-o, 12st.	(Mr Dabbs)	2
Mr J. Tyler's	Venus, 4 y-o, 11st.	(Mr J. Tyler jnr.)	3
Mr -	Patriot	(Mr E. P. Wilson)	-

Betting: 6/4 fav. Kemptown, 5/2 Venus, 3/1 Patriot, 6/1 others.

A MAIDEN HURDLE RACE of 30 sovereigns, for horses that have never won
a hurdle race.
One and a half miles over six flights of hurdles.

Mr T. Wadlow's	Blue Ribbon, 4 y-o, 10st. 7lb.	(J. Davis)	1
Mr F. Brown's	Lyre, 4 y-o, 10st. 7lb	(J. Humphreys)	2
Mr A. Dabbs'	Greenhorn, 4 y-o, 10st. 7lb	(John Deakin)	-
Mr -	Thornton	(Henry Macksey)	-

Betting: 6/4 fav. Thornton, 2/1 Blue Ribbon, 6/1 any other.

1860 – 1879

Tuesday 17th August 1875

THE HURDLE HANDICAP PLATE of 40 sovereigns.
One and a half miles over six flights of hurdles.

Mr E. Dalglish's	**Neptune,** 4 y-o, 10st. 8lb.	*(T. Wheldon)*	1
Mr A. Dabbs'	**Pretty John,** aged, 11st. 6lb.	*(Owner)*	2
Mr J. Batson's	**Nancy,** aged, 10st. 9lb.	*(W. Daniels)*	3
Mr -	**Stanton**	*(F. Lynham)*	4
Mr -	**Stella**	*(Mr E. P. Wilson)*	5
Mr -	**Julian**	*(J. Fox)*	6

Betting: 5/2 favs. Stanton and Stella, 3/1 Neptune, 4/1 Julian.

OPEN HUNTERS HURDLE PLATE of 30 sovereigns for hunters qualified under
the Grand National Hunt Rules.
Two miles, over eight flights of hurdles.

Mr J. Poinon's	**Revenge,** aged, 13st. 3lb.	*(Owner)*	1
Hon. E. Jervis'	**Jack Frost,** 5 y-o, 12st. 4lb.	*(Owner)*	2
Mr C. Halford's	**Lady Lockinge,** 5 y-o, 11st. 7lb.	*(Daniels)*	3

Betting: 4/6 fav. Revenge, 2/1 Lady Lockinge, 5/1 Jack Frost.

THE BRADFORD PLATE (HANDICAP)
of 5 sovereigns each, with 50 added. Six furlongs.

Mr Shepherd's	**Lille,** 3 y-o, 7st. 2lb.	*(Jonas Jarvis)*	1
Mr J. Walker's	**Industrious,** 4 y-o, 8st. 12lb.	*(H. Macksey)*	2

Only two ran.

THE MEMBER'S SELLING STAKES of 5 sovereigns each, with 30 added.
Five furlongs.

Mr J. B. Oerton's	**Lucerne,** 5 y-o, 8st. 3lb.	*(T. Skelton)*	1
Mr J. Batson's	**Keepsake,** 3 y-o, 7st. 11lb.	*(C. Mallows)*	2
Mr W. Walker's	**Claude Duval,** 2y-o, 6st. 3lb.	*(J. Jarvis)*	3

Five ran. Betting: 4/6 fav. Lucerne, 3/1 Keepsake.

THE SECOND HUNTERS PLATE of 19 sovereigns,
for hunters duly qualified under the Grand National Hunt Rules. Gentlemen
riders only. Two miles on the flat.

Mr G. Dodson's	**Cash Box,** 4 y-o, 11st.	*(Mr E. P. Wilson)*	1
Mr Thomas'	**Sea Messenger,** 6 y-o, 12st. 3lb.	*(Mr Trewent)*	2
Mr G. Dodson's	**Patriot,** 6 y-o, 12st. 3lb.	*(Mr J. Poinons)*	3

Betting: 4/5 fav. Cash Box, 7/4 Sea Messenger, 4/1 any other.

THE TOWN WELTER HANDICAP PLATE
of 50 sovereigns. Six furlongs.

Mr Shepherd'	**Emmeline,** 4 y-o, 10st.	*(J. Fox)*	1
Mr J. Raworth's	**Sylvanus,** 5 y-o, 9st. 10lb.	*(Job Toon)*	2
Mr J. Batson's	**Nancy,** aged, 9st. 7lb.	*(C. Fletcher)*	3
Mr -	**Snowdrop**	-	-

Betting: Evens fav. Emmeline, 5/2 Sylvanus, 8/1 any other.

THE INNKEEPER'S HANDICAP PLATE of 50 sovereigns.
Five furlongs.

Mr Cockin's	**Rattener,** 4y-o, 7st. 12lb.	*(G. Ashworth)*	1
Mr W. Walker's	**Woodcut,** 5 y-o, 8st. 7lb.	*(Henry Macksey)*	2
Mr Shepherd's	**Emmeline,** 4 y-o, 8st.	*(Thomas Skelton)*	3
Mr J. Batson's	**Bras de Fer,** 5 y-o, 8st. 7lb.	*(J. Fox)*	4

Betting: 5/4 fav. Rattener, 5/2 Bras de Fer, 3/1 Woodcut.

1876

As far as the Race Committee and the people of Walsall were concerned, it was business as usual regarding the annual race meeting. Few people realising that this would be the final official meeting on the Long Meadow.

On Monday August 7th on the racecourse, was the annual auction sale of the sites for the booths and tents organised by Farrington and Son, auctioneers. The old brick grandstand did not feature in the sale, being let by private contract prior to the auction. The temporary grandstand, which had stood for a great many years, received an opening bid of £25, before being sold to Mr Medlicott of Shrewsbury for £48. Many inferior sites were sold at prices ranging from £1 5s to £10.

Abel Grove, chairman of the Race Committee placed his customary advertisement in the local newspaper, shown above, thanking the public for their generous subscriptions towards the cost of the Races. The meeting was all set for Monday 14th and Tuesday 15th August.

The weather played its part at the final meeting, being very fine and hot on both days. Many times over the years, the going on the Long Meadow had been very soft. This year it was the reverse, thanks to a prolonged sunny spell it was hard, even *'baked'* in places as The *Walsall Observer* put it. The crowds were as large as ever, with an equally large rough element being in attendance too.

John Sheldon from Birmingham remained as Clerk of the Course, with Mr T. Lawley taking dual role of Clerk of the Scales and judge. The Stewards in attendance were Earl Poulett, Major J. N. Browne and Charles Forster, the latter being a regular supporter of the meeting for many years.

Several of the owners of the booths and tents dotted around the course were unhappy when they discovered the licenses that they had only allowed drink to be sold during the hours of noon until 9.00 p.m. Many of them were so disgruntled, they surrendered their pitches altogether, as they thought they should be able to sell drink from 12 noon to 12 midnight. For the sake of three hours less sales, they lost out completely.

The programme consisted of the usual twelve races, six on each day, but on Monday the card was cut to five events only

---

WALSALL RACES, 1876.

THE REFRESHMENT DEPARTMENT of the Grand Stand (inside and out) and the Ground for Booths will be LET BY AUCTION, on MONDAY, August 7th, 1876, on the Race Course, at Three o'clock p.m. Conditions as usual.

FARRINGTON & SON,
Auctioneers.

Mr. A. GROVE, Chairman.

WALSALL RACES.

THE Committee beg to thank the Public for the very liberal response they have given to their canvass for subscriptions, and to ask for a continuance of the same on the part of those who have not yet been called upon.

A. GROVE, Chairman.

1860 - 1879

The only known photograph of the grandstand around the time of the final meeting in 1876. The timber in the foreground is believed to the remnants of Ginnett's Circus. In between the right hand side of the stand and the small building across the road, can just be seen Stemmer Steps, the footbridge over the railway. (Reproduced by permission of Walsall Local History Centre)

when the Tradesmen's Plate was declared void as all of the entries withdrew.

The Walsall Plate opened the meeting with just two runners, Keepsake, now owned by J. B. Oerton, taking the prize from Mr Grace's Epicure. Needless to say, the winner was seriously backed down to 4/6 and won by over ten lengths, leading from start to finish.

The five furlong All-Aged Plate produced a good race with its seven runners. In the field where a pair of two year-olds, Mr Grace's Royalty and D. Lawrence's Pemmican, the 6/4 favourite. After an even start, Royalty made the early pace tracked by Dryad, Pemmican, Mungo Park and Quietude. Near home Royalty was pushed on by his jockey Mallows with Pemmican challenging. At the line, Royalty held on to the lead to win by half a length and a starting price of 5/1.

Pretty Bird, who ran at last years meeting obviously liked the fast ground, winning the Trial Selling Plate for her owner, R. E. Pemberton. When the flag fell, all five runners got away together, Jessamine making the pace tracked the 6/4 favourite, Porridge, and Sphynx. Nearing home, Thomas Skelton got to work on Pretty Bird (5/1). He drove his mount through the field to win by half a length from Surprise, with Porridge a further head back in third place.

The Rushall Hunter's Stakes produced another good race from the six starters, favourite was Mr Walter's Rochester at 6/4. Although he won, it was left rather late by the amateur rider, Thomas Hale. The horse that finished third, P. H. Taylor's Cardigan led for the majority of the two miles until nearing home when Latitat took it up, appearing to everyone as the potential winner. Mr Hale had a different idea as to who should be first, however, sending Rochester through to take the victory by a neck.

Hurdle races in the past had attracted quite a few runners, but in recent years starters were becoming increasingly difficult to find. In the final race of the day, the Maiden Hurdle Race, it became a match between Mr Grace's Epicure and J. B. Oerton's Red Rose, a seemingly unbeatable favourite at 2/5. Mr Grace, successful earlier with Royalty, repeated the process with Epicure who beat the favourite easily.

On Tuesday, the first race of any note was the second on the card, the Innkeeper's Welter Handicap Plate over five furlongs. Seven horses started, including Keepsake, a winner the previous day over the same distance. That victory wasn't enough to convince the backers he could repeat the process. Instead the money went on E. W. Taylor's Red Huntsman and Debonnaire, who closed as joint favourites at 2/1. The runners got away to a even start with the outsider, Patty (6/1) leading for almost the whole trip, the speed the mare was travelling at making it difficult for the others to match. As they reached the line, a determined effort on the part of James Orbell, jockey on Red Huntsman saw him close on Patty and pass her just before the line. The winning margin was declared as two lengths between the winner and Patty, with Sphynx, half a length further back.

The Member's Selling Stakes with seven runners, finally got off after a considerable delay due to several false starts. The runners included three also rans from the previous day, Red Rose, Surprise and Porridge and an earlier winner, Pretty Bird. The choice of the backers in the ring, however, went to Porridge, installing him as 5/2 favourite. When the start was made it was somewhat ragged with Red Rose heading the group. As the post neared, Thomas Skelton, riding Red Rose quickened to fend off a challenge from the favourite, winning by a length, to give J. B. Oerton his second winner of the meeting.

The jockey Thomas Skelton wasn't having too bad a meeting either. Already on two winners, he completed his hat trick when winning the two horse race for the Bradford Plate on F. Gretton's Algebra beating James Hopwood's horse, Bloxwich by a length.

The Handicap Hurdle Race over a mile and a half with six flights was the penultimate race of the meeting, attracting a large field for a hurdle race in recent years with eight starting. The betting saw Moselle the favourite with the backers at 2/1. Au Bac was second choice at 4/1 with Keepsake, trying his luck over hurdles for Mr Oerton at 5/1. At the start Kemptown led from Keepsake, Verity and Elmina, at the turn, Verity moved up to lead followed by Elmina and Kemptown. As the runners turned into the straight, Au Bac began a run that saw him come through the pack to win by a length from Verity. Keepsake took third place, with the favourite who never showed, well beaten.

When the time came round for the final race at five o'clock, the programme was running around half an hour late, due to false starts earlier in the afternoon. As the four runners hacked and cantered down to the six furlong start of the Town Welter Handicap Plate no one on the Long Meadow, spectator, participant, official or vendor realised they were about to make history. The four horses were all previous runners at the meeting, Red Rose, Algebra, Bloxwich and Debonnaire. Algebra was the only previous winner and the backers saw him as the one to carry the burden of favourite at 6/4, Debonnaire was second choice at 2/1. The starter stood with a raised flag in his hand, waiting patiently for the four to appear in something that resembled a line. When he was satisfied, with a shout of 'go gentlemen' the flag dropped and they were away for the final time. In the early stages Bloxwich made the pace followed by Debonnaire, Algebra and finally Red Rose. On fast ground, the leader maintained his advantage, the favourite passing Debonnaire in the closing stages. At the line, Bloxwich, ridden by James Hopwood junior, son of the Hednesford trainer, came home a length in front of Algebra with Debonnaire third, Red Rose still at the rear.

One of the many thousands of spectators cheering Bloxwich home was a young Billy Meikle, who watched the races with his pals from their favourite vantage point, Stemmer Steps. This was the footbridge over the railway before the road went under Bridgeman Street. Meikle later became a famous amateur historian, photographer and watercolour artist in Walsall, recording much of the town's past that has long since disappeared.

As Billy and his pals made their way home after the last race, along with thousands of other racegoers, none of them realised they had witnessed history in the making, after at least one hundred and twenty two years, Walsall Races had finally run their last event.

For those people, and newspapers, that had prematurely prophesied the demise of Walsall Races for many years, finally they could say, 'I told you so,' even if they didn't know it yet!

The official results of the final meeting were:

Monday 14th August 1876

THE WALSALL PLATE (HANDICAP) of 50 sovereigns.
Five furlongs, straight.

| Mr J. B. Oerton's | **Keepsake**, 4 y-o, 7st. 7lb. | (C. Mallows) | 1 |
| Mr Grace's | **Epicure**, 6 y-o, 7st. 9lb. | (Selman) | 2 |

Two ran. Betting: 4/6 Keepsake.

THE ALL-AGED PLATE of 50 sovereigns. Five furlongs.

Mr Grace's	**Royalty**, 2 y-o, 6st. 11lb.	(C. Mallows)	1
Mr Lawrence's	**Pemmican**, 2 y-o, 7st. 4lb.	(Greaves)	2
Mr J. Richards'	**Dryad**, 3 y-o, 7st. 13lb.	(Jones)	3
Mr Hopwood's	**Generosity**, 3 y-o, 7st. 13lb.	(Weston)	-
Mr T. Butler's	**Mungo Park**, 2 y-o, 7st. 7lb.	(J. Hopwood)	-
Mr J. Toon's	**West End**, 4 y-o, 8st. 5lb.	(J. Jarvis)	-
Mr T. Stevens'	**Quietitude**, 2 y-o, 7st. 4lb.	(T. Skelton)	-

Seven ran. Betting: 6/4 Pemmican, 2/1 Quietitude, 5/1 Royalty.

THE TRIAL SELLING STAKES of 5 sovereigns, with 30 added.
Five furlongs, straight.

Mr Pemberton's	**Pretty Bird**, 5 y-o, 8st. 11lb.	(T. Skelton)	1
Mr R. Rodley's	**Surprise**, 3 y-o, 8st. 4lb.	(Horne)	2
Mr T. Stevens'	**Porridge**, 2 y-o, 6st. 4lb	(Jonas Jarvis)	3
Mr W. Saunders'	**br.f. by Paul Jones**, 2 y-o, 6st. 4lb.	(Graves)	-
Mr W. Collins'	**Sphynx**, 3y-o, 7st. 10lb.	(Frost)	-

Five ran. Betting: 6/4 fav. Porridge, 5/2 Sphynx, 3/1 Pretty Bird

---

> ### CORRESPONDENCE.
>
> **EXTENSION OF TIME AT THE RACES.**
> *To the Editor of the Walsall Observer.*
>
> Sir,—Heaven (I suppose for good reason) permits Satan to torment the earth; but why do our Borough Justices help him and inflict upon the town their annual curse? Why do they specially license the sale of drink upon the Racecourse and allure the the people to idleness, drunkenness, and debauchery? Who are the magistrates who sign these "permits," and do they ever think of the crimes they cause to be done? We know
> "Evil is wrought by want of thought,
> As well as want of heart;"
> but those who are placed in authority over us, the should-be civic fathers of the people, ought to think.
> I am, Sir, your obedient servant,
> W. H. DUIGNAN.
> Walsall, 11th August, 1876.

One person who wouldn't be sorry to see the last of the Races, according to the context of his letter to The Walsall Observer in August 1876, was William Henry Duignan, solicitor and historian.

1860 - 1879

THE TRADESMEN'S PLATE - Race declared void.

RUSHALL HUNTERS STAKES of 3 sovereigns eac.
For hunters duly qualified under the Grand National Hunt Rules. Gentlemen riders only. Two miles on the flat.

Mr Walter's	Rochester, 5 y-o, 12st. 1lb.	(Mr T. Hale)	1
Mr Anslow's	Latitat, aged, 12st. 10lb.	(Owner)	2
Mr P. Taylor's	Cardigan, aged, 11st.	(Mr Harper)	3
Mr -	Patriot	-	-
Mr -	Spelling Bee	-	-
Mr -	Royston	-	-
Mr -	Black Joe	-	-

Betting: 6/4 fav. Rochester, 4/1 Royston and Latitat.

A MAIDEN HURDLE RACE of 30 sovereigns, for horses that have never won a hurdle race.
One and a half miles over six flights of hurdles.

| Mr Grace's | Epicure, 6 y-o | (G. Sly) | 1 |
| Mr J. B. Oerton's | Red Rose, 4 y-o | (J. Fox) | 2 |

Tuesday 15th August 1876

THE HUNTERS SELLING PLATE of 40 sovereigns, for hunters duly qualified under the Grand National Hunt Rules. Two miles on the flat.

Sir. W. Milner's	Pirouette, 5 y-o, 11st. 8lb.	(Mr J. Goodwin)	1
Mr Thorne's	Black Joe, aged, 11st. 10lb.	(Mr E. Wilson)	2
Mr Moore's	Hussar, aged, 12st. 3lb.	(Mr Trewent)	3

Betting: 1/2 fav. the winner

THE INNKEEPER'S HANDICAP PLATE of 50 sovereigns.
Five furlongs.

Mr E. Taylor's	Red Huntsman, 3y-o, 8st. 11lb.	(G. Orbell)	1
Mr S. Shaw's	Patty, 3 y-o, 8st. 2lb.	(Horne)	2
Mr W. Collins'	Sphynx, 3 y-o, 7st. 10lb.	(J. Jarvis)	3
Mr J. Oerton's	Keepsake, 4 y-o, 9st.	(Graves)	-
Mr Cobden's	Kemptown, 6 y-o, 8st. 9lb.	(Mr T. Hale)	-
Mr S. Davis'	Debonnaire, 3 y-o, 8st. 7lb.	(S. Darling)	-
Mr Hopwood's	Generosity, 3 y-o, 7st. 10lb.	(Graves)	-

Betting: 2/1 favs. Red Huntsman and Debonnaire, 3/1 Keepsake and Sphynx, 6/1 Patty.

THE MEMBER'S SELLING STAKES of 5 sovereigns each, with 30 added. Five furlongs.

Mr J. B. Oerton's	Red Rose, 4 y-o, 8st. 7lb.	(T. Skelton)	1
Mr T. Stevens'	Porridge, 2 y-o, 6st. 3lb.	(Jonas Jarvis)	2
Mr R. Rodley's	Surprise, 3 y-o, 8st.	(Horne)	3
Mr J. Toon's	West End, 4 y-o, 8st. 2lb.	(Graves)	-
Mr Esches'	f. by Le Marechal, 2 y-o, 6st. 3lb.	(Frost)	-
Mr P. H. Taylor's	Pretty Bird, 5 y-o, 8st. 7lb.	(Crickmere)	-
Mr E. W. Taylor's	Almon, 6 y-o, 8st. 7lb.	(G. Orbell)	-

Betting: 5/2 fav. Porridge, 3/1 Red Rose and Almon.

THE BRADFORD PLATE (HANDICAP)
of 5 sovereigns each, with 50 added. Six furlongs.

| Mr F. Gretton's | Algebra, 5 y-o, 8st. 11lb. | (T. Skelton) | 1 |
| Mr J. Hopwood's | Bloxwich, aged, 8st. 3lb. | (Hopwood, jr.) | 2 |

Only two ran. Betting: 4/7 fav. the winner.

HURDLE HANDICAP PLATE of 40 sovereigns.
One and a half miles, over eight flights of hurdles.

Mr G. Jarvis'	Au Bac, 6 y-o, 11st. 2lb.	(Murphy)	1
Mr J. Ragg's	Verity, 5 y-o, 10st.	(James Hopwood, jnr.)	2
Mr J. Oerton's	Keepsake, 4 y-o, 10st.	(Weston)	3
Mr Cobden's	Kemptown, 6 y-o	-	-
Mr -	Moselle	-	-
Mr -	Elmina	-	-
Mr Grace's	Epicure, 6 y-o	-	-
Mr -	Nettle	-	-

Betting: 2/1 fav. Moselle, 4/1 Au Bac, 5/1 Keepsake.

THE TOWN WELTER HANDICAP PLATE
of 50 sovereigns. Six furlongs.

Mr Hopwood's	Bloxwich, aged, 9st.	(James Hopwood, jnr.)	1
Mr F. Gretton's	Algebra, 5 y-o, 10st. 1lb.	(T. Skelton)	2
Mr S. Davis'	Debonnaire, 3 y-o, 8st. 7lb.	(S. Darling)	3
Mr T. Stevens'	Red Rose, 4 y-o, 9st. 9lb.	(J. Jarvis)	-

Betting: 6/4 fav. Algebra, 2/1 Debonnaire, 4/1 Bloxwich.

1877 - 1879

Through the long nights of the autumn and winter of 1876/77, Abel Grove, chairman of the Race Committee and his fellow members met in the smoky atmosphere of a 'boozer' in Upper Rushall Street to discuss the plans for the meeting the following year, not realising the land on which the racecourse stood would have been sold by the time the meeting came round in August.

No doubt rumours were rife in the town regarding the intended sale of the land to the Midland Railway Company. On February 14th 1877, the death sentence was finally passed on the Races when the General Purposes Committee voted by seventeen to one in favour of the proposed sale.

The railway company had submitted a Bill before Parliament showing their intentions for expansion, and the Council had not objected to these. They considered the increase in rail traffic would be of great importance to the trading and commercial interests of the town. If the Bill went through, it gave the company powers to obtain all of the land known as the Long Meadow and Mill Furlong, a total of 21 acres. Lord Bradford's land agent, Peter Potter junior, had negotiated a fee of £800 per acre with the company on his Lordship's behalf. The Council, who owned the Lammas rights, settled for £300 per acre. The only person opposing the intended sale was Councillor Aulton. He had no objection in principle to the sale, nor had he any objection in allowing this new railway company into the town. His opposition lay in the fact that the company had not indicated exactly they wanted the land for, his question was *'what do they intend to use this land for, a shunting yard, coal wharves, a station, what?'* No one could tell him, and until he had answer from someone, his vote would remain against the motion. A few other dissenting voices were heard in the chamber, but this concerned the price negotiated for the Lammas rights, of which one or two members thought it should have been more than £300 per acre. Their objections were quickly put down when the Mayor, Councillor W.

1860 - 1879

Bayliss, said that the majority considered the offer to be *'a handsome sum for the rights.'*

In the *Walsall Observer* of Saturday February 17th, a very lengthy report of this Council meeting was published with not a single reference to the effect the sale would have on Walsall Races. One hundred and twenty two years of history must not stand in the way of progress, those in the town that opposed the meeting for many years, and for a variety of reasons, had finally got their way.

When the news seeped through to the 'boozer' in Upper Rushall Street, the Nag's Head, it must have been a bitter blow to the Race Committee, Abel Grove in particular, to realise that the Races had finally ended.

The Races were gone and nothing more would be said of them, certainly not when it came to the columns of *Walsall Free Press* and the *Walsall Observer*. The only reports in both newspapers concerned the Wake and Fair, another piece of Walsall heritage that they both thought should go the same way as the races, and the sooner the better.

Races or not, the town was still troubled by bad, behaviour. In September 1878, the *Walsall Observer* published a letter from an irate citizen which read:-

'Sir, - I wish the attention of the authorities of the town was directed to the cocoa-nut throwing nuisance. The number that are allowed to indulge in this low and demoralising game every market evening is anything but creditable. The language used is anything but pleasant, whilst the exhibition itself is a disgrace to what it is supposed to be one of our most respectable centres. Surely that is not the purpose for which Lammas rights were given to the freeholders, nor that which our boasted People's Park Committee are endeavouring to devote the lands. Unquestionably it ought not longer to be allowed that a number of ruffianly fellows should come and squat on our property, and use it for the purpose of annoyance to the residents and those passing by.
Yours, &c,. Freeholder.

This was a problem that had been a concern for sometime. Shortly after the time of the final race meeting, residents in the area of the course had asked Lord Bradford, via his agent Peter Potter junior, to tell the inhabitants of the grandstand to refrain from throwing cocoa-nuts about. Obviously, this was something that the demise of the Races couldn't stop.

Three years after the course closure, all that remained of Walsall Races were many memories, and the remnants of the old grandstand. After June 10th 1879, there remained only the memories. On that day the grandstand was sold by Farrington and Sons, Auctioneers. The two local newspapers reported the sale in their columns, the *Walsall Observer* reporting in their matter of fact way with the *Walsall Free Press* being much more eloquent in their description of the sale, which is quoted in its entirety:-

THE OLD GRAND STAND - One by one the old landmarks of Walsall are being obliterated, and the town itself so metamorphosed that it will soon be difficult for an old resident, long absent from the town to recognise it again. But few parts of the town have of late years undergone a greater change than has the locality of the Bridge. Capacious shops now occupy the space where stood some tumble down old buildings and a blank wall, while what was a garden is now occupied by buildings of no mean pretensions. Still, the visitor to Walsall amidst all those changes had only to turn into Bradford Street and there the glorious green sward of the meadows with their graceful undulations gladdened his eye, and at once enabled him to again recognise old Walsall. But, alas, the verdure of the meadows is gone for ever, and the glory of the Lammas Land departed. The race course will no longer be an attraction for the young nor a place of resort for the aged, for the turf has been removed and the soil, that has lain undisturbed for ages has been rudely torn up preparatory to the 'iron' way being constructed; and notice boards have been put up prohibiting trespassers, upon pain of prosecution, from walking upon the Lammas grounds. On Tuesday last, Mr Farrington sold by auction the materials of the old grandstand. The stand was purchased, we believe, by the Midland Railway Company, who gave it to the Corporation, and it was by the order of the Council that the materials were sold - the conditions being that all the materials be removed and the ground cleared within a month of the date of the sale. The biddings commenced at £20; and very quickly rose to £72, at which price the old grand stand was knocked down to Mr Isaiah Kendrick, who purchased the stand on behalf of Mr J. H. Williams. We believe it is just 75 years since the stand was erected, so that the purchase money was at the rate of just under a £1 per annum for every year the stand has been in existence. Well, such is the transitory glory of all earthly things. The racecourse, with all its reminiscences, has become a thing of the past, and the fleet Azalain has been constrained to give place to the still fleeter and stronger 'iron horse.' And the steam engine and the express train have swept the course and out-vied all rivals - what a pity they have not swept every racecourse in the kingdom in the same way'

For many years, the *Walsall Free Press* rarely hid their displeasure regarding horse racing. The final sentence from their report of the grandstand sale shows exactly what they thought of the 'Sport of Kings.'

Whilst researching updates for this revised edition I came across an article in the *Worcester Journal* on Saturday 1st October 1892 for an event I had never heard of before. The article concerned an application for licenses to sell liquors at a forthcoming race meeting at Bescot during Walsall Annual Wakes. The Chief Constable objected most strongly to the granting of such licenses. He did not object to legitmate race meetings like those of old but this was an unofficial gathering which excluded thoroughbreds and was in fact pony and galloway racing. The residents of Pleck had pleaded with him to object to this meeting and the granting of liquor licenses as there were three licensed houses within 250 yards of the proposed course. The Bench agreed with the Chief Constable and refused the application.

The meeting did go ahead with nine races over the two days and was described as having good number of entries but the organisation and arrangements were 'very bad.'

WALSALL RACES

Chapter Six
THE 1940s REVIVAL

In the first edition of this book in 2005, Chapter Six was titled The 1942 Revival, little did I know at the time that there had not been one meeting in the 1940s but nine!

It was by pure accident when researching for another project in late 2014 I discovered the other meetings. As the original meeting in 1942, the additional ones were all in aid of the Mayor's War Aid Fund, except the final one in 1946 which was part of the victory celebrations.

1942

Sixty-six years after the last race was run on the Long Meadow, the town saw a revival of its race meeting to raise funds for the war effort.

The meeting was held close to The Dilke Arms on the Aldridge Road on Bank Holiday Monday, August 3rd 1942. It was organised by the Mayor of Walsall's War Aid Fund Entertainments Committee, not only to raise money for the cause, but also to boost the moral of the towns people during this uncertain period.

The W.A.F. Entertainments Committee, was comprised of Councillor Baron Power (chairman), Miss M. Wallis (Hon. secretary), Mr and Mrs. N. Dunton, Alderman J. Cliff Tibbitts, D. Pedley, T. E. Bennett, B. M. Lyons and A. W. Cotterell. The committee also received help in organising the meeting from Oscar Johnson, F. Hawley, H. Glaze, H. Fullwood, S. T. Abbots, H. D. Webb, J. Upton, C. Bardell, J. Parker, H. Spruce, and A. W. Smith.

It was estimated that four to five thousand people attended the event, which was somewhat disappointing as many more were expected. This was due to the weather which was poor; after all, it was August, and a Bank Holiday.

The gates were opened at one o'clock, with the first of the nine events beginning at three o'clock. Included in the list of events were two trotting races, rarely seen in Walsall before. The programme consisted of:-

W.A.F. Stakes of £20 and a cup. One mile.
Dilke Stakes of £10. One mile.
Longwood Stakes of £10. One mile.
War Charity Trotting Handicap of £10 and a cup.
The Mellish Trotting Handicap of £10.
Tradesmen's Turnout Class of £5 and a cup.
Pleasure Turnout Class of £5 and a cup.
Children's Pony Race of £5.
Walsall Stakes of £20 and a cup. One and half miles.

The cups that were presented to the proud winners of some of the events by the Mayor, Councillor C. S. Moore, had been on display in the window of *The Walsall Observer* in the week prior to the event.

Although the event was strictly of an amateur nature, it was well organised with all the necessary officials present. The starter and handicapper, Mr J. Price had journeyed up from Merthyr Tydfil in South Wales to officiate. Refreshments were available from several mobile canteens erected around the course with live music supplied by the band of the North Staffordshire Regiment. Members of the regular and special police were on duty, along with the Civil Defence Forces and the St. John's Ambulance Brigade. The services of the latter being required when a horse in the last race jumped a fence into the crowd, injuring two women in the process. They were taken to the Manor Hospital and detained with concussion and abrasions.

For many Walsall people the meeting provided their first taste of anything that resembled the 'sport of kings,' even if it was on a limited scale.

A section of the spectators at the Bank Holiday meeting. In the background can just be seen the bookmaker's stands. (From the now defunct Walsall Observer)

THE 1940s REVIVAL

One of the entries for the Pleasure Turnout Class with an unusual jockey. (From the now defunct Walsall Observer)

Inevitably, the 'gentlemen of sharp practices' were also in attendance. Always on the look out for the unsuspecting 'mugs' who would join in their three card trick. Several of these gangs were on the course accompanied by their 'spotters' who kept their eyes sharply peeled for anyone who resembled a policemen. As in the past, law or not, they still managed to relieve several citizens of a naive nature of the odd pound or two.

The results were:-

W.A.F. Stakes (Open weights) One Mile.

1	Cheeky Face	Mr A. Green, Elton	2/1
2	Snowball	Mr Oscar Johnson, Walsall	3/1
3	Polly	Mr Elton	10/1

Tradesmen's Turnout Class.

1 Mr R. E. Wright, Beacon Farm, Barr Beacon
2 Messrs. Goulden Brothers, Walsall
3 Walsall & District Co-operative Society

War Charity Trotting Handicap. One mile.

1	Scottie, 140 yds.	Mr D. Loverock, Aldridge	8/1
2	Bowlegs, 75 yds	Mr W. Cole, Bilston	7/1
3	Jack Fox, 135 yds	Mr O. Johnson, Walsall	7/1

The Walsall Stakes. One mile and a half.

1	Polly	Mr Elton	5/1
2	Snowball	Mr Oscar Johnson, Walsall	3/1
3	Pilot	Mr G. Price, Netherton	3/1

The Pony Race (Children up to 15 years old)

1	Nib	Master T. Johnson
2	Dolly	Master J. Mars)
3	Skylark	Master G. Gamble

The Dilke Stakes, all carrying 9st. One mile.

1	April Queen	Mr O. Johnson, Walsall	Evens
2	Delmar	Mr N. Groves, Walsall)	3/1
3	Blany	Mr A Barnes, Chase Terrace	5/1

Pleasure Turnout Class.

1 Mr H. Field, Walsall
2 Mr H. Matthews, Four Oaks
3 Mr J. Smith, Great Barr

The Mellish Trotting Handicap, all carrying 8st. One mile.

1	Scottie	-	2/1
2	Bowlegs	Mr W. Cole, Bilston	6/1
3	Jack Fox	-	4/1

The Longwood Stakes. One mile.

1	Our Hope	Mr A. Hall, Cressage	5/1
2	Duke of York	Mr C. Hales, Walsall Wood	2/1
3	Maloga	Mr D. Loverock	5/1

Just like the official races of old, this meeting gave pleasure to a great many Walsall folk on that damp Monday in August. No doubt there are many people in the town and surrounding districts who remember that day as though it were yesterday.

Easter 1943

On Easter Saturday 24th April another race meeting was held in aid of the War Aid Fund but on a different course from last year. The course was on The Meadows at Stencils Farm (see map on page 116) on the opposite side of the road from The Dilke, last year's venue. The *Walsall Observer* wrote:-

'A far cry this meeting from the old Walsall racecourse which, so one reads, stretched from the present LMS goods yard to Corporation Street West, with its grandstand and Victorian customs. Here at Stencils Farm, the green fields patterned with hawthorn hedges, decked in springtime splendour, the Entertainments Committee of the War Aid Fund had discovered a good course, not so narrow as the one on the other side of the road used for the last meeting, and giving all the crowd a better view. The crowd was not so large, probably due to it being a Saturday, when many go a-marketing.'

Even during wartime Walsall market with all its rationing continued to pull in the crowds!

The *Observer* reporter appeared to be enjoying himself as he wrote enthusiastically about the events taking place:-

*'Outstanding features of the gathering were,
The Mayor, who backed four losers and one winner.
A horsey gentleman who has a bloodsucking remedy!
A horse who threw his jockey, jumped the rails and hurt a lady spectator.
A riderless horse that went the full race distance.
A Corporation official who was tipped to win one of the races!
Truly an entertaining combination of humour and drama, a characteristic cross-section of a British holiday crowd having a flutter.'*

THE 1940s REVIVAL

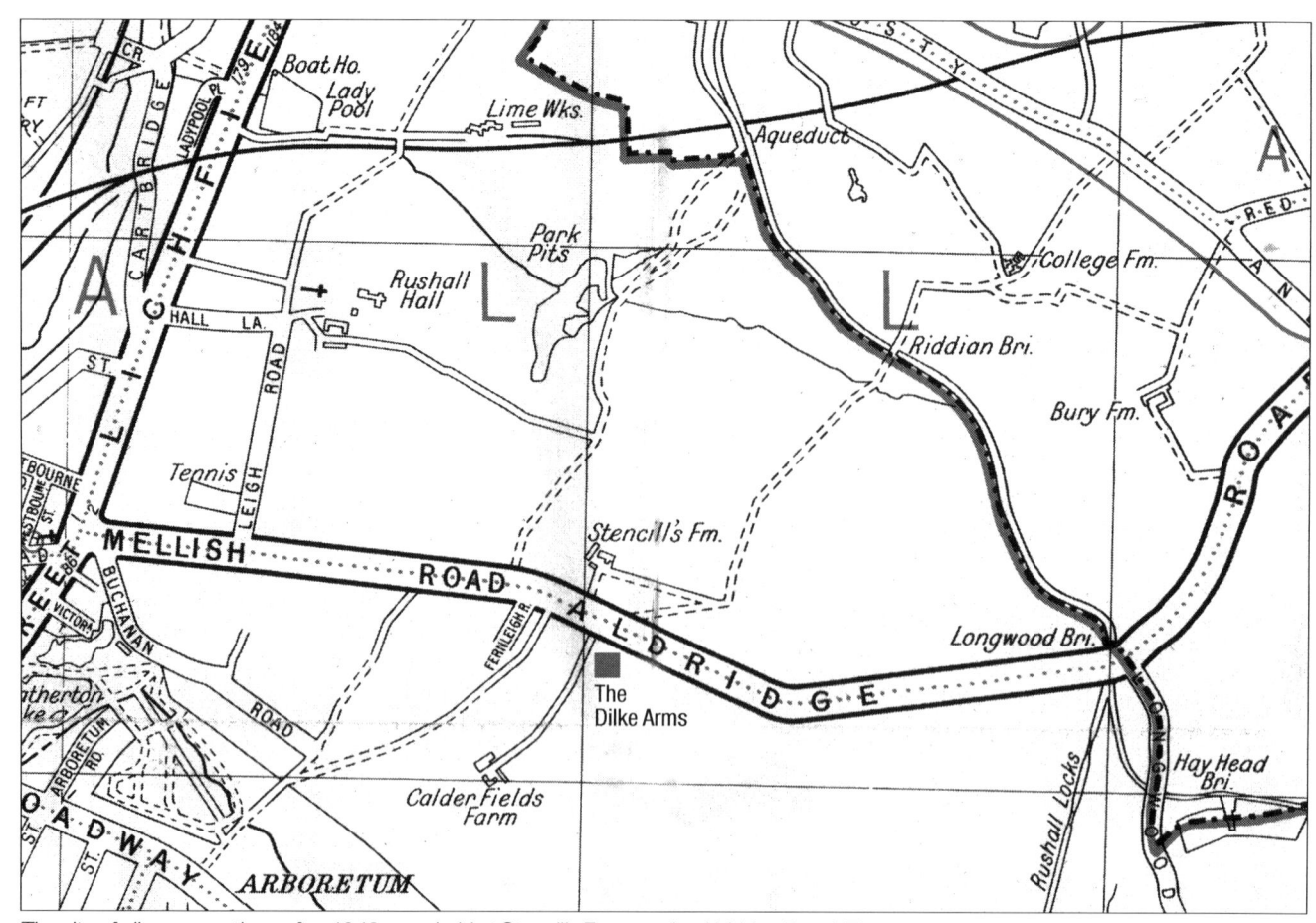

The site of all race meetings after 1942 were held at Stencil's Farm on the Aldridge Road. The course of the canal that formed the boundary between Walsall and Aldridge is shown by the bold dark grey line. It was along here spectators stood on the 'natural grandstand', the canal towpath. The meeting in 1942 was held on a course on the opposite side of the road, near the Dilke Arms public house.

The Mayor of Walsall, Mrs A. McShane placed four bets throughout the meeting which all lost, it wasn't until the final race she managed to reduce her losses by backing a winner. The pony Polly obliged by winning the Walsall Stakes in fine style by a short head.

It was no surprise whilst researching these 1940s meetings to find the name of Oscar Johnson involved in them. His family had been involved with horses for over 150 years but this year it was his sons, Oscar junior and Thomas who took the accolades. In 1943 Oscar junior was fifteen years old and Thomas four years younger, as the *Observer* put it *"they were born to the saddle"* with Oscar riding his first winner aged eight and young Tom at nine. It was Tom, riding at seven stone, who had the first winner for the Johnson family when he partnered the bay trotter Phillip to victory in his red and black colours in the War Charity Trotting Handicap. The *Observer* does actually state in the results that the winner was Master O. Johnson but presumably this was a typographical error. Oscar Johnson senior was asked by the *Observer* reporter about the two boys and remarked *"They train 'em and ride 'em in Walsall and I'm proud of 'em both."*

Another point the reporter observed in the paddock was a 'slightly built groom' sucking a wound that his horse had sustained. When the reporter queried the act, the lad replied, *"it's the same with hosses as it is with the whole of the human family; if yer gets a cut, or pricks yer thumb, suck it in the good old-fashioned way and draw the pizen [poison] out. I always does it with me hoss and the wounds never turn septic. There's nothing like a bit of spit to polish off the germs!"*

In an earlier race a rider was thrown and the horse jumped the rails and knocked down a Miss Kennerley of St. Michael's Street, Caldmore. She was taken to the first-aid tent suffering with shock and abrasions and was examined and treated by the police surgeon, Dr. A. B. Davies.

In another race a horse that had lost its rider continued around the course causing mayhem with the other runners as it ran in and out of them.

A War Reserve policeman was positioned to stop the 'free-gazers' although he said he didn't object to the boatmen having a 'free look' as they passed on their barges. The canal ran at the bottom of the Stencils course and the tow-path provided an excellent elevated 'grandstand' to view the action from.

The results were:
Digbeth Sprint. Six furlongs.

1	Tappits	Mr. G. Wilshaw, Hanley
2	Bob	Mr. A. Hall, Cressage
3	Pat	Mr. N. Groves, Walsall

Distances a neck and three lengths

War Charity Trotting Handicap. One mile.

1	Phillip	Master O. Johnson, Walsall
2	Dan J	Mr. R. Hampton, Moxley
3	Good Luck	Miss V. Hall, Leek

THE 1940s REVIVAL

Longwood Stakes. One mile.

1　Take All　　　Mr. G. Wilshaw, Hanley
2　Snowball　　 Master T. Johnson, Walsall
3　Polly　　　　 Mr J. Wood, Elton

Distances a short head and half-a-length.

Pony Race (Children up to 15 years old)

1　Whippet　　Mr. G. Jones, Alveley
2　Nib　　　　 Master T. Johnson, Walsall
3　Jimmy　　　Miss D. Miller, Walsall

War Aid Fund Stakes. Open weight, one mile approx.

1　Pat　　　　Mr. N. Groves, Walsall
2　Bob　　　　Mr. A. Hall, Cressage
3　Betty　　　Mr. J. Wood, Elton

Distances a length.

Mellish Trotting Handicap. One mile carrying 8 stone.

1　Good Luck　　Miss V. Hall, Leek
2　Big Bill　　　 Mr. J. Hall, Leek
3　Black Prince　Mr. A. W. Brown, Aldridge

Walsall Stakes. Open weight, one and a half miles.

1　Polly　　　 Mr. J. Wood, Elton
2　Take All　 Mr. G. Wilshaw, Hanley
3　Our Hope　Mr. A. Hall, Cressage

Distances a neck and a neck.

The officials at the meeting were:- Judges, Alderman Tibbits and J. F. W. Upton and F. N. Bower. Starter and handicapper Mr. J. Price. Clerk of the course, Mr. B. Dickinson assisted by H. D. Webb and S. T. Abbotts. Stewards, Coun. Baron Power, F. Hawley, S. T. Abbotts, H. Glaze, H. D. Webb and B. Dickinson. Veterinary Surgeon, Mr. W. B. Brownie. Clerk of the scales, Mr. H. Fullwood. Publicity Officers T. E. Bennett and C. Bardell. Flag Steward, Coun. H. F. Truman. Announcer, Mr. B. M. Lyons.

August 1943

Just over three months later another race meeting was held on the same course over two days, Bank Holiday Monday and Tuesday, 2nd and 3rd August. Inevitably many of the runners were by now familiar names to the public as they had also run at the Easter meeting.

The *Walsall Observer* sent along a reporter to cover the events and he opened with:-

> *'The students of form and the pick-em-out-with-a-pin punters were at the Walsall Bank Holiday races at Stencil's Farm on the Aldridge Road on Monday and Tuesday. So were the "friends" of someone who knew the second cousin twice removed of one of the jockeys, and those who were led to back their fancy by signs and portents!'*

One punter thought he had found the elusive secret to backing winners. The first race was won by horse number 13, the astute punter noted the second race had 13 runners! How could he fail, it was number 13 for him. Sadly no one

---

The Mayor of Walsall War Aid Fund Committee

WALSALL
HORSE RACES

"The Meadow," Aldridge Rd., Walsall

AUGUST BANK HOLIDAY
MONDAY and TUESDAY

Commencing at 2.30 p.m.

TOTAL PRIZE MONEY £300

Tradesmen's and Private Turn-outs, August Bank Holiday Monday only.

Entries (last day July 24th) and all information, please apply to:
H. T. Glaze, Bloxwich Road, North Walsall, Walsall.
Telephone: 2532 Walsall

ADMISSION: 2/6, 5/- and 10/-
H.M. and Allied Forces, and Children, 2/-

An advertisement from the Lichfield Mercury for the 1943 races.

told the horse of the punter's method of selecting winners by mathmatical equation......it was beaten by inches in a very close finish.

A lady when asked how she had made her selection said she had noticed a ladybird land on her racecard. She saw the little beetle as a sign of good luck and backed the horse of the same name in the Boston Trotting Handicap. This method of selection proved more reliable as Good Luck did in fact trot up at very long odds although the reports do not state what the odds were.

An estimated 5000 spectators turned out on the first day, swelling the War Aid Fund considerably, but the *Walsall Observer* reported that the numbers were down due to transport difficulties and other causes that kept the viewing public away. What exactly these difficulties were is not stated. The newspaper classed it as an austerity meeting, as there were no sideshows and the refreshment stands were limited to those selling 'only sandwiches and temperance drinks'.

In attendance at the meeting was the Mayor of Walsall, Mrs A. McShane with the Mayoress, Miss Moira McShane and the M.P. for the Borough, Sir George Schuster with his wife.

The results were:

First day, Monday 2nd August

Spitfire Stakes.

1　Broughton Boy　Mr. J. Jones, Wick
2　Polly　　　　　 Mr. James Wood, Elton
3　Snowball　　　Master O. Johnson, Walsall

THE 1940s REVIVAL

Wellington Trotting Handicap
1 Good Luck   Miss V. Hall, Leek
2 Phillip   Master T. Johnson, Walsall
3 Sunny Girl   Mr. J. W. Roberts, Prestatyn

Hurricane Stakes
1 Snowball   Master O. Johnson, Walsall
2 Barda   Mr. G. Price, Neenton
3 Polly   Mr. James Wood, Elton

Sunderland Stakes
1 Farmer's Boy   Mr. W. Matthews, Ludlow
2 Bob   Mr. A. Hall, Cressage
3 Maloga   Mr. D. Loverock, Aldridge

Boston Trotting Handicap
1 Good Luck   Miss V. Hall, Leek
2 Dan J   Master T. Johnson, Walsall
3 Phillip   Master O. Johnson, Walsall

Fortress Stakes
1 Farmer's Boy   Mr. W. Matthews, Ludlow
2 Our Hope   Mr. A. Hall, Cressage
3 Pat J   Mr. P. Groves, Walsall

Tradesmen's Turnout
1 Scribbans Purity Bread Limited
2 Guest Keen & Nettlefold Limited, Darlaston
3 Midland Counties Dairy, Walsall

Pleasure Turnout
1 Mr. Joseph Smith, Four Oaks,
2 Mr. T. J. Goulden, Barr Common
3 Ditto

Second day, Tuesday 3rd August

Stencil Stakes
1 Tappits   Mr. G. Wilshaw, Hanley
2 Bob   Mr. A. Hall, Cressage
3 Sunny   Mr. C. R. Birch, Shrewsbury

Hatherton Trotting Handicap
1 Big Bill   Mr. James Hall, Leek
2 Miss Dillon   Miss Worrall
3 Flo Dewey   Master O. Johnson

Pony Race (Children up to 15 years old)
1 Little Star   Mr. G. Jones, Alveley
2 Nib   Master T. Johnson

War Aid Stakes
1 Broughton Boy   Mr. J. Jones, Wick
2 Take All   Mr. G. Wilshaw, Hanley
3 Pat J   Mr. P. Groves, Walsall

Trotting Handicap
1 Flo Dewey   Master O. Johnson
2 Good Luck   Miss V. Hall, Leek

Victory Stakes
1 Doubtful   Mr. G. Price
2 Take All   Mr. G. Wilshaw, Hanley
3 Polly   Mr. James Wood, Elton

The officials at the meeting were: Judges, Alderman J. Cliff Tibbits, J. F. W. Upton and F. N. Bower. Turnouts Judge, Geoffrey Bennett (London). Starter and Handicapper Mr. J. Price. Clerk of the Course, Mr. B. Dickinson assisted by Mr. S. T. Abbotts. Stewards, Baron Power, F. Hawley, S. T. Abbotts, H. Glaze, Mark Ryan and B. Dickinson. Hon. Surgeons, Dr. A. B. Davies and Dr. J. E. Underwood. Hon. Veterinary Surgeon, Mr. W. B. Brownie. Clerk of the Scales, Mr. H. Fullwood. Financial Stewards, W. A. Smith, H. Spruce and T. Madeley. Publicity and Sales, T. E. Bennett and C. Bardell. Plan of the course by Mr. J. T. Parker. Flag Steward, Coun. H. F. Truman. Announcer, Mr. B. M. Lyons. Paddock Steward, Mr. Mark Ryan. Turnouts Steward, Mr. C. Gough.

Easter 1944

The meeting was again run on just the one day but this year it was on the Easter Bank Holiday Monday, 10th April, as opposed to the Saturday the previous year. The venue was again The Meadows, Stencils Farm on the Aldridge Road.

The programme consisted of six races all named after famous allied aircraft of the era. In previous years although some of the attendances were not quite as expected they had all raised considerable amounts of money for the Mayor's War Aid Fund. This year continued in the same vein because the *Walsall Observer* in its opening paragraph mentions the programme sales alone contributed £118 to the Fund. At the end of the meeting a cheque for almost £1000 was handed over to the Mayor. The money collected was given to the Red Cross and the St. John's Fund.

The occasion was the first time the Mayor and Mayoress, Councillor and Mrs David Jones, had experienced the 'Sport of Kings'. The Mayor commented to the *Observer* reporter, *'I have never been on a racecourse before and I must say it is quite an experience'*.

Another visitor to the course was a member of the US Forces serving over here who, in peacetime, was a leading journalist in the trotting world back in America. According to the report he was surprised at how many people had attended such a small meeting and also commented, *'I thought the rowdier element would be much more in evidence instead of being conspicuous by their abscence'*.

In the States trotting is a much bigger and better organised sport than it has ever been over here but he was nevertheless taken with Walsall's attempt at staging such a meeting. He later commented that he thought of staying over here after the war and perhaps shipping a few American horses over and developing the sport in Britain.

A very surprising thing happened after the first race, something virtually unheard of. The bookies made a mistake and paid out on the wrong horse! The horse they paid out on certainly had the right name, Doubtful! Apparently the bookies decided that Doubtful was the winner before it had

THE 1940s REVIVAL

been officially announced, they then discovered the winner was actually young Tom Johnson's Snowball. Several punters felt guilty about obtaining money by false pretences and returned their winnings to the bookies but one punter was last seen heading back towards town as fast as his legs would carry him clutching thirty quid!

The only other occurrence of any note happened in the final race of the day, The Fortress Stakes. Just four runners went to post and at the off Farmer's Boy and Take All set off at a pace leaving the other two runners nowhere. They kept this pace up for the whole distance of one and half miles but as they entered the straight one of the stirrup leathers of Farmer's Boy broke. The horse swerved off the course away from spectators before his jockey was thrown very hard into the turf. Although severly shaken and bruised those were the only injuries he sustained.

The results were:-

Spitfire Stakes (7 furlong sprint)

1	Snowball	Master T. Johnson, Walsall
2	Doubtful	Mr. G. Price, Ludlow
3	Pale Face	Mr. J. E. Arnold, Walsall

Wellington Handicap (1 mile trotting)

1	Flo Dewey	Master T. Johnson, Walsall
2	Big Bill	Mr. J. W. Roberts, Prestatyn
3	Grape Fruit	Mr. P. Vaughan, Llandiloes

Hurricane Stakes (1 mile open weight race)

1	Doubtful	Mr. G. Price, Ludlow
2	Pink Gin	Mr. G. Wilshaw, Hanley
3	Snowball	Master T. Johnson, Walsall

Sunderland Stakes (1 mile start race)

1	Barda	Mr. G. Price, Ludlow
2	Pat J.	Master O. Johnson, Walsall
3	Girl Pat	Mr. R. Whiteley, Market Drayton

Boston Stakes (6 furlong trotting handicap)

1	Big Bill	Mr. J. W. Roberts, Prestatyn
2	Grape Fruit	Mr. P. Vaughan, Llandiloes
3	Good Luck	Miss V. Hall, Leek

Fortress Stakes (1½ miles weight race)

1	Take All	Mr. G. Wilshaw, Hanley
2	Betty	Mr. James Wood, Elton
3	Polly	Ditto

Tradesmen's Turnout

| 1 | Mr. H. Field |
| 2 | Goulden Brothers |

The officials at the meeting were: Judges, Lady Dartmouth, Alderman J. Cliff Tibbits, and F. N. Bower. Turnout Judges, E. J. Spare and W. E. Dicken. Starter and Handicapper, Mr. J. Price. Clerk of the Course, Mr. B. Dickinson assisted by Mr. S. T. Abbotts. Stewards, Baron Power, F. Hawley, S. T. Abbotts, H. Glaze, Mark Ryan and B. Dickinson. Hon. Surgeons, Dr. A. B. Davies and Dr. J. E. Underwood. Hon. Veterinary Surgeon, Mr. W. B. Brownie. Clerk of the Scales, Mr. H. Fullwood. Financial Stewards, W. A. Smith, H. Spruce and T. Madeley. Publicity and Sales, T. E. Bennett and C. Bardell. Plan of the course by Mr. J. T. Parker. Flag Steward, Coun. H. F. Truman. Announcer, Mr. B. M. Lyons. Paddock Steward, Mr. Mark Ryan. Turnouts Steward, Mr. C. Gough.

August 1944

The second meeting of the year was scheduled for Monday and Tuesday, the 7th and 8th August. An advertisement promoting the races appeared in the *Walsall Observer* on the Saturday prior to the event with a list of the runners for the two days, the amount of entrants appears to be the most yet. For the flat races thirty-eight horse were entered along with eighteen for the trotting races.

Excellent weather greeted the spectators when racing began at 2.30 p.m., admission to the Course was 3/6d (17.5 pence), the Paddock for 10/- (50 pence) with children and members of the Forces 2/- (10 pence) and 5/- (25 pence).

The *Observer* advertisement also told of the '*Special Buses Every Few Minutes from The Bridge*' and '*Refreshments On The Course*'.

At the Easter meeting a few months earlier the name of Lady Dartmouth appeared in the list of officials, now it was the turn of Lady Dudley. Not content with officiating her Ladyship rode, and won, the first race, although not without incident. The *Observer* reports:-

'Having won in fine style the ladies seven furlong race, Lady Dudley's mount, Barda, owned by Mr. Price of Ludlow decided to prolong the pleasure of having her ladyship on his back. Nothing her ladyship could do would induced the horse to realise that the race was won. In an effort to bring the racer to a standstill grooms and jockeys ran on to the course and waved and shouted to the horse, but Barda appeared to be enjoying himself and neatly swerving past them, continued on his way. In the meantime Lady Dudley was pulling hard on the horse's reins, and it was not until he had completed four extra circuits of the course that Barda condescended to pull up.'

Once again, as on previous occasions, the meeting proved to be a great success with much money being raised for the War Aid Fund Committee who were all in attendance. Accompanying the Mayor and Mayoress, Mr and Mrs David Jones, were Lord Dudley, Lord Rothermere, the Duchess of Marlborough and Lady O'Neill who all apparently enjoyed the meeting and entered into the spirit of the proceedings.

Although the bookmakers were swamped with people placing bets the odds quoted were short, so short one experienced punter was overheard saying '*it's like buying money!*'

Monday's racing was marred by a sad incident involving the horse the bookies wrongly paid out on at the Easter meeting, Doubtful. Mr. Price's horse started well for the Hurricane Stakes and soon built up a good lead, looking a certain winner. After completing around a circuit of the

THE 1940s REVIVAL

course spectators were surprised to see Doubtful slow down to walking pace as the rest of the field flashed past him. His jockey dismounted and began to lead the now hobbling Doubtful back to the Paddock. After examination by the vet, Mr. W. B. Brownie, it was discovered Doubtful had fractured his off hind leg just above the fetlock. Sadly, Mr. Brownie had no alternative but to put the horse down.

After the distressing incident spectators were made to smile again at the antics of one of the runners in the Sunderland Stakes. Thirty-nine runners had been original entered for this race but only four came under starter's orders. With the jockey mounted, a mare called Daisy owned by Mr Underwood from Sutton Coldfield flatly refused to move a muscle. All inducements to make the mare move proved unsatisfactory and with that the hapless jockey dismounted and led Daisy back to the Paddock. The race was won by a horse familiar to racegoers by now, Barda, with young Thomas Johnson's Snowball a good second, the other runner, Patience, was officially classed as a 'very poor third'.

The final race, the Fortress Stakes over one and a half miles on Monday proved to be the best of the day. With ten declared runners, Abbot's Romance led from start to finish closely followed by Take All who briefly threatened the winner before settling for second place.

Although the good weather continued into the second day the crowd was not quite as large as that on Monday but nevertheless made a considerable amount to add the previous days four figure sum.

Another first occurred at the course in the Hatherton Trotting Stakes that had just four runners. Miss Lawrence and her horse Spitfire came in last only to find after a few minutes that they were the winners! The Stewards decided the first past the post, Mr. Hampton's Traveller had actually galloped round the course and not trotted and so disqualified him. Second was Oscar Johnson junior's Annette with Miss Hall's Good Luck third, but the Stewards decided both runners had set off before the starter's flag had been dropped.

In the final official race of the day, the Victory Stakes, another shock was about happen. Since the resurrection of Walsall Races there had been no greater certainty at Stencil's Farm than Mr. Wilshaw's Take All......I seem to have heard that before! The old racing adage of 'favourites are there to be beaten' was about to happen. Some bookmaker's were so sure of victory for Take All they wouldn't lay it, those that would gave ridiculously short odds. The winner, Jean, set off at a good pace followed by the odds-on favourite in second place and that is how it finished with Jean winning by a length. Sadly there is no report of Jean's starting price.

The takings for the two days amounted to over £2,000 with a profit of about £1,500.

The result were:-

First day, Monday 7th August

Spitfire Stakes (6 furlongs)

1	Doubtful	Mr. G. Price, Ludlow
2	Abbot's Romance	Mr. T. H. Morgan, Clementstone
3	Tappits	Mr. G. Wilshaw, Hanley

Ladies Race (7 furlongs)

1	Barda	Mr. G. Price, Ludlow, rider Lady Dudley
2	Monty	Dickenson & Son, Rushall, rider Miss Ward
3	Pat	Miss V. Lawrence, Walsall, ridden by owner

Wellington Handicap (1 mile trotting)

1	Annette	Master O. Johnson, Walsall
2	Good Luck	Miss Hall, Leek
3	Grape Fruit	Mr. P. Vaughan, Llandiloes

Boston Stakes (6 furlongs trotting handicap)

1	Good Luck	Miss Hall, Leek
2	Joey	Mr. D. Loverock, Aldridge
3	Annette	Master O. Johnson

Second day, Tuesday 8th August

Stencil Stakes (6 furlong sprint)

1	Tappits	Mr. G. Wilshaw, Hanley
2	Monty	Dickenson & Son, Rushall
3	Daisy	Mr. E. Underwood, Sutton

Pony Race (1 mile, children up to 15 years old)

1	Gold Dust	Mr. F. Wall, Craven Arms
2	Gay Rabbitt	Mr. F. Westley, Rushall
3	Little Star	Mr. G. Jones, Alveley

Dilke Stakes (7 furlong sprint)

1	Barda	Mr. G. Price, Ludlow
2	Tappits	Mr. G. Wilshaw, Hanley
3	Snuff Box	Miss M. Ward, Walsall Wood

Hatherton Handicap (1 mile trotting)

| 1 | Spitfire | Miss V. Lawrence, Walsall |

Three other runners all disqualified.

War Aid Stakes (1 mile)

1	Pink Gin	Mr. G. Wilshaw, Hanley
2	Charlie	Mr. A. Hall, Cressage
3	April Son	Mr. G. Jones, Alveley

Walsall Handicap (6 furlong trotting)

1	Grape Fruit	Mr. P. Vaughan, Llandiloes
2	Good Luck	Miss Hall, Leek
3	Joey	Mr. D. Loverock, Aldridge

Victory Stakes (1½ miles)

1	Jean	Mr. Phil Wall, Craven Arms
2	Take All	Mr. G. Wilshaw, Hanley
3	April Queen	Master T. Johnson, Walsall

The officials at the meeting were: Judges, Mr. J. F. W. Upton, Alderman J. Cliff Tibbits, Coun. F. H. Truman and W. V. Weston. Turnout Judges, E. J. Spare and T. Hickinbottom. Starter and Handicapper, Mr. J. Price. Clerk of the Course, Mr. B. Dickinson assisted by Mr. S. T. Abbotts. Stewards,

THE 1940s REVIVAL

Baron Power, F. Hawley, S. T. Abbotts, H. Glaze, Mark Ryan and B. Dickinson. Hon. Surgeons, Dr. A. B. Davies and Dr. J. E. Underwood. Hon. Veterinary Surgeon, Mr. W. B. Brownie. Clerk of the Scales, Mr. H. Fullwood. Financial Stewards, H. Spruce, L. Davis and A. Anderton. Publicity and Sales, T. E. Bennett and C. Bardell. Plan of the course by Mr. J. T. Parker. Flag Stewards, J. Christie and H. Glover. Announcer, Mr. B. M. Lyons. Paddock Steward, Mr. Mark Ryan. Turnouts Steward, Mr. C. Gough.

Easter 1945

The first day of the Easter race meeting had a feel of victory in the air about it with just over a month to go before WW2 ended. The spring weather for early April was kind to the organisers with plenty of sunshine but accompanied by a strong cool wind.

After over five years of war the spectators, it was said, seemed to be in a more relaxed mood than at previous meetings. The *Walsall Observer* reported over 4,000 paying spectators had gathered to enjoy the sport, they also commented how at this meeting they saw far fewer spectators dressed in khaki than in previous years, in particular American khaki.

With Field Marshall Montgomery leading the troops into Germany it was inevitable a horse of the same name would be victorious in the first race, the Roosevelt Stakes. For once the omens were correct, 'Monty' trained by the Dickinsons from Rushall beat off his rivals to win easily, seemingly with half of the population of Walsall backing it!

The winner of the second race was a horse called Good Luck. It wasn't long before a few jokers in the crowd began chanting 'Good Luck - Monty' at the top of their voices, hoping the message would carry over The Channel, into the Low Countries and eventually Germany itself spurring our troops on.

The *Observer* reporter got into conversation with a chap referred to as 'little George' who swore he had the perfect system for picking winners and was prepared to share his secret with anyone. In the early years of the war 'little George' met up with a soldier on leave from India who 'gave' him a small spinning top. George placed it on the racecard and spun it, whichever horses name it stopped closest to, that was the selection! 'Little George' was emphatic about this method, *'never failed yet'* he told the reporter, *'I've won quite a bit of money with it'*. No doubt there were a few in earshot of George who also saw two pink pigs in overcoats flying over The Dilke!

The spectators thought happier days were just around the corner and this was confirmed when they let out a mighty cheer when a flight of about thirty heavy bombers passed over the course in between the races. The *Observer* reporter commenting on the sight suddenly became quite eloquent, describing it thus, *'the aircraft forged steadily through the wisps of cloud high above us, looking like small silvery toys'*. Bet the enemy didn't think that when they arrived over their target!

The Mayor and Mayoress, Mr and Mrs John Whiston, who were in attendance presented a cup given by the Borough M.P., Sir George Schuster to the owner of the winner of the Schuster Handicap, Mr. O'Sullivan from Newport, Monmouthshire.

The six races on the card for the first day provided the odd thrilling moment with two close finishes and a bit of suspense too. Many backers were kept waiting when there was an objection against the first horse in the Eden Stakes, Miss Hall's Good Luck. Over ten minutes elapsed before the red flag was hoisted on the number board was replaced by a white flag indicating the objection had been upheld. The second horse, Annette, owned by Oscar Johnson junior was declared the winner.

The only mishap of the day came in the very last race when the jockey, Ted Davis from Bromyard, took a crashing fall while riding Mr. Bayliss's horse George. He received attention on the course from Dr. Davies and Dr. Underwood assisted by members of St. John's Ambulance Brigade. He was concussed in the fall and was thought to have broken some ribs.

The weather for the second day, Tuesday, was most unfavourable. It was much cooler than the previous day and although it was dry for the first race some heavy showers moved in for the rest of the afternoon making proceedings very unpleasant for both riders and spectators. The fields were smaller than the previous day and there appeared to be one runner in each race that was firmly established as favourite. The *Observer* reporter comments that not even the bookmakers seem keen on conducting any business. That must have been a first! Inevitably, when short priced favourites are supposedly in abundance there will be a few shocks, sure enough there were!

The Cunningham Stakes was the first race to bring a surprise result when Polmont the red hot favourite dead heated with an old friend from previous meetings, Barda. In the *Observer's* report it was stated Polmont and his owner, Mr. Scott, were from Newcastle-Upon-Tyne which seems an awfully long way to come for a £20 prize! Should that read Newcastle-Under-Lyme?

In the Tedder Stakes, a six furlong trotting race, Aircraft the much fancied and short priced favourite was beaten easily by Big Bill. The owner of Aircraft objected to the winner but the Stewards over ruled him and Big Bill kept the race.

The results were:-

First day, Monday, 2nd April

Roosevelt Stakes (Six furlong sprint, £40)

1	Monty	Dickinson and Son, Rushall
2	George	Mr. H. S. Bayliss, Bromyard
3	Pat J	Master Johnson, Walsall

Attlee Handicap (One mile trotting, £25)

1	Good Luck	Miss V. Hall (Leek)
2	Big Bill	Mr. J. W. Roberts, Prestatyn
3	Annette	Master Johnson, Walsall

Stalin Stakes (One mile open weights, £40)

1	Moggy	Mr. George Price, Ludlow
2	April Queen	Mr. H. S. Bayliss, Bromyard
3	Windsor Boy	Mr. Wilson Brace, Abertridwr

THE 1940s REVIVAL

Schuster Handicap (Seven furlong sprint, £40 and cup)

1	Broughton Boy	Mr. M. O'Sullivan, Newport, Mon.
2	Frisco	Mr. T. Sutton, Short Heath
3	Barda	Dickinson and Son, Rushall

Eden Stakes (Six furlongs trotting handicap, £25)

1	Annette	Master Johnson, Walsall
2	Good Luck	Miss V. Hall, (Leek)

Churchill Handicap (One and half miles race, £50)

1	Pat	Mr. George Price, Ludlow
2	April Queen	Mr. H. S. Bayliss, Bromyard
3	Maloga	Master Johnson, Walsall

Second day, Tuesday 3rd April

Montgomery Stakes (Six furlong sprint, £15)

1	Broughton Boy	Mr. M. O'Sullivan, Newport, Mon.
2	Monty	Dickinson and Son, Rushall
3	Wee Jimmy	Mr. G. Wharton, Cobridge

Eisenhower Handicap (One mile trotting, £20)

1	Big Bill	Mr. J. W. Roberts, Prestatyn
2	Grape Fruit	Mr. P. Vaughan, Llandiloes
3	Good Luck	Miss V. Hall, Leek

Cunningham Stakes (One mile open weights, £20)

Dead heat between

1	Polmont	Mr. Scott, Newcastle-upon-Tyne
1	Barda	Dickinson and Son, Rushall
3	Miss Judy	Mr. Arthur Birch, Derby

Mountbatten Handicap (Seven furlong sprint, £15)

1	Frisco	Mr. T. Sutton, Short Heath
2	Moggy	Mr. George Price, Ludlow
3	Sunny	Miss M. Day, Elton

Tedder Stakes (Six furlong trotting handicap, £15)

1	Big Bill	Mr. J. W. Roberts, Prestatyn
2	Grape Fruit	Mr. P. Vaughan, Llandiloes
3	Good Luck	Miss V. Hall, Leek

Portal Handicap (one and a quarter mile race, £20)

1	Windsor Boy	Mr. Wilson Brace, Abertridwr
2	April Queen	Mr. H. S. Bayliss, Bromyard
3	Star Dust	Mr. S. Parker, Prestatyn

August 1945

The meeting was to take place on Bank Holiday Monday 6th and Tuesday 7th of August. With the war in Europe over for almost three months, the first day of the meeting would go down in history as it was on the morning of the sixth the Americans dropped the first deployed atomic bomb on Hiroshima. As the spectators made their way to Stencils Farm for the second race meeting of the year they were probably oblivious to the fact until later that day or possibly Tuesday.

The *Walsall Observer* comments that although record entries for the races had been received the actual number of horses that arrived on the course was very much lower than expected. Up to twenty cancellations were made at the last minute due to transport problems with many trains being unable to carry the horse boxes. The weather also didn't help as it had been very unpredictable leading up to the meeting with a heavy thunderstorm abating just before racing.

With small fields of, in some cases, only three or four runners the racing did not live up to expectations from a spectators point of view. As at the last meeting at Easter, one horse in each race was made a very hot favourite and in most cases they won but there was the odd upset or two. The only punters to make a profit were those that followed the money and backed with big stakes for a small return. Many of the less experienced racegoers continued to back the outsiders in the hope they would prevail, sadly few did. With plenty of rain prior to the start of the meeting the course was rather slippery in places causing a few runners to part company with their riders. Fortunately both runners and riders escaped relatively unscathed.

The Dickenson family from Rushall with their now familiar horses, Monty and Barda, winning three of the six races on the first day. Second to Monty in the Birchills Stakes was a horse called Mutton Chop, ridden by Miss M. Ward who just failed to get the better of her opponent. The rider's disappointment drifted away when the same horse went one place better on Tuesday beating one of the Johnson's horse, Snowball. It was discovered after the race that Snowball had a severe cut on the off-hind leg as it went round the course.

With the weather being blamed for the smaller attendance there were nevertheless over 2,500 paying spectators on Monday with gate receipts of £521. If the organisers had hoped for better weather on Tuesday they were disappointed as mother nature had other ideas in the form of lower temperatures and persistent rain.

The *Observer* reports that even though attendances were down on previous years the organisers had still managed to cover their expenses to the degree that a cheque was presented to the War Aid Fund for over £500.

The results were:-

Monday 6th August

Bridge Stakes

1	Panarama	Mr. T. Sutton, Short Heath
2	The Jug	Mr. E. Sergeant, Stoke-on-Trent

Bloxwich Handicap

1	Monty	Dickenson and Son, Rushall
2	Wee Jimmy	Mr. G. Wharton, Cobridge
3	Sunset	Mr. T. Sutton, Short Heath

Victory Cup

1	Barda	Dickenson and Son, Rushall
2	Cap	Mr. G. Wilshaw, Hanley
3	Moggy	Mr. G. Price, Ludlow

THE 1940s REVIVAL

Birchills Stakes
1 Monty   Dickenson and Son, Rushall
2 Mutton Chop   Mr. G. Jones, Bridgnorth

Walsall Stakes
1 Gum Chum   Mr. G. Wharton, Cobridge
2 Billy   Mr. A. Hall, Cressage
3 Dusky   Mr. G. E. Fenton, Walsall

Caldmore Handicap
1 Dawn   Mr. G. Price, Ludlow
2 Blackie   Mr. G. Wilshaw, Hanley

Second day, Tuesday 7th August

Harden Stakes
1 Moggy (walked-over)   Mr. G. Price, Ludlow

Hatherton Handicap
1 Aileen   Mr. H. S. Bayliss, Bromyard
2 Bill   Mr. J. Underwood, Sutton Coldfield

Leamore Stakes
1 Cap   Mr. G. Wilshaw, Hanley
2 Grey Lass   Mr. R. Tudge, Worcester
3 Barda   Dickenson and Son, Rushall

Pleck Stakes
1 Mutton Chop   Mr. G. Jones, Bridgnorth
2 Snowball   Master T. Johnson, Walsall
3 George   Mr. H. S. Bayliss, Bromyard

Paddock Stakes
1 April Queen   Mr. H. S. Bayliss, Bromyard
2 Pat   Mr. G. Price, Ludlow
3 Gum Chum   Mr. G. Wharton, Cobridge

Palfrey Handicap
1 Aileen   Mr. H. S. Bayliss, Bromyard
2 George   Mr. H. S. Bayliss, Bromyard
3 Bill   Mr. J. Underwood, Sutton Coldfield

Easter 1946

Easter Monday and Tuesday, 22nd and 23rd of April were the dates set for this meeting.

The *Walsall Observer* concentrates the beginning of their report on an injured soldier just back from Germany who visited the races. The soldier was Driver Norman Harvey of New Road, Aldridge who never expected to be anywhere near his home town on Easter Monday. Having been all through the fighting from North Africa, Sicily, France, Belgium and finally Goblar in Germany and come through it all virtually unscathed. His 'wound' came about in peacetime and all because he trod on a piece of carpet that had no floorboards under it. He fell through turning his ankle badly and was shipped back to a hospital near Swindon for treatment from where he was given a few days leave.

The *Observer* commented:-

'Driver Harvey's was just one of the human stories to be found among the three thousand spectators at the races - a typical section of the holiday crowd who delighted in the opportunity to forget present day anxieties and perhaps win a bob or two'.

The weather was good with plenty of sunshine but rather cool and the going was described by one jockey as *'very hard - like concrete,'* which didn't bode well for any fallers, equine or human! Due to the going fields were again small two of the races only had two runners and the Bloxwich Handicap only attracted three. That race caused a bit of a scene to use the *Observer's* words. An old friend to the regular racegoers at Stencil's Farm, Monty, lead from start to finish with a horse named Bill second and Crusty Loaf third. Monty came home clear by four lengths but an objection was lodged on the grounds of an alleged false start. When it was over-ruled loud booing came from one section of the crowd with one woman becoming very annoyed with the officials.

The reporter for the *Observer* made a point of saying how much improved the course was since it was first used three years ago. He thought in view of this incident, the organisers may well consider a starting gate, although he did appreciate they are not easy to get hold these days. Another point was raised to help things along and that was to place numbers on the saddle cloths as in professional racing. The riders already had numbers on their backs like footballers but sometimes they proved difficult for the judges to see.

One of the runners did sustain an injury whilst running in the Walsall Stakes. Mr. Mast's runner Ogee hurt a foreleg after it came down on its knees. The horse hobbled away but the injury was not thought to be serious.

The final race on the first day, the Caldmore Handicap, was run just as the sun was setting, an appropriately name horse, Sunset, was declared a non-runner leaving the race to be won by one called Dawn!

A good crowd watching the Walsall Stakes as the runners approach the winning post, first was Lady Jane, Jean second and Shamrock third. Earlier in the afternoon Lady Jane had won the County Stakes over one mile with Shamrock again in third place. (From the now defunct Walsall Observer)

THE 1940s REVIVAL

The crowds around the bookmakers stands on Monday afternoon. (From the now defunct Walsall Observer)

Young Thomas Johnson entered another old favourite, the now sixteen year old Snowball in the Pleck Stakes on Tuesday. Old Snowball, ridden by Judy Watkins from Walsall, did the job well coming home by half a length. Judy was a native of South Wales and had worked at Oscar Johnson's stable at Wisemore House for several years where she helped train the horses on the cinder track. Alderman J. Cliff Tibbitts, chairman of the committee presented her with a Newmarket racing bridle. Interviewed during the presentation she told onlookers that she had been riding since the age of eight and she also told of Snowball's liking for warm skimmed milk with a half a dozen eggs mixed with it. Mr Johnson senior said, 'What's more - he doesn't turn his nose up at dried eggs, but they are hard to get these days. We have raced him in many parts of the country, but today I'm giving more credit to the lady [Judy] than to the horse'.

It did rain during the night so the going was slightly better than on Monday which helped when Mr. Richardson's horse, Lorrie, fell in the Harden Stakes. Fortunately neither horse or jockey were injured.

The results were:-

Monday 22nd April

Bridge Stakes (Six furlongs open sprint)

1	Here Again	Mr. G. Wilshaw, Hanley
2	Moggy	Mr. G. Price, Ludlow
3	Barda	Dickinson and Son, Rushall

Won by a length, five ran.

Bloxwich Handicap (Seven furlongs)

1	Monty	Dickinson and Son, Rushall
2	Bill	Mr. E. Underwood, Erdington
3	Crusty Loaf (late Pat J)	Mr. F. Holland, Walsall

Won by four lengths, three ran.

County Stakes (One mile open gallop)

1	Lady Jane	Mr. A Green, Elton
2	Hollands Gin	Mr. G. Wilshaw, Hanley
3	Shamrock	Mr. C. Mast, Coventry

Close finish, five ran.

Birchills Stakes (Seven furlongs, ladies race)

1	Comet	Mr. R. E. Bache, Alveley
2	Barda	Dickinson and Son, Rushall

One length, two ran.

Walsall Stakes (One and a half miles, open)

1	Lady Jane	Mr. A Green, Elton
2	Jean	Mr. P. E. Wall, Craven Arms
3	Shamrock	Mr. C. Mast, Coventry

Close finish, seven ran.

Caldmore Handicap

1	Dawn	Mr. G. Price, Ludlow
2	Bill	Mr. E. Underwood, Erdington

Won easily, two ran.

Tuesday 23rd April

Harden Stakes (Six furlongs, open sprint)

1	Monty	Dickinson and Son, Rushall
2	Moggy	Mr. G. Price, Ludlow
3	Plain Jane	Mr. H. S. Bayliss, Bromyard

Won by five lengths, four ran.

Hatherton Handicap (seven furlongs)

1	Barda	Dickinson and Son, Rushall
2	Tiny	Mr. F. Richardson, Stoke
3	Bill	Mr. E. Underwood, Erdington

Won by four lengths, three ran.

Stencil's Stakes (One mile open gallop)

1	Tiny	Mr. F. Richardson, Stoke
2	June	Mr. H. E. Bayliss, Bromyard
3	Here Again,	Mr. G. Wilshaw, Hanley

Won by four lengths, three ran.

Pleck Stakes ((Seven furlongs ladies race)

1	Snowball	Master T. Johnson, Walsall
2	Barda	Dickinson and Son, Rushall
3	Wee Mac	Mr. J. H. Towers, Birmingham

Won by half a length, four ran.

Paddock Stakes (One and a half mile open)

1	Hollands Gin	Mr. G. Wilshaw, Hanley
2	Tiny	Mr. F. Richardson, Stoke
3	Bill	Mr. E. Underwood, Erdington

Won by one length, three ran.

Palfrey Handicap (One mile)

1	Monty	Dickinson and Son, Rushall
2	Dawn	Mr. G. Price, Ludlow
3	Wee Mac	Mr. J. H. Towers, Birmingham

Won by two lengths, three ran.

THE 1940s REVIVAL

Walsall Victory Races
Saturday 8th June 1946

'Racing in the rain' was how the *Walsall Observer* titled their report on this the final meeting at Stencil's Farm. Once again the great British weather conspired to ruin what should have been a great day in the Victory celebrations calendar organised by the town.

The report from the *Observer* read:-

'*1. Mackintoshes, 2 Umbrellas, 3 Gum Boots, Wet Feet also ran!*

Those were the unpopular 'favourites' at the Mayor's War Aid Fund Entertainments Committee's race meeting on the Stencil's Farm course on Saturday.

What was intended to be one of the chief attractions in the local 'Victory' celebration programme and a source of enjoyment for thousands was converted by the weather into an unpleasant ordeal for a few hundreds, who defied the weather, presumably in the hope of making a profit'.

It began to rain some time before the start and it never stopped while the racing was in progress, to ease the spectators burden there was one question to be answered, 'could they find a winner?' Of the people the *Observer* spoke to few, if any could, as they were too wet to care. One chap was heard to comment as he made his way through the mud and sodden grass, '*If this is Victory celebrations heaven help us if we had lost.*' Every horse he fancied had been beaten, he then commented, '*And I wouldn't mind betting that when I get back into the town there will be no beer and the pubs will be shut!*'

Even the bookmakers, sheltering under their large umbrellas couldn't raise a smile as they had taken very little money. One bookmaker told the *Observer* reporter, '*If we took a pound a piece from everyone who attended it would still be a bad day.*'

All the officials attempted to make the best of a bad day and went keenly about their duties to ensure the meeting went a smoothly as possible. The fields, unsurprisingly, were not large but there was some spirited competition amongst the runners. The race of the day, the Victory Stakes, for which a first prize of £70 was offered, with £20 for the second and £10 for the third produced a very good race from the four runners. At the post it was Mr. Wilshaw's Holland's Gin by a short head from Louise Bonne owned by Mr. Jones who had brought the horse up from the Rhondda Valley.

The members of the organising committee who officiated at this final meeting were: Coun. Baron Power and S. T. Abbotts, C. Bardell, T. E. Bennett, B. Dickinson, H. Fullwood, C. W. Garfield, H. Glaze, I. Hawley, B. M. Lyons, J. T. Parker, Mark Ryan, H. Spruce and H. F. Truman. Honorary Secretary, D. Pedley. Honorary Treasurer, W. A. Smith. Others who assisted were Alderman J. Cliff Tibbitts, A. Anderton, L. Davis, J. Christie, H. Glover, L. Price and H. Mears. Judges, W. V. Weston and J. F. W. Upton. Doctors A.B. Davies and M. G. Robinson. Veterinary Surgeon, W. B. Brownie.

Once again, just like the old meetings of seventy years ago, these wartime unofficial race meetings became history. The Walsall Show continued on Bank Holiday Mondays for many years but the only equestrian pursuits were gymkhanas and show jumping events, or horse leaping as the *Walsall Observer* called it in the late 1940s.

The results were:-

Bridge Stakes (Six furlongs open sprint, £40)

1	Colonel	Mr. A. Hall, Cressage
2	Dawn	Mr. G. Price, Ludlow
3	Here Again	Mr. G. Wilshaw, Hanley

Bloxwich Handicap (One mile trotting, £25)

1	Marshall Watts	Mr D. Fox, Birmingham
2	Alma	Mr. R. Hampton, Moxley

Victory Stakes (One and a half mile open gallop, £100)

1	Hollands Gin	Mr. G. Wilshaw, Hanley
2	Louise Bonne	Mr. D. Jones, Rhondda Valley
3	Discovery	Mr. G. Price, Ludlow

Birchills Stakes (Seven furlongs open sprint, £40)

1	Barda	Mr. H. T. Glaze, Walsall
2	In Time	Mr. P. E. Wall, Craven Arms
3	Robin	Mr. A. Hall, Cressage

Caldmore Handicap (Six furlongs trotting, £25)

1	Jack Fox	Mr. Oscar Johnson snr., Walsall
2	Collier's Pride	Mr. D. Loverock, Aldridge

Walsall Stakes (One mile open gallop, £50)

1	Grey Lass	Mr. R. Tudge, Worcester
2	Discovery	-
3	Jean	Mr. P. E. Wall, Craven Arms

WALSALL RACES

CHAPTER SEVEN
THE JOCKEYS

The identity of many of the jockeys that rode at Walsall in the first seventy years of the meeting is virtually unknown as the *Racing Calendar* rarely published their names.

Jockeys and trainers in those early days were mere servants to the ruling few; their identities were of little consequence. Some early jockeys that did gain notoriety, sometimes for the wrong reasons, were men such as Sam Chifney, Dick and Tom Goodisson, Frank Buckle and Bill Arnull. These jockeys may have ridden in races on the Long Meadow but sadly there are few if any records to substantiate the claim.

It has been mentioned in earlier pages that the jockeys of this era were a pretty rough lot. Many of them had rather dubious reputations and high percentage of them drank to excess, both on and off the racecourse. Those that had weight problems and wasted severely throughout their careers quite often succumbed to an early grave. Due to lack of nourishment many of them died from tuberculosis or by their own hand when depression set in after years of wasting.

An article in the *Sporting Magazine Volume 29*, 1806 by Sir John Sinclair entitled *"On the Training of Jockeys"* gave an excellent insight into how some of the jockeys of this era lived.

'Training lasted from about three weeks before Easter until the end of October, but a week or ten days was quite sufficient for a rider to reduce himself by a stone and a half. To do that they ate very little. For breakfast a small piece of bread and butter with tea in moderation. Dinner would be a very small piece of pudding and less meat, but when fish is taken the pudding and meat disappear. Wine and water is the usual beverage, being one part wine to two of water. Then in the afternoon tea is taken with little or no bread and butter. Finally no supper is taken.

For exercise after breakfast, having sufficiently loaded themselves with clothes, that is, five or six waistcoats, two coats and as many pairs of breeches as possible, a severe walk is taken from ten to fifteen miles. On their return home the wet clothes are removed and dry ones put on. If they are very tired they may lie down of an hour before dinner, after which no exercise is taken. They generally go to bed around nine o'clock and stay there until six or seven the next morning.

Some jockeys do not like the excessive walking and so to lose weight they may take purgatives – two of three ounces of Glauber salts is the usual dose.'

The article gave examples of various jockeys wasting regimes, one being the Prince of Wales jockey, John Arnold. He would abstain from meat and starchy foods around eight days before a big race and commented that he was not injured by wasting at the time and continued in good health. Without the knowledge we have today regarding dietary procedures it is difficult to think that it did not harm him in the long term.

An article in the *Wolverhampton Chronicle* in August 1854 read:-

'A little hot so most pedestrians thought, especially those who, not conversant with the art of turning heavy into light weights, gazed in astonishment on the jockeys out for sweating. Wrapped up in ever so many coats, stout gloves on their hands, a huge wrapper round the neck and face, almost concealing the eyebrows, a jockey out for sweating on a warm morning in August is a being to be wondered at by the uninitiated – such a one, at a sharp trot, would be almost a phenomenon to the general observer on a fine, frosty morning. Certainly, the genus jockey is a strange animal. He never grows fat, never grows old; and then what becomes of him when the season's over, and the Winter's come, until the season opens and Spring bids him come forth?'

Race riding in those days was totally different from that of today, deliberate crossing and jostling was considered to be a legitimate weapon in the jockey's armoury in those days and was encouraged in many cases. As well as their rough habits, their honesty was also questionable. Jockeys could bet on their mounts, or anyone else's, and of course, human nature being what it is, this was a recipe for disaster. Surprisingly, nothing was done to stop this practice for many years to come, with the inevitable consequences. Certain jockeys had reputations for being as bent as the proverbial paper clip. It is not surprising to find that many riders became as renowned for their ability to 'stop' horses as their ability to ride winners.

The style of riding in those days was also considerably different to that we know of today. Jockeys all rode with long leathers, in other words, their legs hung down the side of the horse and they sat upright. It wasn't until around 1900 that the 'monkey-on-a-stick' style of riding came to this country. This new, streamlined style was brought to these shores by the diminutive American jockey named 'Tod' Sloan. Since this

THE JOCKEYS

innovation occurred over one hundred years ago, all jockeys now ride in this crouched style. Almost overnight, Tod Sloan consigned the race riding style of centuries to the history books.

The following pages are devoted to the brief histories of some of the more well known and locally born jockeys that rode at Walsall.

HENRY ARTHUR (Senior)
(1789 - 1844)

Henry Arthur senior was born in Staffordshire in 1789 and his first recorded victory as a jockey came in 1812 when he rode two winners at Chester for Lord Derby and Sir Thomas Stanley. Around 1815 Henry married and one year later the couple had their first child, a daughter in 1816. Their first son Henry Bailey Arthur was born in 1819 and the baptism recorded the father as being a racehorse trainer living in Hednesford. The family actually lived at Hill House (later known as Red House Stables) which is just off today's East Cannock Road, opposite the Globe Inn.

Henry senior was a well known and respected jockey who rode just seven winners at Walsall in a twenty-two year period between 1813 and 1835. Throughout his career he rode well in excess of 240 winners, many of those being horses he also trained as well.

The Chester meeting in early May had always been a favourite with the Hednesford trainers and the Arthurs were no exception. Five times the family name appears as winners of His Majesty's Plate, including one for Lord Derby and another for Sir George Pigot.

It is thought it is he and not his son that assisted Thomas Newton in the design of the lightweight racing saddle. Newton later supplied race saddles to Newmarket made by Tisdale of London which were declared as 'perfect' by the recipients.

Henry, or Harry, as he was also known died on the 31st August 1844.

HENRY BAILEY ARTHUR (Junior)
1819 – 1840

The first of the two sons of Henry Arthur to take up racing, Henry Bailey, was born in 1819 the first son of Jane and Henry Arthur. His first winner was probably at Worcester on August 7th, 1833 when he rode Mr. Griffiths's horse, Repentance, to victory in a Maiden Selling Plate. Bought by Mr. Pickernell, Henry Bailey rode it to several more victories that season. By 1834 he was becoming a competent jockey and managed to win the Liverpool Tradesmen's Cup on Mr. Skipsey's horse, Inheritor, over the new Aintree Course. The season saw him finish with over twenty winners; not bad considering his father was still the favoured stable jockey. The *Wolverhampton Chronicle* reporter said of his ability after winning the Trial Stakes on August 11th, 1834, "Enchantress won after a severe struggle by half a head being excellently jockeyed by young Arthur."

Much like his father, he stayed riding mainly on the Midland circuit only venturing north to Chester, Manchester and Liverpool on occasions. His patrons included Mr. Pigot of Shropshire and Mr. Giffard of Chillington Hall, Brewood, both of whom may still have had horses with the East Cannock Road Stables. However, when his father left the stables around 1835/36 Henry Bailey began to ride for Thomas Carr. Unfortunately his career was to last only until 1837 and the young jockey seemed to have been struck down with some debilitating illness. It may very well have been tuberculosis due to the inclement position of the stables.

By 1840 young Henry Bailey had died and a once very promising career in the saddle had come to a sudden end.

WILLIAM ARTHUR
1826 - 1885

A younger brother to Henry Bailey, William's story was to be almost as tragic. He was born in 1826 and by the time he was fourteen years old he became an apprentice in Thomas Walter's yard. His first winner came in 1842 on Viola at Hereford on 24th August. It was at this same meeting the Hednesford jockeys and trainers won no less than six of the races at the two day event. His record at Walsall was not as good as his fathers or that of his elder brother as he rode just two winners.

With the death of his father in 1844 it seemed that William moved to the Wadlow Stables at Stanton, Shropshire and 1845 saw him win his first major race when he easily won the Chester Cup on Mr. Skerratt's Intrepid. A reporter from the *Wolverhampton Chronicle* described the finish of the race in the following terms, "At the Grosvenor turn Intrepid took the lead at a rattling pace and to the amazement of the "betting ring" went in a winner by three lengths amidst general cries of "Who is it?" The race, being worth £1625, was contested at first by Mr. Gully, another Shropshire trainer, whose horse, St. Lawrence, finished second. He objected citing the fact the Intrepid was "a thoroughbred". The stakes were withheld, but later Gully withdrew his objection.

In the same year William went on to win the Queen Anne Stakes at Ascot on 12th June, riding Mr. Hill's The Libel, also trained by Wadlow. He was to stay with the Wadlow until the late 1840s when he returned to Hednesford and was registered in *Ruff's Guide 1850* as a trainer himself while still riding. In the August of 1850 he won the Chillington Stakes for maiden two year olds at Wolverhampton on William Saunders's Calculator.

Unfortunately his riding career came to a sudden end in 1851 when he was committed to an asylum in Lichfield. The only other surviving brother, Thomas, had moved to Walsall to work as a clerk and he lodged at premises in Mountrath Street with his sister, Maria, and her husband, Edmund Smith. Interestingly Sarah Massey from the Cross Keys joined them as a lodger and stayed until she died in 1852.

William later moved to Walsall also and became licensee of the White Hart public house in Walhouse Street around 1861, he remained there until his death on 11th March 1885. His wife Polly took over as licensee on his death. In 1887 she married Francis Stokes and the couple continued to run the premises until 1893.

THE JOCKEYS

THOMAS ASHMALL
1838 – 1875

Thomas Ashmall was born in 1838 at Farewell Hall, near Lichfield and only a few miles from the Hednesford training grounds. His father, a farmer, came from quite a well to do family in the area, consequently, young Thomas had a good education, not only from an academic point of view. His boyhood school friend was John Porter, the young Rugeley lad who eventually became the greatest of the Victorian racehorse trainers. In school holidays and at weekends the pair would be up on Hednesford Hills together watching the goings on, and eager to be a part of it. Thomas' uncle was the trainer Thomas Carr, so the boys were didn't have to wait long to be in the thick of things. They became friendly with the jockeys George Whitehouse, Charles Marlow and Robert Denman who would tell the excited boys stories that fired their imagination. After a growing up in that environment it wasn't difficult to see why both boys knew exactly where their destiny lay from an early age.

Rather surprisingly, Thomas didn't become apprenticed to his uncle but chose to go to the trainer Thomas Taylor at Newmarket. Not only was this association good from a professional point of view but also from a personal view too. On the 20th August 1861 he married Thomas Taylor's youngest daughter Emily at St. Mary's Church in Newmarket. His address at the time of his marriage was given as Chesterfield House, Newmarket.

Being based at racing's headquarters, Ashmall was an infrequent visitor to Walsall rode just the one winner on the Long Meadow, an un-named colt by Ithuriel in 1854.

As well as riding the winner of the French Derby he later trained in France. As with many jockey of this era, he died young, on the 22nd May 1875 aged thirty-seven.

Ashmall's sister, Lucy Jane, married John Adey and his other sister Mary, married George Palmer, both Hednesford trainers.

Classic and big race winners:
The Oaks on Governess in 1858.
2,000 Guineas on The Wizard in 1860 and again on The Marquis in 1862.
1,000 Guineas on Governess in 1858 and on Hurricane in 1862.
Ascot Gold Cup in 1855 on Fandango
Steward's Cup in 1854 on Pumicestone.
Goodwood Cup in 1857 on Monarque.
Northumberland Plate in 1854 on Grapeshot
The Yorkshire Oaks in 1865 on Klarinska.
Park Hill Stakes in 1858 on Hepatica.
Nassau Stakes on Instructress in 1855 and Go-Ahead in 1858.
Ascot Derby in 1859 on Gamester.
French Derby in 1857 on Lupin.

GEORGE ASHWORTH
1854 - 1900

George Ashworth was born in Prestwich, Lancashire in 1854 and by the age of fourteen he was an apprentice to Thomas Cliff at Hednesford.

It was around this time Cliff was losing his stable jockey, Samuel Kenyon. Ashworth, along with another young jockey, Job Toon, took over from Kenyon.

Ashworth's first ride in public was on Mr. Lincoln's Hereward at Sutton Park on 9th July 1869. Just over a month later he rode his first winner, Lincoln's Prince in Her Majesty's Plate at Derby on 31st August. His first winner at Walsall came just over a year later on the 3rd October 1870 when he partnered Young Rose to victory in the Bradford Handicap Plate. Also riding in that race was the young jockey Ashworth had replaced, Samuel Kenyon.

In the 1872 season Ashworth rode 21 winners, the best tally of any Hednesford jockey for that year. *Ruff's Guide* show his best season was in 1873 when he rode 27 winners with 18 seconds and 19 thirds.

His races ranged throughout the country and also in Ireland where he was particularly successful at the Curragh, mostly for Mr. Lincoln. When Cliff retired from training in 1874 after his accident, Ashworth stayed at the stables under the new trainer and his one-time competitive opponent, Job Toon. Always a favourite jockey of Mr. Lincoln, Ashworth won his last major race, and most prestigious, in 1875 for his patron when he was victorious on Innishowen in the Irish Derby.

After that his rides became less frequent as Job Toon saw fit to ride himself or let members of his family do so.

By 1881 he was back in Prestwich, his home town, living with his widowed mother and two unmarried sisters. In the census of that years he lists himself as 'Jockey (Unemployed)'.

In December 1882 he was involved, with several others, in a betting offence at the Old Nag's Head in Foregate Street, Chester, regarding a donkey race that was to take place at the forthcoming Chester races. Possibly gambling was the reason Ashworth lost his way in the racing world or was it the jockey's other curses, weight and drink?

Whatever had happened to George had been dramatic, ten years later he was living with forty other men in lodgings in London Road, Manchester where he was employed as a groom. It has been reported he had his last ride in public at Chester on 9th May 1893 but to achieve this he would have to have been in possession of a jockey's licence.

He died in Manchester on 21st July 1900 aged 46 leaving just £80 in his will.

Big race winners:

Cambridgeshire Handicap in 1872 on Playfair.

THE JOCKEYS

Liverpool Cup twice on Wynyard in 1871 and on Indian Ocean in 1872.

Shrewsbury Cup in 1872 on Indian Ocean.

Irish Derby in 1875 on Innishowen.

CHARLES FRANK BOYCE
1827 – 1868

Charles was born into a racing family, his father being the jockey Francis Boyce (1804 – 1836). Boyce senior won two Classic races, the first in the year his son was born on Gulnare in the Oaks. His other victory came in 1829 in the 2,000 Guineas on Patron.

For young Charles, growing up in this environment it was inevitable that he to wanted to become a jockey. His parents both died when Charles was only young, but the seed had already been set. After his parents death he was allowed entry to the Bluecoat School and upon leaving was invited to visit the veteran Tom Oliver. Boyce became very keen on hunting and racing and showed such great aptitude as a rider that it wasn't long before he was riding as a steeplechase jockey.

Boyce rode only two winners at Walsall, both in 1850 partnering the same horse, The Streamer on each occasion. Both horse and rider showed their versatility, the first win came in the hurdle race and the second on the flat.

Seven years later Boyce won the Grand National on Emigrant, a horse once owned by the wily old character Ben Land who had several runners at Walsall over the years. Land was horses through and through. He had ridden them in 'chases in his younger days, later trained, owned, dealt and gambled with them. It was the latter instincts that cost him the 'National this year, he lost the horse in a game of cards whilst attending Shrewsbury races. Boyce not only had what it takes to be a jump jockey; he also had quick thinking brain. The weather on 'National day was atrocious, and the start was even worse, at the seventh attempt the twenty-six runners finally got away. As Emigrant came to Valentines, Boyce spotted some firm ground running along side the canal, which was the towpath, giving him quite an advantage. As the runners came onto the racecourse proper for the last time, Emigrant was leading; Boyce eased the horse to give him a breather and then pushed him on again to win by three lengths. In second place was a horse named Weathercock … owned by Ben Land! As if to rub salt into Mr Land's wounds, it only became known after the race that Boyce had ridden with the upper part of his one arm strapped to his side due to an injury sustained in an earlier fall. Because of Boyce's courage, horsemanship and use of the towpath, the grateful owner gave him £1,000. Any jockey intending to use Boyce's ruse in future 'Nationals would be disappointed, the Aintree management instructed that flags would be erected at the extremities of the fences.

Charles Boyce may have been an excellent jockey in his day, but he was no businessman. When he retired he moved to Melton Mowbray to run a hotel, but the ventured failed. On 12th December 1866 he was declared bankrupt at Wigston Magna in Leicestershire and creditors seized all of his furniture and belongings in payment of debts, leaving Boyce and his wife destitute.

He died from congestion of the lungs following a cold at Ball's Pond, London on the 5th January 1868 aged forty. The Sporting Life on Saturday 11th January 1868 said of him:-

'He has left a wife but no family. By marriage he was connected to the Day family (a famous racing family). Charley as he was invariably called, was a good-hearted, honest, sociable fellow and through these qualities made a large number of friends, by whom he will be greatly missed.'

Big race winners:

Grand National in 1857 on Emigrant.
Birmingham Grand Annual in 1853 on Shinrone.
Liverpool Autumn Steeplechase in 1863 on Reporter.

GEORGE CALLOWAY
1803 – 1871

Calloway was born in Stratford-on-Avon on 24th April 1803, and little is known of his early career in the saddle. By the time he married Mary Emery in 1831 at St. Mary's Church, Lichfield, his career as a jockey was already well established and it is thought he was attached to Flintoff's stable at Hednesford.

His first recorded victories were at Worcester in early August 1825 when he rode two winners, one for Mr. Wood and the other for Mr. Steward. He straight away showed his skill in the saddle when Mr. Steward's horse, Man Friday, had its stirrup leather break almost at the start of the second heat. Calloway neatly gathered it in his hand and rode for over three and a half miles to win the race.

Jockeys today travel around the country riding at two meetings a day, in George Calloways day, they worked pretty hard too. An example of Calloways dedication to riding winners is no better illustrated than in the following article taken from the *Sporting Magazine* of 1832 and titled, Smart Work:-

'Calloway, after riding Birdcatcher, which ran second for the Great St. Leger at Doncaster on Tuesday 18th September, set off post haste for Shrewsbury, and rode Clarion, which ran third for the Gold Cup on Wednesday. The moment he dismounted and past muster at the scales, he set off again on his return to Doncaster, where he was engaged to ride on Thursday. The distance from Doncaster to Shrewsbury is 160 miles.'

Although Calloway only rode eleven winners at Walsall between 1830-1840 he is remembered also for being

THE JOCKEYS

the judge at the course, a position he held at other local racecourses also. He was a busy man, as well as the positions mentioned he was also a publican and a racehorse trainer, the latter only being on a small scale. The *Sporting Magazine* of 1835 mentions that he was 'not the most popular jockey.' Quite what this statement means is difficult to understand. Being a publican it is hard to think that it was anything to do with his attitude towards people.

Up until 1840 he was landlord at the Turf Tavern in Bore Street, Lichfield, and then moved a few yards down the same street to take over at the Old Crown Inn where he remained for the next thirty years.

Cecil, one of the correspondents of the *Sporting Magazine*, wrote in 1840 of Calloway's establishment: -

'When journeying to Atherstone, my route being through Lichfield, I took up my quarters for one night at the house kept by Calloway, the jockey, and I must do him the justice to declare that I never was made more comfortable, nor could the essentials necessary in the cavalry department be more assiduously catered for. Independently of the twofold character of landlord and jockey, Calloway has combined that of trainer, having the old Lichfield racecourse to exercise upon, which for a limited number of horses is well adapted for the purpose: he has already got three or four horses at work, and there is no doubt that he will bring them to the post with credit to himself and justice to his employers.'

George Calloway rode many winners throughout the country, but only one Classic race winner came his way. The horse was Touchstone, the 40/1 outsider who won the St. Leger in 1834. The horse was owned and bred by Lord Westminster, and made his debut as a two year-old at Lichfield in a walkover. The same year he came third in the Champagne Stakes, the connections of the horse were impressed by this run, as he was by no means fully trained. On the morning of the St. Leger, Lord Wilton an owner well known at Walsall, was the only one to back Touchstone to beat the 10/11 odds-on favourite, Plenipotentiary. Lord Wilton obviously knew what he was doing, much to the dismay of the other gentlemen of his class, in particular, Lord Westminster, as he left Doncaster an even richer man. The *Sporting Magazine* commented on Touchstone's win with the following, '... *Touchstone won very easily, much to the astonishment of his jockey, who seemed almost petrified at his good fortune.'*

Touchstone ran until he was a six years old and was then retired to stud duty. By 1843, six years after being retired he had already sired the winner of the 1843 St. Leger, Blue Bonnet.

When Calloway won the St. Leger it should have been the catalyst that took his career to another level but sadly, due to circumstances beyond his control, it wasn't.

In August 1835 he sued Mr. Dunn the proprietor of the Swan Hotel in Lichfield for damages and loss of earnings due to a stagecoach crash the previous year. A very lengthy article appeared in the *Staffordshire Advertiser* on 8th August 1835 giving very explicit details of the case at Stafford Assizes.

On 21st September 1834 Calloway took the Quicksilver coach from Lichfield to Walsall, a trip which usually took around an hour. Shortly after the coach had passed Muckley

The winner of the 1834 St. Leger, Touchstone. It is not known if the jockey in the illustration is intended to be Calloway or not.

Corner and entered a dip in the road it began to gather speed. When the horse on the near side veered suddenly to the left the coach fell on its side throwing the luckless jockey out and breaking his leg in the process.

The court case hinged around the fact that Mr. Dunn had been told several times by various drivers and passengers about the behaviour on one of the horses pulling the coach. It was said the near horse was not a match for the off side one and they should not have been paired. Mr. Dunn was having none of it and continued to use the horses as a pair.

Calloway brought many witnesses to court to validate his claim and they all said the horse was not a coach horse and should not have been used as such. Equally Mr. Dunn, the defendant, bought as many witnesses to argue against the animal being to blame for the accident.

One witnesses for Calloway was his brother-in-law, Hednesford trainer Thomas Flintoff. He stated that it was a full nine months after the accident before Calloway could ride any of his horses. The Marquis of Westminster paid Calloway £150 annual retainer plus a fee of 3 guineas for riding each horse, 5 guineas if the horse won and a percentage of the stake money. During the nine months recovery time Flintoff employed William Lear the jockey from Brewood to replace Calloway whom he paid £35.

Calloway argued, and rightly so, the accident had cost him many valuable and influential rides and felt he was due recompense. The other problem associated with an injury of this sort is immobility which caused Calloway to gain around ten pounds above his riding weight of 7st. 9lbs. (47kg). Flintoff told the court of how severe the training would be to lose the weight gained, commenting, '*Training [for jockeys] is very severe exercise; with five or six great coats, and flannel waistcoats and trousers, he must suffer very much.*'

Several witnesses were called to testify they had seen Calloway since the accident and they commented that walking caused him great pain due to the swelling of the

THE JOCKEYS

injured leg which had taken a considerable time for the bone to knit together.

In summing up the judge, Lord Denman, left it to the Jury to decide if it was a case of negligence or not and if Calloway was due compensation. The Jury decided in favour of the jockey and he was awarded damages of £210.

Another famous horse associated with Calloway was Harkaway. The horse was bred in 1834 at Sheepbridge in Ireland by Thomas Ferguson in whose ownership the horse remained throughout his racing career. Harkaway was brought to England after a successful racing career in his home country in 1838. Whilst the horse was in England he was based at one of the Hednesford training stables, for his raids on the English racecourses. Harkaway won the Goodwood Cup in 1838 ridden by Christopher Wakefield. By mid August Calloway had partnered the horse to victory in the Cleveland Cup at Wolverhampton and Her Majesty's Plate at Doncaster in September. The partnership was to continue during 1839 with victories at Chester in the Stand Cup, Cheltenham in the Tradesman's Cup and culminating with a second victory in the Goodwood Cup.

On August 13th Calloway rode the horse in the Cleveland Cup at Wolverhampton again, but, despite it being odds on favourite, it was beaten in a two horse race. The reporter from the *Wolverhampton Chronicle* wrote, '*Kremlin led throughout, and when Calloway called upon his horse, near the stand, it was in vain; he was beat by about a head. It is said Harkaway has not been right since Goodwood.*' In fact the horse was only to appear once again on an English racecourse, at Liverpool in 1840 where he was beaten into third place in the Tradesman's Cup. Ferguson then returned to Ireland where after a few races Harkaway was retired to stud. However, he produced few horses of any real quality.

Whilst continuing to train his own horses he also rode for Flintoff and Saunders in the early 1840s, but with less success and fewer rides. By 1846 *Ruff's Guide* lists him as a freelance jockey still living at Lichfield.

It was sometime during the late 1840s that he retired from riding, his last victories being at Shrewsbury in May, 1847 with The Wizard owned by Mr. Davies who had his horses with Flintoff. By the early 1850s he had almost stopped training. He continued with officiating at various local races until the early 1860s when he retired. He was Starter at Lichfield in 1859 and then Secretary in the 1860 season. Calloway's final association with Walsall Races ended in 1860 when he retired as judge at the course.

He continued as landlord of the Old Crown Inn for many years before moving to a house in Stafford Road, Lichfield where he died from an asthma attack on 9th September 1871.

Classic winner and big race winners:
St. Leger in 1834 on Touchstone.
Knutsford Gold Cup twice on Halston in 1829 and Birmingham in 1831.
Cleveland Cup *(Wolverhampton)* in 1838 on Harkaway.
Her Majesty's Plate *(Doncaster)* in 1838 on Harkaway.
Stand Cup *(Chester)* in 1839 on Harkaway.
Goodwood Cup in 1839 on Harkaway.

THOMAS CHALONER
1839 – 1886

Chaloner was born in Manchester on 2nd June 1839, the son of a baker. He became apprenticed at fourteen to the famous trainer, John Osborne senior at Middleham in North Yorkshire and father of the equally famous jockey John junior. His first ride was on a horse named The Spinner at Warwick in October 1854, owned and trained by his master. Chaloner arrived in Walsall in 1856 with John Osborne senior, and two horses, Miss Tiff and Elastic. The two horses ran twice, once on each day of the meeting and John Osborne left Walsall with three wins from four starts. The aspiring young jockey rode Miss Tiff in both of her races, coming third on the Wednesday afternoon and going two places better twenty-four hours later when the horse won the penultimate race of the meeting over one and a quarter miles. Elastic's partner on both occasions was William Bearpark.

Osborne was not only a good trainer of horses; he knew a thing or two about jockeyship and passed his knowledge on to the young Tom. Throughout his career Chaloner was a modest and unassuming man well-known for his honesty and reliability. In all he rode ten Classic winners, winning the Derby and Oaks once, the St. Leger five times and the 2,000 Guineas on three occasions.

Chaloner married one of the daughters of his governor and they had six sons, four of whom became jockeys, George, Richard, Philip and Harry. He took up training in later life at Newmarket and on his death on 3rd April 1886, another of his sons, Thomas junior, took over the running of his stables. His funeral service was conducted by his brother-in-law, the Rev. George Osborne with many people from the racing world in attendance.

Classic and big race winners:

2,000 Guineas in 1863 on Macaroni, in 1868 on Moslem (a dead heat) and again in 1873 on Gang Forward.
The Derby in 1863 on Macaroni.
The Oaks in 1862 on Feu de Joie.
St. Leger in 1861 on Caller Ou, in 1862 on The Marquis, 1867 on Achievement, 1868 on Formosa and in 1875 on Craig Miller.
Royal Hunt Cup in 1858 on Hesperithusa.
Lincolnshire Handicap in 1861 on Benbow.
Ebor Handicap in 1869 on Fortunio.
Portland Handicap in 1855 on Manganese.
Northumberland Plate in 1856 on Zeta, twice on Caller

THE JOCKEYS

Ou in 1863 and 1864.
Goodwood Cup in 1875 on Aventuriere.
Cesarewitch in 1867 on Julius.
Great Metropolitan Handicap in 1858 on Telegram.
City & Suburban Handicap in 1862 on Sawcutter.
The Middle Park Stakes in 1869 on Frivolity.
Doncaster Cup in 1857 on Vedette, in 1860 on Sabreur, in 1863 on Macaroni and in 1876 on Craig Millar.

ROBERT DENMAN
1812 – 1896

Robert Denman was born in Farnsfield, Nottinghamshire on 17th November 1812 and arrived in Hednesford some time around 1835. Over a sixteen-year period he rode only four winners at Walsall and appears, from census records, to have been associated with several of the better known stables in the Hednesford area at one time or another. In 1841 he was living at the Cross Keys Inn and was most probably with Thomas Walters's stable at first. The 1846 *Ruff's Guide* has him at Wadlow's stable at Stanton in Shropshire, but that was not to last and shortly afterwards he was back in Hednesford.

Like Charles Marlow he married, Charlotte, one of the daughters of Thomas Saunders and had at least three children – Robert born in 1855, Fanny in 1861 and Charlotte in 1862. Robert, junior, was to become a leading trainer in France during the early part of the twentieth century.

Never one of the leading jockeys in the area he nevertheless continued to ride well into the 1860s though mostly preferring to ride at minor Midland meetings. The 1857 *Ruff's Guide* listed him as a freelance jockey living in Hednesford and by the 1861 Census he was listed as *'jockey, trainer and publican'*, but which public house he ran is difficult to say, unless it was the Castle Inn in Littleworth Road. Which ever premises it was proved to be his financial downfall as in late 1861 he was declared bankrupt. *Perry's Bankrupt Gazette* of Saturday 21st December 1861 reported:-

'Robert Denman, beer-house keeper and trainer of racehorses, formerly of Hednesford, now Church-bridge, Cannock.'

The horses he did train were possibly stabled at Littleworth Stables which were run by Thomas Eskrett. Several of them ran at Walsall and Wolverhampton, but were not very successful.

By 1871 he had moved to Anglesey Terrace (now Anglesey Street) and was still listed as a jockey/trainer though he had finished both careers. In the 1881 Census he had once again moved home and was lodging with his brother-in-law,

William Saunders, at Hazel Slade Stables and listed as an ex-trainer. It would seem from his career that he spent nearly all of his life around horses barely making a living, but the love of the sport forced him to continue. Racing was certainly in his blood. He died on 26th April 1896 at Chantilly, France aged eighty three.

While Robert senior was not a very successful trainer his son, Robert junior (1856-1929), right, who was born in Hednesford, most certainly was. He trained at Chantilly in France and between 1883 and 1926 he trained the winner of the Poule d'Essai des Poulains (the French 2,000 Guineas) no less than eleven times, a record which still stands today. In 1924 he trained the French horse, Sir Galahad the Third, to win the Lincolnshire Handicap; the horse had won the Poule d'Essai des Poulains the year before. Robert junior remained in France until his death at Maison Lafitte, France in 1929.

Photograph of Robert Denman junior above reproduced by courtesy of Patrick Breen, France.

JOHN DODGSON
1803 – 1875

John Dodgson was born in Tadcaster, Yorkshire around 1803 and began his racing career as a jockey in the North some time in the early 1820s. First records showed him riding at York in 1825 for Mr. Smith. He probably first came to the Midlands in the 1831 season where he first met and rode for John Beardsworth at Lichfield. Presumably he returned North for a few years, but by 1835 he was again in the Midlands. It is not known exactly where he lived in the area, but it is most likely that he was in Hednesford as nearly all of his rides were for the Flintoff stable from 1836 to 1840. He was especially successful later on John Fowler's horses which were trained by Flintoff. During the same period he also rode for Thomas Carr and Thomas Walters. It was around this time he rode three winners at Walsall.

He arrived as a married man, but unfortunately his wife Betsy, died very young aged just 32 and was recorded as having died on January 15th, 1840 and she was buried at St. Luke's, Cannock. Curiously the 1841 Census did not have him registered as living in Hednesford, but on the Land Title Map produced around 1838 he had a cottage on Hill Top, Hednesford (possibly today's Carmel Cottage). It is quite possible that he was away at a race meeting on the Census day and his empty cottage was presumed unoccupied. The land surrounding that cottage belonged to Thomas Flintoff and John probably rented his home from him.

Ruff's Guide of 1846 recorded him as a freelance jockey living in nearby Rugeley, but by 1851 he was once again back in Hednesford living in Splash Lane with David Miles and his family. In the 1861 Census he had moved back to his native

THE JOCKEYS

Yorkshire living as a groom at the home of Charles Danson a local doctor in Pocklington. Ten years later he was in lodgings in Union Street, Pocklington and is listed as a retired jockey. After retiring he vowed never to get on a horse again and apparently kept his word up to the day he died.

Although never a prolific winner of races he still managed to earn a living at his trade and was a competent jockey. However, most of his winners came from the Midland race courses and many of those winners were in minor races. Like many of his successors he eventually moved into steeplechase riding having some of his final victories for Thomas Eskrett at the Sutton Park course.

He died in Pocklington in 1875 aged 72.

GEORGE FORDHAM
1837 – 1887

It is a matter of opinion as to which was the best horse ever seen at Walsall, some would say Independence, others Blue Mantle, or maybe King Cole. When the same question is asked about jockeys, there is no dispute, it has to be George Fordham, even if it was only a fleeting glimpse of the great jockey.

Fordham visited Walsall only once, in 1855, the year he first became champion jockey at the age of eighteen. His only ride on the course was a winning one, aboard Mr Leech's colt, Cockspur in the Saddler's Stakes. Cockspur ran twice the following day, winning one of the races, but by this time Fordham was long gone, the substitute jockey on that occasion was Christopher Prior.

He was born at Cambridge on 24th September 1837 the son of a grocer. Surprisingly he became apprenticed to Richard Drewitt's stable at Mickleham Downs in Surrey at the age of ten. Surrey seems an unusual choice considering Newmarket was only twelve miles away from his home.

His first winner came at the age of fourteen at Brighton in 1851 and the same course saw him ride his final winner in 1883. He first came into the public eye in 1853 when he won the Cambridgeshire Handicap on Little David, who it is said carried the young jockey all the way into Newmarket town before it pulled up! In between those years he rode 2,587 winners and was champion jockey fourteen times, including nine successive championships between 1855 and 1863. Fordham won sixteen Classic races, winning the Oaks five times, the 2,000 Guineas three times and the 1,000 Guineas seven times. Rather surprisingly, he never won the St. Leger and won the Derby only once, on one of the worst horses he ever rode in the race, Sir Bevys in 1879.

To show his versatility, he rode a horse called Nelly in a two mile steeplechase at Warwick on November 21st 1867, beating his only rival, Wasp, ridden by Tom Cannon. Fordham was given a great ovation on his return to the winners enclosure.

His great rival in later years was the legendary Fred Archer; even today it is discussed as to whom was the better of the two of them. A great many fellow jockeys and trainers of that time had little hesitation in awarding the laurels to Fordham. Both men had the ability to win races on horses that would have had difficulty pulling a cart around, but it was said Archer was much more severe on his mounts than Fordham. It is a fact that Archer always had a great deal of difficulty beating Fordham in a tight finish. Fordham was known on the racecourse as 'The Demon' or 'The Kidder', and with good cause. Many times he won races by allowing the other jockeys to think his horse was a spent force, only to see the 'spent force' come with a fearful burst of speed at the finish.

One famous incident between the two great men came in a match at Newmarket at the end of Fordhams career on 10th May 1883. Archer was riding a horse called Reputation for the Duke of Portland, Fordham was on a horse called Brag. Earlier in the same week, Archer had already lost a match to Fordham and was determined to settle this one in his favour. As Reputation and Archer went out onto the course someone called out, *'Mind the old man [Fordham] don't do you again.'* Archer replied, *'I'll be half way home this before the old gentleman knows where he is.'* This quip of Archers was reported to Fordham who there and then decided to show the young man again why he was called 'The Kidder.' When the race was run, it was Fordham who took the contest by a neck from Reputation. Archer was not impressed, he stormed into the weighing room, threw his saddle at the valet and shouted, *'I can't beat that kidding bastard!'*

Archer himself had a grudging respect for the 'old man,' even having a photograph of him flanking his fireplace. The great trainer, Mat Dawson, Archer's boss and partner said of Fordham: *'Undoubtedly, George Fordham was the best of the jockeys that have come within my knowledge.'*

Fordham was an unsophisticated, rough and ready character, but one who was utterly dependable, honest and loyal. He didn't enjoy the high life that surround racing, much preferring to occupy himself playing whist with friends, a game he played as well as he rode horses. During the winter he enjoyed hunting and shooting, being an excellent shot. Outside of racing he rarely talked about the sport, and refused to let his son have anything to do with it. Fordham's one major failing, like many jockeys, was drink. By 1875 he was drinking considerably and decided to retire to his home at Slough. Three years later, due to some poor foreign investments, Fordham was back in the saddle. Cajoled into a comeback by the owner, Sir George Chetwynd, he began riding again, at ten pounds lighter than when he retired. At the age of forty, he could still do 7st 5lbs. Fordhams 'second coming' saw him add a further 482 winners to the list, including five more Classic victories.

THE JOCKEYS

In 1883 he decided to call it a day once more. His final race was at Brighton, the course where it all began, on 31st October. His mount was his old favourite, Brag. Once again Brag came through to win, this time by five lengths, in second place was the odds-on favourite, Geheimniss, ridden by his arch rival, Fred Archer. Game set and match George Fordham.

Two weeks after his fiftieth birthday, Fordham died at his home in Slough on the 12th October 1887.

Classic winners:-

The Derby in 1879 on Sir Bevys.

The Oaks five times on Summerside in 1859, Formosa in 1868, Gamos in 1870, Reine in 1872 and The Bais in 1881.

2,000 Guineas three times on Vauban in 1867, Formosa in 1868 (a dead heat) and Petronel in 1880.

1,000 Guineas seven times on Mayonaise in 1859, Nemesis in 1861, Siberia in 1865, Formosa in 1868, Scottish Queen in 1869, The Bais in 1881 and Hauteur in 1883.

Other big winners include:

Ascot Gold Cup five times on Lecturer in 1867, Mortemer in 1871, Henry in 1872, Doncaster in 1875 and Tristan in 1883.

Royal Hunt Cup three times on Chalice in 1855, See Saw in 1869 and Winslow in 1873.

Cambridgeshire four times on Little David in 1853, Odd Trick in 1857, See Saw in 1868 and Sabinus in 1871.

Ebor Handicap twice on The Grand Inquisitor in 1854 and Rising Sun in 1861.

Stewards Cup three times on Tournament in 1857, Lady Clifden in 1862 and Elf King in 1880).

Lincolnshire Handicap twice on Saucebox in 1855 and Vigo in 1860.

Chester Cup twice on Epaminondas in 1854 and Knight of the Garter in 1869.

Cesarewitch in 1857 on Pryoress (after a run-off).

Sussex Stakes in 1882 on Comte Alfred.

Portland Handicap in 1863 on Welland.

Goodwood Cup five times on Baroncino in 1855, Rogerthorpe in 1856, Starke in 1861, The Duke in 1866 and on Border Minstrel in 1883.

JAMES GRADWELL
1851 – 1909

James Gradwell was born in Manchester in 1851 and by the time he was fifteen he was at the stables in Hill Street run by George Palmer. His first ride was at Radcliffe in July 1866 where he rode Mr. Barber's Helen. He was the first of Palmer's jockeys to make the long trip north to the Scottish races and in September 1866 he won two races at Ayr on Helen (his first recorded victories). During the 1867 season he continued to ride for Palmer's patrons, including Messrs. Barber, Rickard and Weaver. The beginning of the 1868 season saw him riding two of Barber's better horses, Alicia and The Clown, winning at Warwick and Chester respectively. Both horses were bought by Sir. F. Johnstone and Gradwell won the Cumberland Plate on The Clown at Carlisle in July, 1868. It was during that season that Gradwell began to ride for many other owners while still remaining with Palmer as one of his stable jockeys.

His best season followed in 1869 when he won the Ascot Stakes in July on Mr. Jacques's Bete Noire and followed that up by winning the Cambridgeshire in the October on Mr. Hodgman's Vestminster. It was this same year that he rode his only winner at Walsall, partnering Mr. Dobson's King's Daughter to victory in the Bradford Handicap Plate at odds of 10/1. Gradwell was still at the Palmer stables at the time, though by then had many other patrons not associated with the Palmer stables. He was still at the stables during the 1871 Census.

In 1869 he had made his first visit to France to race in Paris along with Kenyon and Neale and, unlike those two, seemed to ride a lot more over there than in England. In 1873 he won the Prix de Commerce at Beauvais on Houvari. During the same season he also rode winners at Paris, Abbeville and Caen. He was still riding in France during the 1880s, but in the 1890s he had horses of his own which raced throughout England. It is thought he died in his native Lancashire in 1909.

Big race winners:-

Cambridgshire Handicap on Vestminster in 1869.

Ascot Stakes on Bete Noire.

Northumberland Plate on Taraban in 1871.

(MR) FREDERICK GEORGE HOBSON
1842 – 1899

Frederick Hobson, known in racing circles as 'The Squire', rode several times at Walsall but only registered two winners. Hobson rode on the flat and over jumps and became champion amateur in 1867, one of his thirty-six winners was gained at Walsall when he rode Quirina to victory.

In 1877 he won the Grand National on his own horse Austerlitz. Many people advised him not to ride in the great race, but his lifelong friend, the trainer Arthur Yates, thought otherwise and persuaded him to take the mount. One reason for the lack of confidence in his ability was Hobson's habit of holding onto the cantle of the saddle when taking a fence, this gave him the appearance of being a rather nervous rider.

THE JOCKEYS

The whole of Aintree was aghast at Hobson's unorthodox style as he set off at the front of the pack in what was to be his one and only National ride. It turned out to be a winning one, after four and half miles he was still there, coming home by four lengths.

Off the racecourse he was capable of making headlines too. Victorian society was as aghast as the Aintree crowd when 'The Squire's' wife of ten years divorced him and married his old friend Arthur Yates.

JOSEPH KENDALL
1836 – 1892

Joseph Kendall was born in York in 1836, the son of Charles Kendall, a carter. Kendall became a well-known rider under both codes of racing but his one and only winner at Walsall was on the flat on a horse trained by the Hednesford trainer, William Saunders in 1857. Like many aspiring jockeys of this era, he became an apprentice at a very early age, although the exact details of early life are unknown.

Kendall's first big race win came in 1851 at the age of fifteen, when he won the Chester Cup on a horse called Nancy. It is reputed that he was given a large 'present' as a reward for this victory. A year later he won the City and Suburban Handicap at Epsom on Butterfly and in 1858 he rode Ventre St. Gris to victory in the French Derby at Chantilly.

Ruff's Guide 1857 listed him as living in Hednesford and jockey for Henry Lister who had moved to Hednesford from Yorkshire and was living at Hednesford Lodge. He also still rode horses for William Saunders during that time. Kendall was probably staying at the Cross Keys Inn where in the 1861 Census he was listed as a lodger. In 1861 he showed his riding versatility by winning the Grand National on Jealousy, the same horse that he won the Doncaster Grand National on in 1859. To cap a momentous year he married Elizabeth Wilkins, the daughter of the Cross Keys landlord on December 18th. Several historians have made the mistake of stating that Jealousy was trained at the Cross Keys in Hednesford by John Wilkins. This is incorrect, Jealousy was trained in the south of England by John Balchin.

In 1863 he tangled with the Jockey Club over his riding of a horse named Brilliant at Chester on 8th May, in consequence was 'warned off' as a jockey for six-years. It was during this time that Kendall became a trainer. St. Luke's Baptism Register had him signing himself as a trainer on August 15th, 1864 when his son, John, was born. In 1869 his jockey's license was restored and he won on his first ride back at Croydon with a horse named Balder, owned by Mr. Case. By that time he had moved from Hednesford and was living in Staines with his wife and one son, Charles, aged two. Besides riding over hurdles and steeplechase he also rode on the flat down South, namely for Mr. Burnham, but his career as a jockey was soon to end. Already carrying a permanent leg injury sustained in a fall early in his career, Kendall went blind in one eye in the spring of 1871, later in the summer of the same year, he lost the sight of the other eye. As his career was now effectively over, a fund was set up for him and his family which allowed them a pound a week for life.

It has also been stated that Kendall had the dubious distinction of being 'warned off' not only as a jockey, but also as a trainer due to the running of a horse at Walsall Races. Efforts to determine which horse and race this was have proved inconclusive. The only horse and rider, no trainer is mentioned, that were reported to the Stewards occurred in 1874 about the running of a horse named Over, owned and ridden by a Mr Ameys. The local Stewards not being happy with the explanation given by Ameys referred the matter to the Grand National Hunt Committee. It seems unlikely that this is the incident that saw Kendall 'warned off' for a second time, as he had been totally blind for three years.

Joseph Kendall lived for nineteen years on his pound a week pension and died in the city of his birth, York, on 21st March 1892.

Big race winners:-

Grand National on Jealousy in 1861.

Doncaster Grand National on Jealousy in 1859.

Chester Cup on Nancy in 1851.

City & Suburban Handicap on Butterfly in 1852.

French Derby on Ventre St. Gris in 1858.

SAMUEL KENYON
1849 – 1872

Samuel Kenyon only rode three winners at Walsall, but would have undoubtedly ridden more had it not been for his death at the age of twenty-three.

He was born in Manchester in 1849, the son of a tailor and became apprenticed to Thomas Cliff, the Hednesford trainer at the age of eleven. Cliff must have thought highly of the young lad as he gave him his first ride in public when only a few months into his apprenticeship. The ride was on a horse called Jeannette on which he finished second at The Curragh in Ireland. The weight Kenyon carried in this race was 3 stone 5 pounds. His first winner came in August 1862 at Ludlow on a horse called Acre; this was only his second ride, so Cliff's confidence in the lad was fully justified.

Over the next three years Cliff used his young apprentice jockey to great effect throughout the Midlands and nationally. By 1866 Samuel had become a firm favourite with Lord Westmoreland winning races for him all over the country and his patronage of the young jockey continued for some years. It is not clear whether Thomas Cliff trained any of Westmoreland's horses during that period. Also in 1866 Mr. Chaplin became a patron and in 1867 the Duke of Newcastle and Lord Wilton.

Kenyon's greatest triumphs were to happen during 1866, when he became Champion Jockey riding 123 winners in the season aged seventeen, and he still had a year to go before finishing his apprenticeship. He is Hednesford's only Champion Jockey who was still living there at the time of his achievement. Despite riding over a hundred winners in 1867 and 1868 he never again won the championship. During 1867 he also found time to travel to France to ride at Amiens and Paris, the first of the local jockeys to venture abroad.

THE JOCKEYS

He rarely rode in any of the five Classics during his four years of prowess, 1866-69, securing only four rides out of a possible twenty during those years. Of the four rides that he did secure his best effort was second on Mr. Merry's Belladrum in the 1869 2000 Guineas. In 1868 he had ridden the Duke of Newcastle's Speculum in the Derby and finished third to Sir J. Hawley's Blue Gown ridden by John Wells. In fact the same two horses met again in the Ascot Gold Cup in the June with Kenyon and Speculum being beaten once again, Cameron that time riding Blue Gown.

From 1868 until 1870 he continued to ride for the Cliff stables mainly riding for Cliff himself, Mr. Lincoln and Mr. Lawrence, who both had horses at the Hednesford stables. In 1871 he showed his versatility as a jockey when he rode Mr. Lawrence's horse, Young Rose, to victory in a hurdle race at Walsall on October 3rd. His final ride came fittingly at The Curragh in the Madrid Handicap. All the jockeys were suspended after the race for a month due to misconduct at the start. It was during that enforced layoff that Kenyon died at Southport on July 13th, 1872.

Samuel was well liked by both owners and trainers for his honesty and was considered totally trustworthy by everyone who had dealings with him; qualities which were in short supply with a lot of his contemporaries. Because of those qualities Samuel became a very rich young man and managed to leave over £3,000 in his will. Having never married that money went to his parents.

Big race winners:-
Liverpool Autumn Cup on Beeswing in 1866.
City & Suburban Handicap on Delight in 1866.
Goodwood Stakes on Rama in 1866.
Manchester Cup on Retrousse in 1866.
Doncaster Cup on Rama 1866 and Achievement in 1867.
Stewards Cup on Tibthorpe in 1867.
Goodwood Cup in 1868 on Speculum in 1868.
Middle Park Stakes on Green Sleeve in 1867.
Ascot Stakes on Emigration in 1868.

CHARLES MARLOW
1814 – 1882

Charles Marlow was born in 1814 at Thorney Lanes in Staffordshire, the son of Richard Marlow, a groom, which meant that his childhood was surrounded by horses. By the late 1820s he had decided to become a jockey and he probably arrived in the Hednesford area, joining the Hazel Slade stables run by Thomas Carr, junior. His first public ride was in 1828 at Newmarket and his first winner was thought to be at Cheltenham in the Sherbourne Stakes on July 20th, 1831 on Gab, a horse owned by Yates. The records showed 'a lad' as the jockey. His first definite winner was at Walsall on September 29th, 1831 on Lord Warwick's Water Witch, trained by Carr.

For the next few years he rode winners for the Carr stable and for Yates and by the mid 1830s he was also riding for Thomas Walters with Alderman Copeland's horses. It was Copeland's horse, King Cole, which gave Marlow his first major victory winning the Chester Cup in 1838. During that time he also began riding for the Saunders's family, a new partnership which was to prove a happy one because on December 28th, 1844 Marlow married Mary Anne Saunders, daughter of Thomas. The newlyweds moved into Marlow's cottage in Hazel Slade, near the site of today's Hazel Slade Inn which he rented from Thomas Carr. A few months later on 13th July 1845, Marlow's sister Ann married Alderman Copeland's trainer William Shepherd at Rugeley.

Such was his growing reputation as a sound jockey that during the 1842 season he began riding for other patrons beginning with Mr. Mostyn. In 1862 The Druid, author of the book, *Silk and Scarlet* wrote,

'Marlow was a very nice, but not perhaps a brilliant horseman, with good hands, very patient and most resolute mode of riding them out. 'A race is never won till you're past the post' was his invariable motto; and hence he always persevered while there was an ounce of squeezing powder left. Few but him could have brought home the Knight of Avenel in the Port Stakes, or landed Elthiron and Phlegethon at Ascot. Still, his style, like his seat, was not firm and close; and his set-to was so high, that he often seemed to have the horse's head as well as his own in his hands.'

In 1844 he won the Royal Hunt Cup at Ascot on Mr. Bulkeley's Bishop Romford's Cob, but it was the next year which began probably the best period in his racing career because his new patron was Lord Eglinton whose trainer was Fobert in Yorkshire. In 1845 he won the Goodwood Cup on Eglinton's Van Tromp and 1848 began his partnership with The Flying Dutchman when he won at Liverpool on July 12th. By July the pair had won the July Stakes at Newmarket and followed that up with the Champagne Stakes at Doncaster in the September.

In 1849 Marlow won his first Classic when he partnered The Flying Dutchman to victory in the Derby and the pair followed that up with victory in the St. Leger. Marlow became the first jockey to win both Classics on the same horse. An article in the *New Sporting Magazine 1850* by Turfina has it that Marlow possibly did not win the Derby, but that it was more than likely won by his friend, Walsall's own George Whitehouse, another of the Hednesford jockeys. In his article Turfina wrote:-

'Many still assert that The Dutchman never won the Derby at all, and ground their assertion on the fact that Nat, who was only half a length behind, felt so sure that Whitehouse (who did not know his own number on the telegraph) had won, that

he rode up to him and congratulated him; and there is a story that Marlow, when appealed to by them jointly for his opinion, said, with a melancholy air – "I really don't know, but I think it's a dead heat.'

However, there is another story attached to this that reads slightly differently, particularly the last sentence. In the book *Portraits of Celebrated Racehorses of Past & Present Centuries, Vol. IV*, the author, Thomas Henry Taunton M.A. wrote:-

'……*The Dutchman seemed altogether muddled and confused in the deep holding ground, and perfectly inactive in comparison with his two year old movement. Hotspur,* [ridden by George Whitehouse] *on the contrary, went over the dirt like a swallow, and showed no signs of coming back till within three strides of home, when Marlow, who had a length to make up, struck The Dutchman twice (the only time he ever touched him), and the last stride gave him the short neck victory. Whitehouse always maintained that he had won; and the only response Marlow ever made to this bold assertion was, "You won at the wrong place, George; you didn't win at Judge Clarke."'*

The *New Sporting Magazine 1850* also reported on a race regarded as one to discover the best horse in the world at that time. The correspondent wrote, "And now cometh a real event of the occasion – a race to decide the sporting question. "Which is the best horse in the world?" Five were found to dispute it, subject, "A Piece of Plate, value 500 sovereigns, the gift of His Majesty the Emperor of All the Russias." The Champions were The Flying Dutchman, Jericho, Canezon, Little Jack and Peep-o-day Boy.

They went off, the Irish horse making all the running. Presently the mare took it up, but when the fullness of time was come Marlow, letting out the reef, shot past the fleet and won in a canter, by eight lengths. I have little doubt that, on the day, and with the field in its then form, he could have distanced the lot."

However, it was another contest which would capture the sporting nation's imagination. A year after winning the Derby The Flying Dutchman came up against Voltigeur, the 1850 winner of the Derby and St. Leger, in the Doncaster Cup. Both horses were unbeaten when they met. Voltigeur was ridden by Elnathan (Nat) Flatman, an excellent jockey and probably the best match rider of his day. The Flying Dutchman, conceding nineteen pounds to the younger horse, was once again ridden by Marlow and was hot favourite at 1 to 4 on.

When the two runners came on to the racecourse it was apparent to those around that The Flying Dutchman had another handicap – Marlow appeared to be quite drunk. When the race began Marlow shouted across to Flatman, *"I'll show you what I have under me today!"* and with that he set off at a lung-bursting pace totally disobeying his racing orders. He had been instructed to ride a waiting game, but instead went off like a man possessed. The gallant horse hung on to the lead for as long as he could, but fast running out of energy he was beaten by half a length at the post. Fortunately for Marlow Lord Eglinton forgave his jockey and was seen to be consoling a tearful and much distraught Marlow after the race.

The racing world felt duped and demanded a rematch. That took place on Tuesday May 13th, 1851 on the Knavesmire at York for £1,000 a side. That time The Flying Dutchman was only conceding eight and a half pounds to Voltigeur and Charles Marlow was stone cold sober. At the start it was Flatman who uncharacteristically made the running and as the pair went round the course The Flying Dutchman shadowed Voltigeur. Nearing the line Marlow made his move and timed it perfectly, winning by a length. The crowd cheered wildly – Marlow had made up for his earlier mistake.

Those contests became so engraved in racing history and public discussion, particularly the second match, that at least two paintings of the contest were commissioned.

Besides his great partnership with The Flying Dutchman Marlow also won the Ascot Gold Cup on Eglinton's Van Tromp in 1849. In 1850 *Ruff's Guide* registers him as riding for Lord Eglinton first claim, Alderman Copeland second claim and the Wadlow stables in Shropshire, third claim, but he also rode the occasional race for Lord Exeter. It was on Lord Exeter's horse, Nutcracker, that he won the St. James's Palace Stakes at Ascot in 1850 and the Nassau Stakes at Goodwood on Nutmeg. The same year he won the Ascot Gold Cup with The Flying Dutchman and the Ayr Gold Cup on Eglinton's Elthiron. For the Wadlow stables he won the Gimcrack Stakes at York on Lord Caledon's Aaron Smith. For Marlow 1850 was to be his heyday, but other major victories were to follow.

In 1851 he won the King Edward VII Stakes on Lord Exeter's Phelgethon and in the same year won the Ayr Gold Cup for a second time on Lord Eglinton's Elthiron. During 1852 he continued to ride for Eglinton and local stables at Hednesford, adding Mr. Merry to his list of patrons. Incidentally, his first connection with Mr. Merry was in 1848 with the horse, Chanticleer, at Goodwood, the same horse that Metcalf had walked from Yorkshire. William Day in his book *Reminiscences of the Turf* said that Bumby should have ridden the horse, but the ride was given to Marlow on the morning of the race and it won. With Bumby on board it had not been favourite and Fred Swindell, Merry's agent, had persuaded the owner to change jockeys.

1853 was to be his last year for any major successes and he won his third Classic race, The Oaks, on Mr. Wanchope's Catherine Hayes. In the June he won the Coronation Stakes at Ascot with the same horse which had been purchased by Lord J. Scott. During that year he also partnered Mr. Megson's horse, Weathergage, to victory in the Audley End Stakes at Newmarket and was successful in other races.

His career was to come to a sudden and violent end in 1855 during the running of The Oaks. He had been engaged by his brother-in-law, William Saunders, to ride the filly Nettle owned by Dr. William Palmer, the "Rugeley Poisoner". Almost at the start of the race Nettle bolted and swerved, going headlong into the chains, he then fell and threw Marlow. Unfortunately he broke his thigh badly and he was carried from the course. Amid groans of pain he was supposedly overheard to have said, *"It serves me damn well right. What business had I to ride a poisoner's horse."* Like many other tales told after Palmer's trial its truthfulness probably lies in the realms of fantasy!

What wasn't a fantasy however was Charlie's popularity. Always well liked by his fellow jockeys, trainers and owners

THE JOCKEYS

for his honesty and integrity a collection was made on his behalf by them and deposited at Tattersalls. In less than a week over £400 had been donated into the fund. The sum would equivalent to around £30,000 today!

It was that injury which shortened Marlow's racing career, but he was still riding for local owners, particularly Alderman Copeland who described him as one of his favourite jockeys. In 1857 he was only riding for Copeland and still living at Hazel Slade. However, by the early 1860s he had moved south and had become head lad at Tom Olliver's stable and had the occasional ride for Mr. Parr in 1863. Obviously struggling with his disability things deteriorated during the 1870s and by 1881 he was living in the Highworth and Swindon Workhouse. The entry for him stated,

"Charles Marlow, widower aged 66. Pauper, inmate, jockey. 1849 winner of the Derby with The Flying Dutchman."

Just over a year after that entry Marlow died, neglected and forgotten in the Wiltshire County Asylum at Devizes on October 23rd, 1882 aged sixty eight.

Why did he not return to Hednesford where he at least had family? His two sons, Charles and Henry, were still at Hazel Slade and working for William Saunders as jockeys/stable lads. They had followed their father into the business, but never had the same skills. Their appearances on the racecourse were few and far between.

Classic winners:-

The Derby and **St Leger** in 1849 on The Flying Dutchman.

The Oaks in 1853 on Catherine Hayes.

Other big race winners:

Ascot Gold Cup twice on Van Tromp in 1849 and The Flying Dutchman in 1850.

Chester Cup on King Cole in 1838.

Royal Hunt Cup on Bishop Romford's Cob in 1844

Ayr Gold Cup on Elthiron in 1851.

Champagne Stakes on The Flying Dutchman in 1848.

Goodwood Cup on Van Tromp in 1848.

City & Suburban Handicap on Elthiron in 1851.

Gimcrack Stakes on Aaron Smith in 1850.

THOMAS SKELTON
1856 – 1900

Thomas Skelton was born in Lichfield on 21st November 1856 into a family of horse breakers. Growing up in an environment such as this, it was no surprise to find that he became an apprentice jockey with the trainer Thomas Stevens and during his time there he became the leading apprentice in the country. On his first ride in public he came third on Congratulations at Bromley on 2nd October 1868. His first winner came as a twelve year-old riding a horse called Cameroon at St. Albans on 17th May 1869.

His early career as a jockey concentrated on riding on the flat only, but in later years he switched to National Hunt racing, probably due to weight problems. Skelton rode his first winner at Walsall in 1871 aboard Magdala, his second and third wins at the course followed the same afternoon. In the five years that Skelton rode at the course he recorded a treble on four occasions.

It was when he turned to jumping that he was most successful in terms of big races wins. In 1886 he partnered Old Joe to victory in the Grand National, the owner of the horse, A. J. Douglas was so delighted with the victory he gave Skelton the race prize money of £1,380, and the trainer, George Mulcaster £1,000. It must be assumed from the owner's generosity that he made a tidy packet from the ring, at even longer odds than the horse's starting price of 25/1. In 1887, Skelton and Savoyard failed by six lengths to win their second Grand National, being beaten by the gallant Gamecock, ridden by William Daniels who was born in Cradley Heath. The same year Skelton won the Grand Sefton Chase and the Lancashire Chase on Savoyard. In 1888 he won the Sandown Grand Prize on Astrakhan, his final big race win came in the following year in the Prince of Wales Chase riding Scottish Minstrel.

In 1890 he lost his left eye in a shooting accident and was forced to retire from the saddle. After retiring he became landlord at the Black Horse in Kidderminster for awhile before moving back close to his birthplace. Tragedy hit the family again in 1895 when his young daughter drowned in the garden pond at his home in Hednesford.

After a short but successful career in which he rode 177 winners on the flat and 83 under National Hunt Rules, he died at Mildenhall in Suffolk, six days after his forty-fourth birthday on 27th November 1900.

Big race winners:-

Grand National on Old Joe in 1886.

Grand Sefton Chase on Savoyard in 1887.

Lancashire Chase on Savoyard in 1887.

Prince of Wales Chase on Scottish Minstrel in 1889.

Sandown Grand Prize on Astrakhan in 1888.

JOHN SPRING
1802 – 1837

John Spring was born in Ireland in 1802 and came over to England at a very young age to work as a stable lad. When exactly he began racing is not known, but his first recorded appearance was at Walsall Races on September 24th, 1817 when he rode Mr. E. J. Littleton's bay filly Miss Hembery in a sweepstakes race, finishing last. He eventually rode a total of seven winners at Walsall.

During the early 1820s he began his association with Mr. Yates and Edmund Peel riding a considerable number of winners for the former. He also rode for John Massey of the Cross Keys, especially the horse, Ynysymaegwyn. It was during the match race between Orator and Don Carlos at Epsom in 1825 that Nimrod gave his impression of Spring's riding ability. He said, "The first race was a match between Orator and Carlos, the old horse being ridden by the Irish jockey, John Spring, whom I saw make his debut at Chester.

THE JOCKEYS

He is esteemed a fair rider in the country, but I did not think him brilliant on Orator. He kept looking behind him, for which there could be no necessity: and if he had it in him, he ought to have made more running for the young one; of when it came to the spurt of speed, old Cliff, who rode to admiration, had no trouble to win."

It was rare for Spring to venture South to ride and perhaps the occasion just got the better of him. Desperate probably to not fail for his patrons, Yates and Peel, he was obviously nervous. It was probably that incident which decided Spring to keep to the Midland and Chester circuits where he was very successful during the 1820s and early 1830s. At some Midland meetings he almost dominated the proceedings. At the Stafford Races of October 6th/7th, 1823 he won all 4 major races bringing the following comments in the *Wolverhampton Chronicle,* "A fine race won cleverly, an excellent race and a capital race" due to Spring's riding skill. In 1827 he won seven of the races at Shrewsbury, six of the races at Burton-Upon-Trent and four at Newcastle under Lyme. Of those victories twelve were for Mr. Yates while five were for another of his patrons, Sir T. Stanley.

When Edmund Peel had moved his stable to Hednesford Lodge Spring became his stable jockey and their association was to prove very successful, culminating in 1836 with Spring's victory in the Chester Cup riding Tanworth. That was to be his only major success because unfortunately his racing career was abruptly brought to an end in the same year when he was seriously injured in an accident while driving back to his home in Cannock from Rugeley Races. He never recovered from that injury and died the following year. He was buried at St. Luke's in Cannock on April 19th, 1837.

While obviously not one of the leading jockeys of his day, as far as we can discover he did manage to win over 240 races during his career and probably many more that went unrecorded. Had his career not been brought to such an abrupt end he would no doubt have had many more successes.

NEPTUNE HENRY STAGG
1824 – 1877

Neptune Stagg was baptised at Bingham in Nottinghamshire on 4th July 1824, the son of George and Henrietta.

At a young age, Nep or Ned as he became known, was an apprentice jockey to Thomas Saunders's stable at Hednesford but living at the Cottage Stables just above the Cross Keys. Although riding regularly for Hednesford trainers for much of his career, and riding regularly at Walsall, he only rode the just the two winners there.

An engraving of Cruiskeen, winner of the first Cesarewitch with what looks like a small child riding him!

On 16th October 1839 at the age of fifteen he rode the inaugural winner of the Cesarewitch Handicap on the Irish trained Cruiskeen, a horse that landed a big gamble for the owner Lord Milltown. The race is still run for today and its reputation for landing large gambles is as prevalent today as it was in Stagg's day. Two years later, riding Cruiskeen again, he landed the Chester Cup at the May meeting. His other major success was in a race 'over-the-sticks,' when he won the Manchester Grand Steeplechase in 1849 on Fanny Grey, shown in the engraving in the oval. As well as riding regularly on the flat, he also rode in steeplechases and hurdle races. He is one of the few jockeys to have ridden in the Derby at Epsom and the Grand National at Aintree, unfortunately not having any success in either race.

Twice in March and July 1847 Stagg sued Lord Milltown for *'wages and travelling expenses as his lordship's training groom'*. These wages and expenses actually went back to the early 1840s when Stagg was still an apprentice with Saunders. Stagg stated to the court he was a trainer and jockey living at Mansfield in Nottinghamshire who had ridden for Saunders and Lord Milltown many times in the past. When he rode for Lord Milltown he was paid a retainer of £50 per annum plus riding fees of 5 guineas for riding a winner or 3 guineas if unsuccesful. As Stagg was still an apprentice in the early 1840s he rode as a lightweight jockey with George Calloway riding the heavier weights for Lord Milltown. Both jockeys were sent to ride his lordship's horse at The Curragh in Ireland. Calloway said that £15 would be a fair sum to travel to Ireland but Stagg had only been paid £8, a sum sufficient only to take him as far as Liverpool. After 'considerable consideration' by the jury the court awarded Stagg £50 but not before stating:-
'...this was a most confusing case which would have been made a lot easier if the plaintiff and defendant has issued and requested receipts although the court realise this is not the done thing within the racing fraternity.' One other question was raised by the defence, *'why has it taken the plaintiff since 1843 to consider enforcing his claim?'* No reason was given! Then the bombshell was dropped as far as Stagg was concerned. For reasons unknown the verdict in favour of Stagg's claim was 'set aside' as the *Staffordshire Advertiser* put it, meaning cancelled presumably because on 21st July the same year a new trial opened at Stafford Assizes.

THE JOCKEYS

The case bought against Lord Milltown was as before, for unpaid wages and expenses for work and labour already completed. His lordship pleaded, 'firstly, he was never indebted; secondly, that he had paid the money; and thirdly, that the claim was settled.'

Saunders had trained horses for Lord Milltown in the past and Stagg had ridden them as an apprentice and of his own accord later on. These later rides were arranged through James Farrell who also trained for Milltown but no one had seen him in this country for several years. Saunders stated Milltown had paid him £56 on account of Stagg in 1839 but had received nothing else since. Stagg this time brought another respected friend and colleague to the stand, Charlie Marlow. He stated that he had ridden in the same races at Chester as had Stagg and he thought £8 was a reasonable sum to attend such meetings. Marlow again told of the 3 and 5 guineas fee but added it was usual for the owner to give a 'present' to the successful jockey. John Dodgson was also called and he told the court the sum asked by Stagg was not unreasonable. Next up on Stagg's behalf was George Calloway who stated exactly the same as he had at the first trial.

After much deliberation, argument and counter-argument the court found in favour of Stagg again and awarded him £164 this time with £2 costs, which was not 'set aside'!

In December 1850 Stagg married Elizabeth Taylor, second daughter of the late Joseph Taylor, of the Coach and Horses Inn, New Meeting Street, Birmingham. Elizabeth died in 1856 aged thirty-two and Stagg re-married in August 1859 to Mary Ann Lines of Leamington Spa. He remained at the Coach and Horses until 1864. In 1867 Mary Ann died and three years later he married Mary White Knapp. Interesting note, all three women he married were daughters of pub landlords!

In later years he took up breeding and training racehorses, but only on a modest scale.

In November 1874 Stagg was again in court, but this time he was being sued. The plaintiff, Abraham Hoskins claimed an unpaid bill from 1869 for £5 14s. 6d. for 'professional attendance and medicine supplied'. The verdict went against Stagg and he paid the full amount owed.

After leaving the inn he moved to a house in Balsall Heath and remained there until his death by his own hand on 8th February 1877 in the most unusual circumstances, which can be best explained by the newspaper report of the day:-

'Extraordinary occurrence at Balsall Heath. Mr Neptune Henry Stagg, a gentleman of independent means, residing at Cedar Villa, Tindall Street, Balsall Heath, was yesterday morning found drowned in a water-butt. The deceased was missed from his bedroom at a few minutes before seven o'clock, and being somewhat alarmed, Mrs. Knapp, his mother-in-law, went in search of him. She was horrified at seeing the deceased, head downwards, in the water butt, with his feet protruding over the top. An alarm was raised, and Mr Wood, surgeon of Moseley Road was summoned, but although every means was taken, it was found impossible to restore respiration. He was found dressed in his morning clothes and slippers. The deceased, who was fifty-three years of age, was well known in sporting circles and was an owner of racehorses. As a lightweight jockey Mr Stagg rode the first winner of the Cesarewitch. For several years he kept the Coach and Horses' Inn, New Meeting Street, one of the oldest sporting houses in Birmingham.'

Big race winners:-

Cesarewitch Handicap on Cruiskeen in *1839*.

Chester Cup on Cruiskeen in *1841*.

Manchester Grand Steeplechase on Fanny Grey in *1849*.

JOHN TASKER
1829 – 1855

Tasker was born at Hodnet in Shropshire in 1829 and became an apprentice on the flat before increasing weight forced him to turn to 'jumping'. It is believed his career began with one of the trainers at Hednesford, possibly Thomas Flintoff.

He was a little known jockey who rode just two winners at Walsall in 1847, but seven years later he had his moment of fame when partnering the 4/1 favourite, Bourton, to victory in the Grand National of 1854.

The horse was by owned William Moseley and trained by Henry Wadlow, a name familiar to racegoers on the Long Meadow. A year after their victory at Aintree, both horse and jockey were dead. Bourton was sold to a gentleman from Leamington Spa for a mere £50, in the belief the horse was to be retired. Unfortunately, his new owner continued to run the old horse and during a 'chase at Warwick, Bourton fell, injuring himself so badly that he had to be put down. On the 17th October 1855 John Tasker rode a horse named Rosa, coincidentally, in a 'chase, and also at Warwick. Rosa also fell, Tasker, appearing to be uninjured continued to ride and rode Black Swan to victory in the final race of the afternoon. Shortly afterwards the jockey became ill due to the effects of the fall and died eleven days later at Hednesford aged twenty-six. He was buried at St. Luke's Church in Cannock.

Big race winners:-

Grand National on Bourton in *1854*.

Worcester Grand Annual Chase on The General in *1852* and on Bourton in *1853*.

Cheltenham Steeplechase on Trout in *1854*.

Midland Steeplechase (Derby) on Bourton in *1854*.

Leamington Grand Annual Chase on Peter in *1852*.

HENRY TAYLOR
1841 – 1870

Taylor arrived at Thomas Cliff's stables around 1858 and had his first ride in public in November 1859 on Creeper at Shrewsbury finishing second. In March 1860, also at Shrewsbury, Taylor recorded his first victory on Mr. Wilkins Little Jenny. Taylor became Cliff's leading jockey and was to remain so until the emergence of Samuel Kenyon.

Taylor's ability was recognised by Mr. Lincoln, Cliff's most successful patron in the 1860s, and he promptly took the lad with him to Ireland each season where the partnership had great success. It was later discovered that Cockin and Lincoln were the same person. At The Curragh in April 1863 he rode seven winners on Cockin's horses, winning both Royal

THE JOCKEYS

Plates. During the 1860s Taylor rode at least seventeen Royal Plate winners and two Royal Whip winners with horses like Tourist, Selim and Kidderminster. In total he rode well over fifty winners in Ireland.

Sadly he never had the same success back in England but did manage to win a favourable number of races each season including seven at Walsall.

In the September of 1870 Taylor rode at the Sutton Park meeting. On the second day, Wednesday 21st, his mount was Dean of York owned by Mr. Raworth and probably trained by Thomas Eskrett. The horse was reputed to be "awkward" and a dangerous ride (Eskrett's son had ridden him the previous season with some difficulty). The race was a one mile hurdle race over three hurdles and when nearing the first hurdle the horse swerved and collided with Walter White's mount, Marriage. Taylor's mount then pitched and fell at the hurdle with Taylor landing on his back. Unfortunately the horse landed on top of him, severely injuring the jockey. Still unconscious, he was carried on an improvised stretcher to the nearby Bannersgate Cottage where he died the following morning of concussion of the brain. Aged just 29 he left behind a wife and three young children.

An inquest jury, under the supervision of the coroner, the Reverend F. H. Kittoe, returned a verdict of accidental death. Mr. James Cockin who had identified the body 'suggested that in future the committee should cause gorse to be put on the hurdles' because in his experience 'the sight of horses when racing frequently became defective and they had difficulty seeing bare hurdles'. The coroner promised to convey that idea to the race committee.

Big race winners:-
Steward's Cup on Croagh Patrick in 1861.
Grand National Hurdle on Barnabo in 1869.

JOB TOON
1851 – 1896

Job was one of ten children born to Job (senior) and Elizabeth Toon of Atherstone, Warwickshire in 1851.

His first mount in public is thought to have been John Wright's colt by Mr. Sykes at Lichfield in 1865. The first winner came in 1867 on Gunboat at Knutsford. Although more well known for taking over the stable of Thomas Cliff after his accident, Job Toon rode a fair few winners for the stable as well as seven at Walsall between 1867 and and 1875.

Cliff could almost be called the 'jockey maker of his day' as he tutored Henry Taylor, George Ashworth and Job himself making them into fine jockeys. When Taylor and Sam Kenyon who rode for Mr. Cockin in Ireland both died, Cliff relied on Toon and George Ashworth to fill the void created. It was really Mr. Cockin who gave most encouragement to the young Toon and in 1868 he won a number of races on Cockin's Barnabo. The following year he accompanied his patron to Ireland and won both Royal Plates at The Curragh in April on Aneroid. At the same meeting he also won three more races on Cockin's horses. Such was the confidence that Cockin had in his jockey that he preferred him over others to ride Melody, the red-hot favourite for the Irish Derby that year. Bidding for a third Cockin success in four years unfortunately Melody was beaten into second place. However, Toon did win another Royal Plate at the meeting on Cockin's Prince.

The 1881 census has Toon training from Providence House, Hednesford where he employed eleven people. He continued to train for around ten years before becoming the landlord of the New Inn (known as the Pretty Bricks) in John Street, Walsall in 1895. Unfortunately this venture was short lived as Job died at the premises on 29th March 1896. His wife Rosannah took over the licence running the 'Bricks' until 1898.

Job and Rosannah had eight children and the first three boys, Walter, Howard and Herbert all became jockeys, the latter being the most successful.

JOHN WELLS
1833 – 1873

Of all the jockeys associated with the Hednesford training grounds, John Wells was the most successful. During his career he rode eight Classic winners and was champion jockey twice.

Born on Christmas Day 1833 in Sutton Coldfield, Wells became apprenticed to Thomas Flintoff at Prospect House, Hednesford around the age of thirteen. His first ride in public came at Northampton in 1848 on a horse of Flintoff's named Ribaldry. A few months later the same horse gave Wells his first taste of victory in the Birmingham Stakes at Walsall.

At Wolverhampton in August 1849, while Wells was riding Cingari, another of Fowler's horses at the Flintoff stable, John Heitt, a much more experienced jockey, tried to take Wells's

THE JOCKEYS

position on the rails by forcing his mount through. Despite his youth, Wells kept his ground and won the race.

In the following year, 1850, at Stourbridge the *Worcester Chronicle* reporter wrote, *'Wells displayed for a mere child some extraordinary jockeyship and, as also in the Cup race (Gold Cup), was greeted with much cheering.'* The race was the Himley Stakes and he rode Cosachia, another of Fowler's horses. By 1851 he had won his first major race when he partnered Mr. Phillips's horse, Truth, to win the Cambridgeshire. That horse had been trained by William Saunders at Hazel Slade. During that year he had also ridden William Palmer's Goldfinder, also trained by Saunders, to win at Shrewsbury, the year before it won the Gold Cup there.

Whilst getting a reputation for being an excellent jockey another incident was to prove his honesty in the sport. In a clear case of race fixing, the trainer of the horse concerned, Mr. Wetherell wrote a letter to *The Times* explaining his dilemma and also exonerating Wells. It read,

"Sir, - Your love of fair play induces me to trouble you for a corner of your valuable Times to explain my conduct as a public trainer in the affair of Urbanity at Shrewsbury. At Northampton Races Mr. Frail, Clerk of the Course at Shrewsbury, came to me and agreed with me to train two horses for Mr. C. Liley – Urbanity and Heliotrope – and prepare them for their engagements at Shrewsbury.

On August 11th, in the evening I received orders from Mr. Frail that Urbanity was not to start for the Cleveland Handicap, but to run in the Members Plate. On the race being called I saddled Urbanity and gave Wells, the jockey, his orders – to ride and win. The moment before starting Mr. Frail came up and ordered me to tell Wells he must not win the first heat, but wait. I had only just time to give Wells theses orders, which I did, and the mare never tried for the heat, but waited.

After the heat, to my great astonishment, I was ordered to send the mare home. Wells declares that the mare could not have lost the race had she been allowed to run. I was so disgusted with such conduct that I immediately told Mr. Frail and the owner that they should take their horses out of my stable that moment as I would not train for any person who could so forget common honesty.

The horses were taken away that night.

Mr. Wetherell, Mostyn Stables, Holywell, North Wales.

Five years after riding his first winner he became champion jockey at the age of nineteen, riding eighty-six winners and taking the crown from the champion of the previous thirteen years, Elnathan (Nat) Flatman. The following year saw him retain his title with eighty-two winners and also record his first Classic success in the 1,000 Guineas at Newmarket. The horse was Virago, owned by Henry Padwick and trained by William Goater. By this time, Wells had moved south from Hednesford to become stable jockey to Goater who trained at Findon in Sussex. During his time with Goater he met up with John Porter, a fellow Midlander from Rugeley and head lad at the stables. In later years the two came together, along with owner Sir Joseph Hawley to make their mark on turf history.

From his first days as an apprentice, Wells was always

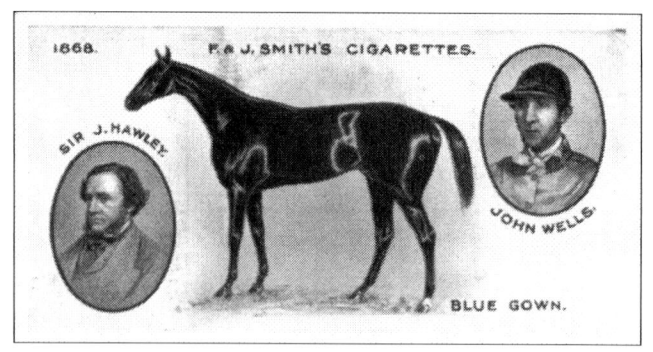

A cigarette card issued by F. & J. Smith Cigarettes in 1913 showing Wells with Blue Gown's owner, Sir James Hawley.

known by the rather predictable nickname of 'Tiny'. He had no problems riding at six stones when he was twenty-two years old, but nature intervened a few years afterwards. He began to grow, not only upwards but outwards too. Like many riders before and after him, Wells from then on fought a constant battle with his weight. Harry Custance, the well known and respected jockey of the same era commented: *'I think Wells was the tallest and biggest man I ever saw ride at eight stones seven. He was a very strong man on a horse and used to lap his long legs round the horse at the finish. He always sat well back in the saddle, kept fast hold of the horse's head, and was a most resolute finisher. Take him altogether, I think he was a good jockey.'*

Wells had an excellent reputation for honesty and loyalty. John Porter commenting some years later said of his stable jockey: *'There is not enough money in the Bank of England to bribe him to ride a crooked race.'* A fine testimony indeed from Porter, at a time when the same could not be said of too many jockeys. One of the few chinks in Wells's armour was his eccentric dress sense and manner. In later life he acquired the second nickname of 'Brusher', this name may well have originated because of the generous sideburns Wells grew. Along with his eccentricities, he was also said to be one of the vainest men ever to set foot on a racecourse. On one occasion when involved in a walk over with Blue Gown at Newmarket he rode the horse dressed in a suit of Gordon tartan, a large Tyrolean hat with a long curly feather, red Moroccan leather slippers and carrying a cane like a billiard cue. One of the friends of Sir Joseph Hawley, owner of the horse, asked him where his hat had come from, Wells replied *'You would like to know so that you can get one like it.'* The person responded quick as a flash, *'If I did, I would be complete and get a monkey and an organ to go with it.'* For all the ridicule thrown at Wells for his dress, it made no difference to him, even when people fell down laughing at him in the street, he put it down to jealousy and never batted an eyelid. Sir Joseph Hawley, who Wells rode five Classic winners for, was one of the few not to be phased by the jockeys strange dress sense and vanity. When questioned about it his only comment was, *'I don't care how he dresses, he is a good enough jockey for me.'*

During the Champagne Stakes in 1867, Wells upset both the owner and trainer of Blue Gown as well as the Senior Steward of the Jockey Club, the formidable Admiral Rous. The night before the race, Wells, in an effort to lose a few pounds in weight, marched off to visit friends who lived four miles from Doncaster. He decided to stay the night and sat up

THE JOCKEYS

into the early hour's playing cards and having the odd drink or two. Because of this lack of self-discipline, he knew he had no chance of making the required 8 stone 10lbs in the race. He was in between a rock and a hard place on this one, he couldn't tell the owner, Sir John Hawley and the trainer, John Porter that he would put up overweight. To say they would have been unimpressed is somewhat of an understatement. Wells decided to be devious, or at least try. He rode the race perfectly, Blue Gown won admirably, as Wells went to weigh in he put his plan into action. He sat on the scales, keeping one foot on the floor in an attempt to stop the weights rising, at the same time dropping a saddlecloth. Unfortunately this old dodge was spotted by another jockey, John Doyle, who had a score to settle with Wells. Doyle made a loud issue of handing back the cloth, saying, *'you weighed out with this, you must weigh in with it.'* Everyone's attention then focussed on Wells; it was discovered he was six pounds overweight. Admiral Rous, within earshot of all this roared, *'get out, I am ashamed of you,'* at the same time cuffing the embarrassed jockey on the back of the head. The owner of Blue Gown, Hawley, also gave Wells the dressing down of his life, the jockey later commented: *'I lost more weight during the twenty minutes I was in that room than I did in the course of any walk I ever took.'* Walking was a favourite method of losing weight in those days. For over a month after the race Wells never wore the colours of the Hawley, but after that it appears Wells had learned his lesson and the matter was forgotten.

John Wells fought many battles over the years with his weight, but he finally lost the war on 17th July 1873. The years of wasting had taken its toll on his body, and at thirty-nine, he was dead. His body is buried at St. Mary's Church, Kingsclere, Berkshire, next to that of his wife Mary, who had died the previous year aged thirty-eight. He made a very good living from the turf, and wisely invested some of the proceeds in a factory making steel pens in Birmingham, ensuring his parents were well provided for.

Classic and other big race winners:
The Derby three times on Beadsman in 1858, Musjid in 1859 and Blue Gown in 1868.
St Leger twice on Saucebox in 1855 and Pero Gomez in 1869.
2,000 Guineas on Fitz Roland in 1858.
1,000 Guineas twice on Virago in 1854 and Tomato in 1864.
Ascot Gold Cup twice on Fisherman in 1858) and Asteroid in 1862.
Cambridgeshire in 1851 on Truth;
Chester Cup three times on Scythian in 1855), Leamington in 1859 and Asteroid in 1863).
Cesarewitch on Weathergauge in 1852.
Goodwood Cup twice on Virago in 1854 and Siderolite in 1870.
City and Suburban four times on Ethelbert in 1853), Virago in 1854, Ireland's Eye in 1855 and Argonaut in 1865.
Great Metropolitan in 1854 on Virago.
Gimcrack Stakes on Rainbow in 1858.

GEORGE WHITEHOUSE
1815 – 1869

George Whitehouse was born in Walsall in 1815. The son of William and Esther Whitehouse of Park Brook, Walsall (now known as Wolverhampton Street) he was baptised at St. Matthews Church on May 7th. His father was a fishmonger, but encouraged George who wanted a career as a jockey. Sometime in the early 1830s he became an apprentice to Samuel Lord at Hednesford and he rode his first winner, Buffalo, for him at Walsall for Mr. T.E. Sharratt in 1834 who had horses with Lord. However, it is likely that before going to Lord he was probably an apprentice with another Hednesford trainer as his most likely first winner was four years earlier in 1830 at Newcastle-under-Lyme with the aptly named Hedgford which was owned by Squire John Mytton. That trainer was mostly likely to be Thomas Flintoff as Mytton had some horses stabled at Prospect House. Most of his early winners before 1836 were owned by John Beardsworth whose trainer was Flintoff and so that seems to confirm that his initial apprenticeship was with Flintoff.

It was towards the end of 1836 that he probably moved to Lord's stable and started to ride for Edmund Peel owing to the accident that had happened to John Spring. For the next few years he rode mainly for Peel and occasionally for Thomas Carr at Hazel Slade. By 1840 he was living with John Spencer at Littleworth as a lodger and in the following year he married Spencer's daughter, Anne, and the pair set up home at Littleworth Cottage. It was during the early 1840s that Mr. Collett became his patron as well as Lord Albemarle, both possibly having horses stabled at Hazel Slade. George also continued to ride for Carr, having ended his association with Samuel Lord and Peel.

It was Lord Albemarle's patronage which gave Whitehouse his first major success in 1844 when he won the Ascot Gold Cup on The Emperor, 1845 saw him retain the Ascot Gold Cup, again with The Emperor, and at the same meeting he won the Queen's Vase on Mr. Hill's Sweetmeat trained by Wadlow. He also won the Doncaster Cup on Sweetmeat in the same year. According to *Ruff's Guide 1846* he was jockey to Lord Albemarle, Lord Chesterfield, Mr. Collett and Lord Spencer in that order of preference and his reputation as a sound jockey was growing in the south. In 1846 he won the Queen Anne Stakes at Ascot on Mr. E. Clark's The Conjuror and the Steward's Cup in 1847 with Mr. Rolt's The Cur trained by French.

THE JOCKEYS

1849 could have been his year for a Classic triumph, but he was pipped at the post by Charles Marlow on The Flying Dutchman. Nat Flatman was convinced that Whitehouse had won, but true to his honesty as a jockey George was not sure and so never objected to the Steward's decision. Up until his dying day, privately, he agreed with Flatman and he too thought he had won. It was strange then that his honesty was questioned by a race on Hotspur in 1850. *The New Sporting Magazine* (July – December 1850) fortunately backs Whitehouse by saying *'The most ridiculous cock-and-bull stories have been told about Hotspur. One was that Whitehouse privately shipped some half a stone of shot ballast before the race, and had it handed to him in a pocket handkerchief as he returned to the scale; the other was that the horse was not the same which ran as Hotspur at two year old. After the Running Rein alias Maccabeus exposure (in the Derby), it was not likely that his owner (let alone all higher considerations) would have run such a risk; and besides this Marlow, who had won a two year old race on him at Bath, very quickly affirmed his identity when the question was put to him.'*

Perhaps that doubt about Whitehouse's honesty came from an incident at Sutton Races on June 19th, 1850 when three horses contested the West Bromwich Stakes. Whitehouse's horse, Clara, won the first heat; La Malhereuse ridden by Yates won the second; and Sara ridden by Turner was awarded the third because both opponents had run the wrong side of the post. The Stewards, after hearing protests from the owners of Clara and La Malhereuse, awarded the race to Clara because they felt that the mistake by the jockeys was not deliberate. That led the *Birmingham Journal* to write, 'No respectable racing authorities continue heats on their grounds; they always engendered ill-feeling, and a congregation of leather-flappers (crooks) in this way is but a certain forerunner of that fraud and robbery, of which the public are the victims.' The incident made the sporting headlines because the crowd were so incensed that the police had to be called in to quieten the trouble-makers. Though not really involved in any decision making Whitehouse's reputation for honesty had been somewhat tarnished simply because he was one of the jockeys.

By 1850 he was still living in Hednesford with his wife and children, Elizabeth, born in 1842, John in 1846, Isabella in 1848, Alfred in 1854 and Louise in 1855. By then his patrons were Lord Chesterfield, Mr. Meeson and John Fowler. In 1851 Whitehouse's frustration with his failure to win a Classic was heightened even more when he narrowly missed both the Derby and The Oaks, finishing second in both races – the Derby on Marlborough Buck and The Oaks on Lord Scott's Miserrima. However, he did win the Jersey Stakes at Ascot on Miserrima and followed that at the same meeting winning the Norfolk Stakes on Lord Scott's Hobbie Noble trained by William Saunders. Hobbie Noble went on to win the July Stakes at Newmarket ridden by Whitehouse and was favourite for the following year's Derby.

The lack of a Classic winner is probably the one and only reason why Whitehouse was somewhat discounted by racing historians during the last century. During the time he was riding it seems he was much more highly thought of. The sporting paper, *The Era* on Sunday 19th February 1843 published a letter written in response to one of their articles from a couple of weeks previous. The letter was written by one who signed himself British Yeoman and the contents of his letter elevates Whitehouse much higher up the ladder than we have been led to believe. The knowledgeable correspondent compiled a table of the twelve most successful jockeys for the years 1840, 1841 and 1842. Whitehouse was in fifth place with 74 winners, only the likes of John Cartwright (77), Jem Robinson (78), Tommy Lye (101) and the great Nat Flatman (162) in front of him.

During his career which spanned twenty-two years from 1834 to 1856 Whitehouse probably rode in excess of 350 winners. His annual winner totals, where known, are as follows:-

1834 to 1839	unknown	1848	23
1840	33	1849	26
1841	26	1850	30
1842	18	1851	20
1843	33	1852	17
1844	unknown	1853	14
1845	unknown	1854	15
1846	31	1855	2
1847	24	1856	2
Known winners total = 314			

In 1852 he won the July Stakes again, that time on The Reiver and in 1853 he won the St. James's Palace Stakes on the same horse. His final prestigious victory came in the same year when he won the Gimcrack Stakes at York on Mr. Saxon's Barrell. By 1857 Whitehouse was living in Lichfield and *Ruff's Guide* listed him as a freelance jockey. It seems that by then he had almost finished riding and had begun to have a few horses of his own like so many other jockeys. His final mount in The Derby came in 1856 on Newington and at the end of that season he more than likely retired. It was thought that his final mount was at Lichfield Races in 1858 but this is incorrect. That jockey 'Whitehouse', with no initial or Christian name, was carrying 6st. 11lbs. and George, although classed as a lightweight jockey, hadn't been that weight for many years and was actually 8st. 5lbs. at his death.

He died at Rose Cottage, Upper St. John Street, Lichfield on 19th February 1869 aged fifty four. The cause of death was said to be through 'general decay'.

Reports of his death in the *Sporting Life* and *Bell's Life & Sporting Chronicle* comment on how popular and genial a character Whitehouse was and also how well respected he was too in the racing world. The publications listed Lord George Bentinck, Lord Albemarle, Lord Chesterfield, Lord George Scott and Lord John Scott as well as Mr. Collett and many others that he had ridden for. The final paragraph of his obituary in the *Sporting Life* reads:-

'To the last he could ride 8st. 5lbs. with ease. His seat was peculiar, and he had none of the regular jockey character about him out of the saddle, in addition to which he was rather knock-kneed. He was a remarkably dapper sort of man, and was seldom seen without the neatest of umbrellas, whatever the day might be. In his conversation he was most genial, and his way of telling anecdotes was particularly racy.'

THE JOCKEYS

His estate was worth just under £5,000 pounds, a considerable amount for the time. His trustees were directed to invest his money in 'some or one of the public stocks or funds and to give the interest to any child who had not reached the age of 21.' He also bequeathed 'the furniture, plate, linen, china, liquors and any housekeeping stores to his wife absolutely'. They were to be shared equally amongst his children on her death.

Big race winners:
Ascot Gold Cup twice on The Emperor in 1844 and 1845.
Doncaster Cup on Sweetmeat in 1845.
Stewards Cup on The Cur in 1847.
Gimcrack Stakes on Barrel in 1853.
Jersey Stakes on Miserrima in 1851.
Norfolk Stakes on Hobbie Noble in 1851.
Queen's Vase on Sweetmeat in 1845.
Queen Anne Stakes on The Conjuror in 1846.

MR) EDWARD POTTER WILSON
1846 – 1918

Although 'Ted' Wilson, as he was commonly known, rode only one winner at Walsall, he doubled that tally at Aintree a few years later and because of that entered the record books. Wilson was a talented and popular amateur rider from Warwickshire who rode Voluptuary to victory in the 1884 Grand National. Not content with that, and to prove it wasn't a fluke, he then partnered Roquefort the following year to win the great race again. He rode his first winner at the age of fourteen on a horse named Starlight at his local course at Stratford-on-Avon. In 1877 and 1883 he was crowned champion amateur jockey.

His riding record was one that made his professional colleagues green with envy. As well as his two 'Nationals, he also won five National Hunt Chases, two Great Sefton Chases, the Scottish Grand National, two Champion Chases, plus many others. At Crewkerne Races in 1878 he rode six winners from seven rides.

Wilson retired from race riding at the age of fifty-two, in 1898. He died at Stratford-on-Avon in January 1918 at the age of seventy-one.

Below is a list of the leading jockeys that rode three or more winners (including walkovers), and the years that they rode them.

George Whitehouse	1834 – 1850	15
Thomas Skelton	1871 – 1876	13
George Calloway	1830 – 1844	11
Walter White	1854 – 1869	11
William Lear	1826 – 1835	9
Charles Marlow	1831 – 1846	9
Richard Spencer	1810 – 1820	8
Henry Arthur senior	1813 – 1835	7
J. Fox	1869 – 1875	7
John Spring	1825 – 1833	7
Job Toon	1867 – 1875	7
Henry Taylor	1859 – 1864	7
Henry Arthur junior	1833 – 1837	6
Mr Friend (amateur)	1834 – 1843	6
William Sharpe	1848 – 1855	5
John Deakin	1873 – 1874	5
Thomas Wadlow	1830 – 1840	4
Robert Denman	1838 – 1854	4
Mr John Shaw Walker (amateur)	1843 – 1851	4
James Knott	1856 – 1866	4
John Dodgson	1836 – 1838	3
William Saunders	1838 – 1845	3
James Bradley	1844 – 1846	3
John Walters	1854 – 1856	3
James Frost	1856 – 1857	3
Thomas	1860 – 1861	3
William Britton	1863 – 1868	3
Samuel Kenyon	1863 – 1870	3
Connor	1864 – 1870	3
Handley	1867 – 1868	3
Mr G. Spafford (amateur)	1868 – 1869	3
George Ashworth	1870 – 1875	3
Thomas Glover	1873 – 1875	3
Alfred Freeborne	1851	3
Gardiner	1859	3
J. Taylor	1859	3
A. Sadler	1860	3
Sait	1861	3
Wardle	1873	3

WALSALL RACES

CHAPTER EIGHT
THE TRAINERS

With Walsall being so close to Hednesford it is not surprising to find that these famous old training grounds supplied a high percentage of the runners, quite possibly, from the concept of the races, right up to the final event in 1876.

One of the first confirmed names to be associated with horse training at Hednesford in the eighteenth century is that of Saunders, a name that would be carried into the next century by another two generations of the same family. The *Racing Calendar* for 1783 states that a Mr Saunders ran two horses, Ne-plus-ultra and Clementina in races at Chester, Liverpool, Nottingham, Lichfield and Stafford. In 1786, at Walsall, a horse named Varges ran second in the Gentlemen's Subscription Purse, owned, trained and possibly ridden by a Mr Saunders. Four years later, in the Staffordshire section of the subscription list in the *Racing Calendar*, two names appeared that confirm Hednesford was indeed about to become an important training ground. The names were William Saunders, father of Thomas and grandfather of William, and James Lord, father of Samuel and James junior, all of whom became trainers in later years.

By 1805 another familiar name was added to the subscription list for Staffordshire in the *Racing Calendar*,

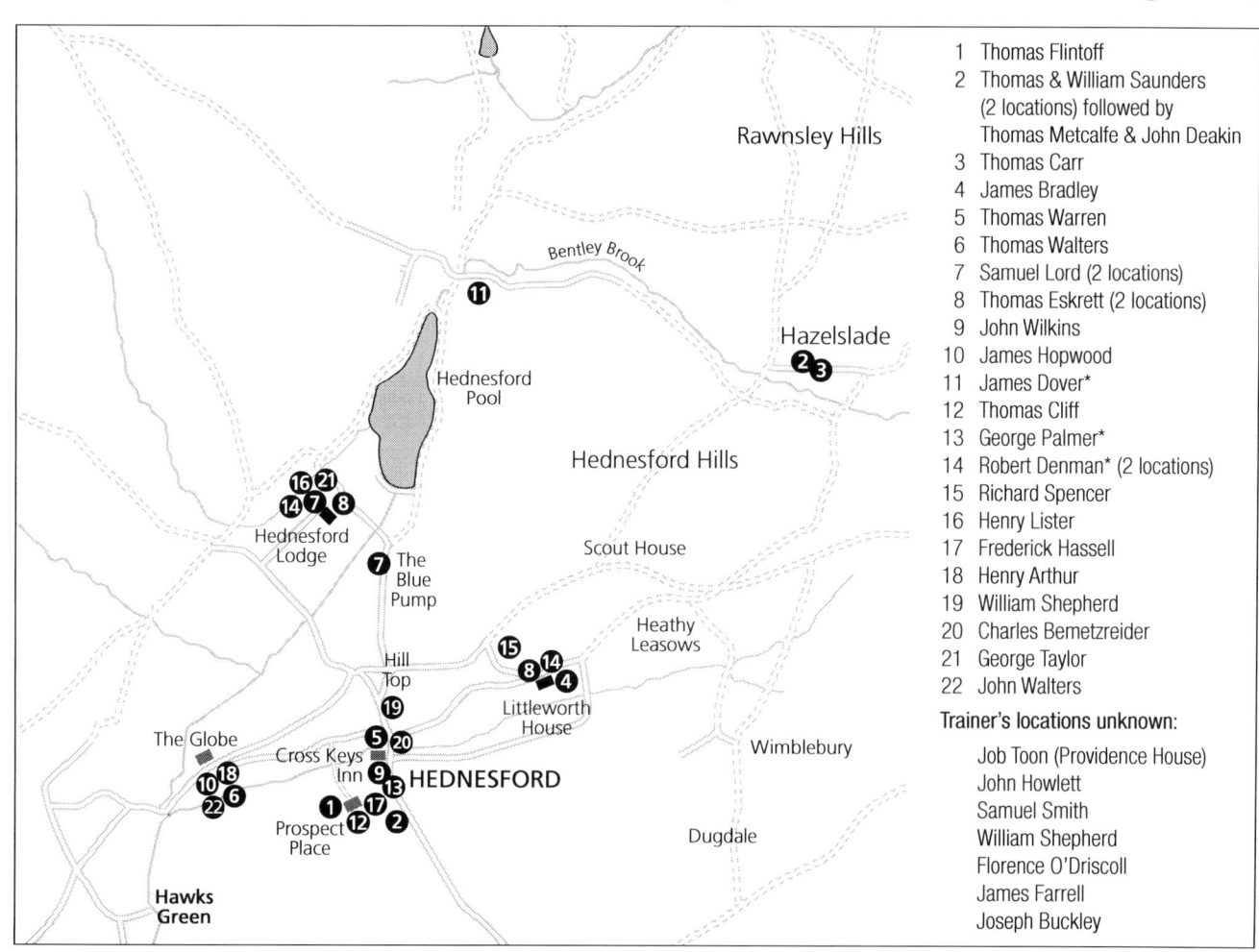

1. Thomas Flintoff
2. Thomas & William Saunders (2 locations) followed by Thomas Metcalfe & John Deakin
3. Thomas Carr
4. James Bradley
5. Thomas Warren
6. Thomas Walters
7. Samuel Lord (2 locations)
8. Thomas Eskrett (2 locations)
9. John Wilkins
10. James Hopwood
11. James Dover*
12. Thomas Cliff
13. George Palmer*
14. Robert Denman* (2 locations)
15. Richard Spencer
16. Henry Lister
17. Frederick Hassell
18. Henry Arthur
19. William Shepherd
20. Charles Bemetzreider
21. George Taylor
22. John Walters

Trainer's locations unknown:

Job Toon (Providence House)
John Howlett
Samuel Smith
William Shepherd
Florence O'Driscoll
James Farrell
Joseph Buckley

146

THE TRAINERS

THOMAS CLIFF
and JOB TOON see also page 141

Another trainer in the area from around 1860 was Thomas Cliff who was born in 1805 at Ketton, near Stamford, Lincolnshire. Cliff occupied the premises vacated by Thomas Flintoff at Prospect House and between 1860 and 1870 he had many runners entered in his name. There are two possible explanations for this; firstly, he may well have trained the horses for himself, or the more likely reason being that he entered the horses to run under his name and not the owners. This was not unusual as many owners during this period ran horses under assumed names for one reason or another.

Little is known of Cliff's early career prior to his arrival at Hednesford, but it is thought he began, like many trainers, as a jockey. His son, also named Thomas, was a jockey and was highly thought of by many people, The Druid described the young man in his book Silk and Scarlet, as 'a very clever young jock.' Thomas junior's career was not to be a long one however, on 14th August 1870, he died at the family home age 30. Another jockey associated with Thomas Cliff senior was the young apprentice from Manchester, Samuel Kenyon, who became champion jockey in 1866 while, it is thought, still at the stables in Hednesford. Cliff could almost be called the 'jockey maker' of his day, included in the stables were Henry Taylor, George Ashworth and Job Toon who later took over Cliff's stables. Henry Taylor rode many of Cliff's horses and died young, as did Samuel Kenyon, Taylor was tragically killed after a fall from a horse named the Dean of York in a hurdle race at Sutton Park races on 22 September 1870, he was twenty-nine years of age. In 1861 the horse Croagh Patrick, ridden by Taylor, won the prestigious Steward's Cup at Goodwood for Cliff.

In the mid 1870s Cliff was involved in a collision with a horse and cart which left him maimed for the rest of his life and ending his training career prematurely. After Cliff's accident there was still a stable to run and that job went to one of his jockeys, Job Toon, assisted by his brother James. Job had been apprenticed to Thomas Cliff and rode many winners for his mentor in the early part of his career, including seven at Walsall between 1867 and 1875. In 1875 the young man achieved a second Classic win for the area when Innishowen, ridden by George Ashworth, won the Irish Derby at the Curragh for his owner James Cockin, a Staffordshire businessman. Prior to this win, Cockin had won the inaugural Irish Derby in 1866 with Selim and the second running of the race in 1867 with Golden Plover. In both cases, the record books give no trainers name, but it is interesting to note that both horses had run in England previously ridden by jockeys associated with Cliff. Thomas Cliff had been training horses for Cockin for about ten years prior to this Classic victory and the majority of the horses he had trained had run in Ireland. Cliff also took the precaution of taking his own jockeys, Samuel Kenyon and Henry Taylor, to the Emerald Isle to ride the horses on the majority of occasions. When these two jockeys died young, the crown fell to Job Toon and George Ashworth to continue the winning streak for the stable. In the 1869 Irish Derby, Job Toon, riding the 4/5 favourite Melody, was beaten a head by The Scout and so just failed to give Cockin a fourth winner in the event. The horses that ran in Ireland under Cockin's name were very successful, on one occasion the trainer/owner partnership won eight races from the fourteen on the two-day card at the Curragh. Cockin won large amounts of stake money in Ireland, so much so the Irish turf authorities amended the rules in an attempt to stop him from winning. Needless to say, they didn't. The authorities stated that horses running in Ireland must be resident in that country for six months of the year. The owner simply sent the horses over and put them into 'lodgings' at an Irish stable for the required duration, thereby complying with the new rules.

Another interesting point that has arisen from the Cliff/Cockin partnership regards the ownership of the horses. When the horses ran in Ireland they were entered under James Cockin's name but when the same horses ran in England the were usually entered in the name of 'Mr Lincoln,' a name familiar to the Walsall racing fraternity. To confuse the situation further, both Cockin and Lincoln had identical racing colours, white jacket with a black cap and second colours of all white. The rulers of racing did not allow this to happen. Many owners had similar colours for the jacket but the cap had to be of a different colour or design. In the annual Racing Calendars for the period, the evidence becomes even more intriguing, both names never appear in the same year, it is always one or the other that is entered. It can only be surmised that James Cockin, preferred, for some unknown reason, to run his horses under an assumed name. It may have come to some reader's attention that it was mentioned earlier that Thomas Cliff was born in Lincolnshire! Was he the elusive Mr Lincoln? James Cockin, spent his last few years in Halifax, the town where he died in 1876. On his death, the stables at Hednesford and his stud were disposed of by public sale.

In 1877 tragedy struck the stables again when the eighteen year old apprentice jockey, Charles Greaves, was killed. After exercising several horses, the riders, as usual took them into Hednesford Pool to bath their legs. Greaves' mount, a horse named Britannia, reared and threw the lad into deep water. Being unable to swim, he clung to the saddle for as long as he could, but drowned before anyone could reach him.

JAMES DOVER

One of Lord's stable men in the 1850s was a young man named James Dover who also became a trainer in Hednesford before moving south to Berkshire in the 1860s. Dover's first employer in the area was James Bradley whom he joined at around twelve years of age. In 1858 Dover was training horses under his own name at stables around the Pool End of the village and also trained what is thought to be his first big race winner. The horse was Eurydice and the race was the 1858 cavalry charge known as the Cambridgeshire Stakes at Newmarket. Thirty-six horses lined up and Dover's charge, carrying the lightweight of 5 stone 7 pounds, was first across the line ridden by his apprentice, George Britton. Dover continued to learn his craft well, by 1866 he had won the

THE TRAINERS

Derby and St. Leger with Lord Lyon and a year later repeated the St. Leger success with the filly Achievement. When the legendary Victorian trainer, Rugeley born John Porter, was taken ill with typhoid fever in late 1865, the majority of his top horses owned by Sir Joseph Lawley, were sent to Dover's stable until Porter was well enough to resume work. What better testimony to Dover's ability with horses than to be sent the charges of the then, leading trainer in the country, and one of the leading owners. It appears the Birmingham born Dover was a far better manager of horses than money, for it is said he died pennyless.

THOMAS ESKRETT

Whilst one National winner has to be discounted (Jealousy in 1861, see J. Wilkins), another is thrown into the spotlight, Chandler, who won the great race in 1848. The man that trained him was Thomas Eskrett, another migrant from Yorkshire. Eskrett also trained in Sussex for a time but he was known to be in the Hednesford/Cannock area in 1848 as he married Yorkshire lass Margaret Smith at St. Luke's Church in Cannock. Thomas is described on the marriage certificate as being a 'training groom,' a term that indicates he was possibly training for someone in a private capacity. In the 1851 census, he is recorded as residing at Littleworth with his wife and two children, plus eight helpers, one of whom was the jockey, Robert Denman. The horse Chandler also had Midlands's connections so the possibility of this being a fourth winner for the area gains some credence.

The horse was bred by Sir Edward Scott at Great Barr Hall and the instant he saw the foal he took a dislike to it calling him 'a fiddled headed brute.' The colt was passed on to a man named Wilkinson in Sutton Coldfield who was engaged as a chandler, hence the horses name. The colt grew up in between the shafts of Wilkinson's cart before being sold to a Mr Garnett of Moor Hill who continued using the future equine hero in the same way. Chandler, as he was now known, regularly pulled Garnett's gig to the Bonehill Harriers meetings and it was at one of these meets that Captain Peel saw him. Peel, a great sportsman of his day was without a mount as his intended steed hadn't arrived and so he enquired if he may ride Garnett's horse. With the owner's permission, the horse was unhitched and saddled up, he gave Peel such a ride that on his return he enquired of Garnett a price for the animal. A fee of twenty guineas was arrived at, plus Peel's other horse which had now arrived at the course. A few days after the deal was done, Garnett returned Captain Peel's horse and so Chandler cost the princely sum of twenty guineas. The next few years saw Chandler being regularly hunted by Captain Peel until he was tried in a 'chase at Birmingham which he finished second. Not only could the horse run, he could jump too. In his next race at Warwick he strolled up twenty lengths in front of his nearest rival and during the course of the race he cleared a brook which was later measured at being thirty-seven feet.

One of Peel's closest friends in the sporting world was another military man, Captain Joseph Lockhart Little, affectionately known as 'Josey.' Little had been down on his luck since losing a great deal of money in a bank crash and Peel gave him the chance of recouping some of his losses when he allowed him to ride Chandler in a 'chase at Worcester. The horse won, and so did 'Josey,' £500 to be exact. Further successes came, which allowed Little to purchase a half share in the horse along with Peel. The co-owners, along with the trainer, put their heads together to form a plan for the 'National as Little had no experience of the race. Captain Peel also rode in the race, maybe to keep a close eye on his investment, but his mount, Pioneer fell, and it isn't known if he managed to get back in time to lead 'his' horse into the winners enclosure. Peel and Little are said to have won over £7000 from the bets laid on the race. Not only did the twelve year old Chandler the give the two men the chance to achieve their lifelong ambitions by winning the 'National, he put one of them back on the road to solvency!

The year of 1850 saw Eskrett gain his first major success on the flat when Musician won the King Edward VII Stakes at Ascot. Sometime after 1851, the exact date is not known, Eskrett moved from Hednesford to train on the Sussex Downs and it was during this period he recorded the majority of his successes in major races on the flat. In 1853 he won the Ebor Handicap at York with a horse named Pantomime and in 1855, the Nassau Stakes at Goodwood with Instructress. In 1858 the trainer became a dual Classic winner with a horse named Governess who won the 1,000, Guineas at Newmarket and the Oaks at Epsom. The horse was owned by the well-known patron of the turf, G. W. Gratwicke. The jockey that partnered Governess was Thomas Ashmall, who had been born at Farewell Hall and as a young boy developed a passion for racing whilst visiting the stables of his uncle, Thomas Carr. The same owner, trainer partnership won the 1860 Coronation Stakes at Ascot with a horse named Allington and it is thought when this horse won, Eskrett was still training in Sussex. On his return from the south of England, Eskrett took up residence in the Anglesey Hotel, where he remained until his death in the 1870s. The Post Office Directory of 1872 has him listed as 'Hotel keeper and trainer,' by 1880, his widow, Margaret was listed in the Kelly's Directory as the hotelkeeper. Although Thomas died many years ago, his name lives on in the area because of the street that bears his name, he his also commemorated by a stained glass window in St. Peter's Church, Hednesford.

THOMAS FLINTOFF

With Hednesford's rich history in horse training, try as it may over many years, it only managed to claim two Classic winners, one English and the other Irish. The man that trained the English Classic winner was Thomas Flintoff and the race was the Great St. Leger in 1830 with a horse appropriately named Birmingham.

Like many trainers in the Hednesford area, Flintoff was a Yorkshireman, born around 1792, he moved into the area around 1824. He trained for two of the most flamboyant characters in racing at the time, John Beardsworth and the infamous, and near insane, John Mytton, although the latter did have horses with other trainers in Shropshire. The horse

THE TRAINERS

that finally broke Hednesford's 'duck' was a brown colt named Birmingham, owned by John Beardsworth, whose first ever runner was at Walsall in 1818. Birmingham was bred by Mr Lacy of Colwick near Nottingham and was by Filho da Puta out of Miss Craigie (by Orville). Beardsworth owned a very successful business in Birmingham known as the Union Horse Repository and Carriage Mart, and the colt was sold out of one of the sales to a Mr Dickinson for 45 guineas. Immediately after the sale, Beardsworth offered Dickinson a further ten guineas on top of what he had paid and the deal was done.

It is worth noting, at this same sale a yearling called Independence was also sold to a Mr Lockley, this horse was also purchased by Beardsworth and went on to become a great servant to both owner and trainer. Some years later Beardsworth commented that of the sixty-four horses sold at that sale in November 1827 the only two that were any good were the two that he eventually owned. Modesty was never Mr Beardsworth's strong point.

Shortly after Birmingham was purchased he became very ill and it was only by the tender care of Mrs Beardsworth that he pulled through. Her husband wanted to have him destroyed, but she would have none of it and nursed the colt for many weeks, night and day. Beardsworth commented that it was the one and only time his wife ever showed any interest in a horse in her life. When the colt had fully recovered he was sent to Hednesford and put into training with Flintoff at that famous old landmark, Prospect House (or Place). Birmingham's first sight of a racecourse was at Ludlow on 1st July 1829 where he finished third of five runners. It was well worth the trip to Ludlow however, Beardsworth's other runner, Independence, won his first race. Just over a month later Birmingham appeared again, this time at Wolverhampton, where he won the Chillington Stakes very easily. Flintoff and Beardsworth must have realised at this point they had something special on their hands with this one. When the St. Leger came round on Tuesday 21st September 1830, Birmingham had run in thirteen races winning ten of them. Beardsworth was so confident of winning the great race he stationed horses at regular intervals between Doncaster and his home town so the result could be relayed to the townspeople as fast as possible. Twenty-eight runners lined up for the start, and amazingly for such a large field, they started at the first time of asking. The early pace was slow with Emancipator taking the lead, followed by a group of ten horses including Birmingham and the 11/10 favourite Priam. At the Red House (a point on Doncaster racecourse) several runners were already disappointing their connections as they faded away. The early leader continued in front with Maria, Pedestrian, and The Cardinal tracking close behind, with Birmingham, Mimic and the favourite following. Nearing the distance pole the first group, all except Emancipator, began to fade, as the pole approached, Patrick Conolly, Birmingham's jockey made a strong effort. That wise old jockey Sam Chifney on Priam seeing the move pushed on and as the three approached the stands Birmingham went past Emancipator with the favourite following. Chifney began whipping and spurring for all his worth, Conolly on the other hand continued working at his horse but without use of the whip. At the line it was Birmingham, who started at 15/1, from Priam by half a length, with Emancipator third. Immediately the result was known Beardsworth sent

Above left, an engraving of the Thomas Flintoff trained Birmingham (a brown colt by Filho da Puta out of Miss Craigie), owned by John Beardsworth. Hednesford's only English Classic winner, victorious in the 1830 Great St. Leger at Doncaster and ridden by Patrick Conolly.

A side view of Prospect House with the stable block on the far left. After Flintoff left the premises they were occupied by Thomas Cliff and later by the jockey and trainer Frederick Hassall.

THE TRAINERS

the first rider off with the result. Almost eight hours later, the news had reached Birmingham and the town was rejoicing at Beardsworth's success all through the night. After Birmingham's victory several 'gentlemen of fine breeding' were what can only be described as green with envy, they rounded on the triumphant owner in an effort to make sure the jockey, Conolly, would only get a small 'present.' 'No!' replied Beardsworth,'I consider myself quite as much indebted to his honest and skilful riding as I do to the goodness of the horse and its skilful training; and I cannot better show my sense of his conduct than by presenting him with a £500 note.' Always true to his word, Beardsworth did exactly that, including further 'presents' to Conolly of £50 each from Beardsworth's son and son-in-law, £50 from Colonel Peel and many other gifts of a similar sum. It is said the jockey came away from Doncaster £1,500 richer. In those days the stakes of the race were worth £1,700, but Beardsworth won over ten times that amount in bets, a conservative estimate puts the figure at around £19,000. With all of this cash flying round it was inevitable Flintoff was going to get his share too. Several reports, although not stating a figure, estimate the sum to be 'considerable.'

Flintoff won numerous Gold Cups and Plates at many English racecourses for his owners as well as three Chester Cups with Halston in 1829, owned by John Mytton, Independence in 1831 and Colwick in 1832, both owned by John Beardsworth. The Cesarewitch Handicap of 1855 was another of his successes with the horse, Mr Sykes, owned by E. R. Clark and ridden by F. Bates. Three years later the same trainer/owner partnership won the Lincolnshire Handicap with Vandermulin, ridden by Tommy French. Another great patron of Flintoffs was the owner John Fowler who placed many horses with the trainer, whilst not attaining the success that Beardsworth had, his horses won a great number of the less prestigious races.

Further testimony to Flintoff's skill as a trainer is shown in an article from the *Sporting Magazine* in 1839 where it is stated that the last time Flintoff had a horse break down in running was in 1824. An admirable testimony by any standards, and when it is considered how many horses he had trained during that period, it speaks volumes for his knowledge and dedication to the welfare of his horses.

JAMES HOPWOOD

Visitors to Hednesford in the mid nineteenth century, chatting with a group of trainers at the Cross Keys may well have thought they had mistakenly got on the York coach as so many of the trainers were from that part of the world. James Hopwood was another who came south and he trained the horse Bloxwich to win the final race at Walsall in 1876, ridden by his son James junior. Hopwood was born around 1815 and began his career as a jockey, riding in his native Yorkshire and the rival county of Lancashire. Exactly when he came to Hednesford is unknown, but he first appears in the Kelly's Directory of 1860 and in the 1861 census, employing eleven staff. His stables were known as Rest Brook House and were situated on the site of the present day enamelling factory, opposite The Globe public house. By 1901 Hopwood, who was now 87, had retired from training but remained in the area, living in lodgings at West View, Rugeley Road, Hednesford. The twentieth century trainer, Lawrence Rooney, later occupied the premises when they were known as the Red House Training Establishment.

JOHN HOWLETT

A trainer that came to the area around 1860 was John Howlett who was born at Newmarket in 1825. He is thought to be the jockey of the same name that rode successfully for many years before trying his hand at training. Howlett won many 'a fifty' as a jockey and came close to winning the 2,000 Guineas on a horse named Winchelsea who finished third in 1845. He had won three times on the same horse prior to the Newmarket Classic and the contemporary race reports are most complimentary with regard to his riding ability. A naturally small man, he was known for being able to ride light, when he was in his early twenties he could do weights of around five and half stone easily. In 1843 he rode Gorhambury, winner of the Queen's Vase at Ascot and in 1845, he partnered Guaracha to win the Coronation Stakes at the same course. As a trainer little is known of him and there is no record of horses running under his name, and no racing colours were registered. It is possible that he was a private trainer employed by an unknown affluent owner.

SAMUEL LORD

Edmund Peel who built the Hednesford (Anglesey) Lodge in 1831 had his own private trainer in residence, Samuel Lord, whose father James had been associated with the area for many years. Samuel's elder brother, also named James, was involved in horse training but it is believed he died quite young. Lord trained for Peel for at least ten years and picked up some valuable prizes over the years in the form of Gold Cups and Plates, plus numerous smaller prizes. Their best known win

The Blue Pump, one time residence of Samuel Lord.

THE TRAINERS

came in the Chester Cup of 1836 when Peel's appropriately named horse Tamworth won, ridden by John Spring. The same horse won the Gold Cup at Walsall, also in 1836, in the easiest way possible, with a walkover. Peel also bred the majority of his racehorses at Hednesford Lodge from mares he owned. In 1839 one of the stallions brought to the Lodge by Peel was Doctor Faustus, an excellent racehorse and sire of many future winners. The census of 1851 has Lord training from premises on the Rugeley Road (now Uxbridge Street), and it is thought near, or at, the licensed premises known as the Blue Pump. Lord died on 11th January 1857, coincidentally, the day the legendary jockey Fred Archer was born. It is thought that because Peel had vacated the premises long before Lord's death, the latter had reverted to public training.

CHARLES MARSON

Another trainer known to have been in the area around the mid 1850s is Charles Marson, a man that remains a complete mystery. Somewhat inconveniently from a researchers point of view, Marson arrived, and departed, from Hednesford sometime in between the 1851 and 1861 censuses, the directories from that period do not list him. He is known to have been in the area as his name, and signature, appears on the poster displaying the rules and regulations for the training grounds in 1857 (see pages 147 and 148). Whilst this is thought to be the same man, there is no conclusive evidence to say it is the same man that trained successfully at Newmarket for many years. His list of major race wins between 1825 and 1847 makes impressive reading. Two 1,000 Guineas winners, three 2,000 Guineas winners and one Oaks victory, followed by wins in the Queen Anne Stakes, the Queen's Vase, the Ascot Gold Cup, the July Stakes three times, and the Doncaster Cup. If this is proved to be the same trainer, his successes in his time at Hednesford were well below the standard of his earlier years as nothing has been recorded against his name of any significance.

GEORGE PALMER

It is said that George Palmer trained in the area for forty years, mainly from stables in Hill Street, but history records his 'fifteen minutes of fame' as the day in 1853 when he rode the winner of the Cesarewitch on Haco. Palmer married Mary Ashmall, the sister of the famous jockey Thomas.

In 1867 Palmer trained several horses for a Mr. Barber, one, who was named Fan and ridden by Thorpe finished second in the Grand National five lengths behind the winner Cortolvin. Palmer remained in the area until his death at the age of sixty-eight in September 1904. His son William Henry Palmer also became a jockey in the 1890s holding a licence to ride under both codes of racing.

THOMAS AND WILLIAM SAUNDERS

Thomas Saunders, born in Hednesford in 1796, had moved back to the area from Huyton in what was then Lancashire to resume training on the Hills as his father had done before him. In 1841 both Thomas and his son William are listed in the census as being trainers, also listed as occupying the same premises were James Farrell and Florence O'Driscoll, also listed as trainers. Two's company but four are far too many, shortly afterwards the father and son team moved to the stables in Hazel Slade previously occupied by Thomas Carr. William was also a jockey, riding on the flat initially and then gaining recognition as also being a very good 'jump jockey'. By 1861 William Saunders had been in sole charge for some years after his father's death. Both father and son trained for some well-known owners, the most famous being Dr. William Palmer who put many of his racehorses with the Saunders family for training, always running his horses under the name of 'Mr Palmer.' In 1853 Palmer's horse Goldfinder won the Chester Cup, it is reported that Palmer won £12,000 in bets on the race, so the horse certainly lived up to its name. The jockey Charles Marlow, William Saunders brother-in-law, was riding many of the trainer's horses at this time and it is thought he was the partner of Goldfinder for the race. When Palmer and Saunders arrived back in Hednesford, a right old knees-up was had by one and all at the Cross Keys, 'with enough brandy drunk to sink a boat that night,' was one comment. After Palmer was hung, his horses were auctioned off by Tattersalls, one of them, Staffordshire Nan, a three-year-old, was bought by a Mr Bryant for 300 guineas. Saunders and the horse were reunited when the new owner put her back into training at Hazel Slade.

Reputedly, one of the best horses seen on the Hills for many years was the Saunders trained Hobbie Noble, owned by Lord John Scott. It wasn't only the owner and trainer that thought very highly of the colt's abilities either. Throughout the winter of 1851 the horse was ante-post favourite for the Derby the following year. The favouritism was fully justified, in his first racing season Hobbie Noble won two of the most coveted trophies for two-year-olds, the New Stakes at Ascot and the July Stakes at Newmarket. It is said crowds of onlookers came to the Hills from neighbouring towns to see the horse work, but William Saunders, like many trainers, preferred a little more privacy. To give the public what they wanted, Saunders substituted Hobbie Noble for a similar looking horse, a practice that didn't confine itself to the training ground. When the 'touts' had been satisfied they had seen the horse work, they departed the scene. Immediately the all clear was sounded, out came the real Hobbie Noble who was then put through his paces in relative privacy. When the potential of the horse became apparent, it is thought, he was sent for training as a three-year-old to the legendary Newmarket trainer, Matthew Dawson as his victories in 1852 are credited to him. Although the horse was now many miles from Hednesford, Dawson chose little George Whitehouse to ride him in the majority of his races that season, and an excellent job he did according to the contemporary press reports. When the Derby came round in early June it was Whitehouse who got the mount, but for whatever reason, the colt never performed on the day and finished unplaced. The previous year Whitehouse had finished second in the Oaks on a filly named Miserrima, also owned by Lord John Scott and trained by Matt Dawson, and this association alone proves how highly Whitehouse was thought of.

THE TRAINERS

Saunders won the Cambridgeshire Handicap twice, the first time in 1851 with a horse named Truth, owned and bred by Edward Phillips of Bushbury, the jockey that rode the winner was the trainers talented apprentice John Wells. Twenty-one years later, in 1872, Saunders repeated the victory with Playfair, a horse ridden by George Ashworth, an eighteen year old apprentice at Thomas Cliff's yard. In the same year the combination carried off the Shrewsbury Cup and the Liverpool Summer Cup with Indian Ocean and in 1873 they won the Liverpool Autumn Cup with a horse named Whinyard. After Charles Marlow and George Whitehouse had departed from Hednesford, James Knott became the jockey for the stable and rode many winners nationwide for Saunders. A native of Radford in Nottinghamshire, Knott came to the trainer as a young boy around 1848, his progress from stable boy to stable jockey was a relatively slow one but it appears he was well thought of by Saunders and the owners that patronised his stables. Knott rode just four winners at Walsall between 1856 and 1866, but within four years of riding his last winner on the Long Meadow, he was dead. Like many jockeys before and after him, Knott become a victim of consumption or tuberculosis, which claimed his life on the 7th March 1870 aged just thirty-six. Listed in the 1861 census were two other aspiring young jockeys at the stables, the sons of Charles Marlow. Charles junior aged fifteen and Henry, aged thirteen, both nephews of William Saunders. It is thought neither of them had inherited their father's ability in any great abundance, although Henry did have several rides in public and the odd winner.

Other owners that patronised Saunders were Lord Derby, Captain Lamb, a high profile sportsman of his day, along with Joseph Painter from Stafford and Edward Phillips from Bushbury; both well established and respected bloodstock breeders in the racing world. After a long and distinguished career in horse racing, both as a jockey and a trainer, William died at Hazel Slade on the 23rd March 1884, aged sixty-four. It is believed the yard was taken over by Saunders head lad for many years, Thomas 'Badger' Metcalfe, a native of Crake Hall near Bedale in Yorkshire who arrived at Hednesford around 1845 and remained in the area until his tragic death on the 6th August 1888. Whilst riding over the Hills to collect the post from Hednesford, his horse fell and rolled on him, he died from injuries sustained in the fall. Metcalfe came to the area with a very good grey horse named Chanticleer, who, along with Hobbie Noble, was considered to be two of the best horses in training at this time. In 1848 Chanticleer won the Northumberland Plate (the Pitman's Derby), the Goodwood Plate and the Doncaster Cup. Whilst being a talented racehorse he also had a dreadful temperament, bringing the remark from one observer, '*He was the most evil thing ever to have grown four legs and a tail.*' After Metcalfe's death, the stable was then taken over by the Tamworth born jockey John Deakin.

RICHARD SPENCER

One of the first people from the area to become well known nationally for his excellent horsemanship was Richard Spencer who lived and trained at Littleworth. In 1810 Richard Spencer rode the winners of all five races at the Walsall meeting, although one was a walkover. Little is known of his training career, but it is thought he trained horses for Lord Stamford, Richard Dyott from Lichfield and John Tomes from Warwickshire. At the Chester spring meeting in May 1820 Spencer won His Majesty's Plate on one of Tome's horses, Duplicate, the following year he again caught the judges eye on the same horse, but this time at a less prestigious venue, the Long Meadow at Walsall. He continued to ride and train up to his death in 1838.

JOHN WALTERS

The trainer John Walters remains something of a mystery, although the Racing Calendar records many horses that ran in his name, there appears to be few of any significance. Walters son, also named John (circa 1833 - 1915) is thought to be the person that rode three winners at Walsall, he was also the jockey of Whitelock, winner of the Northumberland Plate at Newcastle-upon-Tyne in 1855.

The winner of the 1866 Grand National, Salamander, was trained by a John Walters, whilst this is thought to be the same man, the evidence is not conclusive. It is certain that if this is the same man, Salamander was not trained in the Hednesford area.

The yard and stables around 1970.

THE TRAINERS

THOMAS WALTERS

In the 1840s, one of the famous owners associated with the Hills at this time was Alderman William Taylor Copeland, head of the china company, W.T. Copeland and Sons of Stoke, whose horses were trained, it is thought, by Thomas Walters. Of the two trainers named Walters in the area, Thomas and John, historical evidence points to the former as being the one that trained the Alderman's horses. Walters became the third trainer from the area to win the Chester Cup when Copeland's five-year old King Cole won this prestigious race in 1838. King Cole was a very good horse that won many 'a fifty,' and considerably more, for his owner. The crowds on the Long Meadow were fortunate enough to see King Cole win twice, as well as coming second in the Gold Cup of 1839, ridden on each occasion by Charles Marlow. Another horse of good pedigree owned by Copeland and trained by Walters was The Prime Warden who won many stakes and in 1846 was standing at stud with a fee of 10 sovereigns for thoroughbreds and half that for half-breeds, plus 10 shillings for the groom.

Thomas Walters almost got himself into serious trouble with the Jockey Club, which wasn't difficult to do, over the running of a race at Bridgnorth in July 1842. The incident was reported in the Sporting Magazine with scathing criticism of Walters and also the rules that allowed him to get away with it. The race was the Members Plate with eight runners, three of which were connected to Walters. W. T. Copeland owned Guzbeg, and as the Sporting Magazine put it, 'Mr Copeland, one of the most straightforward patrons of the turf, needless to say was not implicated in these disgraceful proceedings.' The remaining two horses, Miss Winney and Country Lass were owned, or part owned by Walters. The race was over three heats and it was in the second that the incident occurred. In first heat Copeland's horse Guzbeg was well beaten and withdrawn, the heat being won by a horse name Rebecca. As the second heat neared its end, Country Lass, ridden by a young Robert Denman was leading from Walters other horse, Miss Winney. In between the distance pole and the winning post, Denman pulled back his mount to allow Miss Winney to pass him, and win. It then became apparent to everyone where the 'Hednesford money' had been laid; everyone it seems except the Bridgnorth stewards, who did nothing. The Sporting Magazine's correspondent was incensed and laid all of the blame squarely on Thomas Walters. Denman, who was described as 'mere stable boy,' was exonerated due to his 'inexperience' and was, after all, only following the orders of his employer. Quite why the magazine took this hard line approach when practices of this sort were an everyday occurrence is unknown, other than the fact one of their correspondents had witnessed the scene for himself. After this blatant 'pulling' of Country Lass, the magazine concluded the report with the following statement: - 'How much longer such absurd exhibitions will be allowed to disgrace a British racecourse remains to be proved.'

Officially, Walters had nothing to worry about from the rulers of racing but it may well have put doubt into Alderman Copelands mind. In 1843 another incident occurred when a horse of Copelands was beaten because the orders for the running had been disobeyed, this led to some 'extreme unpleasantness' as the Sporting Magazine put it. This, along with the earlier incident may well have been a contributory factor in the removal of Copeland's horses from Walters in 1844 when they were all transferred to the Newmarket trainer William Beresford.

Copeland returned some of his horses in later years to William Saunders for training. In 1858 one of the china magnates horses, The Argosy won the Yorkshire Oaks at York.

THOMAS WARREN

Thomas Warren, the initiative behind the Hednesford race meetings trained the Cross Keys Inn. Although described in the newspapers of the day as 'the well-known trainer,' unfortunately, little is known of his individual training exploits.

JOHN WILKINS

It is well documented that three Grand National winners were trained in the Hednesford area, some have credited a fourth to John Wilkins of the Cross Keys who is reputed to have trained Jealousy to win the event in 1851. Wilkins did train horses at one time or another from the premises, but many racing historians credit John Balchin, whose stables were in the south of England, as the trainer of Jealousy. The rider of Jealousy, Joseph Kendall was associated with the area, but that is the nearest the area came to this 'National winner. Little is known of Wilkins training career other than the fact he is listed on the 1857 poster explaining the rules and regulations of the training ground.

Of the other trainers that occupied stables in the area, **John Adie or Adey, Charles Bemetzreider, Joseph Bickley, James Farrell, Henry Lister, David Miles, Samuel Smith, William Shepherd and George Taylor,** little is known of their individual training careers.

In a male dominated profession it is interesting to note the presence of a female trainer in 1841, Florence O'Driscoll, but unfortunately, nothing is known of her career.

As the nineteenth century drew to a close there were just four trainers listed in the *Kelly's Directory* of 1900, Thomas Coulthwaite, Laurence Rooney, Frederick Hassall and Henry Lawless. Hassall trained at Prospect Place, made famous by Flintoff and Cliff before him. He trained his own horses and combined this with a career as a National Hunt jockey. Hassall was killed in a fall on the gallops in 1909, aged 44. Henry Lawless completed the training scene in Hednesford at this time, little is known of him and it appears from the 1901 Census that he had left the area.

By 1910 just three trainers remained in the area, Coulthwaite, Rooney and a new name, William Woodland. Predominately, all three trained under National Hunt Rules although Rooney did train Billy The Verger to win the Royal Hunt Cup at Ascot in 1908. It seems that Rooney was as well known for his vile temper as training racehorses.

Walsall Races

Chapter Nine
THE COLOURS

The following pages show some of the more well known owner's and trainer's racing colours that must have brightened up the dullest of September days on the Long Meadow.

Lord Anglesey	Lord Anson	John Beardsworth	Sir Edward Buckley
George Clement	Thomas Cliff	John Clifton	Ald. William Copeland
Vincent Corbet	Henry Crocket	James Dover	Thomas Eskrett

156

THE COLOURS

Thomas Flintoff	John Fowler	Thomas Giffard	Lord Grosvenor
Frederick G. Hobson	John Kellerman	Captain Douglas Lane	R. Law
Mr. Lincoln	Edward J. Littleton	Mr. Meiklam	Edward Moncton
Captain Moss	John Mytton	Mr. Orme	John Osborne senior
Lord Alexander Paget	Lord Henry Paget	Edmund Peel	J. H. Peel

THE COLOURS

Mr. Pettit

Edward Phillips

Sir George Paget

Lord Rossmore

William Saunders

William Scott

Mr. Skelton

C. Skelton

Lord Stamford

Sir Thomas Stanley

E. W. Taylor

John Tomes

Lord Uxbridge

Francis Villiers

Thomas Wadlow

Lord Warwick

Lord Westmoreland

Lord Wilton

Colonel Yates

Mr. Yates

158

Bibliography

A Long Time Gone - Chris Pitt, 1996
A Race Apart - Reg Green, 1988
Baily's Racing Register, Vols. 1, 2 and 3 - Baily brothers, 1845
Bloodstock Breeding - Sir Charles Leicester, 1957
Book of Sports - Pierce Egan, 1835
Bye-Lanes and Downs of England, with Turf Scenes and Characters - Sylvanus, 1859
Encyclopaedia of Sport - Charles Harvey, 1958
Great Jockeys of the Flat - Michael Tanner and Gerry Cranham, 1992
History of the Racing Calendar and Stud Book - C. M. Prior, 1926
History of Walsall - Frederic W. Willmore, 1887
It Ay 'Ere Our Kid - Ann French, 2000
Jump Jockeys 1830-1950 - Chas. Hammond, 2003
Kingsclere - John Porter, 1896
Racecourses of Great Britain - James Gill, 1975
Racing Calendars (various) - C., J., E., and J. P. Weatherby
Ruff's Guide to the Turf - 1880 to 1907
Running Racing, The Jockey Club Years since 1750 - John Tyrrel, 1997
Sam Darling's Reminiscences - Sam Darling, 1914
Silk and Scarlet - The Druid, 1862
The Badminton Library - Racing - Earl of Suffolk and Arthur Coventry, 1885
The Best of Cannock Chase - M. Wright (Pitman), 1933
The Breedon Book of Horseracing Records - Edward Abelson and John Tyrrel, 1993
The Derby - Michael Wynn Jones, 1979
The Friendship of Cannock Chase - M. Wright (Pitman), 1935
The History and Directory of Walsall - Thomas Pearce, first published 1813
The Jockeys of Vanity Fair - Russell March, 1985
The Life of Fred Archer - E. M. Humphris, 1930
The Life of John Mytton - Nimrod, (C. J. Apperley) 9th edition, 1936
The Post and the Paddock - The Druid, 1856
The Roodee, 450 years of racing in Chester - R. M. Bevan, 1989
The Rugeley Poisoner - Dave Lewis, 2003
The Sport of Kings - Ralph Nevill, 1926
The Staffordshire Encyclopaedia - Tim Cockin, 2000
The Turf - Roger Longrigg, 1975
The Turf - Alfred E. T. Watson, 1898
The Turf of Old - Denzil Batchelor, 1951
Thomas Newton, a pioneer of the Walsall leather trade - Ann French, 1995
We Day Arf 'Ave Fun - Ann French, 1998
When Birmingham Went Racing - Chris Pitt and Chas. Hammond, 2005

Newspapers and periodicals:
Aris's Gazette
The Field
The Birmingham Daily Post
The Sporting Magazine and The New Sporting Magazine
The Staffordshire Advertiser
The Walsall Free Press
The Walsall Observer

Internet:
jockeypedia a great website run by George Wheeler
www.britishnewspaperarchive.co.uk/

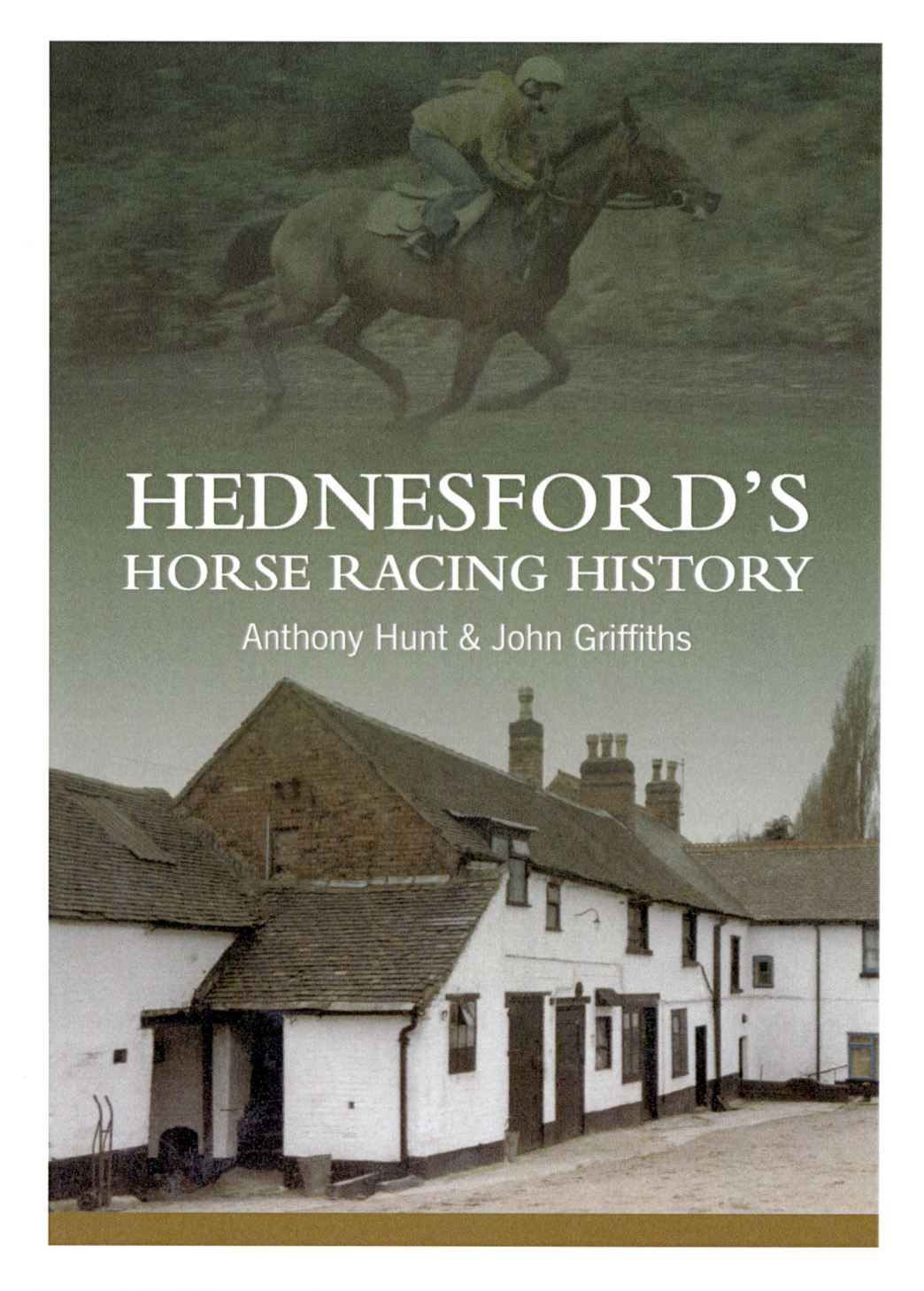

HEDNESFORD'S HORSE RACING HISTORY
Anthony Hunt & John Griffiths

When *A Complete Record of Walsall Races* was first published in 2005 it had a chapter titled the Hednesford Training Grounds 1775-1900. In this revised edition the chapter has been deleted and now covers just the individual trainers in the area.

The reason for this was that in 2008 a joint project was launched between myself and well-known local historian from Hednesford, Anthony Hunt, to produce a book that dealt in depth with all aspects of the horse racing history in the area.

The book was published by Mount Chase Press in 2010 and titled,
Hednesford's Horse Racing History (ISBN 978-0-9551382-2-5).
It measures 175mm x 250mm (B5) and contains 180 pages with 112 photographs, 4 in colour, and 11 maps.

Copies are available at £11.99 plus P & P of £2.
To purchase please email - jw418@btinternet.com